Medical-Legal Evaluation of Hearing Loss

Second Edition

Robert A. Dobie, M.D., F.A.C.S.

SINGULAR

✦ ™

THOMSON LEARNING

Medical-Legal Evaluation of Hearing Loss, Second Edition

by
Robert A. Dobie

Business Unit Director:
William Brottmiller

Acquisitions Editor:
Marie Linvill

Developmental Editor:
Kristin Banach

COPYRIGHT © 2001 by Singular, an imprint of Delmar, a division of Thomson Learning, Inc. Thomson Learning™ is a trademark used herein under license

Printed in Canada
2 3 4 5 XXX 06 05 04

For more information contact Singular,
401 West "A" Street, Suite 325
San Diego, CA 92101–7904.
Or find us on the World Wide Web at http://www.singpub.com

Executive Marketing Manager:
Dawn Gerrain

Channel Manager:
Kathryn Little

Executive Production Editor:
Barbara Bullock

Production Editor:
Brad Bielawski

Library of Congress
Cataloging-in-Publication Data

Robert A. Dobie
  Medical-Legal Evaluation
  of Hearing Loss, Second
  Edition/
  Robert A. Dobie—2nd ed.
    p.; cm
  Includes bibliographical
  references and indexes.
  ISBN 0-7693-0052-9
    (hardcover: alk. paper)
  1. Forensic audiology.
    I. Title.
  [DNLM: 1. Hearing Loss,
  Noise-Induced—diagnosis. 2. Disability Evaluation. 3. Expert Testimony.
  4. Hearing Tests.
  WV 270 D633m 2001]
  RA1062.8 .D63 2001
  614'.1—dc21

NOTICE TO THE READER

Publisher does not warrant or guarantee any of the products described herein or perform any independent analysis in connection with any of the product information contained herein. Publisher does not assume, and expressly disclaims, any obligation to obtain and include information other than that provided to it by the manufacturer. Nothing in this work is to be construed as medical advice; health care professionals are solely and individually responsible for determining the impact, if any, that this and other works may have on their practice.

The reader is expressly warned to consider and adopt all safety precautions that might be indicated by the activities herein and to avoid all potential hazards. By following the instructions contained herein, the reader willingly assumes all risks in connection with such instructions.

The Publisher makes no representa[tion ....]kind, including but not limited to, the warranties of fitness for particular purpose or merchantability, nor are any such representations implied with respect to the material set forth herein, and the publisher takes no responsibility with respect to such material. The publisher shall not be liable for any special, consequential, or exemplary damages resulting, in whole or part, from the readers' use of, or reliance upon, this material.

To the memory of my parents, Geraldine Frances Dobie
and RADM Ernest William Dobie, Jr., USN (Ret)
And to my wife, Christine Jones Dobie

Contents

Acknowledgments
(first edition)

Many thanks to members of my staff for their invaluable assistance in putting this book together. Connie Sakai took the book over (after initial typing by Julie Estrada) and skillfully and cheerfully wrestled with references, styles, correspondence, appendices, abbreviations, and countless other details. Mike Wilson prepared the figures with his usual eye for accuracy, consistency, and clarity.

Jack Snyder, Tom Jayne, and Howard Pelton contributed excellent chapters; their contributions are reviewed in Chapter 1 (Introduction and Overview). They have my sincere thanks.

Dr. James P. Hughes, formerly medical director of Kaiser Aluminum and Chemical Corporation, first got me interested in noise-induced hearing loss and hearing conservation, and encouraged me to write this book, for which I am grateful.

Finally, I must acknowledge the contributions of dozens of colleagues whose published works provide a solid body of knowledge for discussion. I hope that these colleagues and others who read this book will tell me about the errors they will inevitably find, so that they can be corrected in subsequent editions.

List of Contributors

Thomas R. Jayne
Thompson & Mitchell
St. Louis, Missouri

Howard K. Pelton, P.E.
Pelton Marsh Kinsella
Dallas, Texas

Jack M. Snyder, Ph.D.
Professor Emeritus
Department of Otolaryngology—Head and Neck Surgery
University of Washington
Seattle, Washington

Preface to the Second Edition

In the seven years since the first edition of this book went to the printers, hearing research has made great strides, and this is the main reason why the book needed to be revised. In 1993, otoacoustic emissions were mostly a laboratory curiosity; today they are part of the clinical toolkit, and are particularly useful for medical-legal evaluation. Interrelated genetic aspects of age-related and noise-induced hearing loss were then reasonable speculations; now they are facts. We know much more about the biology of hearing loss than we did; the roles of oxidative stress, conditioning exposures, and the olivocochlear efferent reflex are beginning to be understood, and drug and nutritional interventions that may prevent noise-induced and ototoxic hearing loss have been identified. Motorcycles, automobile airbags, and even acoustic reflex testing have recently been implicated as non-occupational causes of hearing loss. All these advances and many others are discussed in the new edition. Every chapter has been revised and updated, with over 150 new references cited.

Along the way, some errors have been corrected and some gaps have been filled. For example, hearing protection devices and the amount of attenuation they can be expected to provide are now discussed at some length in Chapter 9, along with the advantages and pitfalls of noise exposure measurement using dosimeters. Evaluation of tinnitus is now briefly covered in Chapter 12.

The American National Standards Institute has published as ANSI S3.44 an American version of ISO-1999 (published by the International Organization for Standardization in 1990), including a new database (Annex C) for estimating the effects of age-related hearing loss. Research on both sides of the Atlantic increasingly suggests that the highly-screened database A (in both the ISO and ANSI standards) is inappropriate for purposes of medical-legal analysis, and the examples in the book reflect that point of view.

Chapter 13 has been extensively revised. It is shorter, with fewer figures, examples, and formulas; I hope it is also easier to read. The clinical, judgmental nature of allocation in individual cases has been emphasized, with quantitative methods providing useful inputs to that process. The ISO/ANSI model provides a useful benchmark for diagnosis of noise-induced hearing loss, and supports the use of audiometric trajectory analysis to determine the relative contributions of aging and noise. For cases without an extensive audiometric record, estimates of the relative contributions of aging and noise (based on age, sex, and exposure history) can be easily calculated using the median-ratio method.

Legal changes, including Supreme Court decisions regarding the Americans with Disabilities Act and expert testimony, and new federal hearing conservation regulations, have been summarized. Appendix B reproduces (with permission) a very new survey of state and federal workers' compensation program practices.

Finally, many thanks to the readers and reviewers who gave the first edition such a friendly reception, making a second edition viable, and to my new publisher, Singular Thomson Learning, for supporting this project.

Chapter 1

Introduction and Overview

THE PROBLEM

About 23 million Americans (8.3 percent of the population) report some difficulty with hearing (Anon., 1999). Most hearing losses are associated with aging, excessive noise exposure, or both, without any other detectable ear disease. Age-related hearing loss is neither preventable nor treatable. Noise-induced hearing loss (NIHL), whether caused by occupational or recreational exposure, is by definition preventable, but is not medically treatable. Good prevalence data for NIHL are scarce, but in one large Swiss clinic, about 18 percent of hearing loss cases received a diagnosis of NIHL (alone or with some other diagnosis; Spillmann and Dillier, 1983). If these data are representative of the population at large, there would be about 4 million Americans with NIHL severe enough for them to report hearing difficulties. Prevention of NIHL (by noise level reduction, exposure reduction, and use of personal hearing protective devices) would probably do more to reduce the societal burden of hearing loss than medical and surgical treatment of all other ear diseases combined.

Somewhat surprisingly, NIHL doesn't seem to be going away. Perhaps this is because NIHL develops slowly and insidiously, or because the problems of the hearing-impaired are not adequately appreciated by most people. The existence of NIHL was probably widely known in occupational medicine circles by about 1950, although a contemporary textbook (Johnstone, 1948) mentions neither noise nor hearing loss! Hearing conservation programs (HCPs) began appearing in the military and in industry during the 1950s and 1960s, but were hampered by a lack of consensus about harmful levels of noise. Based on discussions with senior occupational physicians, fewer than half of American workers with hazardous noise exposures were covered by HCPs as late as 1975 or 1980. Franks (1988) estimated that about 40 percent of these workers were in HCPs with audiometric monitoring by 1975. Although occupational noise exposure has been extensively regulated at the national level since 1971, some industries are exempt, and the Occupational Safety and Health Administration (OSHA) has not aggressively enforced existing regulations (detailed specifications for HCPs were not promulgated by OSHA until 1983). HCPs can be expensive, and there has been little financial incentive for industry to prevent NIHL other than the desire to avoid compensation costs, which until recently have been modest.

The financial risks faced by companies with noise-exposed workers are rising. More workers are filing for and receiving awards from state workers' compensation systems as awareness of NIHL spreads within the general population. Workers in industries not covered by workers' compensation systems are suing their employers in court and receiving some very large judgments. Groups of workers constrained from suing their employers by workers' compensation coverage have filed suit against the manufacturers of the noisy machines used in their workplaces.

Certainly, medical-legal assessment of allegedly noise-damaged workers is increasingly required to assist courts and compensation boards in determining the extent of loss and work-relatedness. NIHL is not the only issue; suits claiming hearing loss from head injury, neck injury, and medical malpractice are common, and expert medical assessment and testimony are required in these cases as well. The principles of assessment, diagnosis, and allocation are the same, whether NIHL or other types of injury are at issue.

The natural experts for medical-legal assessment of hearing loss are otolaryngologists (physicians who have completed five years or more of postgraduate training in the diagnosis and management of disorders of the ears, nose, throat, and head and neck). Some otolaryngologists limit their practices to otology (ear disorders); otologists have usually had additional training in medical and surgical treatment of ear disease, but are not necessarily more qualified to assess medical-legal hearing loss cases than other otolaryngologists. Many otologists and otolaryngologists feel ill-prepared in the medical-legal arena, primarily because their training has emphasized treatable disorders, especially those that are surgically treatable. The principal goal of this book is to assist these physicians in providing medical-legal assessments that are scientifically based, rational, practical, and quantitative (where that is possible). The book should also be of interest to audiologists, occupational physicians, attorneys, industrial hygienists, engineers, safety experts, insurance and risk management professionals— all of whom play important roles in the management and prevention of hearing loss claims.

THE SCOPE OF THE BOOK

Chapters 2 and 3 present elementary discussions of acoustics, the ear, and hearing tests. While most of this material is most likely superfluous for otolaryngologists and audiologists, it is essential for members of other professional groups who wish to use this book to become better informed consumers of otologic reports.

The subtle and often-frustrating art of detecting and managing exaggerated hearing loss is discussed in Chapter 4 by Jack Snyder, an audiologist with extensive experience and great skill in this area. Hearing loss is measured, and the compensation amount is determined in most cases, in terms of pure-tone thresholds—the softest sounds that a subject admits to hearing. The validity of these thresholds depends on a subject's honesty and best efforts, neither of which can be assumed in the medical-legal arena. Too many audiograms are simply accepted at face value, without considering whether they may portray a more severe loss than really exists or even a hearing loss where none exists.

Chapter 5 explores the complex relationships among hearing loss, hearing impairment, and hearing handicap. The fundamental question here is how best to estimate the impact that hearing loss has on an individual. Job-related issues, such as the ability of a hearing-impaired person to hear warning signals and carry out the communicative demands of a job, will be discussed, but the majority of the chapter deals with the more general problem of interference with speech understanding in everyday life. The most frequently used methods for determining hearing handicap use pure-tone thresholds for those frequencies judged most important for speech perception, but there is considerable controversy in this area.

Even in the absence of hazardous noise exposure and other types of trauma or ear disease, virtually all people develop significant hearing loss as they age. The term *presbycusis* has been used to describe this phenomenon, but means different things to different authors. Thus, Chapter 6 discusses age-related hearing loss (ARHL) in terms of anatomical and physiological changes, possible mechanisms, and epidemiological studies. Some people lose hearing more rapidly than others, of course. It is essential to consider the *distribution* of severity of ARHL at each age in order to understand the studies of NIHL in Chapter 7, and in order to make reasonable estimates of the relative contributions of aging and noise in individual cases.

Chapter 7 presents the topic of NIHL from occupational exposure. The effects of continuous noise are distinguished from those of impulsive noise and acoustic trauma. Interactions with other forms of hearing loss, especially ARHL, are discussed, along with epidemiological studies comparing the hearing of noise-exposed subjects to that of nonnoise-exposed control subjects. The International Organization for Standardization and the American National Standards Institute have recently published nearly identical documents (ISO-1999 and ANSI S3.44, respectively) summarizing the combined effects of age and noise exposure on hearing at different frequencies. The ISO/ANSI formulae facilitate the prediction of the distributions of hearing loss to be expected, given age, gender, exposure level, and duration.

In almost all claims for compensation for alleged NIHL, it is important to consider both aging and occupational noise exposure as possible causal factors. A third important factor, often overlooked, is nonoccupational exposure. Chapter 8 reviews the evidence that such exposures, especially through hunting and target shooting, are both common and hazardous. "Dose-response" data (like those in ISO-1999 and ANSI S3.44) relating severity of exposure to magnitude of hearing loss are not available for gunfire, but a history of regular shooting must be considered as contributory in noise-exposed workers.

In Chapter 9, Howard Pelton, an experienced and prominent acoustical engineer, discusses hearing conservation in industry, appropriately stressing the preeminent role for noise reduction when feasible. When workplace exposure levels can be brought below 85 dBA, occupational NIHL will be negligible and claims can be strongly defended. Even when exposure levels cannot be kept below potentially hazardous levels, a well-managed hearing conservation program can minimize occupational NIHL and can provide data regarding exposures (both occupational and nonoccupational) and serial audiometry which can be quite helpful in defending exaggerated claims. Otologic referral during the course of employment, based on baseline abnormalities or shifts seen on annual testing, also yields information useful for both prevention and defense of claims. On the other hand, a poorly-managed effort, or one that merely documents hearing loss without preventing it, leaves an employer deservedly vulnerable to successful claims.

While most medical-legal claims for hearing loss involve occupational noise exposure or acoustic trauma, some will involve claims of head or neck injury or ototoxicity, and, in others, all or part of their losses are attributable to any of a variety of ear disorders unrelated to the legal claim. Chapter 10 surveys the spectrum of causes for hearing loss other than noise (including blast injury) and aging. Some of these disorders cause otolaryngologists little diagnostic difficulty—for example, chronic otitis media or temporal bone fracture. Otolaryngologists vary substantially in their criteria for diagnosing other disorders, such as Ménière's disease. There is even controversy over whether some ear disorders exist at all: hearing loss caused by diabetes and vascular disease, for example. We hope otologists and otolaryngologists will find useful summaries of relevant literature in this chapter, while nonphysician readers will find it helpful in interpreting physicians' reports.

Chapter 11 summarizes the legal aspects of hearing loss claims. Tom Jayne is an attorney with wide experience in hearing loss litigation; in this chapter he discusses the different ways in which hearing loss claims are adjudicated and paid in the United States. Variation among different jurisdictions is wide, regarding issues such as formulae for hearing handicap, allowance for presbycusis, consideration of tinnitus, and aggravation of preexisting loss.

Chapter 12 describes what happens when the claimant comes to the otolaryngologist's office. A structured interview is essential, and questionnaires are very useful. Review of prior audiograms and noise exposure measurements is also essential, when available. The otolaryngologist should work closely with the audiologist to gather a data set that will permit valid conclusions regarding severity and causation of hearing loss. This sometimes requires repeat visits to resolve issues of functional hearing loss or reversible outer and middle ear conditions.

The otolaryngologist has no laboratory test or X-ray available to assist in the diagnosis of NIHL or ARHL; these diagnoses rely primarily on history (including noise exposure history and serial hearing tests). In fact, most patients claiming compensation for NIHL have both NIHL and ARHL. Chapter 13 describes the well-known process of differential diagnosis (identifying the cause or causes of hearing loss) and the much less well-known process of allocation (estimating the relative contributions of different causes to the total hearing loss, or more appropriately, to the total hearing handicap). The allocation methods presented in this chapter are based on epidemiological data (especially the ISO/ANSI standards) and common sense, and use the hearing handicap formula proposed by the American Academy of Otolaryngology (AAO) in 1979 (later adopted by the American Medical Association). Several case studies illustrate the use of these methods, which do not usually require calculations more complex than those used in the AAO hearing handicap formula. However, sound professional judgment is essential to determine when to allocate, which method to use, and how to use it.

The physician's report must completely and succinctly describe the data collected, the conclusions reached, and (often omitted) the reasons for those conclusions. Chapter 14 continues the use of case studies to demonstrate the elements of good medical-legal reports in hearing loss cases.

Chapter 15 covers an area many physicians and audiologists find uncomfortable: testimony in deposition and in court. Most cases never come to this, but any clinician seeing medical-legal cases will be in court sooner or later. A competent expert witness with a valid point to make can create a poor impression without some understanding of courtroom demeanor, procedures, and strategy.

Appendix A contains tables of typical noise levels for workplaces, machines, tools, vehicles, firearms, and the like. Appendix B gives a tabular summary of current (2000) state and federal hearing loss compensation regulations.

This is not a book about NIHL per se. Very little of the basic science of NIHL is discussed, except to the extent that these data are necessary to understand NIHL as a clinical (and specifically medical-legal) problem. In addition, other ear disorders are prominently discussed, and the assessment and allocation methods proposed are not unique to NIHL. In particular, it would be illogical to devise methods for hearing handicap assessment and compensation that would be suitable for one ear disorder and not for others. Readers interested in additional in-depth study of NIHL are urged to consult the books and papers cited in the appropriate chapters. Nonauditory effects of noise (annoyance, sleep disturbance, physiological changes) are discussed only briefly.

This is not a book on forensic otology. Such an undertaking would require much more extensive treatment of vestibular disorders, tinnitus, facial nerve disorders, and medical malpractice than attempted here. Rather, the focus is on hearing loss, with these other otologic topics discussed only to the extent that they are relevant to hearing loss. Although many inner ear disorders affect both hearing and balance, vestibular dysfunction is not extensively treated in this book for several reasons. First, most hearing loss claims involve NIHL, in which vestibular damage is rarely at issue. Second, vestibular function testing is complex, controversial, and of questionable value in estimating handicap and disability. Third, in almost every area of clinical epidemiology—prevalence, relative risk, aging effects, and so on—too little is known about vestibular disease and injury to permit more than educated guesses about causality and allocation. Fourth, and most important, what is known about hearing loss is more than enough for this book.

We hope this book will be useful both as a didactic text and as a reference. Relevant literature has been selectively and critically reviewed, as it is impossible to even attempt an exhaustive review of the subjects treated. Topics of potential medical-legal importance have naturally been discussed in a more detailed and well documented fashion than those that are primarily of didactic interest. We have erred on the side of selecting recent publications over older ones, accessible publications over those that are obscure or abstruse, and (in some areas) review articles over primary publications. In some cases, these policies may promote clarity and the reader's convenience at the expense of fair acknowledgment of original research contributions, but we have tried to accurately describe the history of the field: When was a particular fact known widely? (This is often important in medical-legal cases.) In reviewing the state of knowledge, we have attempted to distinguish certainty (or at least consensus) from controversy. Multiple case studies are worked through in Chapters 13 and 14 to show the reader how to solve actual problems in practice.

Many legally important topics have been addressed by more or less authoritative governmental and professional groups, including the Occupational

Safety and Health Administration, the American National Standards Institute, the American Academy of Otolaryngology–Head and Neck Surgery, the American College of Occupational Medicine, the National Institutes of Health, and many others. The pronouncements of these groups are liberally referenced and discussed in various chapters, both because some of them are legally binding in some circumstances and because they often illustrate areas of professional consensus.

THE AUDIENCE

The most appropriate users of this book will be otologists and otolaryngologists, who can use the information and methods presented to more skillfully perform medical-legal assessments in hearing loss cases. It should go without saying that this book cannot replace, but can only supplement, the training in otologic disease, diagnosis, and management that is an integral part of residency in otolaryngology. Of course, the same is true for audiologists, attorneys, engineers, and so on: No book can substitute for professional training in any of these disciplines.

Medical-legal assessment of hearing loss is best approached by a team effort involving an audiologist and an otolaryngologist. The role played by each will vary from one team to another, and many audiologists may choose to learn and use the methods presented in this book in conjunction with their medical colleagues. Other audiologists are actively involved in hearing conservation program management, consulting, and litigation work, and will find some helpful information in these pages.

On the other hand, many readers will be consumers of medical-legal reports. Attorneys need to be able to interpret, evaluate, and critique the information provided to them by physicians. Insurance professionals and corporate risk management personnel need to assess the magnitude and nature of risk in hearing loss cases, and to understand the role a good hearing conservation program can play in reducing risk. Occupational physicians, industrial hygienists, and engineers will primarily approach this subject from a prevention point of view, but may profit from a better understanding of otologic evaluation, even if they are not frequently involved with medical-legal cases. In fact, many medical-legal claims can be forestalled by timely otologic referral early in the employment history, as a part of the occupational hearing conservation program.

Nothing in this book requires more background than high school science and eighth grade mathematics. Basic discussions of acoustics and hearing are included for those needing them, so that none of the professional groups listed above should have any difficulty with the rest of the book.

REFERENCES

American Academy of Otolaryngology–Committee on Hearing and Equilibrium and American Council of Otolaryngology–Committee on the Medical Aspects of Noise. 1979. Guide for the evaluation of hearing handicap. *JAMA* 241(19):2055–2059.

American National Standards Institute. 1996. *Determination of Occupational Noise Exposure and Estimation of Noise-Induced Hearing Impairment, ANSI S3.44-1996.* Acoustical Society of America, New York.

Anonymous. 1999. Current estimates from the National Health Interview Survey, 1996. *Vital Health Stat. Series* 10 (200).

Franks, John R. 1988. Number of workers exposed to occupational noise. *Semin. Hear.* 9(4):287–298.

International Organization for Standardization. 1990. *Acoustics: Determination of Occupational Noise Exposure and Estimation of Noise-Induced Hearing Impairment, ISO-1999.* Geneva: International Organization for Standardization.

Johnstone, C. T. 1948. *Occupational Medicine and Industrial Hygiene.* Chicago: C. V. Mosby.

Spillmann, Thomas and Norbert Dillier. 1983. Der internationale klassierungscode (ICD) in der audiologie. *VIII. Audiosymposium, Rexton, Zurich:* 147–159.

Chapter 2

Acoustics

Sound means two different things. To the physicist, it is a propagated change of density and pressure in an elastic medium (such as air). To the psychologist, it is a perception commonly associated with acoustic stimulation of the ear. Usually the two definitions coexist: Striking a tuning fork causes both a measurable sound (in the physical sense) and a perception of sound (in the psychological sense). Either one can exist without the other, though. Sounds outside the range of human hearing and those produced in the absence of a human observer produce no sensation. Conversely, a person can perceive a sound when none is physically present—this is called *tinnitus*, and, when persistent, it is usually the consequence of damage to the auditory system. This chapter will deal mostly with acoustics, the branch of physics covering sound. However, we will briefly discuss issues in psychoacoustics, the branch of psychology that describes the relationships between acoustic stimuli and perception, since our underlying interest is in the effects physical sounds have on humans.

Obviously, given space restrictions and our commitment to keep this book accessible to professionals from several different disciplines, this chapter can only offer a cursory and descriptive introduction to the science of acoustics. The reader will *not* become an acoustician or acquire the ability to perform acoustic measurements. The goal of this chapter is to impart only as much information as is necessary to understand and use the material to be presented in later chapters. Many readers, especially otolaryngologists, audiologists, and engineers, may be able to skip this chapter, but will still find it useful for reference purposes.

Sound (in the acoustical sense) requires an elastic medium, such as air, water, or solid material; unlike light and radio waves, sound cannot travel in a vacuum. At rest, the molecules in the medium (in the case of air, mostly nitrogen and oxygen molecules) are more or less evenly dispersed, moving to and fro in a random fashion. At each point in space, both the density (number of molecules per unit volume) and pressure (the force the molecules exert per unit area) are approximately uniform.

Imagine now that a tuning fork begins to vibrate in the air. Each time the tuning fork moves to the right, it compresses a layer of air molecules on its right side so they are more closely packed, exerting greater pressure (called *condensation*), and pulls the molecules further apart on its left side, reducing the air pressure (called *rarefaction*). Both the condensation and the rarefaction move outward, as the high pressure compresses adjacent layers of air on one side, while the low pressure rarefies adjacent layers of air on the other. If the tuning fork now moves to the left, it creates zones of condensation on the left and rarefaction on the right. As the fork oscillates, alternating waves of rarefaction and condensation move outward to both the right and left. This is illustrated in Figures 2–1 and 2–2, which show the variations in pressure and

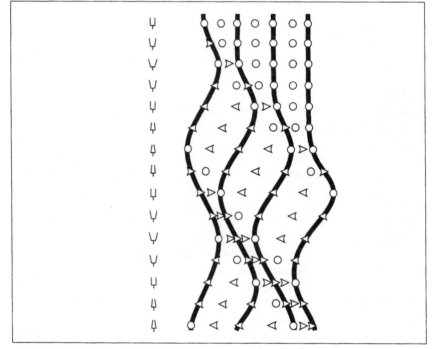

Figure 2–1. As the tuning fork (left) vibrates, air molecules are alternately pushed together (compression) and pulled apart (rarefaction). At successive instants in time, represented from top to bottom, individual molecules move back and forth (arrows indicate their direction of movement), while the rarefaction and condensation waves move outward.

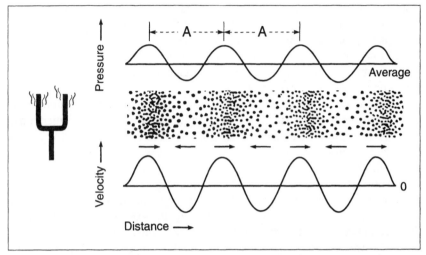

Figure 2–2. The dots represent individual air molecules at various distances from a vibrating tuning fork, at one instant in time. As the upper graph indicates, air pressure is highest where the molecules are closely packed. Positive velocity (lower graph) means movement away from the fork; negative velocity means movement back towards the fork. The distance (A) between condensation peaks is the wavelength. (Source: U.S. Environmental Protection Agency–Office of Noise Abatement and Control, 1976)

particle velocity at increasing distances from the right side of a tuning fork at successive moments in time.

As mentioned, sound can travel in any elastic medium. We will focus our discussion on airborne sound, but will need to consider sound in water at a later time because the hair cells that convert sound energy into nerve impulses in the inner ear are immersed in a watery fluid. The middle ear exists solely to facilitate the transfer of acoustic energy from air to water; without its impedance-matching function, almost all the energy would be reflected back into the air. Acoustic impedance, sound transmission across media, and impedance matching will be briefly discussed in Chapter 3.

FREQUENCY

The *frequency* of a sound is simply the number of complete oscillations or cycles completed each second; usually frequency is expressed in units of hertz (Hz) or kilohertz (kHz). For example, a tuning fork completing 2,000 cycles each second makes a sound with a frequency of 2,000 Hz or 2 kHz. At best, humans can hear sounds between 20 Hz and 20 kHz; sounds with frequencies below and above these limits are called *infrasound* and *ultrasound*, respectively. Within the range of frequencies we can hear, frequency (a physical, measurable variable) is closely related to pitch (a perceptual variable). A piano produces tones with fundamental frequencies from about 28 Hz to 4.1 kHz. Each doubling of frequencies corresponds to the musical interval of an octave, and the piano's range is a little more than seven frequency doublings, or octaves.

The *period* of a sound is the time interval required for a single complete cycle (the time between successive condensations or successive rarefactions), and can be simply calculated as the inverse of the frequency. A sound of 500 Hz has a period equal to $1 \div 500 = 0.002$ sec, while a 2 kHz tone has a period of 0.0005 sec. For convenience, periods are usually expressed in milliseconds (msec); thus, the 500 Hz and 2 kHz tones have periods of 2 and 0.5 msec, respectively. If we know the speed of sound in a particular medium (it is about 1,100 ft/sec in air), we can also easily calculate the *wavelength* of a sound, the distance between successive condensations (or rarefactions; refer back to Figure 2–2). Wavelength is equal to speed divided by frequency; a 1 kHz tone has a wavelength in air of $1,100 \div 1,000 = 1.1$ ft, or about 13 inches.

A tuning fork is an unusual and artificial object: When properly struck, it emits what is called a pure tone, the result of "simple harmonic motion" of its tines. The variation of pressure for a pure tone is equal to the tone's peak pressure multiplied by the sine (a trigonometric function) of the product of frequency and time (or distance). For this reason, a graph of pressure versus time (or distance) for a pure tone is called a sine wave (e.g., the upper and lower curves of Figure 2–2).

Most real vibrating objects produce complex sounds when struck, plucked, or otherwise made to emit sound. A violin string, for example, moves to and fro as it is dragged in one direction by the bow, then snaps back, only to be dragged again. This creates a sound pressure wave that is periodic (repeating itself at regular intervals), but is not a smooth sine wave. The resulting sound can be considered as composed of multiple sine waves with frequencies (called *harmonics* or *overtones*) that are integer multiples of a fundamental frequency. If the violin string completes 250 cycles of its irregular pressure wave each second, the resulting sound will contain strong acoustic energy at 250 Hz (the fundamental) and much weaker energy at 500, 750, 1,000 Hz, and so on (the overtones). The pitch of the tone will be the same as for a tuning fork emitting a 250 Hz tone, but the quality or timbre of the violin tone will be distinctively different. In fact, it is the relative strength of the overtones that permits us to distinguish different musical instruments playing the same musical note, or one vowel from another.

The fundamental frequency of the sound produced when an object is struck depends on its mass and stiffness. Smaller, stiffer objects emit high-pitched sounds, while larger, less stiff objects emit low-pitched sounds. This preferred frequency of an object is called its *resonant frequency*. Some objects, like tuning forks, are highly tuned and emit a single frequency or a very narrow band of frequencies, for a long time. Other objects, such as a piece of wood, are broadly tuned because of high internal damping (friction) resulting in a very brief emission of a sound containing multiple frequencies. Columns of air can generate sounds, too: Wind instruments such as the flute depend on this phenomenon. The resonant frequency of an air column depends on its length. Resonances also determine how freely an object or air column will vibrate when driven mechanically at different frequencies. If broadly tuned, there will be response to many different frequencies, but the strongest response will be to tones at or near the resonant frequency.

These observations about resonance are important in order to understand human hearing and noise-induced hearing loss. We are most sensitive to tones between 1 and 5 kHz because of the combined resonances of the ear canal (an air column) and the middle ear bones (vibrating objects), as will be discussed in Chapter 3. Not surprisingly, the damaging effects of excessive sound are greatest in a similar frequency range (3–6 kHz), as we will see in Chapter 7.

Many natural sounds, such as wind and surf, are sustained but not periodic, that is, there is neither regular waveform repetition nor a definite musical pitch. When the air molecules are moving back and forth in a more or less random fashion, we call the resultant sound "noise" ("noise" also refers to "unwanted sound," among other definitions). Truly random air movement produces white noise (containing equal energy at all frequencies), but noise can also be limited to more or less narrow frequency bands. For example, the speech sounds "s" and "sh" represent noises produced by blowing through an oral cavity that is narrowed by tongue placement either far forward ("s") or further back ("sh"); the varying resonant properties of the oral cavity cause the resultant noise to have relatively more high-frequency ("s") or low-frequency ("sh") energy.

INTENSITY

So far, we have treated sound as propagated changes in pressure over time in an elastic medium, but must now recall that the molecules in the medium are also moving back and forth together at any point in space. The amount of sound energy depends on both pressure and net molecular flow. Since *pressure* is defined as force per unit area (e.g., pounds/square inch or newtons/square meter), acoustic *intensity* is similarly defined as the flow of energy per unit time per unit area, and is expressed as watts per square meter. Acoustic intensity is equal to the product of sound pressure and a quantity called volume velocity, and is analogous to electric power. Sound pressure and volume velocity are analogous to voltage and current, respectively.

In practice, pressure is easy to measure and volume velocity extremely difficult. Fortunately, it's not necessary to measure both; for a given medium, pressure and volume velocity are always proportional: Volume velocity (V) equals pressure (P) divided by the acoustic impedance (Z) of the medium (impedance is the opposition offered by the molecules to imposed pressure). Intensity (I) can thus be easily calculated, as it is proportional to pressure squared:

$$I = PV = (P)\frac{P}{Z} = \frac{P^2}{Z}$$

Just as frequency (physical) is correlated with pitch (perceptual), acoustic intensity correlates with loudness: The more intense a sound, within limits of audibility, the louder it will be. It is essential to remember the distinction between acoustic and perceptual variables. In hearing-impaired persons, for example, the relationship between intensity and loudness may be abnormal. Soft sounds audible to normal listeners may be inaudible to impaired listeners, while more intense sounds may be equally loud to both normal and impaired listeners. This abnormally rapid growth of loudness for a given increase in intensity is called *recruitment*.

Let us return to our vibrating tuning fork to consider changes in intensity with increasing distance from a sound source. Assume no sound energy is lost as it radiates out in a spherical fashion. The total sound power (energy per unit time) at any specified distance would then be the same as at any other distance, but spread out over spherical surfaces of varying area. Since the surface area of a sphere is proportional to the square of its radius, sound *intensity* (power per unit area) is inversely proportional to the square of the distance from the sound source. This is known as the *inverse square law*. Recall that intensity is proportional to pressure squared; sound *pressure* is thus inversely proportional to distance (not its square). If the distance is doubled, the intensity will be one fourth as great, and the pressure will be halved. These relationships are illustrated in Figure 2–3; some examples are shown in Table 2–1.

The general rule that sound pressure is inversely proportional to distance must be modified by two additional factors. First, even in an unbounded medium, there is some conversion (dissipation) of sound energy to heat through friction as it radiates out. This effect is greater for higher frequencies. Second, in enclosed spaces such as factories, there is considerable reflection of sound from interior walls; in such reverberant environments, sound pressure may drop off much less rapidly as distance increases than would be predicted by the inverse square law.

The Decibel

The standard metric unit of pressure is the pascal (Pa), equal to one newton/square meter. In acoustics, the micropascal (μPa) is more commonly used. The softest sounds that are audible by humans have sound pressures of

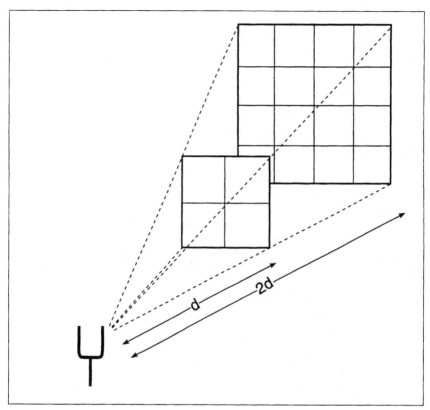

Figure 2–3. As sound energy radiates outward, it is distributed over areas which are proportional to the square of the distance from the source. Sound intensity (energy flow per unit area) at a distance of 2d is only one quarter as great as at a distance d.

about 20 μPa (about one billionth of normal atmospheric pressure). The loudest sounds we can tolerate have sound pressures of about 20 million μPa. Obviously, the great range of audible intensities makes it cumbersome to record sound pressure levels directly. In such situations, physicists resort to logarithmic representations; an example familiar to most readers is the pH scale used to measure acidity.

TABLE 2–1
Intensity and Pressure Changes with Distance

Distance Ratio	Intensity Ratio	Pressure Ratio
1:1	1:1	1:1
2:1	1:4	1:2
10:1	1:100	1:10

The logarithm of a number is the power to which the "base" (usually 10) must be raised to equal that number. The logarithm of 1,000 is 3, because 10^3 (10 to the third power) equals 1,000; the logarithm of 10,000 is 4. For numbers between 1,000 and 10,000, a scientific calculator will show logarithms between 3 and 4.

The first attempts to compress the measurement scale for sound involved a unit called the *bel* (named for Alexander Graham Bell), defined as the logarithm of the *ratio* between the sound intensity of interest and a reference sound intensity. If the ratio of sound intensities were one million to one, the more intense sound would be designated as "6 bel" re: reference level, since $10^6 = 1,000,000$. The bel proved to be too large a unit and was replaced by the decibel (dB), each of which is one-tenth of a bel.

$$10 \, dB = 1 \, bel$$

Thus, the number of decibels is equal to 10 times the logarithm of the intensity ratio. An intensity ratio of 1,000,000 to one is equal to 60 decibels (count the zeroes, multiply by 10). Recall that sound intensity is proportional to sound pressure squared. That same 1,000,000 to one intensity ratio is equivalent to a 1,000:1 pressure ratio. To arrive at the same 60 dB result using a pressure ratio, we must count zeroes and multiply by 20. Since it is usually pressure rather than intensity that is measured, the most familiar formula for the decibel is:

$$dB = 20 \, log_{10} \frac{P}{P_\emptyset}$$

where
    log_{10} means logarithm with base 10

and
    $P_\emptyset$ is the reference sound pressure.

A reference level in common use is 20 µPa; decibels calculated relative to this reference are referred to as dB SPL (sound pressure level). It is essential to remember that dB always refers to a ratio and that a reference level must be specified. A sound with pressure equaling 20 µPa would be 0 dB SPL (since the logarithm of 1, the pressure ratio, is 0. Clearly 0 dB SPL does not mean the absence of sound; rather, it means a sound equal to the reference level. Negative dB values mean that the sounds in question are less intense than the reference sound.

Table 2–2 and Figure 2–4 show some examples of intensity and pressure ratios and corresponding decibel values.

Calculating with decibels is easy for amplification and attenuation. An amplifier that doubles sound pressure level adds 6 dB (see Table 2–2); an earplug

TABLE 2–2
Decibels as Intensity and Pressure Ratios

Intensity Ratio	Pressure Ratio	dB
1:1	1:1	0
2:1	1.4:1	3
4:1	2:1	6
8:1	2.8:1	9
10:1	3.1:1	10
100:1	10:1	20
1:100	1:10	−20

that excludes 99 percent of sound energy, for an intensity ratio of 1:100, gives 20 dB of attenuation. Thus, a sound initially at 50 dB SPL is amplified to 56 dB SPL (or in the case of the earplug, attenuated to 30 dB SPL). Recalling our earlier discussion of attenuation with distance, every doubling of distance cuts the sound pressure in half and reduces the decibel value by 6 dB.

Many people have difficulty with decibels when multiple sound sources are present. If one machine emits 80 dB SPL at a measurement point, and a second machine (also emitting 80 dB SPL, but not synchronized to the first machine) is turned on at an equal distance from the microphone, the resultant sound pressure level is 83 dB SPL, not 160 dB SPL. This is true because the *intensities* add, and a doubling of intensity means a 3 dB increase in level.

Although loudness increases as intensity increases, it seems to grow somewhat more slowly. Most people judge one sound to be twice as loud as another when the two sounds are about 9 to 10 dB different. This is equivalent to a threefold difference in pressure and a tenfold difference in intensity.

The SPL reference is based on best human hearing, but is used across the frequency range, even at frequencies where humans hear poorly or not at all. A 30 dB SPL tone at 2 kHz could be heard by any normal listener, while a 30 dB SPL tone at 50 Hz is inaudible. A different decibel reference level is needed to specify sounds in terms of normal human hearing. As Figure 2–5 shows, the softest sounds humans can hear are near 0 dB SPL in the 1 to 5 kHz range, but rise substantially for lower and higher frequencies. The Hearing Level (HL) reference levels are designed for testing hearing; for each frequency from 125 Hz to 8 kHz, 0 dB HL is defined as the average threshold of hearing of young normal adult subjects free of otologic disease (ANSI S3.6-1996). For example, at 250 Hz, 0 dB HL = 25 dB SPL (measured as earphone output into a standard calibration coupler; specified levels vary slightly for different types of earphones). A subject who can barely hear a 250 Hz tone at a presentation level of 55 dB SPL has a threshold that is 30 dB worse than average normal (55–25); his threshold would be reported as 30 dB HL.

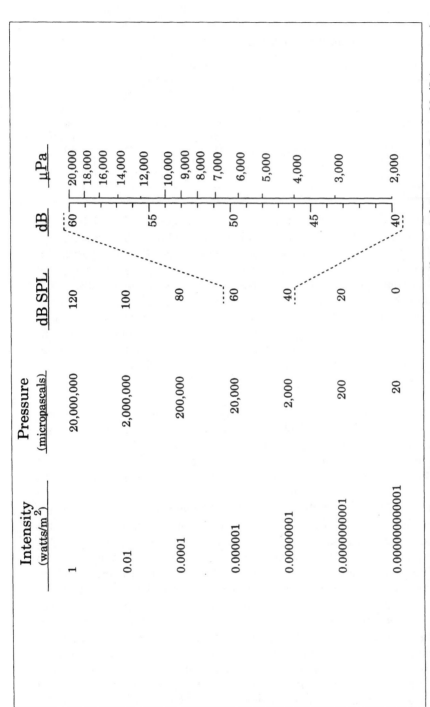

Figure 2–4. By convention, 0 dB SPL equals 20 micropascals (pressure) or 10^{-12} watts/m^2 (intensity). Every 20 dB increase is equivalent to a 10-fold increase in pressure and a 100-fold increase in intensity. The logarithmic nature of the dB scale is illustrated by the expansion, at right, of the 40–60 dB SPL region.

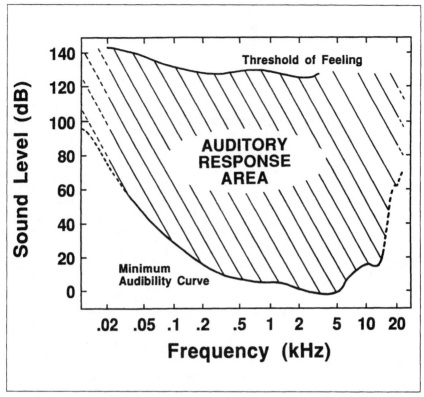

Figure 2–5. The range of human hearing is indicated by the hatched area. Sounds below the minimum audibility curve (e.g., 20 Hz, 40 dB SPL) can't be heard. (Source: Dobie and Rubel, 1989)

A 250 Hz tone of 75 dB SPL (50 dB HL) is 20 dB above that subject's threshold—this tone is said to be 20 dB SL (sensation level) for that subject.

In summary, the decibel is a relative measure that always refers to a *ratio* of two sounds. It is proper to speak of two sounds that are 10 dB apart, or of a 20 dB amplification or a 30 dB attenuation; all these usages imply relativity. It is improper—or at least ambiguous—to speak of a "30 dB sound" without specifying the reference level. Some commonly used reference levels are 20 µPa (dB SPL), normal human hearing for a particular frequency (dB HL), and an individual's own hearing (dB SL). Decibels are also handy for comparing the intensities of a desired sound (signal) and an unwanted sound (noise). A *signal-to-noise ratio* (SNR) of +3 dB means that the signal is twice as intense as the noise. If the SNR is −10 dB, the noise is 10 times as intense as the signal. Effective speech communication depends not only on a speech signal that is audible to the listener, but also on a good

SNR; depending on the difficulty of the speech message and other factors, communication begins to break down when SNR approaches zero or becomes negative (Webster, 1978).

MEASUREMENT OF SOUND

In this section we will consider a commonly used method of measuring overall sound pressure levels across frequencies in a way that approximates effects on human listeners. Most real-world occupational noises are broad spectrum: They contain significant sound energy across a wide range of audible frequencies. In its simplest operating mode, a sound level meter measures overall sound pressure level (dB SPL); it actually measures not the *peak* pressures, but the "root mean square" pressure (the pressure that, if constantly present during the measurement interval, would deliver the same amount of sound energy as the varying pressure actually present). However, this measurement is of limited usefulness for assessing risk to hearing because it gives equal weight to all frequency ranges, including those where human hearing is quite poor and where even very intense sounds pose little or no risk. This problem was recognized decades ago, and early attempts to assess damage risk relied on making separate measurements for each of several octave bands (e.g., 707–1,414 Hz, 1,414–2,828 Hz), using filters that excluded frequencies outside the band of interest prior to measurement. Each of these bands was then given a weight corresponding to the risk potential of sounds in that frequency range.

Since the 1960s, a simpler solution has been almost universally accepted. Sound level meters are equipped with weighting networks that do not totally exclude any band of frequencies, but rather attenuate them to varying degrees. The "A"-weighting network (Figure 2–6) gives essentially full weight to frequencies between 700 and 9,000 Hz (within 3 dB), but gives much less weight to lower and higher frequencies (ANSI S1.4-1983). For example, noise in the 100 Hz region is given about 20 dB less weight than noise in the 2 kHz region. The similarity of the A-weighting response to the human audibility curve shown in Figure 2–5 (inverted) is no coincidence. A-weighted measurements give a reasonably accurate idea of the relative loudness and damage risk of different sounds because they emphasize the frequencies humans hear well and de-emphasize those we hear poorly. Decibels measured using the A-weighting network of the sound level meter are referred to as dBA.

Risk to human hearing for eight-hour daily exposures begins at about 85 dBA. For shorter daily exposures, higher sound levels can be tolerated without appreciable risk, but the appropriate trading relationship between time and intensity is not universally agreed on. One approach is to assume that equal sound energy means equal risk. Intensity is energy per unit area

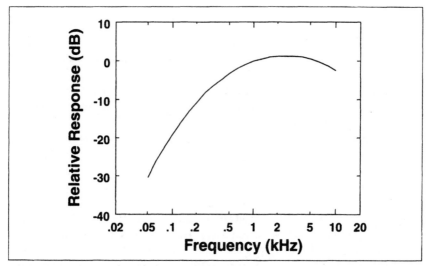

Figure 2–6. The A-weighting network causes a sound level meter to give different readings than unweighted sound pressure level (re: 20 micropascals), by the amounts shown in this graph.

per unit time; it follows that total energy delivered per unit area would be equal to the product of intensity and time, and a doubling of intensity (a 3 dB increase; see Table 2–2) or of time would double the total energy delivered. Conversely, if intensity is increased 3 dB and exposure time is cut in half, the overall energy is unchanged—and so is risk, if the equal-energy hypothesis is correct. As will be discussed in Chapter 7, shorter exposures tend to be intermittent throughout the day, and interrupted exposures cause less hearing loss than continuous exposures of equal duration. For this reason, the Occupational Safety and Health Administration of the U.S. Department of Labor specifies a 5 dB trading rate instead of the 3 dB suggested by the equal-energy hypothesis (OSHA, 1983).

Noise dosimeters are wearable integrating sound level meters that can assess the overall risk of an individual's workday exposure. The dosimeter measures A-weighted levels throughout the day, then reads out a time-weighted average (TWA): the A-weighted level that, if continuously present for eight hours, would pose risk to hearing equivalent to the varying exposure measured by the dosimeter. With 5 dB trading, a dosimeter exposed for four hours to 95 dBA would read out 90 dBA-TWA; two hours at 95 dBA would produce a reading of 85 dBA-TWA. OSHA requires hearing conservation programs (where it has jurisdiction) when daily exposures exceed 85 dBA-TWA. Noise dosimeters do not always provide the best estimates of risk; some measurement pitfalls are discussed in Chapter 9.

REFERENCES

American National Standards Institute. 1996. *American National Standard Specifications for Audiometers, ANSI S3.6-1996*. New York: Acoustical Society of America.

American National Standards Institute. 1983. *American National Standard Specification for Sound Level Meters, ANSI S1.4-1983*. New York: Acoustical Society of America.

Dobie, Robert A. and Edwin W. Rubel. 1989. The auditory system: Acoustics, psychoacoustics, and the periphery. In *Textbook of Physiology: Volume 1, Excitable Cells and Neurophysiology*, 21st ed., eds. Harry D. Patton, Albert F. Fuchs, Bertil Hille, Allen M. Scher, and Robert Steiner, pp. 365–385. Philadelphia: W. B. Saunders Company.

U.S. Department of Labor—Occupational Safety and Health Administration. 1983. Occupational Noise Exposure: Hearing Conservation Amendment; Final Rule. *Federal Register* 48(46):9738–9784.

U.S. Environmental Protection Agency—Office of Noise Abatement and Control. 1976. *About Sound*. Washington, DC: U.S. Government Printing Office.

Webster, John C. 1978. Speech interference aspects of noise. In *Noise and Audiology*, ed. David L. Lipscomb, pp. 193–228. Baltimore: University Park Press.

Chapter 3

The Ear and Hearing Tests

STRUCTURE AND FUNCTION OF THE EAR

The human ear, like those of other mammals, can conveniently be divided into three parts with different functions. The *outer ear* collects sound; the *middle ear* acts as an impedance-matching transformer so that airborne sound can be efficiently transmitted into the inner ear fluids; and the hearing organ in the *inner ear* changes sound energy to mechanical energy, then into nerve impulses that travel to the brain. Figure 3–1 shows the outer, middle, and inner parts of the ear in coronal section, that is, as if the head were separated into front and back halves.

Outer Ear

The outer ear has two parts. The *pinna*, or *auricle*, is a delicately shaped flap of cartilage covered by skin on both sides and projecting from the side of the head. While the pinna is functionally important for many mammals, funneling sound to the ear canal and moving from side to side to enhance directional hearing, it is mostly decorative in humans. Because of its complex shape, the pinna slightly increases or decreases sound transmission at different frequencies depending on the direction from which the sound is coming. An individual who lost both auricles would be unable to localize sound in the vertical plane, that is, tell whether a sound was coming from near the ground or from above the horizon, but would have no difficulty with horizontal plane (right-left) localization. Loss of one auricle would have negligible effect unless the

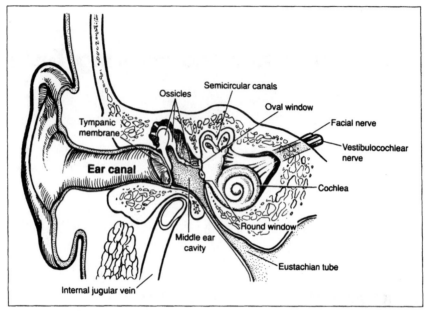

Figure 3–1. This coronal section of the right ear, from the front, shows the outer ear, middle ear, and inner ear.

opposite ear had poorer hearing; in that setting, the individual would lose both vertical plane and horizontal plane localization from the combination of unilateral hearing loss and loss of the pinna.

The ear canal is a skin-lined tube beginning at the pinna and terminating at the tympanic membrane (eardrum), which separates the ear canal from the middle ear. Like any tube closed at one end, the ear canal (or rather the column of air within it) has a resonant frequency determined by the length of the tube. For adult human ears, that resonant frequency is about 3 kHz (kilohertz). Sounds in the 2 to 5 kHz range are boosted by 10 dB or more in the ear canal, compared to sounds below 500 Hz (hertz). (Readers uncomfortable with resonant frequencies and decibels should read or reread Chapter 2 before continuing with this chapter.) Narrowing or partial blockage of the ear canal by cerumen (earwax), infections, tumors, or foreign bodies has almost no effect on hearing, but a complete blockage produces a substantial hearing loss.

Middle Ear

The tympanic membrane is thin and almost transparent, lined by skin cells on its outer surface and by mucous membrane on its inner surface. It is attached to the outermost of a chain of three small bones called the *ossicles:* malleus (hammer), incus (anvil), and stapes (stirrup). The ossicles are delicately suspended from the bony walls of the middle ear cavity. Sound traveling down the ear canal strikes the eardrum, causing it to vibrate and to transmit those vibrations to the ossicular chain and then into the inner ear (the footplate of the stapes is in direct contact with the inner ear fluid). Two of the ossicles—the malleus and the stapes—have small muscles attached to them that contract in response to loud sounds, stiffening the chain and reducing the amount of low-frequency sound that can pass to the inner ear; this is the *acoustic reflex*. The middle ear is normally an air-containing space, but is lined by a mucous membrane that continuously absorbs air, requiring that air be periodically supplied by the eustachian tube leading from the upper part of the throat (nasopharynx) to the middle ear.

Why such a fancy arrangement—why not just have the eardrum contact the inner ear fluid directly? The answer is found by considering the *acoustic impedances* of air and water. Different conducting media have different acoustic impedances, just as they have different electrical impedances or resistances. Air is a low-impedance medium; it takes very little pressure to cause high particle velocities. Water is a high-impedance medium: For a given sound intensity level, pressure will be high and particle velocity low (the speed of the to-and-fro movements of the "particles"—molecules in the air or water—is not to be confused with the speed of the sound wave traveling through the medium, which is actually much faster in water than in air). When sound traveling in one medium strikes a boundary with a medium of different impedance, efficient transmission does not occur. If the first medium is low-impedance, sound pressure will be insufficient to move the particles rapidly in the second medium. If the first medium is relatively high-impedance, particle velocity is insufficient to generate high pressures in the second medium. In either case, most of the sound energy will be reflected from the interface, with little energy passing into the second medium. The acoustic impedances of air and water are different enough that ordinarily less than 0.1 percent of sound energy is transmitted; this corresponds to a 30 dB loss (1,000:1 ratio) of sound intensity.

The eardrum and ossicles convert low-pressure, high-particle-velocity sound (in air) to high-pressure, low-particle-velocity sound (in water). This occurs primarily because the area of the eardrum is so much larger than the area of the stapes footplate. Although the total *force* applied at the eardrum by incoming sound is about the same as the force applied by the footplate to the inner ear fluid, the *pressure* (force/unit area) is much increased, allowing much of the energy that would otherwise have been reflected to be transmitted. In engineering terms, the middle ear acts as an impedance-matching transformer, similar in principle to the transformers used to connect electronic devices of different impedances (e.g., antenna or cable to a television set).

The middle ear, like any mechanical system, has mass and stiffness and a resonant frequency; it works best in the range between 1 and 2 kHz. This resonance and the ear canal resonance combine with the inherent inability of the inner ear to respond to very high and very low frequencies to determine the normal human sensitivity curve (see Chapter 2), with best hearing between 1 and 5 kHz and none outside the 20 Hz to 20 kHz range.

Conductive Hearing Loss

Since the middle ear prevents about 30 dB of energy loss caused by impedance mismatch and reflection, we predict that loss of the middle ear transformer would result in a 30 dB hearing loss relative to normal. Indeed, this is the approximate result when, as sometimes happens, the ossicles are eroded by chronic infection and the eardrum comes to rest directly on the stapes footplate. This is one type of *conductive hearing loss*, in which sound is not adequately conducted into the inner ear.

Conductive losses have multiple causes—cerumen blockage of the ear canal, ossicular erosion and fixation, fluid filling the middle ear, and perforation of the eardrum, among others. They never exceed about 60 dB, even with total absence of the ear canal and middle ear, because sounds above 60 dB SPL (sound pressure level) cause the entire skull to vibrate strongly enough to transmit sound into the inner ear; this is called *bone conduction*, in contrast to the normal *air conduction* pathway of sound to the inner ear. Conductive hearing losses are usually correctable by medical or surgical treatment of the outer ear or middle ear.

Inner Ear

The inner ear is a fluid-filled labyrinth of cavities hollowed out of the solid petrous bone, containing the organs of hearing and balance. The vestibular labyrinth includes three semicircular canals for the detection of head rotation and two otolith organs that detect linear movement and tilt. Disordered or absent vestibular function often leads to symptoms of imbalance and vertigo.

The hearing part of the inner ear is called the *cochlea* (Greek: snail) because of its spiral shape. Within the cochlea, two connecting chambers (the scala vestibuli and scala tympani) contain *perilymph*, a fluid much like spinal fluid, while a third chamber (scala media or cochlear duct) contains *endolymph*, a potassium-rich fluid like no other extracellular fluid in the body (Figure 3–2). The organ of Corti runs the entire length of the cochlear duct and contains the hair cells that actually transduce sound-induced movement into auditory nerve impulses. Both the membranes of the cochlea and the hair cells are mechanically tuned (based on mass and stiffness), so that each region of the organ of Corti responds best to a particular frequency: High-frequency

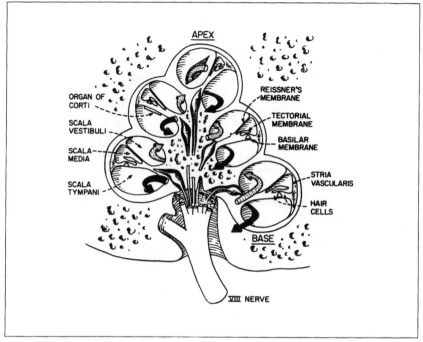

Figure 3–2. A cut through the axis (for modiolus) of the cochlea yields a view of all three turns of the cochlea, from base to apex. The VIIIth nerve fibers innervate the organ of Corti through tiny channels in the bony modiolus. (Source: Dobie and Rubel, 1989)

sounds preferentially activate the basal region, while low-frequency sound activates the apex of the organ of Corti. This *tonotopic organization* permits the inner ear to segregate sounds of different frequency content, which in turn permits the listener to recognize complex sounds (e.g., speech) based on the patterns of frequencies present. Damage limited to a single region of the organ of Corti will usually cause hearing loss limited to the range of frequencies best transduced by the damaged region.

Progressively higher-powered looks at a cross section of a single turn of cochlear spiral (Figure 3–3) show that within the organ of Corti, in the cochlear duct, are three rows of outer hair cells and a single row of inner hair cells. The outer hair cells are essential for the detection of soft sounds and are particularly vulnerable to any number of noxious agents, such as excessive noise and ototoxic drugs. However, most of the nerve fibers going to the brain from the cochlea are attached to the inner hair cells. When outer hair cells are lost, soft sounds can no longer be heard, but more intense sounds may not only be heard, but may be as loud as before. This phenomenon is called

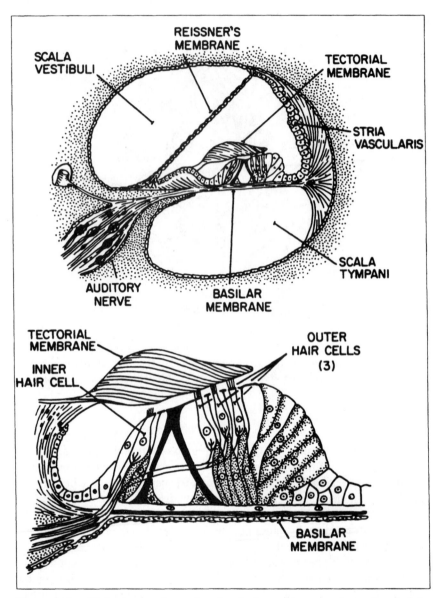

Figure 3–3. High-power schematics of a single cochlear turn (upper) and of the organ of Corti (lower). Most of the nerve fibers running to outer hair walls are not sensory; rather, they carry messages from brain to hair cell which help to "tune" the inner ear. (Source: Dobie and Rubel, 1989)

recruitment (an abnormally rapid growth of loudness) and is one factor making inner ear hearing losses difficult to manage. For example, a hearing aid that amplifies soft sounds enough to be audible may make more intense sounds too loud for comfort. The stria vascularis is a strip of metabolically highly active cells on the outer wall of the cochlear duct that supplies electrical energy to the organ of Corti by pumping potassium ions into the cochlear duct; this in turn produces a large electrical voltage in the endolymph, which is essential for proper hair cell function.

Sensorineural Hearing Loss and Tinnitus

Hearing losses originating in the inner ear, auditory nerve, or, rarely, the brain are called *sensorineural*. In contrast to conductive hearing losses, they are usually not amenable to medical or surgical treatment. While some cases show fluctuation or spontaneous improvement, most are either stable or progressive. The third basic type of loss is a *mixed hearing loss*, in which a conductive loss and a sensorineural loss coexist.

Any ear (or brain) disorder that causes hearing loss can also cause *tinnitus*, a sensation of sound (often described as ringing) in the absence of any external, physically measurable sound. Tinnitus, like vertigo, is difficult to measure, and even more difficult to relate to handicap. Tinnitus is often an early warning symptom for noise-induced hearing loss and other insidious disorders; patients may notice tinnitus before they notice hearing loss.

The auditory nerve leaves the inner ear and travels to the brainstem where its fibers make extraordinarily complex connections with groups of brain cells involved in analyzing the multiple dimensions of the incoming sound. The brainstem auditory centers send projections to the cerebral cortex. Within the brainstem, there are extensive side-to-side connections, so that a sound entering only the right ear (e.g., by earphone) elicits brainstem and cortical activity on both sides of the brain. One reason for this extensive binaural representation in the auditory brainstem is to support the localization of sounds: By comparing small differences in the timing and intensity of sounds at the two ears, the brain can determine whether the sound source is closer to one ear than the other, and, more specifically, the angle of the source relative to the listener. Because of this, injuries and other lesions on one side of the brain, while they may impair localization of sound, rarely cause measurable hearing loss for tones presented to either ear.

This has been a necessarily superficial discussion of auditory physiology, but covers those areas important for medical-legal assessment of hearing loss. Readers wishing a more complete treatment may wish to read Dobie and Rubel (1989).

HEARING TESTS

We cannot directly observe hearing in others, in the sense that we observe the form or movement of some part of the body. Usually, the simplest way to learn whether or how well a person has heard something is to ask him. When we deliver a tone or word to the subject's ear and the subject responds by raising a finger or by repeating the word, we observe (see or hear) the subject's *behavior* and infer that the stimulus has been heard. *Behavioral* tests of hearing are not only simple and rapid; they provide in most cases the best information available to characterize a person's hearing.

We can also observe and measure involuntary, *physiological* responses to sound, ranging from middle ear muscle contractions to cochlear "echoes" to electrical brain waves. As we will see, tests based on physiological responses are quite useful as "site-of-lesion" tests to determine the location (middle ear vs. inner ear vs. auditory nerve) of the abnormality causing a hearing loss. They are not usually necessary for measuring the severity of a hearing loss, although some exceptions will be discussed in Chapter 4 (Audiologic Evaluation for Exaggerated Hearing Loss). A good introductory text for those who want to read further is by Campbell (1998).

Behavioral Tests

Pure-Tone Air-Conduction Thresholds
In Chapter 2, we discussed frequency, intensity, the decibel, and several dB reference levels: sound pressure level (SPL), hearing level (HL), sensation level (SL), and A-weighted (A). Recall that dB HL refers to the intensity of a sound relative to the average intensity of the softest sounds audible to young adult normal listeners. Implicit here is the idea of a *threshold*, an intensity level above which a sound is audible and below which it is inaudible. 0 dB HL is the level just audible to the average healthy young adult for sounds presented by *air conduction*, using earphones, in a laboratory setting; some will have higher thresholds, that is, require more sound, and an equal number will have lower thresholds. These latter thresholds are negative, for example, −5 dB HL. Standard deviations for pure-tone thresholds in healthy young adults are approximately 6 dB (Hardick et al., 1980); this means that about two thirds of these subjects have thresholds between −6 and +6 dB HL. Ninety-five percent have thresholds between −12 and +12 dB HL. Thresholds up to +15 dB HL are considered normal for young adults in clinical testing.

Present standards for audiometric zero (0 dB HL) were set by the International Organization for Standardization (ISO) in 1964 and adopted by the

American National Standards Institute in 1969 (ANSI S3.6-1969, 1970). This standard has recently been updated (ANSI S3.6-1996), but the reference threshold levels are unchanged. Before 1969, American audiometry was based on a different standard set by the American Standards Association, ANSI's predecessor (ASA Z24.5-1951). The ASA-1951 levels for audiometric zero were, on the average, about 10 dB higher than ANSI-1969; in other words, the ASA-1951 standard assumed normal hearing was about 10 dB worse than was subsequently found to be true. An individual with 20 dB HL thresholds under ASA-1951 would have 30 dB HL thresholds under ANSI-1969. Table 3–1 shows the actual changes between the two standards.

This change in standards sometimes creates problems in case analysis when comparing two tests that may have been based on different standards. Many clinics began using the ISO-1964 standard prior to the promulgation of ANSI S3.6-1969. It is safe to assume that a test done before 1964 was based on ASA-1951 and that after 1970, ANSI-1969 was in universal use. For tests done between these years, the standard should be stated.

Accurate measurement of thresholds requires a very quiet test room, so that ambient noise will not mask the soft test tones. The lower the thresholds to be measured, the quieter the room has to be. A patient with 50 dB HL thresholds will hear a 50 dB HL tone quite well even in a typical office environment. Another patient, with a −5 dB HL threshold in a very quiet room, may not hear a tone below 10 dB HL in a less quiet room. ANSI (S3.1-1999) has specified permissible octave-band noise levels for pure-tone audiometry under earphones, which will permit the recording of thresholds as low as 0 dB HL (Table 3–2).

The Occupational Safety and Health Administration (OSHA) of the U.S. Department of Labor permits ambient levels 13–25 dB higher, for 500–8,000 Hz, for audiometry in occupational hearing conservation programs (U.S. Dept. of Labor, 1983). Individuals with very good hearing may have slightly inaccurate thresholds in these noisier rooms; for example, a person with a 0 dB HL threshold in a clinical setting may show a 10 dB threshold, because of masking by ambient noise.

TABLE 3–1
Reference Threshold Levels, dB SPL (ASA-1951 vs. ANSI-1969; TDH-39 earphone)

	Frequency (Hz)						
	125	*250*	*500*	*1,000*	*2,000*	*4,000*	*8,000*
ASA-1951	54.5	39.5	25.0	16.5	17.0	15.0	21.0
ANSI-1969	45.0	25.5	11.5	7.0	9.0	9.5	13.0
Difference	9.5	14.0	13.5	9.5	8.0	5.5	8.0

TABLE 3–2
Maximum Ambient Noise Levels for Audiometry, dB SPL (ANSI S3.1-1999)

Test Frequencies (Hz)	Octave Band Center Frequency (Hz)						
	125	250	500	1,000	2,000	4,000	8,000
125–8,000	35	25	21	26	34	37	37
500–8,000	49	35	21	26	34	37	37

While the idea of a threshold is simple, measuring it is not. For a given individual on a given day, there is a *range* of intensities below which a sound is never audible and above which it is always audible (under specified conditions of ambient noise and assuming properly functioning equipment). Within that range, the probability of our subject responding to the sound will depend on several factors, including:

- Instructions to the subject
- Testing technique used
- Subject's familiarity with the test
- Subject's motivation, effort, and attention
- Tester competence

For example, if a subject believes he is to respond only if he is certain a tone is presented, the measured threshold will be much higher than if he responds whenever he thinks there may have been a tone.

Several methods of pure-tone audiometry are in common use. In *manual audiometry*, the tester controls the frequency and intensity of the test tone, its duration, and the interval between tones, usually from a separate room, while watching the subject's responses. *Microprocessor audiometers* (used widely in industry) attempt to imitate the procedures followed in manual audiometry; the instrument automatically selects tone frequency, intensity, and so forth, then varies intensity according to fixed rules based on the subject's response (a button press) to the previously presented tone. *Self-recording audiometry* is also automatic: The audiometer constantly decreases (or increases) the tone's intensity, depending on whether the subject's last response was to hold the button down (indicating he is hearing a tone) or to release the button (he no longer hears it). An example of the tracing produced by a self-recording audiometer is shown in Figure 3–4.

An approved method for manual audiometry (also applicable to microprocessor audiometers) was published in 1978 and republished in 1997 (ANSI S3.21-1978). Recommended procedures include:

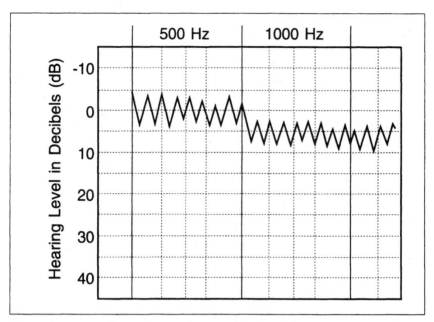

Figure 3–4. In self-recording audiometry, the intensity of the test tone alternately increases and decreases, controlled by the subject's responses.

- Preliminary inspection of the ear canal for blockage or collapse
- Use of two responses (e.g., raising and lowering a finger) for each test tone, one at the start and one at the end of the tone
- Tone duration = 1–2 seconds
- A 5 dB step size
- Level changes of 5 dB up after each failure to respond and 10 dB down after each response
- Definition of threshold as lowest level at which responses occur for half or more of ascending trials (minimum = three trials)
- Begin and end with 1,000 Hz (to check for reliability)

This method of threshold estimation tends to identify a level at which the subject responds more than half the time, because the criterion is most often met by two responses out of three presentations. In contrast, thresholds for self-recording audiometry are estimated at the halfway point between the peaks of the tracings (Figure 3–4), where a subject would respond about half the time. For this reason, all else being equal, self-recording thresholds tend to be 2–3 dB better than those recorded manually or by microprocessor audiometers.

Thresholds can be recorded in tabular fashion, but it is also helpful to show them on a graph. The *audiogram* is a graph of thresholds for several frequencies between 125 and 8,000 Hz. Figure 3–5 shows the conventional format, with intensity increasing as we go *down* the vertical axis. Thus, normal hearing would be recorded by a series of symbols across the top of the audiogram, and hearing loss would result in elevated thresholds marked further down on the scale. In Figure 3–5, the right ear has normal hearing and the left ear has a mild hearing loss. Colors (red for right, blue for left) are often used to indicate ears, but can create ambiguity when photocopied. The symbols and conventions of Figure 3–5 will be used throughout this book, and will be explained as we go along.

Table 3–3 shows the adjectives most commonly used by audiologists and otolaryngologists to describe different degrees of hearing loss (Goodman, 1965), with respect to the average hearing level at 0.5, 1, and 2 kHz. The region from 15 to 25 dB should probably be called "borderline"; thresholds in this region are not statistically normal for young adults, but are not significantly handicapping for adults (as will be discussed in Chapter 5).

Many factors can affect the quality of audiometric data. The American Academy of Otolaryngology–Head and Neck Surgery *Guide for Conservation of Hearing in Noise* (1988) lists these:

1. Physical variables
   a. Improper calibration of audiometer
   b. Improper placement of earphones

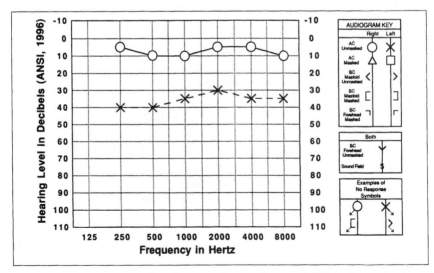

Figure 3–5. Conventional audiometric format (see text). Mild left hearing loss.

TABLE 3–3
Degrees of Hearing Loss

Pure-Tone Average (dB HL)	Adjective
≤ 25	normal
26–40	mild
41–55	moderate
56–70	moderately severe
71–90	severe
> 90	profound

    c. Excessive ambient noise levels in test room
    d. Equipment variables, such as accuracy of attenuator steps, type of earphone cushions, hum, noise, and other factors

2. Physiological variables
    a. Age and sex
    b. Pathologic condition of auditory organs
    c. General health of subject
    d. Temporary threshold shift
    e. Tinnitus
    f. Collapsed ear canals caused by earphone pressure

3. Psychological variables
    a. Motivation of subject
    b. Momentary fluctuations of attention
    c. Attitude toward the test situation
    d. Personality attributes
    e. Intellectual factors
    f. Comprehension of instructions
    g. Experience in test taking of any sort

4. Response conditions
    a. Type of response required of subject (e.g., button pressing, finger raising, verbal response)

5. Methodologic variables
    a. Tester competence
    b. Testing technique used
    c. Time interval between successive tests
    d. Instructions to subjects
    e. Order of presentation of frequencies

Annual pure-tone air-conduction audiometry is an essential part of the hearing conservation program mandated by OSHA for workers with potentially hazardous noise exposures (see Chapter 9). Air-conduction tests in industry are often performed by nurses and other individuals who have completed a 20-hour course and are certified by the Council for Accreditation in Occupational Hearing Conservation. The remaining tests to be described—bone conduction, masking, speech audiometry, impedance, otoacoustic emissions, the auditory brainstem response—are beyond what is required or appropriate in the industrial setting. These tests are usually performed by audiologists, although many are carried out by physicians and their staffs or by hearing aid dealers.

Bone Conduction

Earlier in this chapter we introduced the concepts of conductive hearing loss and bone conduction (BC). When the inner ear is normal, but sound is not adequately transmitted through the middle ear, a conductive hearing loss is present. The patient will hear normally if the entire skull is set into vibration, for example, by a tuning fork held against the forehead or teeth (BC), but will have elevated thresholds for sounds delivered by air conduction (AC) to the ear canal. This principle can be used in audiometry to distinguish conductive losses from sensorineural losses. A standardized BC vibrator, held to the head with a metal band, delivers tones directly to the skin over the mastoid (the bone behind the pinna). As for AC, thresholds for young healthy subjects form the basis for specifying 0 dB HL; patients with sensorineural hearing loss will have elevated BC thresholds, to about the same degree as their AC thresholds. Conversely, patients with pure conductive losses will have normal BC thresholds, but elevated AC thresholds.

One might expect AC and BC thresholds to be identical for normal subjects and for persons with sensorineural losses. However, individuals vary with respect to the relative efficiency of AC and BC pathways, and it is normal to have threshold differences of 5 to 10 dB—in either direction—between AC and BC. When AC is 15 dB or more worse than BC (under good test conditions), a true "air-bone gap" exists, and a conductive hearing loss is probably present (Figure 3–6; note that the BC thresholds are indicated by symbols introduced in Figure 3–5). As suggested earlier, one never sees air-bone gaps greater than about 60 dB, because at this point the earphone and cushion used in the AC test begin to cause the skull to vibrate, activating the BC pathway.

An individual who has both a conductive loss and a sensorineural loss is said to have a *mixed hearing* loss (Figure 3–7). In this case, the bone conduction thresholds show approximately what the individual's hearing would have been like if the external and middle ear were normal; they also predict the results of successful medical or surgical treatment of outer or middle ear disease, for example, removal of middle ear fluid.

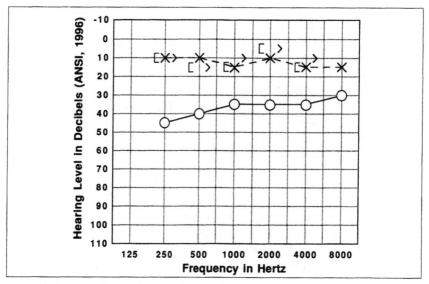

Figure 3–6. Conductive hearing loss, right.

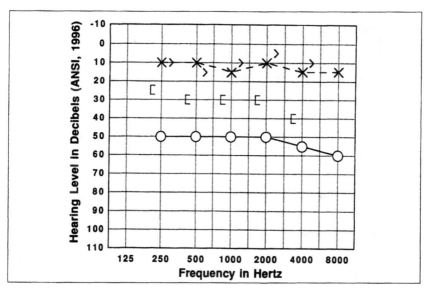

Figure 3–7. Mixed hearing loss, right.

Masking

When the two ears have similar AC thresholds, these thresholds can usually be accepted at face value, but this is not true when there is a large difference in hearing between the ears. If the right ear is completely deaf, sounds presented to it at high intensity will still be heard—in the *left* ear, since some of the sound can escape between the earphone and pinna and travel around to the good ear, or stimulate it by bone conduction. This usually requires sound levels about 40 to 60 dB more intense than the good ear's threshold. The problem of *acoustic crossover* can be solved by presenting masking noise to the non-test (better) ear to prevent it from hearing sounds presented to the test (worse) ear. Usually, masking is required for AC testing whenever the difference between ears on initial unmasked testing exceeds 40 dB (actually, it is the difference between the better BC threshold and the worse AC threshold that determines the need for AC masking). Figure 3–8 shows an example of a unilateral loss that is mild at lower frequencies—requiring no masking—but severe at higher frequencies. Note that the masked AC symbols (refer back to Figure 3–5) are used for the left ear from 4 to 8 kHz.

Masking is required for BC testing whenever an apparent air-bone gap of 15 dB or more is present. If one ear hears more poorly than the other, initial unmasked BC testing of the poorer ear will show an apparent air-bone gap whether the loss is sensorineural or conductive. This is true because a BC vibrator applied to one mastoid shakes the whole head and stimulates both cochleas with nearly equal efficiency. Masking noise presented by AC to the better ear will permit the worse ear's BC threshold to be properly estimated. When both ears hear equally poorly but only one has a conductive hearing loss, both ears will show apparent air-bone gaps when unmasked BC thresholds are

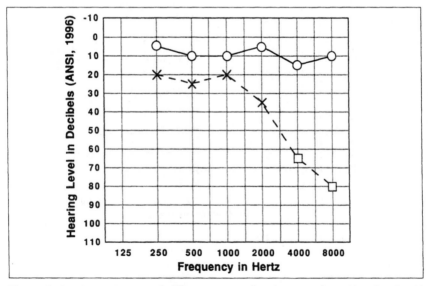

Figure 3–8.   Large interaural differences require the use of masking for 4 and 8 kHz, left ear.

obtained. In this case, each ear's BC thresholds must be measured with masking presented to the other ear.

When hearing is poor in both ears and at least one ear has a large conductive component, it can be difficult to obtain valid AC and BC thresholds, even with masking. This is called a "masking dilemma"; the basic problem is an inability to find a level of masking that is high enough to mask the non-test ear without stimulating the test ear by bone conduction. Using insert earphones (instead of the conventional earphones that are held against the pinna by an elastic band) will often solve this problem.

Most cases of medical-legal interest are relatively symmetrical sensorineural hearing losses, in which unmasked AC and BC thresholds are adequate. For simplicity, we will omit the BC symbols in this book except in examples of conductive or mixed losses. Masked AC thresholds will be shown when appropriate, as in Figure 3–8.

Speech Audiometry

Basic hearing evaluation in the clinical setting usually includes testing with speech sounds, in addition to pure tones. Although we use our sense of hearing for detection, identification, and localization of many types of sound, speech is obviously the most important. One goal of testing hearing with speech is to assist in estimating the degree of difficulty a hearing-impaired individual may have with speech communication. Less obviously, speech testing provides a cross-check of the validity of the pure-tone test results and also helps to distinguish inner ear disorders from disorders in the auditory nerve or brainstem. In fact, these latter benefits are probably more important than the former; as we will see in Chapter 5, speech testing adds surprisingly little information (regarding real-world communicative difficulties) to that provided by pure-tone testing.

Spectral analysis of speech reveals that most acoustic energy is contained in the frequency region below 500 Hz, but frequencies above 500 Hz contribute at least 75 percent of speech intelligibility, for two reasons. First, sounds below 500 Hz are relatively poorly heard (refer back to Figure 2–5). Second, most of the information in speech is contained in the consonants, which are relatively high-frequency, low-intensity sounds. Figure 3–9 shows an audiogram with the spectral peaks of selected speech sounds superimposed. For example, the vowel "o" at normal conversational level has its peak energy at about 500 Hz, about 50 dB HL (above normal threshold), while the "t" sound has its peak energy at about 4 kHz and 20 dB HL (it is important to recognize that each of these speech sounds contains energy for a wide range of frequencies; for example, the "f" sound has a nearly flat spectrum from 2 to 6 kHz). The shaded area represents the range of intensities present from moment to moment at different frequencies. This graph makes it easy to understand why people with high-frequency hearing losses complain that they can

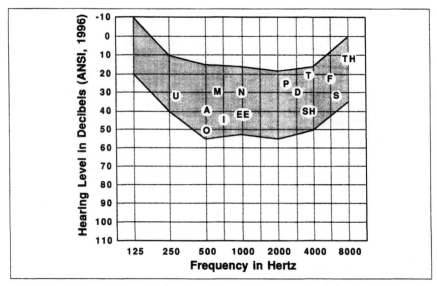

Figure 3–9.   Peak energies for several speech sounds, along with the typical energy envelope for running speech (shaded area) are superimposed on the audiogram.

hear but cannot understand: They are missing consonants which are essential to the message, for example, "tone" versus "phone."

In the example above, the inability to distinguish the "t" sound from the "f" sound could cause a message ("Can you hear the phone?") to be misunderstood. However, the context may provide sufficient clues for the listener to be pretty sure what the missing sound was. For example, the speaker may be pointing to a telephone while asking the question. Speech communication is normally rich with this sort of *redundancy* at multiple levels. When a particular speech sound is inaudible or misheard, the listener often can choose from a quite limited repertoire of possibilities, based on the subject under discussion, the grammatical context, and so forth.

These considerations of context and redundancy are of obvious relevance in constructing and interpreting hearing tests using speech materials. Tests using sentences or connected discourse are much easier than those using words in isolation. Spondees (two-syllable words in which each syllable is a word in its own right) are relatively easy, since there are only a few of them in English (baseball, cowboy, railroad, etc.) and one can usually guess the whole word having heard either half. Monosyllables are harder, but are still pretty guessable; there are only a couple of words in English that rhyme with "pal," so a listener who missed the "p" would still have a good chance to guess correctly. The hardest speech materials use nonsense syllables, so that a missed speech sound almost certainly leads to a scored error.

There are two types of speech tests in common clinical use. The first uses spondees (easy words) to estimate *threshold* for speech, the lowest sound level at which substantial speech information is available to the listener. The second uses monosyllables at various intensities to determine the listener's best speech perception performance in a quiet background.

Speech sounds, like pure tones, are presented at intensities specified as dB HL. 0 dB HL is the average level at which young healthy subjects can correctly identify 50 percent of spondees, and corresponds to 19 to 20 dB SPL peak level, depending on the earphone used (ANSI S3.6-1969, 1970). Since 0 dB HL is so similarly defined for pure tones and for spondees, we might expect that thresholds for spondees would be similar to pure-tone thresholds at frequencies important for speech understanding. Indeed, this is usually the case, for both normal and hearing-impaired subjects. A well-established clinical convention holds that the speech reception threshold (SRT; also called spondee threshold or ST) and the average threshold for 0.5, 1, and 2 kHz (pure-tone average or PTA) should be within 6 dB. In cases of steeply sloping losses, Fletcher (1950) pointed out that the SRT was closer to the "best two out of three" of these frequencies (almost always, 0.5 and 1 kHz) than to the three-frequency PTA; the two-frequency average is a "Fletcher-corrected" PTA.

When the SRT and PTA do not agree, the validity of the test is open to question. Probably the most common reason is a subject's failure to respond to the softest sounds he can hear. A desire to feign (or exaggerate) a hearing loss, a misunderstanding of the tester's instructions, or other factors, may lead a subject to respond only when the stimulus reaches an appreciable loudness level. Since loudness grows more rapidly for speech sounds than for pure tones for a given dB increment in intensity, such a subject is likely to respond to (and identify) spondees at lower levels than pure tones. Pure tone-speech reception threshold discrepancies will be further discussed in Chapter 4.

Monosyllabic words are more difficult to identify than spondees and are used in the second main class of speech tests in general clinical use: tests of *speech discrimination* (also referred to as "word recognition tests," as in Chapter 4). These tests use lists of monosyllabic words that are commonly used in spoken English and are, as a group, phonetically balanced; that is, they represent the speech sounds of the language in the approximate proportions found in normal speech. The most popular lists are the "W-22" (Hirsh et al., 1952) and "NU-6" (Tillman and Carhart, 1966) lists. A set of 25 or 50 of these words is presented to the listener using either a recording or the tester's live voice delivered through the audiometer at specified intensities, and the percent correctly repeated is scored.

Ideally, a different set of monosyllables is presented for each of several intensity levels, beginning at the listener's SRT, and continuing to 40 to 50 dB above SRT. Percent correct can then be plotted against intensity to obtain a *performance-intensity* (P-I) function. The P-I function rises to a plateau 20 to 40 dB above SRT in normal listeners, in those with conductive hearing loss, and even in most patients with sensorineural hearing loss. Patients with disorders affecting the auditory nerve or brain (called *retrocochlear* disorders) typically display an initial rise in discrimination score to a maximum level, which is often lower than would be expected for the degree of hearing loss present (Dubno et al., 1995), followed by a decrease at higher intensities (*rollover*). As we will see in Chapter 4, the P-I function can also be useful in suspected functional hearing losses.

Testing at multiple intensity levels to obtain a P-I function is quite time-consuming, and is not ordinarily done unless there is reason to suspect a retrocochlear problem. Usually, speech discrimination is tested at a *single* presentation level; unfortunately, there is no consensus regarding the choice of level. If the goal is to estimate ability to hear in "normal" situations, a 50 dB HL level is often chosen; this is the approximate level of normal conversational speech. For a subject with SRT greater than 25 dB, many audiologists choose a level of 25 to 40 dB SL (e.g., SRT + 30 dB), seeking to hit the point on that person's P-I function where percent correct will be at its maximum. Some audiologists present the monosyllables at the subject's most comfortable level. This is often well below the level at which they perform best, but may predict how well they would perform with a hearing aid (which often is adjusted more for comfort than for maximum speech discrimination). When looking for rollover, one alternative to a full P-I function is to measure performance at two levels, for example, 25 to 40 dB SL (at or near maximum performance) and 90 dB HL. When comparing speech discrimination tests from different facilities, it is crucial to note the presentation level, as well as other factors that may affect performance, such as the test materials used.

One might expect that speech discrimination scores would correlate well with self-reported hearing handicap, but this doesn't seem to be true. High, Fairbanks, and Glorig (1964) found that SRT and PTA (threshold measures) were better predictors of communicative handicap than discrimination score. Weinstein and Ventry (1983a, 1983b) found that speech discrimination scores correlate less well than pure-tone thresholds with scores on their Hearing Handicap Inventory for the Elderly. Monosyllable tests, as conventionally administered for the past 40 years, do not simulate real-world listening situations very well. In one sense, they are too difficult, removing most of the redundancy normally present in running speech. In another sense, they are too easy, because the words are presented in a quiet background, while real-world communication is often contaminated by noise. A third problem is variability; even when a 50-word list is used, percent-correct scores can differ by as much as 18 points without that difference reaching statistical significance at the 95 percent level (Thornton and Raffin, 1978; variability is worse for shorter lists). There have been many attempts to develop speech tests that more validly simulate communicative handicap, but none has achieved wide acceptance.

Site-of-Lesion Inference

Audiological tests alone never permit a determination of the cause of an individual's hearing loss, but they can determine the affected level of the auditory system. We've already seen how the comparison of AC and BC thresholds allows the tester to distinguish conductive (outer and/or middle ear) from sensorineural losses. Most sensorineural losses are caused by inner ear disorders, but the few caused by auditory nerve and brain disorders usually show reduced speech discrimination scores, out of proportion to the degree of pure-tone loss, or rollover on P-I functions. Thus, pure-tone and speech audiometry can go beyond measuring the severity of a hearing loss to provide significant localizing information.

Impedance Testing

Measurements of middle ear impedance are extremely useful adjuncts to pure-tone and speech audiometry, helping to identify different types of middle ear disorders, as well as retrocochlear disorders. Figure 3–10 shows schematically the instrumentation for impedance measurement (sometimes referred to as "immittance" or "admittance" measurement). An airtight probe seals the ear canal except for three tiny tubes. One is connected to a small loudspeaker and delivers a low-frequency sound to the ear canal, a second is connected to a pump, permitting the air pressure in the canal to vary, and a third is connected to a microphone to record the sound level in the ear canal.

When the middle ear is working properly, much of the sound delivered to the probe passes through into the middle ear and relatively low sound levels are recorded by the microphone. The eardrum and ossicular chain can be temporarily stiffened by introducing positive or negative pressure with the pump, reducing the efficiency of sound transmission and increasing the amount of reflected sound present at the microphone. The sound level measurements are converted into compliance (the opposite of stiffness) and plotted as a function of ear canal pressure in a graph called a *tympanogram* (Figure 3–11).

The tympanogram is a sensitive indicator of middle ear disorders. Eustachian tube blockage causes first a partial vacuum in the middle ear, followed by accumulation of fluid from the lining membranes. Various diseases may cause the ossicular chain to become abnormally loose or too stiff. Tympanometry reveals the presence of all these problems, sometimes before a significant air-bone gap can be seen on pure-tone audiometry.

Loud sounds presented to either ear elicit the previously described acoustic reflex, which can be recorded using tympanometric equipment and provides evidence for intact hearing and brainstem processing. In patients with retrocochlear disorders, the reflex is often lost, reduced in strength, or shows rapid decay when a long tone is used as a stimulus. These reflex abnormalities, along

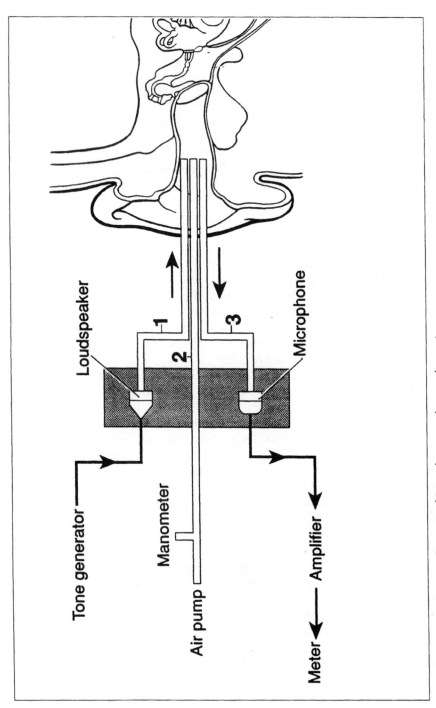

Figure 3–10.   Schematic diagram of impedance testing equipment.

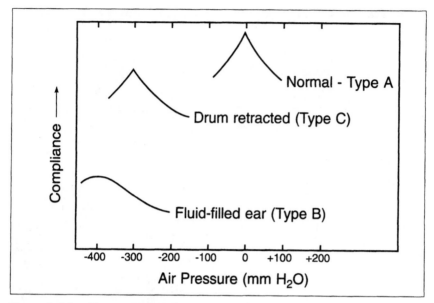

Figure 3–11.   Tympanograms showing normal curve (A), middle ear fluid (B), and negative pressure (C).

with the reduced speech discrimination previously discussed, are quite helpful in detecting retrocochlear problems, such as acoustic neuromas (Chapter 10).

Otoacoustic Emisssions (OAEs)

Healthy ears have outer hair cells that are exquisitely tuned and highly sensitive, and can respond to very faint tones. Some of these cells, in the healthiest ears, emit tones at the frequencies to which they are tuned; these *spontaneous* otoacoustic emissions are sounds that are usually too faint to be heard but can be recorded by placing a tiny microphone in the ear canal. Emissions can also be *evoked*, in almost all ears with good hearing, by delivering sound to the ear; transient sounds such as clicks will evoke an echo recordable a few milliseconds later. An example of a transient-evoked otoacoustic emission (TEOAE) recording is shown in Figure 3–12. TEOAEs are now in wide use in clinical audiology for hearing screening, for site-of-lesion inference (intact TEOAEs indicate functioning outer hair cells), and for medical-legal purposes (see Chapter 4). A third type of emission is produced when two tones of different frequencies (e.g., 2,000 and 2,400 Hz) are delivered to the ear, and the ear canal microphone records a "distortion product" at a third frequency, lower than the two tones presented, such that the three tones are evenly spaced (in this case, the third tone would have a frequency of 1,600 Hz). Distortion-product otoacoustic emissions

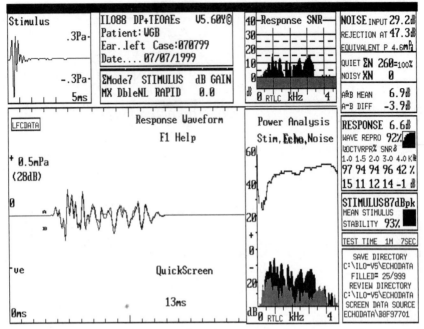

Figure 3–12. Two replications of a distortion-product otoacoustic emission recording overlap nearly perfectly (above the word "QuickScreen"); reproducibility is 92 percent and amplitude is 6.9 dB.

(DPOAEs) can be recorded from slightly less healthy ears, with AC thresholds up to about 50 dB HL in some cases, but are less well standardized and are less widely used than TEOAEs.

All types of OAEs require a healthy middle ear as well as functioning outer hair cells, because the faint sound produced in the cochlea must travel backwards through the ossicular chain, using the eardrum as a loudspeaker to produce recordable sound in the ear canal. For this reason, tympanometry and/or BC testing is often done prior to OAE testing; middle ear fluid or significant air-bone gaps usually preclude recording OAEs.

Auditory Brainstem Response

The most sensitive audiological test for retrocochlear hearing loss is the *auditory brainstem response* (ABR). When clicks or other brief sounds are delivered to the ear, they elicit a series of tiny electrical waves coming from the auditory nerve and brainstem; these waves are recordable using electrodes attached to the scalp. They can be amplified and measured using computers; even very small increases in latency (length of time from stimulus to response) suggest a slowing of nerve conduction in the auditory nerve or brainstem

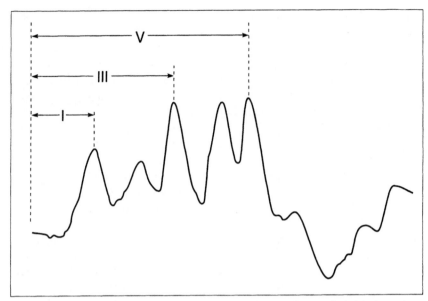

Figure 3–13. Auditory brainstem response. The largest peak (V) is less than 1 μV in height and occurs about 6 msec after the stimulus onset.

(Figure 3–13). The ABR, as well as other auditory evoked potentials, will be discussed further in Chapter 4, in the context of exaggerated hearing loss.

REFERENCES

American Academy of Otolaryngology–Head and Neck Surgery—Subcommittee on the Medical Aspects of Noise of the Committee on Hearing and Equilibrium. 1988. *Guide for Conservation of Hearing in Noise*, rev. ed. Washington, DC: American Academy of Otolaryngology–Head and Neck Surgery Foundation, Inc.

American National Standards Institute. 1970. *American National Standard Specifications for Audiometers, ANSI S3.6-1969*. New York: Acoustical Society of America.

———. 1997. *Methods for Manual Pure-Tone Threshold Audiometry, ANSI S3.21-1978* (R1997). New York: Acoustical Society of America.

———. 1996. *American National Standard Specification for Audiometers, ANSI S3.6-1996*. New York: Acoustical Society of America.

———. 1999. *Maximum Permissible Ambient Noise Levels for Audiometric Test Rooms, ANSI S3.1-1999*. New York: Acoustical Society of America.

American Standards Association. 1951. *Audiometers for General Diagnostic Purposes, ASA Z24.5-1951*. New York: American Standards Association.

Campbell, Kathleen. *Essential Audiology for Physicians*. 1998. San Diego: Singular Publishing Group.

Dobie, Robert A. and Edwin W. Rubel. 1989. The auditory system: Acoustics, psychoacoustics, and the periphery. In *Textbook of Physiology: Volume 1— Excitable Cells and Neurophysiology*, 21st ed., eds. Harry D. Patton, Albert F. Fuchs, Bertil Hille, Allen M. Scher, and Robert Steiner, pp. 365–385. Philadelphia: W. B. Saunders Company.

Dubno, J. R., F. S. Lee, A. J. Klein, L. J. Matthews, and C. F. Law. 1995. Confidence limits for maximum word-recognition scores. *J. Speech Hear. Res.* 38:490–502.

Fletcher, Harvey. 1950. A method of calculating hearing loss for speech from the audiogram. *Acta Otolaryngol. Suppl. (Stockh.)* 90:26–37.

Goodman, Allan C. 1965. Reference zero levels for pure-tone audiometers. *ASHA* 7(7):262–263.

Hardick, Edward J., William Melnick, Nancy A. Hawes, Joseph P. Pillion, Ray G. Stephens, and Deborah J. Perlmutter. 1980. *Compensation for Hearing Loss for Employees Under Jurisdiction of the U.S. Department of Labor: Benefit Formula and Assessment Procedures (Contract No. J-9-E-9-0205)*. Columbus: The Ohio State University.

High, Wallace S., Grant Fairbanks, and Aram Glorig. 1964. Scale for self-assessment of hearing handicap. *J. Speech Hear. Disord.* 29(3):215–230.

Hirsh, Ira J., Hallowell Davis, S. Richard Silverman, Elizabeth G. Reynolds, Elizabeth Eldert, and Robert W. Benson. 1952. Development of materials for speech audiometry. *J. Speech Hear. Disord.* 17(3):321–337.

Thornton, Aaron R. and Michael J. M. Raffin. 1978. Speech discrimination scores modelled as a binomial variable. *J. Speech Hear. Res.* 21:507–518.

Tillman, Tom and W. Raymond Carhart. 1966. *An Expanded Test for Speech Discrimination Utilizing CNC Monosyllabic Words (Northwestern University Auditory Test No. 6), Technical Report, SAM-TR-66-55*. Brooks Air Force Base, Texas: USAF School of Aerospace Medicine, Aerospace Medical Division (AFSC).

U.S. Department of Labor—Occupational Safety and Health Administration. 1983. Occupational Noise Exposure: Hearing Conservation Amendment; Final Rule. *Federal Register* 48(46):9738–9784.

Weinstein, Barbara E. and Ira M. Ventry. 1983a. Audiologic correlates of hearing handicap in the elderly. *J. Speech Hear. Res.* 26(1):148–151.

———. 1983b. Audiometric correlates of hearing handicap inventory for the elderly. *J. Speech Hear. Disord.* 48(4):379–384.

Chapter 4

Audiologic Evaluation for Exaggerated Hearing Loss

Jack M. Snyder

INTRODUCTION

There may be many motivations for a patient to offer voluntary audiometric responses that are worse than his or her "true hearing." The primary gain for such behavior is probably the potential of monetary award for claimed hearing loss. Very few patients display such responses as symptoms of significant psychiatric disorders, as in the classic hysterical deafness category. Secondary (nonmonetary) gains may be less evident, as in attempts to gain sympathy, to be excused for poor performance (vocational, academic, or personal), or to gain attention.

There is a continuum for exaggerated hearing loss, ranging from the malingerer to the true hysteric. The former is purposely lying and knows it; the latter has no conscious knowledge of the action. Many cases, if not most, lie between these two extremes. All audiometric test results and audiologic clues for falsely claimed hearing loss are the same regardless of where an individual may be on this continuum, making it impossible for such tests to accurately place a patient. In many years of practice, I have seen only a handful of patients who indicated that they had not "told the truth." Terms such as *malingering, unconscious*, or *hysteric* are not within audiologic or otolaryngologic practice.

This chapter will use the term *exaggerated hearing loss* (EHL) to encompass the full range of expression described in the previous paragraphs. Other terms similarly used have included *pseudohypacusis, simulated hearing loss, feigned hearing loss, psychogenic hearing loss*, and, more commonly, *functional* or *nonorganic hearing loss*. Those readers who are "splitters" in nosology may refer to Ventry and Chaiklin (1962), Goldstein (1966), and Noble (1987), for discussions of possible meaningful differences among these terms. I have taken the suggestion of my editor and lumped all categories together as "exaggerated hearing loss."

EHL is suspected when behavioral responses are inconsistent with general functional performance, with other behavioral tests (both generally administered tests and those specifically designed for EHL), and/or with physiological tests of the auditory system.

This chapter will focus primarily on the adult patient with possible EHL. The basic audiometric considerations are the same for all ages. A separate specific bibliography for EHL in children is presented after the reference list.

The classic study of EHL was conducted by Ventry and Chaiklin (1965) in a U.S. Veterans Administration hospital. Three subsequent studies of audiometric response in large groups of patients referred with possible noise-induced hearing loss (NIHL) have been reported by Alberti, Morgan, and Czuba (1978), Alberti, Hyde, and Riko (1987), and Rickards and DeVidi (1995). These three reports should be reviewed for supplemental background for this chapter.

DIAGNOSTIC STRATEGIES

The audiologic examination for EHL should include an evaluation of the following:

1. Discrepancies between the patient's description of hearing loss and the history and otologic findings; for example, a claim of severe unilateral hearing loss resulting from industrial noise exposure where one would expect both ears to be affected
2. Discrepancies between test results and the examiner's observations of the patient's performance and behavior; for example, a patient with an audiogram showing severe bilateral hearing loss occasionally responding appropriately to speech presented at low intensity levels (without visual or contextual clues)
3. Bizarre or atypical responses to test procedures; for example, delayed or exaggerated responses, absence of false-positive responses, or refusal to attempt a response as directed by the examiner
4. Intra-test inconsistency; for example, excessive variation of threshold shown across repeated presentations of a test
5. Inter-test inconsistency; for example, threshold for speech is significantly better than for pure tones
6. Departures from acknowledged psychoacoustic principles; for example, absence of appropriate shadow responses in asymmetric hearing loss or

unusually good performance in word recognition tests presented at an intensity level just louder than voluntary threshold

These discrepancies, inconsistencies, and other behaviors are without significance unless the examiner completes the test procedures in a consistent fashion after carefully instructing the patient as to the nature of the test and the type of response. Variation in instructions and procedures may inadvertently lead to inconsistencies falsely suggesting EHL.

The goal of every examination is to provide results that are both reliable and valid. Usually, the specific goal is to determine the amount of threshold elevation at specific frequencies and further to indicate whether the hearing loss is sensorineural, conductive, or a combination of the two. The presence of EHL may make these goals impossible to achieve. In such cases, the examiner may find, after an initial evaluation, that it is appropriate to merely judge the presence or absence of EHL. Better yet, the examiner may be able (and should be satisfied) at this point to state that the hearing levels are at least as good as a specific level (e.g., within normal limits), but that the exact (possibly better) true levels are as yet not established.

Subsequent counseling of the patient regarding inconsistencies and a reexamination at another time is a valid strategy and goal. This allows the patient to reconsider his purposes and allows the examiner the opportunity to efficiently extend the evaluation using appropriate special tests.

CASE REPORTS

The following five case presentations illustrate EHL. Each represents a variant, with discussions of the test strategies and inconsistencies that might be found. These are not atypical cases and reflect common problems and their resolutions in medical-legal audiometric evaluations. These case reports are presented early in the chapter to give the reader an immediate sense of the practical use of techniques, which are explained in detail later in the chapter.

CASE 1

A 62-year-old shipyard worker was referred for otologic and audiologic evaluation upon his retirement. He had filed a compensation claim with his employer for hearing loss incurred during his 18-year work history. His noise-exposure history was sufficient to possibly cause permanent hearing loss. A baseline audiogram obtained by the employer 12 years prior to the worker's retirement showed a mild bilateral high-frequency hearing loss, with the poorest threshold of 30 dB hearing level (HL) at 4,000 Hertz (Hz). Records of annual tests showed a gradual progression of this high-frequency hearing loss to about 60 dB HL, with the mid-frequency range

(500–3,000 Hz) remaining within normal limits. The last audiogram was completed by the employer two weeks prior to retirement. It showed a sudden increased bilateral loss for all frequencies. The employee had no change in noise exposure for several years.

COMMENT   *The history suggested to the examiner that this was possibly a case of EHL for at least three reasons. First, this is an obvious compensation case. Second, the sudden unexplained increased hearing loss at retirement is not consistent with the noise-exposure history and is coincident with his compensation claim. Third, involvement of 500 and 1,000 Hz in NIHL is unusual.*

The otologic history was otherwise negative and the physical examination by an otologist was normal. A tympanogram, the first test given at the audiometric examination, suggested normal middle ear function.

COMMENT   *The possibility of recent conductive hearing loss was essentially ruled out by these examinations and could not account for the sudden, increased bilateral hearing loss.*

The pure-tone air-conduction and speech reception thresholds (SRTs) for each ear were obtained. Reliable SRTs of 8 dB HL and 14 dB HL were obtained (well within normal limits), but the pure-tone thresholds (Fletcher correction; see Chapter 3) averaged 30 dB HL for each ear. The patient was slightly inconsistent in his responses for the pure-tone thresholds (see Figure 4–1A).

COMMENT   *The examiner had been alerted to the possibility of EHL and obtained thresholds after a very careful face-to-face explanation of the procedures. The SRTs were significantly better than the pure-tone thresholds for the frequencies that primarily compose the speech signals. The thresholds were obtained in a fashion that usually enhances pure-tone and SRT discrepancies in EHL (ascending intensities for SRT and descending intensities for pure-tone thresholds).*

Word recognition tests (WRTs) were measured next. These indicated surprisingly good scores at very low intensity levels (10 dB sensation level [SL]): 50 percent for the right ear and 30 percent for the left. (See Chapter 2 regarding SL and HL.) The maximum WRT score was well within normal limits for each ear (94–96 percent).

COMMENT   *These results are not possible given the worker's voluntary pure-tone thresholds. He denied hearing any pure-tone signal at less than 30 dB HL in his right ear, yet he was able to correctly repeat 50 percent of the words at 18 dB HL (a presentation level of only 10 dB*

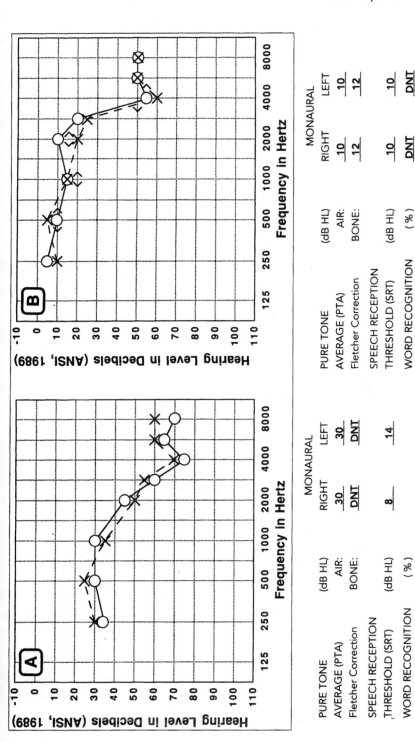

Figure 4–1. Case 1. DNT = did not test.

above his SRT). In fact, this score suggested his true average loss for the important speech frequencies was well within normal limits.

The examiner repeated the pure-tone thresholds after cautioning the patient to respond to the faintest sounds heard. The repeat test responses were more consistent, but again no threshold was found at less than 30 dB HL. Bone-conduction audiometry was omitted as it was obvious that the patient was not giving reliable responses. The patient was counseled that there were gross inconsistencies among the findings. He was told that the examiner did not know why these discrepancies occurred and that these tests would have to be repeated, perhaps with other special tests. Another appointment was scheduled. The patient had been friendly and cooperative throughout the testing.

COMMENT   *A confrontational approach to counseling is usually not productive in a case such as this, at least at this point in the evaluation.*

The patient returned for re-evaluation one week later. His first response upon meeting the examiner was to state that he thought he probably did not fully understand the instructions given to him at the time of the first test, and he felt he could do a much "better job" this time. Pure-tone and SRT testing was repeated (Figure 4–1B). His responses were remarkably clear and consistent and all prior inconsistencies were resolved. WRT scores were not repeated as they previously were shown to be within the range of normal. Because of his consistency and because his loss was consistent with his noise-exposure history in terms of degree, laterality, and configuration, the evaluation was concluded. Other special tests for EHL were felt to be unnecessary. The patient's audiogram was reviewed with him in detail.

COMMENT   *This is a typical case for several reasons. Given the patient's age and noise exposure history, some high-frequency sensorineural hearing loss (SNHL) was expected. A 20 to 30 dB EHL overlay on the true loss is often found in such cases (Alberti, Hyde, and Riko, 1987). It has often proved valuable to inform the patient of discrepancies and then immediately schedule a re-examination so the patient can use the interim period to reflect upon and evaluate his needs and motivation regarding the claimed hearing loss.*

CASE 2

A 42-year-old welder was referred by his employer following an accident at work. The medical history indicated that a spark entered the right ear canal about a month prior to his being seen, which caused great pain and a small tympanic membrane perforation. The injury was treated by an otologist and the perforation was closed. The patient claimed severe hearing loss for the injured ear. Recent tests done elsewhere were inconsistent and suggested a profound hearing loss in the right ear. The physical examination of the right ear (completed just before the audiometry) was reported as essentially normal by the otologist. The pre-examination interview with the audiologist showed a very agitated patient who bitterly complained of his working conditions and the pain he had suffered from the accident. He repeatedly cupped his hand behind the concerned ear during the interview. In a very loquacious manner, he reported many instances of how handicapping his loss was. He was accompanied by his wife and requested her presence throughout the interview and testing. She repeatedly confirmed all aspects of his discussion.

COMMENT   *The nature of the injury and subsequent relatively simple and successful medical treatment (with a paper patch and ear drops) argues against the presence of such a severe hearing loss. A small tympanic membrane perforation usually presents as a mild conductive loss (Anthony and Harrison, 1972; Sheehy and Anderson, 1980). The patient reported working in noise often requiring the use of ear plugs, so one might expect the customary bilateral hearing loss in the higher frequencies. His exaggerated attempt to hear the examiner's voice in a sound-treated room seems inappropriate considering his claims of only unilateral loss. His obvious anger and loquacious behavior seemed inappropriate and suggested EHL.*

Pure-tone audiometry (air-conduction and bone-conduction) was completed first (Figure 4–2A). Hearing in the left ear was normal except for a mild high-frequency SNHL, worst at 6,000 Hz (40 dB HL). The right ear showed a profound loss of 95 to 100 dB HL for air conduction and about 70 dB HL for bone conduction. Note that masking was not used in the left ear while testing the right ear.

COMMENT   *Loud sounds presented to a deaf ear will be heard in the good ear, resulting in a "shadow curve" on the audiogram about 60 dB down from the better ear thresholds. The lack of expected shadow responses from the good left ear when testing the poorer right ear strongly suggested EHL in this case. (See Shadow Responses in Unilateral or Asymmetrical Losses, below, regarding shadow responses.)*

Speech audiometry was then completed. The left ear findings were normal. Gross inconsistencies were shown for the right ear when comparing SRT and WRT findings with the pure-tone threshold results.

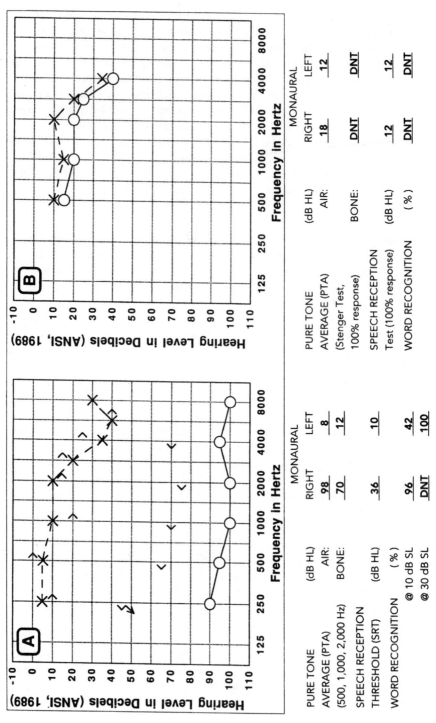

Figure 4–2.   Case 2. DNT = did not test.

COMMENT   *First, the pure-tone average of 500, 1,000, and 2,000 Hz (PTA-512) was 98 dB HL, whereas the SRT was only 36 dB HL. Second, the WRT was presented at 46 dB HL (36 dB + 10 dB) and an improbably good score of 96 percent was obtained.*

A tympanogram for each ear showed bilateral symmetrical findings, which were within normal limits for middle ear function.

COMMENT   *Although the patient's responses so far were not valid, the nature of the injury and the appearance of small air-bone gaps shown for the right ear required tympanometry to help rule out possible conductive involvement.*

Pure-tone Stenger tests and the modified (speech) Stenger test were administered next. The results are shown in Figure 4–2B. They showed hearing in the right ear to be generally within normal limits. The examination was terminated and it was reported to the patient and his wife that the results would be sent to the referring company physician. No interpretation of results was provided to the patient.

COMMENT   *The Stenger tests (see The Stenger Test, below) can be extremely sensitive in showing EHL for cases of claimed unilateral loss. In this case, these tests were of great qualitative as well as quantitative value. The examiner was able to show that hearing in the claimed severe hearing loss ear actually was within normal limits for 500 through 3,000 Hz. The middle ear function also appeared to be within normal limits. Further studies would not contribute to significantly greater understanding and resolution of the case. Any discussion of the findings with the patient would have been confrontational and unnecessary.*

CASE 3

A 56-year-old iron worker was referred for special audiologic evaluation by his otologist with a question of EHL. About two years before, he had suffered a blunt head injury. His major complaints following the injury were chronic dizziness and vertigo with head movement. Subsequently, he noted neck pain and blurred vision. He began to note *bilateral* hearing loss about one year previously, following exploratory surgery for the *left* ear to rule out a perilymphatic fistula. Radiologic evaluation and MRI of the head were essentially unremarkable. Auditory-evoked potentials were within normal limits. A current electronystagmography evaluation was normal. All objective tests for a fistula were negative. He had been unable to work since the accident because of dizziness and was receiving disability insurance benefits. Hearing tests prior to ear surgery showed bilaterally symmetrical high-frequency SNHL, greatest at 4,000 Hz with degree and configuration thought to be consistent with NIHL. Subsequent tests during the previous year showed fluctuating results for each ear and occasional SRT-PTA inconsistencies. In the process of various evaluations, the patient had seen three otolaryngologists in addition to several other physicians and chiropractors. He was wearing binaural hearing aids and spontaneously removed them when he began the pretest discussion with the audiologist.

COMMENT   *The patient had a full history of subjective complaints without any clear history of objective findings. His numerous somatic complaints, including onset of bilateral hearing loss many months following his accident were remarkable as was his choice to discuss his history without use of his hearing aids. The examiner felt he was able to answer questions presented at relatively normal conversational levels when the examiner's face was not in the patient's view. The patient was very sophisticated in routine hearing test procedures.*

A standard audiometric evaluation was completed, as shown in Figure 4–3A. While the reliability of his pure-tone threshold responses was good, inter-test inconsistencies were observed. The pure-tone thresholds showed severe SNHL and were remarkably worse than the SRTs. WRT scores were absolutely normal (a most unusual finding considering the claimed severity of the loss for pure tones) and were obtained at levels (65 and 70 dB HL) at which he denied hearing for pure tones. The patient was told he required additional special tests and was rescheduled.

COMMENT   *The patient was very cooperative and friendly throughout the examination. Bizarre or unusual exaggerated behavior was not noted except for the surprising action of removing his hearing aids before discussion with the audiologist. This was a case of EHL, but his personal behavior did not particularly suggest this finding and his sophistication in hearing tests allowed him remarkable reliability in duplicating puretone thresholds.*

About two weeks later, the patient returned; the repeat tests are shown in Figure 4–3B. Again, he was very friendly and seemingly cooperative. There was no evidence of his hearing aids. All previous discrepancies were again evidenced. However, this time he gave SRTs well within normal limits, and WRT scores were normal for the right and quite good for the left at normal conversational intensities (50–60 dB HL). Tympanograms were within normal limits. Acoustic reflexes were present for 500 and 1,000 Hz at levels from 5 to 10 dB louder than the usual range for normal hearing. Békésy (self-recording) audiograms showed hearing as good as 15 dB HL at 1,000 Hz

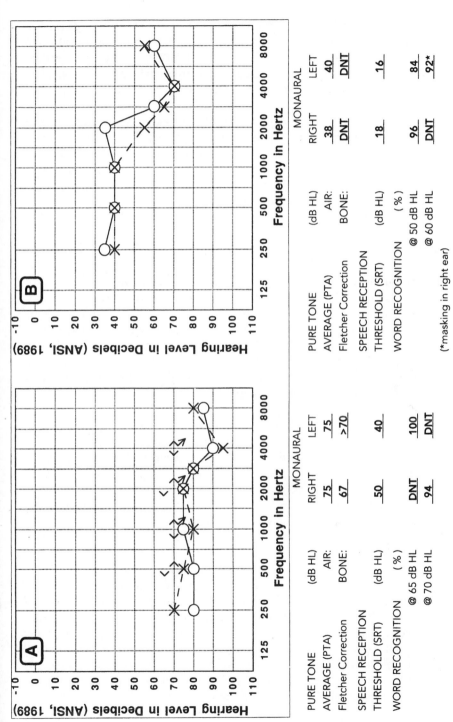

		MONAURAL	
		RIGHT	LEFT
PURE TONE	(dB HL)		
AVERAGE (PTA)	AIR:	**38**	**40**
Fletcher Correction	BONE:	**DNT**	**DNT**
SPEECH RECEPTION	(dB HL)		
THRESHOLD (SRT)		**18**	**16**
WORD RECOGNITION	(%)		
	@ 50 dB HL	**96**	**84**
	@ 60 dB HL	**DNT**	**92***

(*masking in right ear)

		MONAURAL	
		RIGHT	LEFT
PURE TONE	(dB HL)		
AVERAGE (PTA)	AIR:	**75**	**75**
Fletcher Correction	BONE:	**67**	**>70**
SPEECH RECEPTION	(dB HL)		
THRESHOLD (SRT)		**50**	**40**
WORD RECOGNITION	(%)		
	@ 65 dB HL	**DNT**	**100**
	@ 70 dB HL	**94**	**DNT**

Figure 4–3. Case 3. DNT = did not test.

and were "Type V" (supporting EHL) in the 250 to 2,000 Hz range (Figure 4–4; see the Békésy test, later in this chapter). A psychological evaluation had been requested by the otologist associated with this audiometric evaluation. It showed a normal validity scale with strong indications of somatization. The patient was sent back to the referring otolaryngologist.

COMMENT   *The patent showed persistent inter-test results indicating EHL. The final SRTs were within normal limits and these results, along with normal WRT scores, gave quantitative evidence of essentially normal hearing in the 500 to 2,000 Hz range. It was felt that the primary question of the referring physician had been answered, although valid pure-tone thresholds were not obtained.*

CASE 4

A 25-year-old was referred for audiological evaluation with a complaint of left hearing loss following nasal reconstruction. The patient had recently broken his nose when he was struck by a bicycle and fell against a telephone pole. A personal injury claim had been filed by the patient. There was a medical history of mental retardation. The test results are shown as "1981" in Figure 4–5. The results showed normal hearing for the right ear and no response for pure tones in the left ear (even without masking in the right ear). The SRTs for each ear were well within normal limits.

COMMENT   *The motivation for the EHL was unknown. The patient was referred back to the otolaryngologist who performed the nasal reconstruction with a firm summary impression of normal hearing bilaterally based upon SRTs. The responses shown are typical of a very unsophisticated patient whose voluntary responses for pure tones showed a "deaf" ear (with lack of expected shadow responses), but normal hearing for speech. Stenger tests could have been performed, but were felt to be unnecessary with an SRT of only 5 dB HL in the claimed affected ear.*

Ten years later the patient returned to our otologic and audiologic clinic with the complaint that he could not hear his mother, with whom he lived. He stated that his trouble was primarily caused by hearing loss in his left ear. Test results are shown in Figure 4–5, "1991." The otologic examination was unremarkable. The hearing tests again show the typical inconsistencies discussed in previous cases. The best results obtained are shown, but repeated tests showed moderate to severe hearing loss of up to 60 dB HL on the right and 80 dB HL for the left. Note that SRTs (10 dB HL) were normal. Tympanometry measurements also were within normal limits.

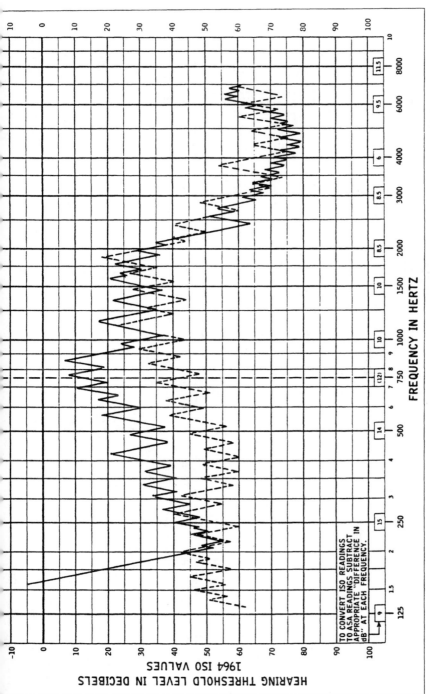

Figure 4-4. Békésy (self-recording) audiometry for the right ear of Case 3 showing a Type V result indicating EHL. A similar finding was obtained for the left ear. The continuous tone trace (—) is at significantly better hearing levels than the pulsed tone tracing (– –) in the range from 250 to 1,000 Hz. Both tracings showed much better hearing than that exhibited on the routine (manual) pure-tone test.

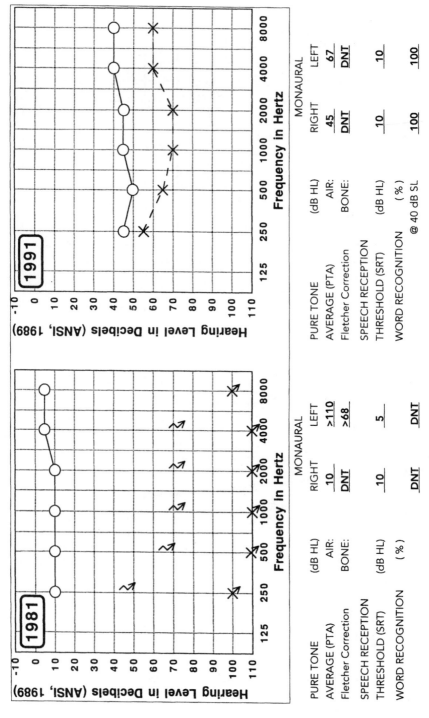

Figure 4–5.   Case 4. DNT = did not test.

COMMENT   *The motivation, primary gain, and secondary gains under-lying this patient's complaints are unknown. He was reassured that his hearing was good, and he was dismissed.*

CASE 5

This is a 50-year-old woman referred by an attorney and a physician associated with the company for which she worked. She had a history of significant industrial noise exposure and had filed a hearing loss claim. Previous audiometric examinations had been cursory and the results were inconsistent. Physical examination of the ears was normal and there was no other aural significant history. The patient stated she had severe bilateral hearing loss caused by years of exposure to industrial noise while working in a paper mill. She stated her company had supplied her with the binaural hearing aids she was wearing. She stipulated early in the pretest discussion that test results must be sent only to her personal lawyer, and that the company physician and lawyer were not to receive the audiometric results or report. She signed a form attesting to these requests. The referring attorney requested a standard test battery and specifically requested the Békésy test for EHL.

COMMENT   *This initial contact was an obvious red flag alerting the audiologist to the possibility of EHL. Early in the preliminary interview the examiner asked the patient to leave her hearing aids at the volume settings she was using and hand them to him. She did so, and the examiner's judgment was that the hearing aids were turned to the lowest volume possible. This was most inconsistent with the severe losses subsequently reflected in her voluntary responses.*

The results on the initial audiometric examination are shown in Figure 4–6 under "September 1988." The patient was remarkably consistent in her threshold responses. These showed a severe bilateral SNHL. The threshold losses were inconsistent with the better functional abilities observed in conversation. The examiner specifically noted that she often correctly answered questions and followed directions given at normal conversational intensities, even when the speaker's face was not visible to her. The SRTs were consistent with PTA-512. The WRT scores, however, were *unusually* good (100 percent) for such severe SNHLs and unusually good for being presented at only 10 dB SL (10 dB above the SRT levels).

COMMENT   *Only two suggestions of EHL are noted here: the examiner's subjective evaluation of exceptional ability to respond to conversation and the subtle finding of exceptional word recognition ability.*

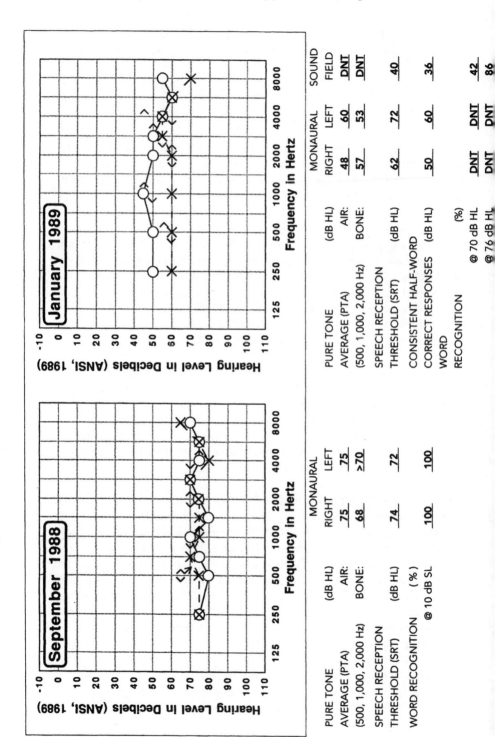

September 1988

Frequency in Hertz

Hearing Level in Decibels (ANSI, 1989)

		MONAURAL	
	(dB HL)	RIGHT	LEFT
PURE TONE AVERAGE (PTA) (500, 1,000, 2,000 Hz)	AIR:	75	75
	BONE:	68	>70
SPEECH RECEPTION THRESHOLD (SRT)	(dB HL)	74	72
WORD RECOGNITION	(%) @ 10 dB SL	100	100

January 1989

Frequency in Hertz

Hearing Level in Decibels (ANSI, 1989)

		MONAURAL		SOUND
	(dB HL)	RIGHT	LEFT	FIELD
PURE TONE AVERAGE (PTA) (500, 1,000, 2,000 Hz)	AIR:	48	60	DNT
	BONE:	57	53	DNT
SPEECH RECEPTION THRESHOLD (SRT)	(dB HL)	62	72	40
CONSISTENT HALF-WORD CORRECT RESPONSES	(dB HL)	50	60	36
WORD RECOGNITION	(%) @ 70 dB HL	DNT	DNT	42
	@ 76 dB HL	DNT	DNT	86

Tympanometry showed some hypermobility of the left eardrum but otherwise was essentially within normal limits for each ear. Acoustic reflexes were obtained at normal levels. Békésy audiograms were clearly and remarkably Type V, indicating EHL and, in addition, showed continuous tone tracings that were 10 to 20 dB better than the standard test first administered for air-conduction pure-tones. The patient was advised that there were some inconsistencies and the results and interpretation would be sent to her lawyer.

COMMENT   *Letters were sent to the referring company attorney and physician indicating that the examination was completed. Results and a brief report were sent only to her attorney. The report to her attorney indicated definite signs of EHL and stated that specific true thresholds could not be reliably estimated at this point.*

The patient's attorney subsequently discussed the case with the audiologist and requested continuation of the examination with whatever other tests might help to quantify the loss. The return appointments were delayed, canceled, and changed by the patient so that she did not reappear until four months later. The results of that study are shown in Figure 4–6 as "January 1989." When she appeared she was *not* wearing her hearing aids and she spontaneously announced she would refuse to take any test involving the use of electrodes. The repeat test showed improved thresholds for pure tones, SRTs that were much worse than PTA-512, and greatly decreased WRT scores to 10 to 28 percent (at the same levels that previously had given 100 percent for each ear). The sound-field measurements (binaural hearing for speech presented over a loudspeaker) for SRT and WRT were remarkably better than the findings from the usual unilateral earphone tests.

COMMENT   *The findings indicating EHL were as follows: (1) She was not using the hearing aids, which she said were of great help in communication. (2) Such remarkable changes on the second test would be improbable for NIHL. (3) The patient gave classic half-word responses for SRTs at low levels of 50 and 60 dB HL (see Unusual Responses on the Word Recognition Test, below). (4) Improved sound-field word recognition compared to unilateral tests is most unusual to the degree shown here, that is, 10 to 28 percent to 86 percent. It is occasionally seen in VIIIth nerve and brainstem auditory lesions, but is improbable in cochlear damage of NIHL. (5) Sound-field SRT was much better than the individual earphone SRTs (40 dB HL versus 62 and 72 dB HL). This is psychoacoustically highly improbable. Other possible tests could not be given against her wishes, were not thought likely to contribute to better quantification of her loss, or were simply felt to be undesirable to attempt with this patient, who became rather belligerent as the second examination continued. The case was subsequently settled out of court. The attorneys agreed to use the 40 dB HL sound-field SRT to estimate the percentage of binaural hearing loss.*

TESTING TECHNIQUES

These case histories have shown that routine hearing measurements often help to identify EHL. Simple threshold tests for pure tone and speech can be enhanced to detect EHL if certain techniques for measurement are followed. Special tests designed to reveal EHL often are extremely valuable, but may not be necessary if the following techniques are followed.

Test Instructions

Instructions to the patient should be given in a face-to-face discussion; that is, instructions over earphones at a level the patient indicates as comfortable should be avoided. (If EHL is present, the patient would set a level to which he would respond and try to remember this loudness level for consistency.) Face-to-face instruction does not allow the patient to control the level and set the standard or reference to which he or she responds on the audiometric speech tests. For all threshold tests it is absolutely required that the patient should be instructed to respond to the faintest signal he thinks he hears. The spondee words used for SRT tests should be those recommended by the American Speech-Language-Hearing Association (ASHA, 1988) and should be made familiar to the patient before the formal test by having him or her either repeat the words as the examiner says them face-to-face, or by reading the list. The patient must be instructed to guess at the words if he is unsure of the response.

Reference Intensity Levels When Establishing Thresholds

In a routine measurement technique, the examiner usually first presents pure tones or spondee words at suprathreshold levels so that the patient recognizes the signals for which he is listening. Subsequently, the tester decreases the signal in a bracketing technique until the 50 percent response criterion level is established. This technique is *not* appropriate for possible EHL. Instead, an ascending technique is strongly advised where the examiner advances from inaudible to audible threshold as acknowledged by the patient. Initial presentations at suprathreshold levels would allow the patient to establish a reference intensity level for loud stimuli.

Intensity Steps to Establish Thresholds

The normal attenuator step increment used in audiometry is 5 dB. Cases of potential EHL often should be tested in smaller intensity increments of 2 or 2.5 dB. To show the value of this technique, assume a patient is being tested who has a normal SRT of 10 dB HL. The patient, however, will not respond until a suprathreshold level is reached that would indicate a significant loss. Using a small step increment of 2 dB, the examiner presents a word at 0 dB HL and increases the intensity with each subsequent word (or small groups of words) until there is a response. The patient begins to hear the words when the examiner reaches 10 dB HL, but does not respond. The patient finally responds when 20 dB HL is reached even though the words were heard at 10, 12, 14, 16, and 18 dB HL. When 20 dB HL is reached, the patient has noted five increasing intensity levels where he heard the words, and finally decides the words are loud enough for a response that indicates hearing loss. If 5 dB step increments were used, again he may not respond until five steps have been made above his true 10 dB HL SRT. Five steps of 5 dB would thus place his initial response at 35 dB HL. Small increment steps with an ascending technique tend to give a more valid indication of true hearing; this is, in this illustration, 20 versus 35 dB HL.

Tone Stimuli Presentation Mode

Patients often indicate that it is difficult to sort out the pure tone for which they are listening from the physiologic sounds of their own body. This is especially true in a sound-treated room or if the patient complains of tinnitus. The difficulty is a legitimate complaint regardless of whether or not EHL is present. In such cases, it is recommended that the examiner present a pulsed or warbled tone to help the patient differentiate the test stimuli. A pulsed rather than continuous stimuli mode is a presentation option on many commercial audiometers; it can also be initiated manually. Warble-tone stimuli with a continuous variation of frequency a few Hertz around the specific tone being tested can be produced only by an audiometer designed for such an option.

INDICATIONS OF EHL ON STANDARD TESTS

Audiometric Configuration

No audiometric configuration is unique to EHL. It has often been suggested that flat and saucer configurations are seen, but these are commonly seen in true losses. If a patient with normal hearing has EHL, these configurations are more often evident (Gelfand and Silman, 1985). When there is EHL over a true loss the sensitivity of this generalization is very weak. Instead, the effect of exaggeration is often to produce a "flatter" or more gently sloping audiogram than would otherwise have been recorded.

Klockhoff, Drettner, and Svedberg (1974) and Alberti, Morgan, and Czuba (1978) have shown that in NIHL a 40 dB or greater hearing level at 500 or 1,000 Hz suggests the presence of other disease *or* EHL. Indeed, Rickards et al. (1996) studied NIHL claimants whose behavioral thresholds had been judged either reliable or unreliable based on evoked response testing (described later); 93 percent of "reliable" cases had behavioral thresholds at 500 Hz of 20 dB HL or better, while 94 percent of unreliable cases had 500 Hz behavioral thresholds of 25 dB or worse.

The audiometric pattern for NIHL has often been profiled in the literature. Figure 4–7 shows the mean hearing-loss configuration for 450 ears reported by Cooper and Owen (1976) (see also Chapters 7 and 13). The configuration is of essentially normal hearing for 250 to 1,000 Hz, followed by a descending curve (more precipitous above 2,000 Hz) to a maximum loss at 4,000 Hz at about 60 to 70 dB HL, with a slight return at 8,000 Hz. The loss is a sensorineural type without significant conductive involvement (bone conduction approximates air conduction ± 10 dB).

Studies have repeatedly suggested that a maximum loss of about 70 dB HL should be expected from NIFIL alone. A somewhat greater loss than that shown is occasionally seen at 8,000 Hz, but this finding is usually seen in elderly patients with accompanying presbycusis or those who have also had

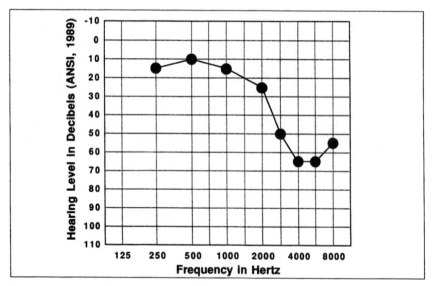

Figure 4–7. Mean audiometric results for 450 ears with uncomplicated noise-induced hearing loss. Adapted from Cooper and Owen (1976).

blast trauma. The maximum loss at 4,000 Hz is thought to be caused by the resonance of the average ear canal as it interacts with general noise frequency components. Patients with ear canals larger than average adult size seem to have the greatest loss around 3,000 Hz, and those with smaller canals tend to have maximum loss at a frequency above 4,000 Hz (Gerhardt et al., 1987).

In cases of bilateral EHL, the degree and configuration of loss tend to be bilaterally symmetrical (Alberti, Morgan, and Czuba, 1978).

The degree of hearing loss and audiometric configuration caused by *blast trauma* can be quite different from those associated with industrial noise exposure. Blast trauma may give a conductive hearing loss (caused by tympanic membrane perforations and/or disruption of the ossicular chain), a mixed conductive-sensorineural loss, or a pure SNHL. It is also usually accompanied by pain, which is not usual in common industrial NIHL. An intense and concussive blast wave can cause ascending low-frequency loss audiometric curves, primarily mid-frequency loss curves, sloping losses greater for higher frequencies, or unusual combination configurations.

Kerr and Byrne (1975a) and Bruins and Cawood (1991) provide overall discussions of blast injuries and more detailed otologic and audiometric: description have been detailed in other studies (Singh and Ahluwalia, 1968; Ruggles and Votypka, 1973; Kerr and Byrne, 1975b; Pahor, 1981; Walby and Kerr, 1986).

During the 1980s, there were several detailed reports of SNHL caused by cordless telephones (see also Chapter 7). The SNHL seen in such cases was most often in the mid-frequencies or in all frequencies and so was not typical of industrial noise exposure (Singleton et al., 1984; Gerling and Jerger, 1985; Orchik et al., 1987). Cordless phone manufacturers have redesigned their instruments so as to prevent such injuries.

Open and closed head injuries are similar to blast trauma in their otologic and audiometric findings in that a variety of types and degrees of loss are found. Complete sensorineural deafness is frequently found caused by fractures of the temporal bone. A monograph edited by Mueller and Sedge (1987) as well as chapters in most otologic texts are references for the reader (see also Chapter 10). Concussive injuries to the brainstem can, in addition, cause bizarre and unusual decreased word recognition ability in these cases *without* loss of pure-tone thresholds at any frequency. A book chapter by Jerger and Jerger (1981) is a succinct summary of material dealing with head trauma and hearing loss.

Test-Retest Reliability

Repeat tests given during a single test session should be consistent with the first test. Threshold tests for pure tones should be replicated ± 5 dB and definitely suggest EHL if there is a 15 db difference at any frequency. SRTs measured using 2 dB increments should show no more than a ± 6 to 8 dB difference.

It has been suggested previously that an ascending intensity technique is the better way to obtain an estimation of true thresholds in EHL. However, a descending intensity technique (from a loud level readily acknowledged by the patient as heard) is a good strategy for repeat tests. This increases the chance of finding a test-retest discrepancy suggesting EHL, and again is enhanced by using small incremental steps. Those with true hearing loss are not affected by the two different approaches and give small test-retest differences (always within 10 dB; Cherry and Ventry, 1976). Those with EHL may have considerable difficulty producing a consistent response when an ascending test is compared to a descending test. Martin et al. (2000) suggest using continuous tones for ascending trials and pulsed tones with lengthened off-time for descending trials, a strategy reminiscent of the "BADGE-LOT" version of the Békésy test, described later in this chapter.

Some patients with EHL (usually those most experienced by prior testing) have an almost phenomenal ability to repeat test results at least during a single test session. This is one of the reasons our clinic ordinarily has chosen to divide evaluation of EHL into two test sessions separated by a few days.

Shadow Responses in Unilateral or Asymmetrical Losses

When a pure-tone or speech stimulus is presented to one ear at intense levels, that sound can cross the skull and be heard by the other ear. Therefore, when testing an ear with complete deafness, the examiner should expect to get shadow responses from the better ear. Ordinarily under such conditions, the tester places appropriate levels of narrow-band noise in the non-test (better) ear to rule out its participation (as discussed in Chapter 3). If EHL is a possibility, the examiner should first test thresholds *without* contralateral masking in order to evaluate the expected shadow responses from the better ear. These levels of expected shadows have received considerable study, and the results of one large study (Snyder, 1973) are shown in Table 4–1. When an examiner is evaluating possible EHL, the *absence* of expected shadows clearly is a significant sign. Note that the skull attenuates sound crossing to the opposite ear by a much lower amount during bone-conduction testing. The attenuation for SRT is the same as the average of 500, 1,000, and 2,000 Hz.

Unusual Behavior or Responses on Speech Threshold Tests

Standard speech material for threshold testing is composed of a group of about 30 spondee-type words; that is, two-syllable words in which each syllable is a word in its own right and is equally stressed when spoken. The words have been selected to be equivalent in familiarity. They are made familiar to the patient prior to the formal test. The patient is advised to guess at each

TABLE 4–1
Level of Audiometric Shadow Responses (in dB) for Dead Ears
re: Thresholds of the Better Ear

	250	*500*	*1,000*	*2,000*	*4,000*	*8,000*	*SRT*
Air Conduction							
Mean	51	58	60	60	63	58	59
Mean + 2 sd	65	71	74	77	80	80	73
Maximum	70	75	75	80	85	80	74
Bone Conduction							
Mean	8	8	7	11	13		
Mean + 2 sd	20	22	20	27	29		
Maximum	20	25	25	35	35		

word regardless of how faint the presentation; the threshold is identified as the lowest level at which 50 percent of words presented are correctly repeated.

Three types of responses on this test should alert the examiner to EHL. First, and possibly most common for EHL, is the half-word response. The patient will give only half of the word and, even when encouraged, will not repeat the full word. For example, the word *baseball* is on the relatively small list of words *and* has been rehearsed with the patient. If at some point the patient repeats "base" or "ball" when asked to repeat the word but will not guess "baseball," it is not considered a reasonable response. A response of "football" would also be bizarre. Second, assume you are performing an ascending intensity technique test and a patient repeats "baseball" correctly at 40 dB HL. Then at a significantly *louder* level of 46 dB HL the patient will not repeat the word. This inconsistency is not valid. Lastly, the examiner occasionally finds a patient who is able to repeat some words correctly over an unusually broad intensity range before achieving a 50 percent criterion. Spondee words usually have a narrow range of about 10 to 15 dB from 0 percent to 50 percent response. Therefore, if words are repeated correctly at 30 dB HL, but a 50 percent correct response was not attained until 50 dB HL, EHL is suggested.

The accepted guidelines and research rationale for determining SRT have been published by ASHA (1988).

Unusual Responses on the Word Recognition Test

If EHL is suspected, it is advisable to first present the phonetically balanced word lists used for these tests at very low sensation levels relative to the SRTs obtained. High scores at low sensation levels (either absolute or relative to those expected for the degree of threshold loss) usually suggest EHL. The cases presented in Figures 4–2 and 4–6 show such findings. Note that at only

10 dB above SRTs, 96 to 100 percent WRT scores were achieved. Functions for the standard WRT have been extensively studied for over 40 years and have shown consistently that a presentation level at least 20 dB above the SRT must be used to achieve such a high score.

Jerger and Jerger (1976) studied over 2,000 patients with varying types and degrees of hearing loss to find the relationship of the SRT to WRT scores. They used recorded Psychoacoustic Laboratories phonetically balanced word lists (Egan, 1948) and correlated PTA-512 and the levels at which 25 percent and 50 percent scores were found on a WRT. They suggested that the average loss for the mid-frequency pure tones was 21 dB better than the level (in SPL) necessary to achieve 25 percent on the WRT and 26 dB better than the level for 50 percent. Thus, a 50 percent WRT at 50 dB HL (70 dB SPL) suggests the PTA-512 is usually about 44 dB HL (70–26 dB) or even better. Hopkinson (1978) suggested a similar comparison to estimate true thresholds; specifically, a 50 percent WRT predicted an SRT at an intensity 10 dB lower.

Inter-test Consistency

SRT-PTA Comparison

The SRT usually should be consistent with PTA-512. In cases of upward or downward audiometric slopes in this range it is appropriate to use the average of the two best of these three frequencies. The "two-best" average is often called the *Fletcher correction* (1950). These two scores (SRT and PTA) should agree within ± 6–8 dB when measuring in 2 dB intensity steps or ± 10 dB in 5 dB steps. Martin (1985) has presented a discussion as to why the SRT is often better than the PTA in EHL.

Standard Manual vs. Self-Recording Audiometry Comparison

In standard audiometry, the examiner controls the procedures. In automatic audiometry, an automated system *and the patient* primarily control the results obtained. Self-recording audiometry is discussed below in the section, "The Békésy Test." It is sufficient to say at this point that results obtained by these two different procedures should reflect comparable thresholds and that greater than 5 dB differences suggest possible EHL.

Sound-Field SRT

Sound-field SRT should be equivalent to the better ear in significantly asymmetrical hearing loss or about 6 dB better with symmetrical loss (Tillman, Johnson, and Olsen, 1966). Case 5, discussed above, is an illustration of an inconsistency in these measures indicative of EHL.

SRT–WRT Consistency
The consistency of SRT with WRT tests has been discussed in Unusual Responses on the Word Recognition Test, above.

SPECIAL TESTS FOR EHL

There are tests that merely indicate the presence of EHL and tests that specifically quantity the true loss. There are behavioral tests that rely upon the voluntary responses of the patient, and there are physiological tests that estimate thresholds without these voluntary responses. All tests, however, require some degree of at least passive patient cooperation.

Some of the qualitative tests for EHL may be of sufficient sensitivity in an individual patient that it is not necessary to provide information on exact thresholds. For example, if results show that all thresholds are within normal limits, it would make no significant difference to determine if the exact thresholds were 0 or 15 dB HL. If that same qualitative test indicates only a 40 dB hearing level when voluntary responses indicate a 60 dB hearing level, it is necessary to use supplementary tests to attempt to quantify further the degree of true loss.

Some tests for EHL may be of academic interest, but are no longer in general use. Tests in common use vary, depending on whether the claimed loss is unilateral or bilateral, the availability of specialized equipment, the expertise of the examiner, and whether at least the passive cooperation of the patient is obtained. Some tests have shown a strong potential power efficiency to determine EHL quantitatively and/or qualitatively, but are not found in general use. The latter group of tests may be found in specialized clinics dealing with large numbers of forensic hearing evaluations, but have not found use in otherwise excellent audiologic clinics that evaluate a relatively small number of such cases.

The tests discussed in the following sections are grouped according to the categories just described. Their detailed procedural techniques and technical descriptions are generally omitted, and the focus is upon the general strategy of their use and usefulness. A selected bibliography of the most contemporary references is provided for each test when appropriate. General references with detailed reports of the tests are available in books by Engelberg (1970), Kramer and Armbruster (1982), Katz (1994), and Silman and Silverman (1997).

Tests in Limited Use

The Lombard Test
This is a gross quantitative test for EHL based upon observations that people raise the intensity of their voices in the presence of noise if they hear the noise *and if* they are without conductive hearing loss. The test is judged by having the patient read a passage. If this voice reflex occurs when noise is introduced

via an earphone at intensity levels below the voluntary thresholds of hearing, the patient obviously hears. This is sometimes a quick screening test but is difficult to interpret and often gives inconsistent results (Silman and Silverman, 1997).

The Doerfler-Stewart (DS) Test

This is a confusion-type test designed to destroy the loudness criteria used by a patient with EHL as the patient responds to SRT, thresholds for noise, and combinations of the two. Those with true hearing loss respond in a reliable fashion consistent with psychoacoustic standards when they repeat spondee words as noise is faded in and out of their hearing range. Hattler and Schuchman (1971) reported results of the test in 725 patients in a clinic with a high incidence of EHL. About 60 percent had normal or mild-loss SRTs, which they felt made the test inappropriate. The remaining patients gave 20 percent false-positive responses and 23 percent false-negative responses for EHL. The poor applicability of the test and the high false-negative rate thus yielded a very low rate of detection of EHL in the total group.

This quantitative test for only binaural hearing is thus weak and, in addition, relies upon the SRT, which is primarily determined by a limited frequency range. It provides no qualitative information regarding the unilateral thresholds for the broader frequency range necessary in forensic evaluation. Hopkinson (1978) and Martin (1985) provide excellent descriptions of the details of procedure and interpretation.

The Swinging Story Test

This confusion-type test evaluates the patient's ability to repeat the elements of a short story given over earphones as the examiner *rapidly* shifts segments of the sentences in the story to either ear or to both ears. Critical elements are presented at intensity levels at which the patient denies hearing in one or both ears. If the patient includes such information in the retelling, the test is positive. The test provides no information on specific frequency thresholds. My experience is that sophisticated EHL patients often will immediately recognize the strategy of the examiner and refuse to cooperate with the test procedure. See Hopkinson (1978) and Martin (1985) for additional discussion and illustration.

Delayed Auditory (Speech) Feedback (DAF)

When a person hears his recorded voice played back to him while he is reading with only a very brief delay (about 0.1–0.2 sec delay time), his vocal rate and intensity may begin to change. There often are brief sound and syllable repetitions or elongations (similar to stuttering), and unusual intensity variations in his speech. The positive criteria for EHL is an increased time in reading a passage under a DAF condition compared with a previous timing made under normal conditions. The patient's delayed voice feedback is presented at intensity levels that are less than the admitted SRT and are gradually increased until the phenomenon occurs. Normal listeners and those with SNHL, unfortunately, have a rather broad range of intensity at which the feedback is effective.

This test was often applied to the EHL patient during the 1950s. It is very weak in several aspects (Hopkinson, 1978) and was essentially discarded by the early 1960s when a modification using pure tones was substituted for the speech stimuli.

Electrodermal Audiometry (EDA)

This was a highly successful quantifying test that was used to obtain specific pure-tone thresholds for any frequency. It was first described about 1950 and used routinely in many clinics until the late 1970s. Its use was halted in most centers because of controversies over the use of noxious stimulus and cessation of equipment production. It was also known as galvanic skin response (GSR) audiometry and psychogalvanic skin response audiometry (PGSA). It is based upon the classic Pavlovian model of unconditioned stimulus (food)–conditioned stimulus (bell ring)–response (salivation). As adapted for EDA, a mild electric shock is the unconditioned stimulus, a pure tone is the conditioned stimulus, and a drop in skin resistance is the response. The entire response is mediated by the autonomic nervous system and requires no voluntary response to obtain thresholds. An increase in the anxiety of the patient causes a decrease in the skin's electrical resistance measured by electrodes attached to two fingers of one hand. The examiner presents a tone acknowledged by the patient as heard, followed by the mildest electrical shock (applied to electrodes on two fingers of the opposite hand) necessary to obtain the criterion change in resistance. Tone-shock presentations are paired until the patient is conditioned to respond to only the tone presentation. The tone is then decreased until no response is obtained and raised in 5 dB steps until the responses are again observed; this is designated as the threshold.

Chaiklin, Ventry, and Barrett (1961) provided the rigid conditioning schedule that was usually used. Engelberg (1970) and Knox (1978) have provided detailed discussions of the use of EDA. Citron and Reddell (1976) reported that 29 percent of 86 patients referred to their clinic for medical-legal evaluation could not be conditioned for the test and three others refused it. The last original report found in a current literature review was by Stankiewicz, Fankhauser, and Strom (1981). They reported successful use of the test in 33 of 35 patients (two patients refused the test). They stated that many tests were useful in identifying the presence of EHL, but none was as useful for establishing valid and precise threshold data by frequency.

The Békésy Test

This is a unique test of self-recording threshold audiometry (see also Chapter 3), with the procedure controlled primarily by the patient rather than by the examiner. The patient traces his threshold by means of a push-button procedure that activates a pen recording on an audiometric form. The test has often been used in industrial settings. The examiner may use a slowly changing frequency tone or may select the recording for a single frequency over a period of time. The former is called *full-sweep* and the latter *fixed-frequency* Békésy. The method has differential diagnostic capability for type of loss if the recording is made with both pulsed and continuous stimuli. The two recordings are made on the same form and the tracings are compared. Four comparison types or patterns have been identified, indicating normal or conductive hearing loss, cochlear loss, and retrocochlear loss (Types I–IV). In these types, the pulsed and continuous-tone tracings overlap, or the continuous-tone tracing shows somewhat greater loss than the pulsed-tone tracing for at least part of the audiogram. A subsequent and unique tracing type (Type V) was identified for EHL wherein the *pulsed* tracing showed the greater loss. A Type V pattern also may be found in only part of a full-sweep audiogram (see Figure 4–4).

Rintelmann and Harford (1967) and Ventry (1971) have provided studies documenting the test in all its aspects. The criterion of at least a 10 dB separation of the two tracings for at least two octaves, or for one-minute on fixed-frequency tests, is recommended to suggest EHL. The sensitivity of this test is about 75 percent, but there is unfortunately about a 2 to 3 percent false-positive response rate. Also, the more sophisticated (practiced) patient may lower the sensitivity of the test (Martin and Monro, 1975).

Two modifications strengthened the Békésy test for evaluation of EHL. First, Hood, Campbell, and Hutton (1964) applied the previously described ascending versus descending intensity threshold differences seen in EHL to the Békésy test. Because in a Type V result the continuous-tone tracing is better than the pulsed tracing, they appropriately reasoned that the difference could be enhanced by introducing the continuous tone from an inaudible (ascending) level and completing the second (pulsed) tracing from a very loud introduction at a suprathreshold level (descending intensity technique). Their results showed improvement in sensitivity for obtaining a Type V in their EHL patients compared to the standard technique. Their modification is labeled the BADGE test (Békésy ascending-descending gap evaluation).

The second modification involved the pulsed-tone stimuli. The standard pulsed signal has a duty cycle of 50 percent (200 msec on and 200 msec off). Hattler and Schuchman (1970) and Hattler (1971) lengthened the off-time to 800 msec and found increased sensitivity and specificity for EHL patients with a total power efficiency of over 98 percent in a clinic population with a high incidence of this type of loss. They labeled this modification as the lengthened off-time (LOT) Békésy. Hattler and Schuchman (1971) found the test more sensitive (96 percent) than the DS Test (77 percent) and the Stenger test (48 percent).

The two modifications can be combined to complete a LOT-BADGE test, to enhance the sensitivity of the Békésy test for EHL. Martin et al. (2000) describe what is essentially the same strategy using a conventional autiometer.

The Békésy test is basically qualitative, but provides specific frequency information that marks it as more useful than most other qualitative tests. Note in Case 3, the patient was unable to maintain a reference for the false thresholds shown for the standard test when completing a full-sweep Békésy. In the octave interval of 500 to 1,000 Hz the Békésy continuous-tone tracing was as good as 10 to 15 dB HL, whereas the best thresholds by standard manual audiometry for that range were 35 to 40 dB HL. The better thresholds obviously are the more valid and provide quantitative information. Completing the Békésy test also allows another inter-test comparison for reliability with other threshold tests. Unfortunately, Békésy test equipment is now only rarely available in audiology suites, so the test has fallen into disuse.

Tests in Common Use

The Stenger Test

The principle underlying this test is a psychoacoustic one; when a single tone is presented to both ears at the same time and at the same SL, the tone is heard in the middle of the head. When the SL is increased about 10 dB in one ear, the tone is perceived by the subject *only* in the ear with the louder signal. The subject is unaware that the fainter tone is present. The application of this phenomenon in testing for EHL is in the case of claimed unilateral or remarkably asymmetrical loss. The patient is instructed to respond as in the usual unilateral threshold tests and is *not* informed that binaural tone presentations also will be given. Table 4–2 illustrates this application in a normal listener, in a patient falsely indicating unilateral hearing loss, and in a patient with true unilateral SNHL.

The traditional pure-tone Stenger test has been adapted using the spondaic words of the SRT test instead of pure-tone stimuli (speech Stenger test). The techniques are the same, but specific frequency thresholds cannot be evaluated. Silman and Silverman (1991) present a thorough summary of the techniques and procedures involved for both types of presentation.

The test requires an audiometer with two channels and a hearing level dial (attenuator) for each channel. The tone can be produced from a single oscillator or from two oscillators that are synchronized for exact frequency and phase. In either case, the tone should be presented to both ears by a

TABLE 4–2
The Stenger Test (Stimulus: 1,000 Hz tone)

Condition	Right	Left	Subject Responses
Normal Listener			

Thresholds:
  50% criterion
  5 dB step increments
	10	10	UR: Heard right ear
			UL: Heard left ear

Signal increased 5 dB SL to assure 100% response	15	15	UR: Heard right ear UL: Heard left ear Bil: Heard midline or in both ears
Signal further increased 10 dB in left ear	15	25	UR: Heard in right ear UL: Heard left ear Bil: Heard left ear
Exagerated Hearing Loss: Left Ear			
True threshold	10	10	UR: Heard right ear UL: Denies hearing
Admitted threshold	10	45	UR: Heard right ear UL: Heard left ear
Signal increased 5 dB SL to assure 100% response	15	50	UR: Heard right ear UL: Heard left ear Bil: Heard left ear
Stenger Test: Positive Does not recognize tone is in right ear at above threshold level in Bil presentation	15	25	UR: Heard right ear UL: Denies hearing Bil: Denies hearing (perceives only left ear)
True Hearing Loss: Left Ear			
True threshold (50% response)	10	45	UR: Heard right ear UL: Heard left ear Bil: Heard midline or both ears
Signal increased 5 dB SL to assure 100% response	15	50	UR: Heard right ear UL: Heard left ear Bil: Heard midline or both ears
Stenger Test: Negative	15	40 (−5 dB SL)	UR: Heard right ear UL: Denies hearing Bil: Heard right ear

UR: Unilateral presentation of tone only to right ear
UL: Unilateral presentation of tone only to left ear
Bil: Simultaneous bilateral tone presentation

single introducer switch. Some audiometers cannot meet these test requirements. During the test, the tones should occasionally be presented only to
the better ear or only to the poorer ear as if obtaining unilateral thresholds.
It is critical that the patient does not learn that the tone is present in the good
ear during the binaural presentation. The test has superior sensitivity with
naive normal-hearing subjects claiming EHL (Monro and Martin, 1977),
but is much less successful in some sophisticated patients (Martin and
Shipp, 1982).

Studies have shown that from 40 percent to almost 100 percent of patients
with unilateral EHL give a positive response on the test; and that the greater
the degree of EHL and the less the patient is experienced in taking audiometric tests, the higher the percentage of positive responders. The test should always be administered either as a screening (qualitative) test or as a more
thorough study that can give quantitative information (see Case 2). It is so
easily performed and so rapid to administer that it is appropriate in every unilateral EHL evaluation.

Auditory Brainstem Responses (ABRs)

These are a class of early evoked responses that have been used for several
years to screen infants for possible hearing loss and as a differential test for all
ages in the diagnosis of auditory nerve pathway and lower brainstem lesions.
The response class also is known as brainstem auditory evoked potentials
(BAEPs), brainstem evoked response (BSER), and brainstem auditory evoked
response (BAER).

Auditory stimuli are presented by earphone, and the electric potentials
generated in the auditory system in response to the stimuli are picked up by
scalp electrodes. The electrical activity is recorded as an ongoing waveform
with five or more time-locked specific peaks from the auditory system response within 10 msec of the stimuli (see Figure 3–13). Because of ongoing
activity in the auditory system, a single stimulus (at a specific intensity) must
be repeated many times and averaged by a computer in order to identify these
peaks on the waveform. Several hundred repetitions are usually required to
identify the morphology of the waveform from the background "noise" of the
auditory system. The stimulus in general use is a "click-like" sound, which is
required to generate the waveform; its peak intensity is in the higher frequency range. The ABR test is demanding in terms of equipment, procedure,
and expertise for interpretation.

The current standard clinical techniques provide results that correlate
primarily with pure-tone behavioral thresholds only in the 2,000 to 4,000
Hz range. This alone is inadequate for medical-legal evaluation. Brief tone-
pips can be used to obtain threshold estimates for lower frequencies.

Sohmer and Kinarti (1984), Hyde (1988), and Brookhouser, Gorga, and Kelly (1990) summarize the techniques and problems of the use of ABR in forensic evaluation.

Acoustic Reflex Test

The acoustic reflex reflects primarily the contraction of the stapedius muscle (see Chapter 3) in response to loud sound, attenuating the sound reaching the inner ear. It is a binaural reflex so that stimulation of either ear normally causes the contraction in both ears.

A tone is delivered to either ear at various intensity levels. When the reflex occurs, it stiffens the middle ear conductive system, causing a change of impedance that can be observed on an immitance bridge audiometer. The change is picked up by a special probe assembly inserted into one car. The instrumentation can be an earphone to one ear and a "pickup" probe on the other ear, or can be combined so that the stimulus and pickup are on the same ear.

A reflex is obtained in normal listeners at an SL of 75 to 95 dB. It is usually absent from ears with even a minimal degree of conductive hearing loss (Jerger et al., 1974a), from some ears with retrocochlear loss, with many cases of VIIth nerve dysfunction, and with some cases of severe cochlear hearing loss. In cases of cochlear type loss, the reflex is obtained at a low SL, but almost never at levels of less than 20 dB SL (Jerger, Jerger, and Mauldin, 1972). When the reflex is obtained at a level fainter than the admitted threshold or at less than 20 dB SL, there most probably is EHL. Thus, the absence of a reflex is non-diagnostic in EHL, but its presence can provide strong diagnostic evidence of EHL. Because the reflex is usually obtained for specific frequencies, there are potential quantitative aspects of interpretation.

Jerger et al. (1974b) proposed an extension of the test that compares the reflex elicited by pure tones to the reflex elicited by broad-band noise. This comparison may be used to estimate true threshold information. This comparison (the Sensitivity Prediction from the Acoustic Reflex [SPAR] Test) has not found clinical utility for EHL in our clinic.

Otoacoustic Emissions

As described in Chapter 3, the outer hair cells of a healthy ear *emit* faint sounds (echoes) when moderate-level clicks or tones are presented to the ear. Transient-evoked otoacoustic emissions (TEOAEs) have become quite widely used during the 1990s, especially for screening babies for hearing loss, and are also helpful in some medical-legal cases. TEOAEs can't usually be recorded when there is a conductive hearing loss, so tympanometry and/or BC testing usually precedes TEOAE testing. TEOAEs can be present in some people with serious hearing loss due to auditory nerve or brain problems (Starr et al., 1996), but in cases of NIHL (a hair cell disorder) the presence or absence of TEOAEs can provide very useful information

The most popular TEOAE instrument (the ILO-88) indicates the reproducibility (R) of the "echo" waveforms (see Figure 3–12). When overall R ≥ 60 percent and response level ≥ 2 dB SPL in persons over 60, pure-tone averages (PTAs) at 0.5, 1, and 2 kHz were always 30 dB HL or better (Bertoli and Probst, 1997). However, only half of their patients with PTAs between 15 and 30 dB had intact TEOAEs, compared with 77 percent of those with PTAs of 15 dB or better.

Using younger subjects (mean age=44), Hurley and Musiek (1994) found that R scores above 70 percent were found in almost all their normal subjects (all thresholds ≤ 20 dB, 500–4,000 Hz) and in almost none of their "hearing loss" subjects (all thresholds > 20 dB, 500–4,000 Hz).

When TEOAEs are present and reproducible despite PTAs exceeding 30 dB HL, explanations other than NIHL or other hair cell disorders must be sought, such as neural/brain disorders or EHL. An exception to this rule would be the steeply-sloping audiogram with TEOAE energy present only at lower frequencies.

Uncommon Tests of Potential Value

Pure-Tone Delayed Auditory Feedback
In a previous section, the speech DAF test was described and its usefulness in EHL evaluation was classified as very limited. The original speech test phenomenon has been modified for use as a frequency-specific test. The patient is instructed to tap a continuous pattern with a finger movement on a specially constructed switch that sends a *brief* tone to the patient's earphone. When the tone is simultaneous with the tap (synchronous feedback) at any level above or below the threshold for that tone, there is no change in the rhythm or rate of the pattern. However, if the instrumentation is set to delay the stimulus about 200 msec, the tapping performance is altered if the tone is at about 5 dB SL or louder.

The test requires complicated instrumentation not readily available commercially, and the results must be fed to a strip chart that records the pattern tapped by the patient; it has probably been under-used because of these requirements. The test has high reliability (Cooper and Citron, 1983), is superior to other tests used to evaluate EHL (Citron and Reddell, 1976), and is resistant to patient sophistication (Monro and Martin, 1977). It is often positive at levels as low as 5 dB SL and usually positive at 10 dB SL. This sensitivity, combined with specific frequency information, makes it an excellent test with quantifying capability.

The Slow Vertex Response (SVR)

This is an objective test that evaluates one of the family of auditory evoked responses occurring 75 to 300 msec following the stimulus (Hyde, 1988). It permits a verification of pure-tone thresholds throughout the frequency range, in contrast to the click-evoked ABRs previously discussed, which are primarily determined by hearing in the 2,000 to 4,000 Hz range. It requires only passive cooperation of the patient. It is a quantifying test which can estimate true hearing levels within 10 dB according to Hyde et al. (1986), Alberti, Hyde, and Riko (1987), and Rickards and DeVidi (1995). Hyde and his colleagues report that a four-frequency audiogram for each ear was completed in about 1.5 hours in 95 percent of about 1,200 medical-legal evaluations. The test requires the special equipment required for ABRs, but this is now common in most otologic and audiologic centers. This appears to be an uncommonly sensitive test which has been surprisingly little-used in the United States.

Miscellaneous Other Tests

A plethora of other special tests for EHL has been described. The following group was selected for brief discussion to illustrate the breadth of their variations and procedures.

The Falconer Lipreading Test

This test purports (to the patient) to measure lipreading skill, when it actually uses single-syllable words that are relatively impossible to distinguish from other words by lipreading alone (Falconer, 1966). For example, one set of words was "mud," "bud," "but," and "bun." A correct repetition of any word can occur only if it is heard. The words are presented *both* by audition and by vision (through patient observation of the examiner's face). This deception-type test seemed to be quite sensitive in estimating an SRT considerably below the conventionally-measured SRT in EHL patients. Falconer's original findings were substantiated in a subsequent study (Weiss, 1971).

Conditioned Eyelid Response

Galloway and Butler (1956) suggested an alternative to using shock as the unconditioned stimulus, as in the EDA test. They conditioned subjects to an eyelid blink by combining a flash of light and pure-tone stimuli. Most of their subjects gave conditioned eye blinks as low as 5 to 10 dB SL (at frequencies from 500 to 800 Hz), but required clinically unacceptable training times to establish conditioning.

Yes-No Test

This was described as appropriate for children with EHL (Frank, 1976). The unsophisticated child was told to listen for the tone and indicate "yes" if it was heard or "no" if it was not heard. A brief tone was presented occasionally and periodically at levels both above and below admitted threshold. When the child's "no" response was coincident with a presentation below admitted threshold, the tone obviously had been heard. I have found that unsophisticated and nervous adult patients with EHL will occasionally give such responses as "I didn't hear that last tone."

Forced-Choice Procedure

Haughton et al. (1979) described a test using the classic forced-choice technique of experimental psychology to confirm EHL. The test paradigm used a tone randomly presented to either ear at 15 dB above or below the admitted threshold. A light was turned on at the initiation of the tone and the subject was "forced" to indicate in which ear the tone was presented even though it "might not be heard." Only the -15 dB SL tones were scored. A correct score outside the normal probability range for guessing (for example, two or fewer correct answers in a set of 12 trials) was found in several subjects simulating malingering.

SUMMARY

The examiner must take a flexible approach to the evaluation of EHL. Careful pretest history taking, and explanation and counseling regarding the procedures and goals for the examination are necessary. The goals are best accomplished if the examiner is not judgmental or intimidating in explaining the presence of inconsistencies during the examination. Routine test comparisons are invaluable in both detecting and quantifying the presence of EHL and estimating of true thresholds. The most valuable contribution toward identification of EHL often lies in a strong index of suspicion by an experienced examiner.

Valid and reliable thresholds are more likely to be estimated, and EHL is more likely to be detected, if the following suggestions are followed:

1. Instruct the patient face-to-face, not using the audiometer circuits;
2. Observe and document behavior, especially conversational performance and verbatim responses to speech testing;
3. Begin with SRT testing, using 2 dB steps and ascending presentation levels;
4. WRT testing should initially be performed at low levels, for example, SRT + 10 dB;

5. Estimate pure-tone thresholds (AC and BC) using small step size, and pulsed or warbled tones, *without masking;*
6. Initial AC thresholds can be obtained either with ascending levels (for best estimates) or descending levels (to maximize detection of EHL by comparison with SRT as described by Schlauch et al., 1996); often both should be done;
7. Obtain masked thresholds as needed, but only after recording unmasked thresholds;
8. Use tympanometry, reflex testing, sound-field testing, and special tests as needed.

REFERENCES

Alberti, Peter W., Martyn L. Hyde, and Krista Riko. 1987. Exaggerated hearing loss in compensation claims. *J. Otolaryngol.* 16(6):362–366.

Alberti, P. W., P. P. Morgan, and I. Czuba. 1978. Speech and pure tone audiometry as a screen for exaggerated hearing loss in industrial claims. *Acta Otolaryngol. (Stockh.)* 85(5–6):328–331.

American Speech-Language-Hearing Association–Committee on Audiologic Evaluation. 1988. Guidelines for determining threshold level for speech. *ASHA* 30(3):85–89.

Anthony, Walter P. and Clell W. Harrison. 1972. Tympanic membrane perforation. *Arch. Otolaryng.* 95(6):506510.

Bertoli, S. and R. Probst. 1997. the role of transient-evoked otoacoustic emissions in the evaluation of elderly persons. *Ear & Hearing* 18:286–93.

Brookhouser, Patrick E., Michael P. Gorga, and William J. Kelly. 1990. Auditory brainstem response results as predictors of behavioral auditory thresholds in severe and profound hearing impairment. *Laryngoscope* 100(8):803–810.

Bruins, W. R. and R. H. Cawood. 1991. Blast injuries of the ear as a result of the Peterborough lorry explosion: 22 March 1989. *J. Laryngol. Otol.* 105(11):890–895.

Chaiklin, Joseph B., Ira M. Ventry, and Lyman S. Barrett. 1961. Reliability of conditioned GSR pure-tone audiometry with adult males. *J. Speech Hear. Res.* 4(3):269–280.

Cherry, Rochelle and Ira M. Ventry. 1976. The ascending-descending gap: A tool for identifying a suprathreshold response. *J. Aud. Res.* 16:281–287.

Citron, David, III and Rayford C. Reddell. 1976. Electrodermal response, delayed auditory feedback and lengthened off-time procedures. *Arch. Otolaryngol.* 102(4):204–206.

Cooper, J. C., Jr. and Jeffrey H. Owen. 1976. Audiologic profile of noise-induced hearing loss. *Arch. Otolaryngol.* 102(3):148–150.

Cooper, William A., Jr. and David Citron III. 1983. Delayed feedback audiometry: Reliability of repeated measures. *Ear & Hearing* 4(2):84–87.

Egan, James P. 1948. Articulation testing methods. *Laryngoscope* 58(9):955–991.

Engelberg, Marvin W. 1970. *Audiological Evaluation for Exaggerated Hearing Level*. Springfield, IL: Charles C. Thomas Publisher.

Falconer, George A. 1966. A "lipreading test" for nonorganic deafness. *J. Speech Hear. Disord.* 31(3):241–247.

Fletcher, Harvey. 1950. A method for calculating hearing loss for speech from an audiogram. *J. Acoust. Soc. Am.* 22(1):1–5.

Frank, Tom. 1976. Yes-no test for nonorganic hearing loss. *Arch. Otolaryngol.* 102(3):162–165.

Galloway, F. Thomas and Robert A. Butler. 1956. Conditioned eyelid response to tone as an objective test of hearing. *J. Speech Hear. Disord.* 21(1):47–55.

Gelfand, Stanley A. and Shlomo Silman. 1985. Functional hearing loss and its relationship to resolved hearing levels. *Ear & Hearing* 6(3):151–158.

Gerhardt, Kenneth J., Gary P. Rodriguez, Ernest L. Hepler, and Michael L. Moul. 1987. Ear canal volume and variability in the patterns of temporary threshold shifts. *Ear & Hearing* 8(6):316–321.

Gerling, Irvin J. and James F. Jerger. 1985. Cordless telephones and acoustic trauma: A case study. *Ear & Hearing* 6(4):203–205.

Goldstein, Robert. 1966. Pseudohypacusis. *J. Speech Hear. Disord.* 31(4):341–352.

Hattler, Karl W. 1971. The development of the LOT-Békésy test for nonorganic hearing loss. *J. Speech Hear. Res.* 14(3):605–617.

Hattler, Karl W. and Gerald I. Schuchman. 1970. Clinical efficiency of the LOT-Békésy test. *Arch. Otolaryng.* 92(4):348–352.

———. 1971. Efficiency of the Stenger, Doerfler-Stewart and lengthened off-time Békésy tests. *Acta Otolaryngol. (Stockh.)* 72(4):262–267.

Haughton, P. M., A. Lewsley, M. Wilson, and R. G. Williams. 1979. A forced-choice procedure to detect feigned or exaggerated hearing loss. *Br. J. Audiol.* 13(4):135–138.

Hood, William H., Richard A. Campbell, and Charles L. Hutton. 1964. An evaluation of the Békésy ascending descending gap. *J. Speech Hear. Res.* 7(2):123–132.

Hopkinson, Norma T. 1978. Speech tests for pseudohypacusis. In *Handbook of Clinical Audiology,* 2nd ed., ed. Jack Katz, pp. 291–303. Baltimore: Williams and Wilkins Company.

Hurley, R. M. and F. E. Musiek. 1994. Effectiveness of transient-evoked otoacoustic emissions in predicting hearing level. *J. Am. Acad. Audiol.* 5:195–203.

Hyde, Martyn L. 1988. Auditory evoked potentials. In *Otologic Medicine and Surgery,* Vol. 1, eds. Peter W. Alberti and Robert J. Ruben, pp. 443–485. New York: Churchill Livingstone.

Hyde, Martyn, Peter Alberti, Noriaki Matsumoto, and Yao-Li Li. 1986. Auditory evoked potentials in audiometric assessment of compensation and medicolegal patients. *Ann. Otol. Rhinol. Laryngol.* 95(5 Pt. 1):514–519.

Jerger, James, Lois Anthony, Susan Jerger, and Larry Mauldin. 1974a. Studies in impedance audiometry. III. Middle ear disorders. *Arch. Otolaryngol.* 99(3):165–171.

Jerger, James, Phillip Burney, Larry Mauldin, and Betsy Crump. 1974b. Predicting hearing loss from the acoustic reflex. *J. Speech Hear. Disord.* 39(1):11–22.

Jerger, James, Susan Jerger, and Larry Mauldin. 1972. Studies in impedance audiometry. 1. Normal and sensorineural ears. *Arch. Otolaryng.* 96(6): 513–523.

Jerger, Susan and James Jerger. 1976. Estimating speech threshold from the PI-PB function. *Arch. Otolaryngol.* 102(8):487–496.

———. 1981. Trauma. In *Auditory Disorders: A Manual for Clinical Evaluation,* pp. 169–177. Boston: Little, Brown and Company.

Katz, Jack, ed. 1994. *Handbook of Clinical Audiology,* 4th ed. Baltimore: Williams and Wilkins Company.

Kerr, A. G. and J. E. T. Byrne. 1975a. Surgery of violence. IV. Blast injuries of the ear. *Br. Med. J.* 1(5957):559561.

———. 1975b. Concussive effects of bomb blast on the ear. *J. Laryngol. Otol.* 89(2):131–143.

Klockhoff, I., B. Drettner, and A. Svedberg. 1974. Computerized classification of the results of screening audiometry in groups of persons exposed to noise. *Audiology* 13(4):326–334.

Knox, Albert W. 1978. Electrodermal audiometry. In *Handbook of Clinical Audiology,* 2nd ed., ed. Jack Katz, pp. 304–310. Baltimore: Williams and Wilkins Company.

Kramer, Marc B. and Joan M. Armbruster ed., 1982. *Forensic Audiology.* Baltimore: University Park Press.

Martin, Frederick N. 1985. The pseudohypacusic. In *Handbook of Clinical Audiology,* 3rd ed., ed. Jack Katz, pp. 742–765. Baltimore: Williams and Wilkins Company.

Martin, Frederick N. and Deborah A. Monro. 1975. The effects of sophistication on Type V Békésy patterns in simulated hearing loss. *J. Speech Hear. Disord.* 40(4):508–513.

Martin, Frederick N. and David B. Shipp. 1982. The effects of sophistication on three threshold tests for subjects with simulated hearing loss. *Ear & Hearing* 3(1):34–36.

Martin, J. S., F. N. Martin, and C. A. Champlin. 2000. The COS-SOT-LOT test for nonorganic hearing loss. *J. Amer. Acad. Audiol.* 11; 46–51.

Monro, Deborah A. and Frederick N. Martin. 1977. Effects of sophistication on four tests for nonorganic hearing loss. *J. Speech Hear. Disord.* 42(4):528–534.

Mueller, H. Gustav and Roy K. Sedge. 1987. Audiological aspects of head trauma. *Semin. Hear.* 8(3):191–298.

Noble, W. 1987. The conceptual problem of "functional hearing loss" (editorial). *Br. J. Audiol.* 21(1):1–3.

Orchik, Daniel J., Daniel R. Schmaier, John J. Shea Jr., John R. Emmett, William H. Moretz, Jr., and John J. Shea III. 1987. Sensorineural hearing loss in cordless telephone injury. *Otolaryngol. Head Neck Surg.* 96(1):30–33.

Pahor, Ahmes L. 1981. The ENT problems following the Birmingham bombings. *J. Laryngol. Otol.* 95(4):399–406.

Rickards, F. W. and S. DeVidi. 1995. Exaggerated hearing loss in noise induced hearing loss claims in Victoria. *Med. J. Austr.* 163:360–363.

Rickards, F. W., S. DeVidi, and D. S. McMahon. 1996. Audiological indicators of exaggerated hearing loss in noise induced hearing loss claims. *Austr. J. Audiol.* 18:89–97.

Rintelmann, William F. and Earl R. Harford. 1967. Type V Békésy pattern: Interpretation and clinical utility. *J. Speech Hear. Res.* 10(4):733–744.

Ruggles, R. L. and Ray Votypka. 1973. Blast injuries of the ear. *Laryngoscope* 83(6):974–976.

Schlauch, R. S., K. D. Arnce, L. M. Olson, S. Sanchez, and T. N. Doyle. 1996. Identification of psuedohypacusis using speech reception thresholds. *Ear & Hearing* 17:229–236.

Sheehy, James L. and Robert G. Anderson. 1980. Myringoplasty: A review of 472 cases. *Ann. Otol. Rhinol. Laryngol.* 89(4 Pt. 1):331– 334.

Silman, Shlomo and Carol A. Silverman. 1997. *Auditory Diagnosis: Principles and Applications,* 2nd ed. San Diego: Academic Press, Inc.

Singh, Daryao and K. J. S. Ahluwalia. 1968. Blast injuries of the ear. *J. Laryngol. Otol.* 82(10):1017–1028.

Singleton, George T., David L. Whitaker, Robert J. Keim, and F. J. Kemker. 1984. Cordless telephones: a threat to hearing. *Ann. Otol. Rhinol. Laryngol.* 93(6 Pt. 1):565–568.

Snyder, Jack M. 1973. Interaural attenuation characteristics in audiometry. *Laryngoscope* 83(11):1847–1855.

Sohmer, H. and R. Kinarti. 1984. Survey of attempts to use auditory evoked potentials to obtain an audiogram: Review article. *Br. J. Audiol.* 18(4): 237–244.

Stankiewicz, James, Charles E. Fankhauser, and C. Gordon Strom. 1981. Electrodermal audiometry: Renewed acquaintance with an old friend. *Otolaryngol. Head Neck Surg.* 89(4):671–677.

Starr, Arnold, Terence W. Picton, Yvonne Sininger, Linda J. Hood, and Charles I. Berlin. 1996. Auditory neuropathy. *Brain* 119:741–753.

Tillman, Tom W., Robert M. Johnson, and Wayne O. Olsen. 1966. Earphone versus sound-field threshold sound-pressure levels for spondee words. *J. Acoust. Soc. Am.* 39(1):125–133.

Ventry, Ira M. 1971. Békésy audiometry in functional hearing loss: A case study. *J. Speech Hear. Disord.* 36(1):125–141.

Ventry, Ira M. and Joseph B. Chaiklin. 1962. Functional hearing loss: A problem in terminology. *ASHA* 4(8):251–254.

———. 1965. Multidiscipline study of functional hearing loss. *J. Aud. Res.* 5(3):179–272.

Walby, A. P. and A. G. Kerr. 1986. Hearing in patients with blast lung. *J. Laryngol. Otol.* 100(4):411–415.

Weiss, Betty Goldman. 1971. Predicting organic hearing levels: The Falconer lipreading test for nonorganic deafness. *J. Aud. Res.* 11:223–226.

BIBLIOGRAPHY OF EXAGGERATED HEARING LOSS IN CHILDREN

Behnke, Charles R. and James E. Lankford. 1976. The LOT test and school-age children. *J. Speech Hear. Disord.* 41(4):498–502.

Bowdler, D. A. and J. Rogers. 1989. The management of pseudohypoacusis in school-age children. *Clin. Otolaryngol.* 14(3):211–215.

Brockman, Seymour J. and Gloria H. Hoversten. 1960. Pseudo neural hypoacusis in children. *Laryngoscope* 70(6):825–839.

Campanelli, Peter A. 1963. Simulated hearing losses in school children following identification audiometry. *J. Aud. Res.* 3:91–108.

Leshin, George J. 1960. Childhood non-organic hearing loss. *J. Speech Hear. Disord.* 25(3):290–292.

McCanna, D. L. and G. DeLapa. 1981. A clinical study of twenty-seven children exhibiting functional hearing loss. *LSHSS* 12:26–35.

Peterson, John L. 1963. Nonorganic hearing loss in children and Békésy audiometry. *J. Speech Hear. Disord.* 28(2):153–158.

Rintelmann, William and Earl Harford. 1963. The detection and assessment of pseudohypoacusis among school-age children. *J. Speech Hear. Disord.* 28(2):141–152.

Yamamoto, Minako, Jin Kanazaki, Kaoru Ogawa, and Kyoko Asano. 1991. Psychological aspects of psychogenic deafness in children. *Int. J. Pediatr. Otorhinolaryngol.* 21(2):113–120.

Chapter 5

Impairment and Handicap

DEFINITIONS

The terms *impairment, handicap,* and *disability* are frequently used in discussions of hearing loss. Unfortunately, they often mean different things to different people. Even the term *hearing loss* can be quite ambiguous. On one hand, *loss* implies a change, usually from normal or adequate hearing to abnormal or inadequate hearing. On the other hand, we commonly consider persons who were born with poor hearing to have a hearing loss, although no *change* has occurred. Almost all otologists and audiologists tend to use *hearing loss* and *hearing level* (threshold for pure tones or speech) interchangeably in everyday speech, as in "Mr. X has a 40 dB hearing loss." This usage is illogical, especially if we apply it to a person with normal hearing who has a 5 dB HL (hearing level) threshold, but can't be said to have a 5 dB hearing loss. Davis and Silverman (1960) made a useful suggestion: Don't use "hearing loss" and "dB" together. If dB are involved, we should use either "hearing level" (re: 0 dB HL) or "threshold shift" (re: the patient's previous threshold). Thus, Mr. X may have a 40 dB hearing level, but only a 25 dB threshold shift, if his original hearing level was 15 dB HL. This distinction will be important later on in discussing differential diagnosis and allocation (Chapter 13), and we will try to follow Davis and Silverman's advice throughout this book to avoid ambiguity. Ideally, "hearing loss" should be used in the general sense of poor hearing or the process that causes it.

The American Academy of Otolaryngology–Head and Neck Surgery (AAO–HNS 1988) defines hearing impairment, handicap, and disability as follows:

Permanent (Hearing) Impairment is "function outside the range of normal."

Permanent (Hearing) Handicap is "the disadvantage imposed by an impairment sufficient to affect the individual's efficiency in the activities of daily living. Handicap implies a material impairment; conversely, the concept of material impairment implies that there is a narrow range of hearing impairment, beyond the statistical range of normal hearing, which does not produce hearing handicap."

Permanent Disability is "an actual or presumed inability to remain employed at full wages."

The American Academy of Otolaryngology (AAO), the AAO–HNS's predecessor, in its *Guide for the Evaluation of Hearing Handicap* (AAO, 1979) states that handicap begins at 25 dB HL (for average threshold in the speech frequencies). Thus, these definitions imply that impairment begins at about 15 dB HL, where hearing levels begin to be abnormal (re: young adults); that between about 15 and 25 dB HL the impairment is not "material"; and that above 25 dB HL (for the speech frequencies) there is both *material impairment* and *handicap*. These definitions also imply that for frequencies unimportant for speech, for example, 8 kHz (kilohertz), impairment would begin at 15 dB, but would never be material or cause handicap. *Disability* depends on factors other than just hearing loss, such as occupation and education, and is ordinarily determined administratively or in a legal or quasi-legal setting.

We will use these terms as defined above throughout the book; however, it is essential to first point out some of the variations in definition and usage that exist. The AAO–HNS definitions are substantially unchanged since 1965 (Davis, 1965), but the American Medical Association (AMA, 1971, 2000), in its *Guides to the Evaluation of Permanent Impairment* uses the term "binaural hearing impairment" in place of "hearing handicap." Curiously, the preface to the AMA document accepts the use of "handicap" as a concept intermediate between "impairment" and "disability," referring to the effects of an impairment that substantially limits one or more life activities, but "handicap" is not used in the section of the *Guides* devoted to hearing loss. The AMA also defines "disability" somewhat more broadly, as "an alteration of an individual's capacity to meet personal, social, or occupational demands, to meet statutory or regulatory requirement." The American Speech-Language-Hearing Association (ASHA) uses "impairment" and "handicap" in a fashion very similar to that of the AAO–HNS, except that the concept of material impairment is not made explicit. ASHA defines "hearing disability," however, as "the determination of a financial award for the loss of function caused by any hearing impairment that results in significant hearing handicap" (1981). The World Health Organization (WHO, 1980) proposes definitions of handicap and disability that are nearly opposite those of the AAO–HNS. For WHO, handicap (or disadvantage) limits or prevents the fulfillment of a role that is normal (depending on age, sex, and social and cultural factors) for the individual; disability is "any restriction or lack (resulting from an impairment) of ability to perform an activity in the manner or within the range considered normal for a human being." Many British and European authors use these terms as defined by WHO.

What are the effects of hearing impairment on "activities of daily living"? Most obviously (and most importantly), hearing-impaired persons have difficulty with speech communication. As discussed in Chapter 3, the degree of difficulty in speech understanding depends not only on the severity of the hearing impairment, but also on the difficulty of the communicative task (intensity, signal-to-noise ratio, redundancy, etc.) and non-auditory attributes of the listener (alertness, motivation, intelligence, familiarity with the task, etc.). Nevertheless, there is a strong and predictable relationship between severity of hearing impairment and communicative difficulties. For an impaired listener, speech communication is often slow and frustrating, leading to fatigue, stress, and social isolation. In the elderly, at least, hearing loss is associated with depression (Herbst and Humphrey, 1980) and probably with psychosis (Eastwood et al., 1985).

Hearing impairment can also interfere with the enjoyment of music and with the ability to detect, identify, and localize environmental sounds. Persons with noise-induced hearing loss (NIHL) are particularly likely to report difficulties hearing doorbells, telephones ringing, and birds singing (Hetu et al., 1988). In both daily living and occupational settings, an inability to hear warning signals can occasionally be life-threatening. Lipscomb (1982) suggests that for reliable alerting, such signals need to be at least 9 to 10 dB above background noise levels based on octave band analysis (see also ISO 7731, 1986); obviously, they would also need to be above an individual's detection thresholds by a similar amount.

METHODS FOR ESTIMATING HEARING HANDICAP

Controversies

There is general consensus that hearing handicap (HH) should be assessed in terms of the effects a hearing loss has on speech communication in the activities of daily living, rather than on the hearing of non-speech sounds. However, there is considerable controversy regarding the methods used to measure or estimate HH. Perhaps the thorniest issue is the specification of the communicative environment of "daily living." At one extreme, this would include face-to-face conversation with a friend or family member in a quiet room, talking of familiar subjects—a relatively easy task, even for a person with mild hearing impairment. At the other extreme, many "daily lives" include listening to unfamiliar speakers and unpredictable messages in noisy settings without visual input; even people with perfectly normal hearing miss some words under very difficult listening conditions, and hearing impairment may further degrade performance. What point on this wide range of communicative difficulty best represents "activities of daily living"? Probably it is more reasonable to recognize that a "typical" lifestyle includes several levels of communicative difficulty, but how do we then represent the relative importance of each?

A second level of controversy, closely related to the first, surrounds the choice of pure-tone tests versus speech tests versus self-report measures (versus some combination of these) for the estimation of HH. A third set of controversies deals with the details of HH estimation when pure tones are used. Which frequencies should be included? At what level of impairment does HH begin (low fence)? At what level of impairment is HH total (high fence)? Between the low fence and high fence, does HH grow linearly with increasing impairment? How are the separate impairments of the two ears to be combined to estimate a person's HH, when one ear is worse than the other?

A fourth controversy is often ignored or at least not made explicit: Is the goal to estimate HH for a single type of hearing loss (e.g., noise-induced hearing loss) or for hearing loss, regardless of cause or audiometric characteristics? The AAO (1979) recommends a method that would apply "regardless of the manner in which the handicap was acquired." Others have proposed methods that would be specific to NIHL and would not work well for patients with different types of hearing loss.

Self-Report

Physicians and audiologists routinely interview their patients regarding self-perceived handicap, asking questions such as "Is your hearing good, fair, or poor?" and "In what situations do you have difficulty hearing?" Patients' reports of type and severity of hearing difficulty have been of great value to clinicians over the years in validating audiometric tests. For example, patients who have hearing impairment only at very high frequencies ($\geq$ 6 kHz) do not report speech communication problems. Historically, pure-tone rules for estimating HH derived in large part from the collective experience of otologists who had compared their patients' reports of hearing problems to their audiograms, and then formed opinions regarding which frequencies were important, how much pure-tone threshold loss was needed to cause handicap, and so on.

More formal, detailed interviews and questionnaires have been developed with the intent of providing HH estimates directly from self-report. Schow and Gatehouse (1990) reviewed 19 such instruments: Although they strongly supported the use of self-report questionnaires for hearing screening, assessment of rehabilitative need and potential, measurement of treatment benefit, demographic surveys, and other uses, they did not recommend them for direct use in compensation cases. Rather, they suggested that self-report measures are useful in validating HH measures based on pure-tone thresholds. In other words, the degree of correlation with self-assessment (in cases *not* involving compensation issues) would be an important factor in choosing an HH formula based on pure-tone thresholds (or other audiometric data) for compensation cases. Implicit in this proposal is the concern that direct self-assessment of HH would be excessively prone to exaggeration by individuals seeking compensation.

Accepting the premise that self-report is the most appropriate "gold standard" for measuring hearing handicap in individuals who are not involved in compensation claims, but that it is inappropriate in the context of such claims, the problem is to identify the best surrogate measure—an audiometric measurement that correlates well with self-report in non-claimants but is less subject to exaggeration. There are dozens of studies addressing this issue, and taken together they support three general conclusions (Dobie, 2000):

1. Audiometric measurements correlate moderately well with self-report in non-claimants;
2. Pure-tone thresholds and speech reception thresholds correlate better than speech discrimination scores do with self-report; and
3. The best-performing pure-tone threshold measures are the averages that include 0.5, 1, and 2 kHz, although performance differences among the various pure-tone averages are typically small.

Outside the compensation arena, patients have far less reason to exaggerate their actual level of handicap, although some exaggeration still occurs, for non-monetary motives, and some patients also deny their true handicaps. Tendencies to exaggerate or deny handicap are among the "non-sensory factors" (Demorest and Walden, 1984) affecting self-report measures. Gatehouse (1990) administered the Hearing Performance Inventory (Giolas et al., 1979) and a brief Hearing Disability Questionnaire to 240 middle-aged and elderly subjects with symmetrical normal hearing or mild hearing loss; speech frequency (0.5, 1, 2 kHz) pure-tone averages (PTA-512) were predominantly in the 10 to 40 dB HL range. As expected, PTA-512 was the strongest predictor of self-reported handicap, but personality characteristics were also strongly correlated. For a given PTA, more neurotic subjects reported more handicap. Age and IQ were less strongly correlated; older or more intelligent subjects reported less handicap than younger or less intelligent subjects for a given PTA. These findings do not demonstrate that the self-reported handicap is not genuine, only that it depends on factors beyond the condition and function of the ears.

Speech Tests

Common sense tells us that speech tests ought to be the right way to measure difficulties with speech communication. Indeed, early attempts to estimate HH from pure-tone thresholds assumed that this would be only an interim phase, and that valid and reliable tests of "everyday" speech understanding would soon be available (AMA, 1955). As previously discussed, this goal has been elusive. Hardick et al. (1980) reviewed the literature relating speech discrimination tests to self-reported handicap and concluded that there were "no data as yet available in the literature to indicate that speech perception measures are more predictive of actual difficulty experienced than . . . PTA. " The technical problems underlying this disappointing conclusion include choice of speech materials, variation in linguistic competence, and choice of signal-to-noise ratio (for background noise levels below 70 dBA, most speech communication involves signal-to-noise ratios of 5–15 dB [Pearsons et al., 1977], although these ratios would be higher if expressed in terms of peak speech levels, as in audiometry). As pointed out in Chapter 3, speech tests of reasonable duration have poor reliability. ASHA (1981) also pointed out that exaggeration or faking is more difficult to detect in speech discrimination tests than in pure-tone threshold tests. The Veterans Administration uses the maximum monosyllable discrimination score together with the pure-tone average in a complex system for assessing "percentage hearing loss." No other state or federal jurisdiction is known to this author to use speech test data in compensation cases.

Pure-Tone Thresholds

Almost all professional and governmental groups in the United States and worldwide use pure-tone thresholds to estimate HH for compensation purposes. The underlying principle is simple: The audiogram reflects at least an important part of auditory function quickly, reliably, and with limited susceptibility to exaggeration. Thresholds for frequencies important for speech understanding correlate fairly well with both speech discrimination tests and with self-reported communication problems. There is less agreement regarding the *details* of pure-tone formulas for HH, as we will see.

Frequencies

Identification of the frequencies important for speech communication was a matter of great practical importance to the Bell Telephone Laboratories from the early years of the twentieth century; the wider the range of frequencies necessary, the more expensive and difficult the engineering required for lines and equipment. Bell Lab scientists found that if they excluded variable amounts of high- or low-frequency energy using electrical filters, there were predictable effects on intelligibility of monosyllable nonsense words. Frequencies below 200 Hz (hertz) and above 6,000 Hz were found to be unnecessary; even now, the Federal Communications Commission regulates telephone receiver performance only in the range from 300–3,300 Hz (Code of Federal Regulations, 1996). Subjects could identify over 95 percent of speech sounds if frequencies above 3,000 Hz or below 1,000 Hz were excluded (French and Steinberg, 1947; Fletcher, 1953). At about 1,700 Hz (halfway between 1,000 and 3,000 Hz on a logarithmic scale), they identified a crossover point; exclusion of energy above or below this frequency resulted in equal (but quite mild) performance deficits. Subjects listening to speech containing only frequencies above *or* below 1,700 Hz could identify about 90 percent of speech sounds correctly—yet another manifestation of redundancy in speech. Not only could the frequency spectrum be divided into equally important halves in this fashion, it could be further subdivided into as many equally contributing bands as desired; the total intelligibility of a message could then be predicted by summing the contributions of these bands. This was called the "articulation index" (AI) approach. The American National Standards Institute (ANSI S3.5, 1969) published an official version of the AI—based on data collected by Bell Labs in the first half of the century.

The data used to estimate equally contributing bands for the AI can also be used to develop *frequency-importance* functions; these show the relative contribution made by each frequency region to overall intelligibility. The crossover frequency divides the frequency-importance function in half; the *area* under the portion of the curve to the left is equal to the area under the portion to the right of the crossover frequency.

Frequency-importance functions have been shown to vary with the nature of the test material. ANSI S3.5 (1969) specified a crossover frequency of 1,660 Hz for nonsense syllables. However, Studebaker and his colleagues have developed frequency-importance functions for more realistic speech materials, showing crossover frequencies of 1,314 Hz for monosyllable words (Studebaker and Sherbecoe, 1991) and 1,118 Hz for continuous discourse (Studebaker, Pavlovic, and Sherbecoe, 1987), with or without competing masking noise. These functions are shown in Figure 5–1. Clearly, lower frequencies are more important for words and sentences than for nonsense syllables. There is now a new standard (ANSI S3.5, 1997) that substitutes "speech intelligibility index" for AI; this standard lists frequency-importance functions for several types of speech materials, including the studies described above.

Since the most popular formula for estimating HH (AAO, 1979) uses four pure-tone frequencies to represent overall hearing sensitivity, it is interesting to ask what sets of four frequencies best represent the frequency-importance functions of Figure 5–1. If we let each of the four frequencies represent 25 percent of the area under the importance curve, the frequencies we want will divide these quarters into equal eighths. The lowest frequency of interest will be at the one-eighth point; 12.5 percent of the area under the curve will be to the left, with 87.5 percent to the right. The second, third, and fourth frequencies will be at the three-eighths, five-eighths, and seven-eighths points, respectively. The results of these calculations (using logarithmic interpolation) for the frequency-importance functions of Figure 5–1 and for the nonsense

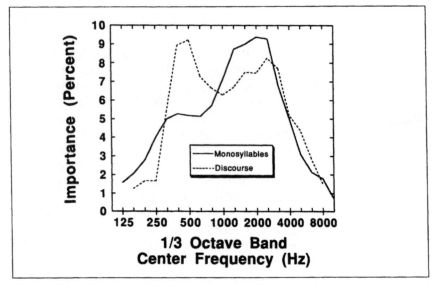

Figure 5–1. Frequency-importance functions for monosyllables and connected discourse.

syllable function embodied in ANSI S3.5 (1969), are shown in Table 5–1. Since speech in everyday life is best represented by sentences, Studebaker's data for connected discourse probably give us the best estimates of important frequencies for estimating HH, from the AI point of view. His estimates, furthermore, were unaffected by background noise, with signal-to-noise ratios as poor as 4.5 dB. 500, 1,000, 2,000, and 4,000 Hz are all a little too high, compared to the values in the last row of Table 5–1; 500, 1,000, 2,000, and 3,000 Hz strikes a compromise, with 3,000 Hz too low and the other three too high.

It is important to remember that AI (percent audibility corrected for relative importance of different frequencies) does not equal performance. Loss of all frequencies above (or below) the crossover frequency would yield an AI of 0.5; only half of the original acoustic information is now present. However,

TABLE 5–1
Most Representative Frequencies (nearest 10 Hz)

	Cumulative Importance			
	0.125	0.375	0.625	0.875
Nonsense syllables	490	1,230	2,130	3,940
Monosyllabic words	310	910	1,820	3,550
Connected discourse	380	760	1,770	3,780

listeners would score over 95 precent correct with sentence materials in either condition (ANSI, 1969).

The AI approach predicts intelligibility for normal listeners when high or low frequencies are excluded by filters—in a sense, simulating hearing loss, although certainly not reproducing the effects of recruitment and other distortions that commonly accompany sensorineural hearing loss. Obviously, a better approach would be to examine patients with hearing losses limited to certain frequencies to determine which frequencies are important for real-world speech communication. Precipitous high-frequency losses are common; there is a strong professional consensus that losses involving 6 and 8 kHz do not affect speech discrimination, and that measurable deficits, especially with speech in noise without visual input, are seen with losses affecting 3 to 4 kHz. Unfortunately, up-sloping losses, preferentially affecting the low frequencies, are uncommon, and *never* display steep slopes, making it much more difficult to dissect out the relative importance of lower frequencies in this way.

Early studies of this type (Harris, Haines, and Myers, 1956; Ward, Fleer, and Glorig, 1961) included patients with varying slopes of high-frequency hearing loss and suggested that hearing loss above 2 kHz was unimportant for speech discrimination *in quiet*. These investigators suggested the use of a 0.5, 1, 2 kHz PTA to estimate HH; adding 3 or 4 kHz did not improve prediction of speech discrimination scores. Subsequent studies by Harris and coworkers (Harris, Haines, and Myers, 1960; Harris 1965) showed that speech that had been distorted in a variety of ways put different demands on hearing: The more distorted the signal, the greater the importance of hearing at 3 and 4 kHz.

Discrimination of speech in noise is also affected by high-frequency loss. Kryter, Williams, and Green (1962) demonstrated that listeners with losses at 4 kHz and above scored lower on sentences and words in noise than normal-hearing listeners, suggesting that the pure-tone average at 2, 3, and 4 kHz (PTA-234) correlates better with discrimination scores than averages using other frequencies. Suter (1978) found the highest correlation coefficients for PTA-124 for speech in quiet or low noise, and for PTA-234 for speech in high noise levels.

Taken together, these correlational studies demonstrate that high-frequency hearing is relatively more important for speech that is distorted or masked than for speech in quiet. They do not, however, establish the relative importance of hearing at 3 or 4 kHz vis-à-vis lower frequencies. When most or all of a study's subjects have normal low-tone hearing, it is obvious that whatever performance deficits are found will correlate better with the high-frequency thresholds. As Webster (1964) noted, correlation depends not only on the strength of association between variables, but also on the *range* of variation of those variables. Analyses based on groups with inadequate variation in possibly important variables (e.g., low-frequency thresholds) may not be generalizable to other populations.

The problem with using correlation coefficients to estimate the relative importance of audiometric frequencies can be further illustrated by an example from the visual domain. One could identify several different and measurable dimensions of visual abilities, such as color vision, night vision, acuity, visual field, and so on. If each of these were measured in a group of patients, and each patient was asked to rate his or her own vision (overall) on a scale of zero (blind) to ten (normal), one could perform an analysis to determine which of our measurable variables correlated best with patients' self-assessment. If the patients were all chosen from a myopia (nearsightedness) clinic, there would be great variation in acuity, but little if any variation in the other dimensions. Clearly, those patients with the worst acuity would rate themselves as having the worst vision, and acuity would have the highest correlation with self-assessment. Another group of patients, selected for diseases that reduce visual field, would probably vary more in this dimension than in the others. Patients' self-assessments would largely be determined by the extent of field limitation, and visual field would emerge from the correlation analysis as the "most important" variable. Obviously, both results are correct for the groups they represent (myopics and field-defect patients, respectively), but neither can tell us which variables are most important to the estimation of visual handicap in general. Returning to the auditory realm, a study involving patients with normal low-frequency hearing and variable high-frequency hearing loss will necessarily identify the higher frequencies as more important (patients with isolated low-frequency losses would yield the opposite result). Appropriate use of the correlation method requires the choice of patients who display appropriate variation for all the dimensions of interest, and this doesn't seem to have been done in the studies discussed earlier.

Subjects with really precipitous losses—normal up to a specified frequency, showing 45 to 50 dB or greater hearing levels at all higher frequencies—have provided data that are somewhat easier to interpret, since the *magnitude* of performance deficit for loss of each frequency can be estimated. In one such study, Lacroix and Harris (1979) presented distorted or masked sentences to 20 normal subjects and to 45 subjects with precipitous losses beginning at either 4 kHz, 3 kHz, or 2 kHz. As seen in Table 5–2, 4 kHz losses were associated with small changes in performance compared to 3 kHz and 2 kHz losses.

TABLE 5–2
Performance Deficits (% performance) re: Normal Subjects

Type of Interferences	Normal	Lowest Involved Frequency		
		4 kHz	3 kHz	2 kHz
Time compression	0	0.5	11.3	37.7
Interruption	0	4.6	8.0	23.1
Noise	0	0.9	12.5	25.8

Aniansson (1974) conducted a similar experiment with 63 subjects, using eight different conditions involving masking noise and competing voices, and measuring discrimination for monosyllabic words. Figure 5–2 shows that, in quiet, there was little effect except for subjects with losses at 2 kHz and above. In more difficult situations, normal subjects and hearing-impaired alike showed decreased performance, with the 2 kHz loss group showing the largest decreases. Averaged over all seven difficult conditions, normal subjects made about 28 percent errors, 4 kHz loss subjects about 10 percent more, and 3 kHz loss subjects about 32 percent more than normals. These data remind us that people with high-frequency loss make more errors than normal subjects, but primarily in situations where normals also make errors. Further, they suggest that 4 kHz hearing is not as important as 3 kHz or 2 kHz hearing, according to the magnitude of deficit associated with the loss of each.

All the studies discussed previously tested subjects' performance without vision; this is analogous to many real-life situations, such as using the telephone, but many everyday situations also permit us to see the speaker. Vision not only makes the task easier, it also puts more emphasis on lower frequencies, because vision supplies clues that are complementary to low-frequency acoustic information and somewhat redundant with high-frequency information. Grant and Walden (1996) degraded speech by removing either low-frequency or high-frequency energy, such that syllable recognition was equally poor when subjects listened to either version without vision. When they allowed their subjects to both listen and watch the speaker on videotape, performance improved more for the low-frequency recording (high frequencies removed).

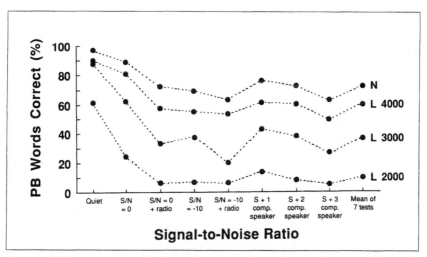

Figure 5–2. Average performance for each of several speech tests is shown for normal-hearing listeners (N), and for listeners with precipitous hearing losses beginning at 4 kHz, 3kHz, and 2 kHz. (Source: Aniansson, 1974)

How do audiograms correlate with patients' own evaluations of their hearing difficulties? Correlational studies, despite the "range of variation" problems described earlier, have generally found that PTA-512 works as well or better as averages including higher frequencies in predicting self-report (e.g., Parving and Ostri, 1983; Newman et al., 1990; Pedersen and Rosenthall, 1991; reviewed by Dobie, 2000).

Finally, expert opinion has been sampled by asking randomly selected otologists and audiologists to assign monetary awards to hypothetical patients who had suffered traumatic hearing loss of varying severity and audiometric shape (Dobie and Sakai, 1998a). Analysis of the experts' awards showed that they considered frequencies from about 500 Hz to 3–4 kHz to be important (the crossover frequency was 1346 Hz), although they gave more weight to frequencies where hearing was better than to frequencies where hearing was poorer.

All these data can be interpreted to support various frequency combinations for estimating HH. PTA-512 predicts both speech performance in quiet and patients' own self-assessment well; adding 3 kHz or 4 kHz matches the AI frequency-importance functions better and incorporates high-frequency information important for distorted or noisy speech without visual input. PTA-5123 is probably the best choice, because real "everyday" speech includes both easy and difficult listening situations, and because 4 kHz losses cause relatively minor deficits even in difficult situations. Another option is to assign different weights to each frequency; 4 kHz might then be substituted for 3 kHz, but with low weight. However, this would probably make the HH calculation method too complex for general acceptance. Some have advocated combinations such as PTA-1234 (ASHA, 1981); these would be unfair to the small number of persons whose losses at frequencies below 1 kHz can be communicatively significant. The ASHA method also gives double weight to the octave between 2 and 4 kHz, and matches up poorly with frequency-importance functions, even for nonsense syllables.

Low Fence

Assume we have chosen PTA-5123. At what hearing level for this PTA does handicap begin? HLs up to about 15 dB are statistically normal for screened young adults, but this doesn't necessarily mean that larger HLs are associated with difficulties in everyday speech communication. Specification of a "low fence," below which there is no handicap, is probably the most controversial aspect of HH estimation. It should be noted, however, that the low fence is related to the frequencies chosen for the PTA. Most subjects applying for compensation have hearing loss that is greater in the high frequencies. Thus, an individual with a 20 dB HL for PTA-512 may have a 30 dB HL for PTA-123. In Suter's (1978) study, PTA-5123 was, on the average, about 5 dB worse than PTA-512.

As in our discussion of choice of frequencies, we will struggle with the definition of "everyday" speech communication, because the more difficult the listening situation, the lower the HL at which subjects begin to experience difficulty. We could not expect a distinct boundary between normal, error-free performance and abnormal performance; even if pure-tone thresholds were perfect predictors of individuals' speech discrimination performance, we would expect instead a continuous curve in which performance gradually worsens as PTA increases, slowly at first, then more rapidly. Add in the confounding factors of test variability; nonauditory subject factors such as intelligence, attention, and linguistic skill; and the intrinsic inability of pure-tone audiometry to completely describe peripheral auditory function, and it becomes clear that the threshold of handicap—the low fence—will be elusive. We cannot pick a low fence without mislabeling some individuals as handicapped when they are not, or vice versa (or, most likely, without making both types of error).

Suter (1978) suggested that appropriate low fences would be about 9 dB HL for PTA-512, and about 19 dB HL for PTA-123; this corresponds to about 14 dB for PTA-5123 for her subjects. These values were obtained by calculating the PTAs halfway between the average PTAs for a group of subjects showing no deficit in a speech-in-noise test, and another group that did demonstrate a deficit. However, Macrae and Brigden (1973) showed that listening tasks could be made sufficiently difficult that even subjects with normal hearing had difficulty. For sentences in random noise (with a −10 dB signal-to-noise ratio), 25 dB HL for PTA-512 was the degree of hearing loss necessary to cause a 10 percent decrease in discrimination. However, sentences in "cafeteria" noise, with the same signal-to-noise ratio, were much more difficult: Even subjects with PTA-512 between 0 and 10 dB HL had average accuracy scores under 60 percent. These studies suggest that people with normal hearing experience performance deficits under difficult listening situations. It is unclear whether these near-normal subjects were aware of any deficit or what impact this would have on daily life.

Another useful approach has been to correlate audiometric data with self-report. Merluzzi and Hinchcliffe (1973) asked subjects whether their hearing was "normal" or "not as good as it used to be," and determined the audiometric boundaries between the two resulting groups of subjects. They found that this boundary varies with age. Forty-five-year-olds began to report poorer hearing at 10 dB HL for PTA-512, while the boundary for 70-year-olds was about 26 dB HL (N.B.: for PTA-5123, these levels would probably be about 15 and 31 dB, respectively).

Schein, Gentile, and Haase (1970) administered the eight-item Hearing Ability Scale (HAS) and a four-point ear rating to over 2,000 subjects and reported the audiometric distributions for subjects with different levels of self-reported abilities. Levels 1, 2, 3, and 4 are particularly relevant here.

Hearing Ability Scale

1. Can you usually hear and understand what a person says without seeing his face if he whispers to you from across a quiet room?
2. Can you usually hear and understand what a person says without seeing his face if he talks in a normal voice to you from across a quiet room?
3. Can you usually hear and understand what a person says without seeing his face if he shouts to you from across a quiet room?
4. Can you usually hear and understand a person if he speaks loudly into your better ear?

Subjects in category 1 (answering "yes" to all questions) had an average *better* ear PTA-512 of about 14 dB, while those in category 2 ("no" to question 1, "yes" to others) had average PTA-512 of about 27 dB (combining clinic and community survey data). However, these investigators also found important age effects: Young adults (18–39) had average PTA-512 of 8 and 18 dB for categories 1 and 2, suggesting that for them, handicap would begin at about 13 dB HL; this is probably equivalent to about 18 dB HL for PTA-5123 in the better ear. However, the validity of question 1 of the HAS as a criterion for normal function in everyday speech communication is debatable. One is not often called upon to hear and understand a whispered voice across a room. A person answering "no" to question 2, however, is clearly experiencing at least a mild handicap (inability to understand normal voice across a quiet room). The boundary between categories 2 and 3 for Schein, Gentile, and Haase's young group was about 25 dB HL for PTA-512 (probably about 5 dB higher for PTA-5123).

Schein, Gentile, and Haase also compared self-rating *by ear* to actual PTA for that ear. Ears rated by their owners as "good" had PTAs of about 17 dB HL, while those causing "a little trouble hearing" or "a lot of trouble hearing" had PTAs of 36 and 56 dB HL, respectively. "Deaf" ears were at 88 dB HL, on the average. The boundary for "a little trouble" would thus be about 26 to 27 dB PTA-512 (higher for PTA-5123).

Robinson et al. (1984) tried to determine a low fence in a study for the British government. Normal and hearing-impaired subjects were given auditory tasks of varying difficulty, and the authors analyzed the relationship of performance to pure-tone thresholds. Not surprisingly, they found that the "threshold" of beginning handicap was dependent on the difficulty of the test, stating that "there are as many potential disabilities as there are activities." They recommended a low fence of 30 dB HL for PTA-123, since only 2 percent of normal subjects would perform as poorly (on any of their speech tests) as subjects with this degree of hearing impairment.

The data are, as we might expect, somewhat inexact. Young subjects begin to be aware of hearing differences between 15 and 30 dB HL (for PTA-5123);

our survey of otologists and audiologists (Dobie and Sakai, 1998b) suggested a low fence of 20–25 dB HL. Older subjects admit to difficulties at higher levels. This may be because they compare themselves to their age-group peers, because their losses have accrued so gradually as to be unnoticed, because their lifestyles put fewer demands on their hearing, or because they wish to deny their handicap.

High Fence

One hundred percent hearing handicap exists when no useful speech communication can take place in everyday circumstances; by common agreement, actual or potential benefit from hearing aids is not considered (AMA, 1955). Typical conversational speech levels are 60 to 70 dB SPL (sound pressure level), with peaks up to 75 to 85 dB SPL. Clearly, such speech would be inaudible to a listener with hearing levels above about 75 dB *HL* (recall from Chapter 2 that *sound pressure levels* are different from *hearing levels*). Loud speech can be audible and partially intelligible to persons with losses up to 85 dB HL (Macrae and Brigden, 1973), and speech shouted close to the ear can be heard and repeated by subjects with losses up to 106 dB HL (Bunch, 1940). Shouted speech at conversational distance is about 18 dB more intense than normal voice level (Price, Kalb, and Garinther, 1989). In self-report studies, the boundary between "a lot of trouble hearing" and "deaf" may be as low as 72 dB HL (Schein, Gentile, and Haase, 1970). However, the former rating category is probably much broader (in dB terms) than the latter, and the true boundary may not be well estimated by the point halfway between the means of the two distributions. "Deaf" may also be interpreted by many subjects as "severely hard of hearing"; Schein, Gentile, and Haase did not define the term for their subjects. In fact, many of their subjects who considered both ears "deaf" acknowledged being able to *hear and understand* loud speech in the better ear; the boundary between this subgroup and those who could not do so was 87 dB HL. It seems likely that 100 percent HH, as we have defined it, occurs for most individuals somewhere between 80 and 100 dB HL. The otologists and audiologists we surveyed awarded money to hypothetical claimants as if the high fence was about 95 dB HL (Dobie and Sakai, 1998b).

Weighting of Ears

When one ear has a mild loss and the other has a severe loss, how is HH to be calculated? Simply averaging the values for the two ears has never made much sense, because even complete deafness in one ear causes only mild handicap— certainly not half as bad as total bilateral deafness. It has been difficult to agree on the correct weighting in favor of the better ear, although Macrae (1974, reported by Hardick et al. [1980]) apparently recommended a 4:1 ratio based on a multiple correlation analysis of the relationship of hearing in each ear to self-perceived HH. Our clinician survey and a British study also suggested a 4:1 ratio (Dobie and Sakai, 1998b; Lutman, Brown, and Coles, 1987).

A BRIEF HISTORY OF AMERICAN HH RULES

The first approach to HH estimation endorsed (at least tentatively) by the American Medical Association was the Fowler-Sabine rule (AMA, 1942; revised, 1947). In the 1947 rule, HH was based on pure-tone thresholds at 0.5, 1, 2, and 4 kHz, with unequal weighting: 40 percent for 2 kHz, 30 percent for 1 kHz, and 15 percent each for 0.5 and 4 kHz. These weights appear to have been based, at least in part, on AI data, as previously discussed (Fowler, 1942). In addition, the relationship between HH and pure-tone threshold was S-shaped, rather than linear (see Figure 5–3, solid line). The low fence was 15 dB HL (converted from American Standards Association [ASA-1951] to ANSI-1969, 1970), but 10 percent HH was not reached until about 33 dB HL (assuming a flat hearing loss). At the high end, 100 percent HH was not reached until 105 dB HL, but there was 90 percent HH at 85 dB HL. The better ear was given seven times the weight of the poorer ear.

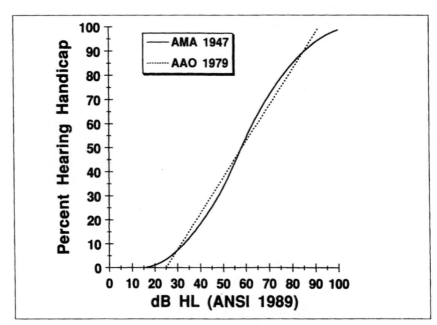

Figure 5–3. The AMA-1947 and AAO-1979 hearing handicap estimation methods are contrasted, after correction from ASA-1951 to ANSI-1989 audiometric zero.

Davis (1971) summarized the subsequent history nicely. The Fowler-Sabine rule was found to have two important flaws: First, it was too complicated, and second, otologists felt that the HH scores overestimated their patients' real handicaps. In part, this may have been because a partial HH was computed for each of the four frequencies (no PTA was computed). Thus, a person with 0 dB HLs at 0.5, 1, and 2 kHz, but a 60 dB HL at 4 kHz (with PTA-5124 = 15 dB), would have an 8 percent HH under the Fowler-Sabine rule. The AMA (1955) subsequently expressed their displeasure with this rule and stated principles and criteria for a new rule. These included the definition of "hearing disability" in terms of "sentence intelligibility" under "average everyday conditions," without the aid of vision or hearing aids. The AMA's 1955 statement also raised the hope (forlorn, we now know) that tests using speech materials would soon be useful, not just to validate pure-tone rules, but also to directly estimate HH.

In 1959, a committee of the American Academy of Ophthalmology and Otolaryngology (AAOO) recommended a new rule that was subsequently adopted by the AMA (1961). The rule was, as requested, much simpler than Fowler-Sabine. "Monaural impairment" for each ear was based on PTA-512, beginning at 25 dB HL and growing linearly at 1.5 percent per dB up to a maximum of 100 percent HH at about 92 dB HL (converted to ANSI-1969 from ASA-1951). Better ear to worse ear weighting was 5:1.

There it stood for 20 years, although already in 1960 there was "considerable sentiment for including somehow the hearing level at 3000 cps . . . in order to recognize to a realistic extent the loss of auditory discrimination that goes with a sharp frequency cutoff at or near 2000 cps" (Davis and Silverman, 1960). In 1979, the American Academy of Otolaryngology (the successor organization to the American Academy of Ophthalmology and Otolaryngology or AAOO, which now has become the American Academy of Otolaryngology–Head and Neck Surgery) recommended just such a change: Use PTA-5123 in calculating HH (AAO, 1979). The reason given was "to reflect a more realistic degree of the understanding of speech, not only in the quiet, but also in the presence of some noise." The AMA accepted this recommendation the same year and the rule is still AMA policy at this writing (2000). As of 1988, 22 states used the AAO-1979 rule, 8 used the old AAOO-1959 rule (AMA, 1961), and 14 left it to the discretion of the examining physician; however, most of the latter group specify AAO-1979 as part of the process (ASHA, 1992). Six states and the District of Columbia used other formulas (4), did not consider NIHL compensable (2), or failed to provide information (AAO-HNS, 1988). The U.S. Department of Labor uses a formula based on PTA-123, and ASHA recommends the use of PTA-1234 (the latter method apparently has not been adopted by any state or federal agency).

The AAO-1979 rule is also illustrated in Figure 5–3 (dotted line), superimposed on the 1947 Fowler-Sabine rule. The comparison is only really valid for flat hearing losses for two reasons: First, the frequencies used are slightly different (3 kHz included in AAO-1979, 4 kHz in Fowler-Sabine); second, AAO-1979 uses PTAs, while Fowler-Sabine assesses partial HH for each frequency. Still, the similarities and differences are instructive. Fowler-Sabine has a 15 dB HL low fence, versus 25 dB for AAO-1979, yet it is not on balance more "generous" than AAO-1979, because of its sigmoid shape. In fact, it almost looks as though the AAO rule was obtained by looking for the straight line that best fits the Fowler-Sabine curve (Davis [1971] acknowledges that this was "not entirely a coincidence")! Nature, it has been said, abhors a vacuum and never draws a straight line; if true, the Fowler-Sabine curve is probably closer to the biological truth. It seems to mute the controversy about the low fence by assigning very low HH (0 to 3 percent) to hearing levels between 15 and 25 dB HL. Nevertheless, Davis' caution is probably still valid; simple rules are best.

EXAMPLE   Figure 5–4 shows the audiogram of a patient with an asymmetrical high-frequency sensorineural hearing loss. The AAO-1979

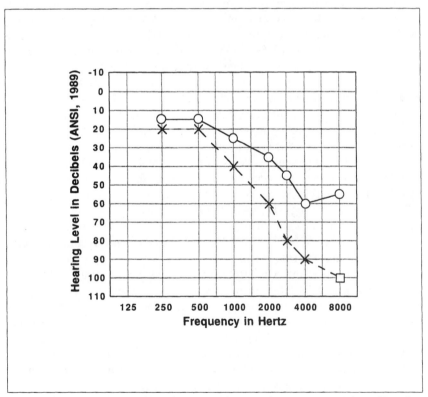

Figure 5–4.   Asymmetric high-frequency hearing loss; see examples of hearing handicap estimation in text.

method estimates HH using PTA-5123 (if the recorded threshold for any of the four frequencies is greater than 100 dB HL, 100 is used in calculating PTA-5123), a 25 dB HL "low fence," and a growth rate of 1.5 percent handicap per dB above 25 dB HL. Actually, an impairment score is calculated for each ear separately, and the overall HH score is then calculated as a weighted average favoring the better ear; in other words, the overall HH is much closer to the impairment score for the better ear than the worse ear.

Right ear

0.5 kHz	—	15 dB HL
1 kHz	—	25 dB HL
2 kHz	—	35 dB HL
3 kHz	—	45 dB HL

$$\text{PTA-5123} = \frac{15 + 25 + 35 + 45}{4} = 30 \text{ dB HL}$$

$$\text{Impairment} = (30–25)1.5\% = 7.5\%$$

Left ear

0.5 kHz	—	20 dB HL
1 kHz	—	40 dB HL
2 kHz	—	60 dB HL
3 kHz	—	80 dB HL

$$\text{PTA-5123} = \frac{20 + 40 + 60 + 80}{4} = 50 \text{ dB HL}$$

$$\text{Impairment} = (50–25)1.5\% = 37.5\%$$

Hearing Handicap (HH)

$$\text{HH} = \frac{5 \text{ (better ear impairment)} + \text{worse ear impairment}}{6}$$

$$= \frac{5 \, (7.5) + 37.5}{6} = \frac{37.5 + 37.5}{6}$$

$$= 12.5\%$$

As previously described, the AAO-1979 method is more widely used in the United States than any other, and is well justified. Many other methods have been discussed in this chapter; the results of some of these for the audiogram in Figure 5–4 are shown below, for comparison:

Method	Frequencies Averaged (kHz)	Hearing Handicap (%)
AAO-1979	0.5, 1, 2, 3	12.5
U.S. Dept. of Labor	1, 2, 3	21.25
AAOO-1959	0.5, 1, 2	3.75
ASHA	1, 2, 3,4	41.25

All these methods use a 5:1 weighting favoring the better ear, and a 25 dB HL low fence. The ASHA method uses a 2 percent growth rate (with the high fence at 75 dB HL) while the others use 1.5 percent and a 92 dB HL high fence. The major difference among the methods is in the frequencies averaged; as the example shows, methods using higher frequencies result in much larger handicap estimates for typical cases of NIHL (or any other high-frequency hearing loss).

Summary of HH Methods

Pure-tone rules are nearly universal in the United States and abroad. The AAO-1979 rule is by far the most widely used and is an acceptable compromise of simplicity and accuracy (Dobie, 2000). Like democracy, it is not perfect, but it's probably better than the alternatives. Subsequent chapters will discuss hearing loss caused by aging, noise, and other otologic conditions almost exclusively with respect to the changes in pure-tone thresholds, because most of the available data are of this type, and because estimation of HH is likely to continue to rely on pure-tone measurements for the foreseeable future.

Aging Effects

Chapter 6 discusses hearing loss accompanying the aging process, and Chapter 7 shows how aging and noise interact. In 1955, the AMA stated that HH rules should include "an allowance for the hearing loss expected with advancing age." However, the AAOO-1959 (AMA, 1961) and AAO-1979 rules rather studiously avoided the subject. Very few states specify correction for aging changes; many, perhaps most, do not permit such corrections. Some believe that the 25 dB HL low fence embodied in the AAO-1979 and AAOO-1959 rules was "deliberately set high enough to account for this aging effect"

(Melnick, 1988), and cite Davis (1971) in support. However, Davis (1971) says nothing of the kind. Rather, he argues against age correction methods that subtract expected hearing levels for age from a worker's actual hearing levels prior to calculation of hearing handicap. His reasoning is compelling:

> Causes other than noise and presbycusis can contribute to a hearing handicap, including otitis media, trauma, otosclerosis and Ménière's disease. Rules must be devised for dealing with multiple causation, and presbycusis should be handled in this context. The general principle is to estimate first the overall percentage handicap. (See how big the pie is.) Then estimate separately the relative contribution of each of two or more causes to the final impairment. (Cut the pie on this basis.) Fortunately we now have good predictive data for presbycusis in nonnoise-exposed populations, . . . and we can reasonably estimate its contribution to the total permanent threshold shift. (The remainder of the pie is charged to noise-exposure or other causes.) The problem of "second injury" in a different employment can be handled in the same way. Pre-employment audiograms are very useful here.

Davis' central concept is that estimation of HH and estimation of "relative contributions" (what I have called *allocation*; see Chapter 13) are distinct and separate processes. Davis (1971, 1973) and the AMA and AAO documents cited earlier make it clear that the HH methods developed in 1959 and 1979 were intended to estimate HH without regard to age or cause of hearing loss.

The AMA *Guides*

The *Guides to the Evaluation of Permanent Impairment* (AMA, 2000) is a comprehensive manual intended to assist physicians in the evaluation of persons with medical impairments. Now in its fifth edition, it has been published since 1971 and contains rules for calculating impairment for all types of medical disorders, including the AAO-1979 rules for HH already discussed. The *Guides*, as mentioned before, uses the term "permanent binaural hearing impairment" where the AAO uses "permanent hearing handicap"; while this can be confusing, the rules are the same, and the two terms are identically defined. Total (100 percent) hearing handicap (or binaural impairment) is considered by the *Guides* to be equivalent to a 35 percent "impairment of the whole person" (compare to 85 percent for total blindness).

Other ear problems are discussed in the *Guides*, but quantitative measures are unavailable for any of these. Loss or disturbance of vestibular function may lead to poor equilibrium or vertigo; persons suffering from these problems are assigned to one of five descriptive categories, with whole-person impairment up to 95 percent. Facial paralysis is assigned 5 percent whole-person impairment, 8 percent if bilateral. Otalgia, otorrhea, and tinnitus are said to be "subjective," and impairment ratings are left to the physician's discretion, although tinnitus may contribute no more than 5 percent to binaural hearing impairment (2 percent to whole-person impairment).

Amelioration by Hearing Aids

The AAO/AMA rules are intended to estimate HH without regard to any improvement possible with hearing aids. Only three states considered hearing aid benefit in their workers' compensation programs (AAO–HNS, 1988). Nevertheless, hearing aids can reduce the effective handicap associated with hearing loss. Conductive hearing losses, such as may occur after head injuries or surgical mishaps, may be completely compensated for by appropriate hearing aids; they are also often amenable to corrective surgery. Sensorineural losses are never completely mitigated by hearing aids because of problems with recruitment and other types of distortion, but hearing aids can still help. In medical-legal settings where mitigation by hearing aids can be relevant, expert assessment should be sought to determine the degree of benefit that is attainable.

JOB FITNESS

At times it is important to know not only an individual's HH (as defined for activities of daily life), but also whether any hearing impairment would interfere with that individual's occupational performance. This requires comparing the individual's abilities with the demands of the job. The degree of hearing impairment is obviously important, as are an individual's speech perception abilities and various "extra-auditory" factors such as intelligence, training, motivation, and familiarity with the auditory tasks required on the job. Those auditory tasks may vary in qualitative ways (speech vs. warning signals, for example) and in quantitative ways (noise level, degree of message redundancy, etc.). In many difficult occupational listening situations, redundancy is deliberately added by requiring workers to repeat back what they have heard, by restricting the set of permissible messages, or by other means. We have already seen how difficult it is to estimate HH—with the thorniest problem being the definition of everyday listening situations. Assessing job fitness is even more difficult if the demands of the job are not well specified.

Price, Kalb, and Garinther (1989) used theoretical models to estimate the job performance deficits likely to be experienced by soldiers with mild (about

30 dB HL) hearing impairment, and concluded that these deficits were clearly *job-specific* (depending on the task) and *graded*. For example, hearing impairment reduced the area in square meters that a soldier could monitor for sounds produced by hostile forces and reduced the warning time available when such sounds were heard.

Many governmental agencies have set hearing standards for entry and/or retention in various jobs; most of these seem to have been devised by professional judgment rather than by job-specific performance studies. Perhaps for this reason, many agencies are more lenient in applying these rules for retention than for entry, reasoning that if an individual can demonstrate competence despite hearing impairment, that fact should carry great weight. Among these agencies (and the covered jobs) are the U.S. Department of Transportation (locomotive engineers and long-distance truckers), the Federal Aviation Administration (FAA; pilots and air traffic controllers), and many police and fire departments. For a first-class pilot's license, the FAA requires thresholds as good or better than 40 dB HL at 500 Hz and 35 dB HL at 1 and 2 kHz. The U.S. Armed Forces have somewhat stricter induction criteria, and each service has specific job categories (e.g., pilot, cavalry scout, missile launch crew) for which even more stringent criteria are applied (Suter, 1989). However, even the most stringent military criteria would pass some individuals whose hearing impairments would exceed the low fence for 0 percent HH of the AAO-1979 rules.

Abel et al. (1982, 1985) have shown that personal hearing protective devices, while not impairing the ability of normally hearing subjects to detect warning signals and discriminate speech in noise, can cause degraded performance for hearing-impaired subjects. In a noisy factory, speech or other signals need to be at or above the noise level to be audible; inserting earplugs reduces both signal and noise levels, but leaves the signal-to-noise ratio unchanged. Therefore, the signal will still be audible, if initial level minus the attenuation of the earplug exceeds the worker's hearing level (corrected to SPL). When hearing level for the frequency of the signal exceeds about 50 dB HL, there is substantial risk that a signal just above the noise level may be inaudible when the worker uses hearing protectors. This can lead to poor speech perception if the high-frequency components of speech become inaudible.

Some of the occupational problems associated with hearing impairment can be mitigated. Workers in quiet but communicatively demanding jobs can use hearing aids—in fact, the military permits personnel in many job categories to use hearing aids as necessary. So-called assistive listening devices can improve communication in many settings; for example, hearing-impaired physicians and nurses can use amplified stethoscopes (Dobie, 1992). In noisy environments, devices that function simultaneously as hearing protectors and audio headsets are available—either with wireless input from a remote microphone or with input from a directional microphone on the headset.

The Americans with Disabilities Act

When fully implemented, the Americans with Disabilities Act (ADA), passed by Congress in 1990, promised to dramatically change the way employers determine job fitness. It applies to almost all nonfederal employers with 15 or more employees. While the intent of the law—to guarantee equality of opportunity to the disabled—is clear, many of its requirements are vague and will probably require years of executive branch rule-making and judicial review for clarification (Anfield, 1992). The ADA also covers public services provided by both governments and private entities (parks, hotels, etc.), and telecommunications (Tucker, 1994), but it is the employment provisions of the Act that concern us here.

In essence, the ADA makes it illegal to discriminate against "qualified" persons with "disabilities," because of their disabilities, with respect to employment or the conditions thereof. "Qualified" refers not only to the usual educational, skill, and experience requirements, but also to the ability to perform the "essential functions" of the job with or without "reasonable accommodation." Each of the terms in quotation marks contains some ambiguity and will provide grist for the legal mills.

The ADA defines "disability" as a chronic physical or mental impairment that "substantially" limits one or more major life activities (hearing and speaking are specifically included). Even a history of past disability or perception by others that one is disabled qualifies an individual for protection under the ADA. However, in a recent decision with obvious relevance to hearing loss (*Sutton* v. *United Air Lines,* 1999), the U.S. Supreme Court held that two nearsighted pilots whose vision was correctible by glasses were not ADA-protected against the airline's policy of requiring excellent uncorrected vision for newly hired pilots.

"Substantial" limitation of hearing in everyday life is itself hard to define, as we have seen, and the ADA offers no quantitative criteria. "Hearing handicap," as defined by the AAO-HNS and the AMA, would be a reasonable yardstick, but where would "substantial" limitation begin? 0 percent? 10 percent? Clearly, ability that is merely below average does not constitute a disability. This leads to a potential paradox: A job applicant with a mild nonhandicapping high-frequency hearing loss (0 percent hearing handicap) could be refused employment more easily than an applicant with a handicapping degree of loss, although the latter applicant presents greater concern to the employer regarding job performance, safety, and potential compensation and insurance costs. However, if the former applicant were refused *because* of his hearing, he would probably be protected by the ADA as someone perceived (by the employer) to have a handicap.

The employer may refuse employment to an otherwise qualified, disabled applicant who can't perform the "essential functions" of the job, even with accommodations. However, the ADA doesn't specify how *well* the applicant must perform. Employers may use nonmedical job simulation tests or job trials to predict future performance, and can use rankings on these tests to select successful applicants, but may not use disability per se as a factor, even if there are data to indicate that individuals with a particular disability perform less well, on the average, in a particular job.

Employment may also be refused if the disabled person would pose a "direct threat" to the health or safety of self or others, if employed. (Actually, the ADA only refers to threats to other persons, while subsequent federal regulations refer to the prospective employee as well.) The degree of risk that constitutes "direct threat" is left in question.

Both job performance and safety/health risk must be considered in the light of "reasonable accommodations." For hearing-impaired workers, these could include use of assistive listening devices, such as amplified telephones, provision of sign-language interpreters (for important events such as job interviews, annual performance reviews, and disciplinary counseling), installation of visible as well as audible safety alarms, and reassignment of "marginal" (nonessential) duties to other employees. Job procedures could be changed, for example, requiring important communications to be verified in writing or repeated back. Obviously, the range of possible accommodations is unlimited, and the employer retains some discretion: Accommodations that would pose "undue hardship" in terms of cost or other disruption of business are not required.

The ADA will probably *reduce* the role played by medical examination in employment decisions. Employers are still permitted to require examinations prior to employment, but only

1. *After* an offer of employment (the offer may be contingent on the results of the examination),
2. If required of all prospective employees entering similar jobs,
3. If medical criteria can be shown to be related to job performance, and
4. If medical records are treated confidentially and sequestered from personnel files, with supervisors' access limited to recommendations regarding restrictions and accommodations.

During the "pre-offer" phase, an employer may describe or demonstrate essential job activities, ask an applicant if (and how) he or she would be able to perform them, and/or require performance tests. For example, a prospective receptionist might be asked to answer the telephone and accurately record messages and appointment data; if accommodation such as a hearing aid or amplified telephone were needed, it would be the applicant's duty to request this. Any relevant disability that was not otherwise apparent would probably be revealed during this process, but the employer may not directly ask about disabilities prior to determining whether a job offer will be made.

A contingent job offer can be withdrawn based on relevant physical examination findings, but the link between these findings and job performance can often be severely challenged. If our prospective receptionist were found to have a 10 percent hearing handicap by audiometry despite performing well on a job simulation test using the telephone, a decision not to hire (if based on the audiogram) would be difficult, perhaps impossible, to defend. If no job simulation test were given, the employer would still have the burden of proving that the audiometric criteria used were appropriate, if the spurned applicant sought relief under the ADA. Pre-offer performance tests based on job simulation or actual job trial will probably be more widely used in the near future; not only will they permit a more defensible decision of noncompetence, they may be used to rank qualified and competent applicants.

REFERENCES

Abel, Sharon M., Peter W. Alberti, Caroline Haythornthwaite, and Krista Riko. 1982. Speech intelligibility in noise: Effects of fluency and hearing protector type. *J. Acoust. Soc. Am.* 71(3):708–715.

Abel, Sharon M., Hans Kunov, M. Kathleen Pichora-Fuller, and Peter W. Alberti. 1985. Signal detection in industrial noise: Effects of noise exposure history, hearing loss, and the use of ear protection. *Scand. Audiol.* 14(3):161–173.

American Academy of Otolaryngology–Committee on Hearing and Equilibrium and the American Council of Otolaryngology–Committee on the Medical Aspects of Noise. 1979. Guide for the evaluation of hearing handicap. *JAMA* 241(19):2055–2059.

American Academy of Otolaryngology–Head and Neck Surgery–Subcommittee on the Medical Aspects of Noise of the Committee on Hearing and Equilibrium. 1988. *Guide for Conservation of Hearing in Noise,* rev. ed. Washington, DC: American Academy of Otolaryngology–Head and Neck Surgery Foundation, Inc.

American Medical Association. 2000. *Guides to the Evaluation of Permanent Impairment,* 5th ed. Chicago: American Medical Association.

American Medical Association–Committee on Medical Rating of Physical Impairment. 1961. Guide to the evaluation for permanent impairment: Ear, nose, throat, and related structures. *JAMA* 177(7):489–501.

American Medical Association–Committee on Rating of Mental and Physical Impairment. 1971. *Guides to the Evaluation of Permanent Impairment.* Chicago: American Medical Association.

American Medical Association–Council on Physical Medicine. 1947. Tentative standard procedure for evaluating the percentage loss of hearing in medicolegal cases. *JAMA* 133(6):396–397.

American Medical Association–Council on Physical Medicine and Rehabilitation. 1955. Principles for evaluating hearing loss. *JAMA* 157(16):1408–1409.

American Medical Association–Council on Physical Therapy. 1942. Tentative standard procedure for evaluating the percentage of useful hearing loss in medicolegal cases. *JAMA* 119(14):1108–1109.

American National Standards Institute. 1969. *American National Standard Methods for the Calculation of the Articulation Index, ANSI S3.5-1969.* New York: Acoustical Society of America.

———. 1970. *American National Standard Specifications for Audiometers, ANSI S3.6-1969.* New York: Acoustical Society of America.

———. 1997. *American National Standard Methods for Calculation of the Speech Intelligibility Index, ANSI S3.5-1997.* New York: Acoustical Society of America.

American Speech-Language-Hearing Association. 1992. A survey of states' workers' compensation practices for occupational hearing loss. *ASHA Suppl.* 34(Suppl 8):2–8.

American Speech-Language-Hearing Association—Task Force on the Definition of Hearing Handicap. 1981. On the definition of hearing handicap. *ASHA* 23(4):293–297.

American Standards Association. 1951. *Audiometers for General Diagnostic Purposes, ASA Z24.5-1951.* New York: American Standards Association.

Anfield, Robert N. 1992. Americans with Disabilities Act of 1990. *J. Occup. Med.* 34(5):503–509.

Aniansson, Gunnar. 1974. Methods for assessing high frequency hearing loss in everyday listening situations. *Acta Otolaryngol. Suppl. (Stockh.)* 320:1–50.

Bunch, C. C. 1940. Usable hearing. *Ann. Otol. Rhinol. Laryngol.* 49(2):359–367.

Code of Federal Regulations, Title 47, Parts 68.4, 68.317. *Federal Register* 61:42184ff., August 14, 1996.

Davis, Hallowell. 1965. Guide for the classification and evaluation of hearing handicap in relation to the international audiometric zero. *Trans. Amer. Acad. Ophthal. Otolaryng.* 69(4):740–751.

———. 1971. A historical introduction. In *British Acoustical Society Special Series: Volume 1—Occupational Hearing Loss,* ed. D. W. Robinson, pp. 7–12. New York: Academic Press.

———. 1973. Some comments on "Impairment to hearing from exposure to noise" by K. D. Kryter. *J. Acoust. Soc. Am.* 53(5):1237–1239.

Davis, Hallowell and S. Richard Silverman. 1960. *Hearing and Deafness,* rev. ed. New York: Holt, Rinehart and Winston.

Demorest, Marilyn E. and Brian E. Walden. 1984. Psychometric principles in the selection, interpretation, and evaluation of communication self-assessment inventories. *J. Speech. Hear. Disord.* 49(3):226–240.

Dobie, Robert A. 1992. Amplified stethoscope for the hearing-impaired physician. *JAMA, Questions and Answers Section* 267(16):2245.

————. 2000. Estimation of hearing loss severity from the audiogram. In D. Henderson et al. (eds.), *Noise-Induced Hearing Loss: Basic Mechanisms, Prevention, and References Control*. London: NRN Publishers.

Dobie, Robert A. and Connie S. Sakai. 1998a. Monetary compensation for hearing loss: Choice and weighting of frequencies. *J. Occup. Hearing Loss* 1:163–172.

————. 1998b. Monetary compensation for hearing loss: Clinician survey. *J. Occup. Hearing Loss* 1:73–80.

Eastwood, M. R., S. L. Corbin, M. Reed, H. Nobbs, and H. B. Kedward. 1985. Acquired hearing loss and psychiatric illness: An estimate of prevalence and co-morbidity in a geriatric setting. *Br. J. Psychiatry* 147(11): 552–556.

Fletcher, Harvey. 1953. *Speech and Hearing in Communication*. New York: D. Van Nostrand Company, Inc.

Fowler, Edmund Prince. 1942. A simple method of measuring percentage of capacity for hearing speech: Fundamental factors in setting up a standard. *Arch. Otolaryngol.* 36(6):874–890.

French, N. R. and J. C. Steinberg. 1947. Factors governing the intelligibility of speech sounds. *J. Acoust. Soc. Am.* 19:90–119.

Gatehouse, Stuart. 1990. Determinants of self-reported disability in older subjects. *Ear & Hearing Suppl.* 11(5):57S–65S.

Giolas, Thomas G., Elmer Owens, Stanford H. Lamb, and Earl D. Schubert. 1979. Hearing performance inventory. *J. Speech Hear. Disord.* 44(2): 169–195.

Grant, K. W. and B. E. Walden. 1996. Evaluating the articulation index for auditory-visual consonant recognition. *J. Acoust. Soc. Am.* 100:2415–2424.

Hardick, Edward J., William Melnick, Nancy A. Hawes, Joseph P. Pillion, Ray G. Stephens, and Deborah J. Perlmutter. 1980. *Compensation for Hearing Loss for Employees Under Jurisdiction of the U.S. Department of Labor: Benefit Formula and Assessment Procedures (Contract No. J-9-E-9-0205)*. Columbus: The Ohio State University.

Harris, J. Donald. 1965. Pure-tone acuity and intelligibility of everyday speech. *J. Acoust. Soc. Am.* 37(5):824–830.

Harris, J. Donald, Henry L. Haines, and Cecil K. Myers. 1956. A new formula for using the audiogram to predict speech hearing loss. *Arch. Otolaryngol.* 63(2):158–176.

————. 1960. The importance of hearing at 3 kc for understanding speeded speech. *Laryngoscope* 70(2):131–146.

Herbst, Katia Gilhome and Charlotte Humphrey. 1980. Hearing impairment and mental state in the elderly living at home. *Br. Med. J.* 281(6245):903–905.

Hetu, R, L. Riverin, N. Lalande, L. Getty, and C. St-Cyr. 1988. Qualitative analysis of the handicap associated with occupational hearing loss. *Br. J. Audiol.* 22(4):251–264.

ISO 7731-1986. Danger signals for work places—Auditory danger signals. Geneva: International Organization for Standardization.

Kryter, Karl D., Carl Williams, and David M. Green. 1962. Auditory acuity and the perception of speech. *J. Acoust. Soc. Am.* 34(9):1217–1223.

Lacroix, Paul G. and J. Donald Harris. 1979. Effects of high-frequency cue reduction on the comprehension of distorted speech. *J. Speech Hear. Disord.* 44(2):236–246.

Lipscomb, David M. 1982. Audibility and the law. In *Forensic Audiology,* ed. Marc B. Kramer and Joan M. Armbruster, pp. 191–222. Baltimore: University Park Press.

Lutman, M. E., E. J. Brown, and R. R. Coles. 1987. Self-reported disability and handicap in the population in relation to pure-tone threshold, age, sex, and type of hearing loss. *Br. J. Audiol.* 21:45–58.

Macrae, J. H. and D. N. Brigden. 1973. Auditory threshold impairment and everyday speech reception. *Audiology* 12(4):272– 290.

Melnick, William. 1988. Compensation for hearing loss from occupational noise. *Semin. Hearing* 9(4):339–349.

Merluzzi, F. and R. Hinchcliffe. 1973. Threshold of subjective auditory handicap. *Audiology* 12(2):65–69.

Newman, C. W., B. E. Weinstein, G. P. Jacobson, and G. A. Hug. 1990. The hearing handicap inventory for adults: Psychometric adequacy and audiometric correlates. *Ear & Hearing* 11:430–433.

Parving, A. and B. Ostri. 1983. On objective criteria for hearing impairment and hearing disability. *Scand. Audiol.* 12:165–169.

Pearsons, K. S., R. L. Bennett, and S. Fidell. 1977. Speech levels in various noise environments. Report No. EPA-600/1-77-025. Washington, DC: Environmental Protection Agency.

Pederson, K. and V. Rosenthall. 1991. Correlations between self-assessed hearing handicap and standard audiometric tests in elderly persons. *Scand. Audiol.* 20:109–116.

Price, G. Richard, Joel T. Kalb, and Georges R. Garinther. 1989. Toward a measure of auditory handicap in the Army. *Ann. Otol. Rhinol. Laryngol. Suppl.* 98[Suppl. 140](5 Pt. 2):42–52.

Robinson, D. W., P. A. Wilkins, N. J. Thyer, and J. F. Lawes. 1984. *Auditory Impairment and the Onset of Disability and Handicap in Noise-Induced Hearing Loss (ISVR Tech. Report No. 126).* Southampton, UK: Institute of Sound and Vibration Research.

Schein, Jerome D., Augustine Gentile, and Kenneth W. Haase. 1970. Development and evaluation of an expanded hearing loss scale questionnaire. *Vital Health Stat.* 2(37):i–viii, 1–42.

Schow, Ronald L. and Stuart Gatehouse. 1990. Fundamental issues in self-assessment of hearing. *Ear & Hearing Suppl.* 11(5):6S–16S.

Studebaker, Gerald A., Chaslav V. Pavlovic, and Robert L. Sherbecoe. 1987. A frequency importance function for continuous discourse. *J. Acoust. Soc. Am.* 81(4):1130–1138.

Studebaker, Gerald A. and Robert L. Sherbecoe. 1991. Frequency-importance and transfer functions for recorded CID W-22 word lists. *J. Speech Hear. Res.* 34(2):427–438.

Suter, Alice H. 1978. *The Ability of Mildly Hearing-Impaired Individuals to Discriminate Speech in Noise (Joint EPA/USAF Study, EPA 55019-78-100, AMRL-TR-78-4).* Washington, DC: U.S. Environmental Protection Agency.

———. 1989. *The Effects of Hearing Loss on Speech Communication and the Perception of Other Sounds (Technical Memorandum 4–89, AMCMS Code 611102.74A0011).* Aberdeen Proving Ground, MD: U.S. Army Human Engineering Laboratory.

Sutton v. United Air Lines Incorporated, #97-1943 (Supreme Court, June 22, 1999).

Tucker, B. P. 1994. Legal rights of hearing-impaired persons under the Americans with Disabilities Act and related federal laws. *Seminars in Hearing.* 15:230–242.

Ward, W. Dixon, Robert E. Fleer, and Aram Glorig. 1961. Characteristics of hearing losses produced by gunfire and by steady noise. *J. Aud Res.* 1:325–356.

Webster, J. C. 1964. Important frequencies in noise-masked speech. *Arch. Otolaryngol.* 80(5):494–504.

World Health Organization. 1980. *International Classification of Impairments, Disabilities, and Handicaps: A Manual of Classification Relating to the Consequences of Disease.* World Health Organization.

Chapter 6

Age-Related Hearing Loss

As humans age, they lose hearing at variable rates. Some of this hearing loss is caused by noise exposure (see Chapters 7 and 8), some by other otologic injuries and diseases (see Chapter 10), but most of it is without apparent cause other than the aging process. This chapter will describe age-related changes in auditory system structure and function, possible mechanisms and causes, and the effects of these changes on aging persons. From the medical-legal point of view, the most useful information in this chapter is probably contained in the graphic summaries of epidemiologic studies of age-related hearing loss (ARHL); these data permit us to estimate, for an individual of a given age and gender, the amount of hearing loss to be expected, in the absence of identifiable otologic trauma and disease, on the basis of age alone. Aging changes in the ear are not limited to the auditory system—deterioration of vestibular function probably contributes to poor balance and falls in the elderly, but this is outside the scope of our discussion.

ARHL is primarily caused by cochlear degeneration, but age-related changes in the outer and middle ear do occur. Cerumen (earwax) obstructions of the ear canal are more common in older people, and can cause substantial conductive hearing losses, which are easily detected and reversed by the removal of the cerumen. More insidiously, old ear canals lose some of their rigidity and may collapse when earphones are placed for audiometric testing; this leads to a spurious conductive hearing loss, greater in the high frequencies, which is present only while the earphones are in place (Randolph and Schow, 1983). Once recognized, the problem can be solved by placing a short length of plastic tubing in the outer part of the ear canal prior to placing the earphones on the head. Old ears are subject to the entire spectrum of middle ear disease described in Chapter 10, but may also display small air-bone gaps related to aging changes in the tympanic membrane, the ossicles, and their joints and ligaments (Marshall, Martinez, and Schlamm,

1983). However, significant outer and middle ear changes are not usually a part of the aging process.

The inner ear degeneration that accompanies aging causes a sensorineural hearing loss that initially affects the highest frequencies in most cases. Men usually have greater losses than women of the same age.

Schuknecht (1964) postulated the existence of four types of presbycusis (literally "old man's hearing"): *sensory, neural, metabolic*, and *mechanical*. In sensory presbycusis, the cochlear hair cells are progressively lost, beginning at the base of the cochlea, where high-frequency sounds are transduced, then moving gradually toward the low-frequency region of the cochlear apex. Patients with these findings on post-mortem microscopic examination usually had steeply-sloping audiograms, with relatively good low-frequency hearing, prior to death. Johnsson and Hawkins (1972a, 1972b) demonstrated that loss of hair cells began even in adolescence. Many animal species show age-related hair cell loss.

Neural presbycusis refers to loss of auditory nerve fibers within the cochlea; Schuknecht argued that this microscopic pattern correlated with speech perception difficulties, which were more severe than would be expected from the degree of pure-tone threshold loss.

Patients with metabolic presbycusis were said to have rather flat audiograms, good speech discrimination, and atrophy of the stria vascularis. In support of this variety of presbycusis, Schmiedt, Mills, and Adams (1987) have found strial atrophy, decreases in the endolymphatic potential (the inner ear voltage, maintained by the stria vascularis, which acts as an energy source for the hair cells), and hearing loss in aging gerbils. Gratton and Schulte (1995) found that strial atrophy in aging gerbils preceded measurable hearing loss, and was accompanied by loss of blood vessels.

There remained some cases in Schuknecht's experience where the inner ears showed no apparent atrophy or degeneration; he theorized that age-related changes in the stiffness of inner ear membranes, not detectable by light microscopy, were responsible (mechanical presbycusis).

Most investigators agree that aging affects several elements in the cochlea—at least hair cells, neurons, and stria vascularis—and that these elements may deteriorate more or less independently. In this sense, ARHL is clearly different from noise-induced hearing loss (NIHL), where (as we will see in Chapter 7) hair cells are virtually the only affected cochlear elements. However, Schuknecht's scheme has proved difficult to apply to clinical data. Pure-tone audiograms in older subjects show variability in shape and severity of loss, but do not naturally segregate into categories (Katsarkas and Ayukawa, 1986). Many investigators (e.g., Gates et al., 1990) have noted a tendency to flatter audiograms in aging women and more steeply sloping audiograms in aging men, but these are only weak statistical trends. (It is impossible to predict the gender of an elderly person from his or her audiogram.) Some microscopic studies of the inner ear in old persons have also failed to support the notion of discrete categories of degeneration correlated to audiometric shape

(Suga and Lindsay, 1976); in one study, almost all aging ears showed hair cell loss (base > apex), with little or no strial atrophy or neural loss (outside of areas with severe hair cell loss) (Soucek, Michaels, and Frohlich, 1986). In contrast, Schuknecht and Gacek (1993) concluded that hair cell loss was "the least important cause of hearing loss in the aged."

In the early days of audiology, some authors (e.g., Hinchcliffe, 1958) believed that age-related degeneration of the brain was an important—perhaps essential—component of ARHL. In part, this theory was advanced to explain the disproportionate difficulty with speech perception some older persons display, which Schuknecht characterized as "neural presbycusis" and Gaeth (1948) called "phonemic regression." Both humans and other animals show age-related loss of cells and other degenerative changes in the auditory brainstem nuclei (Kirikae, Sato, and Shitara, 1964; Hansen and Reske-Nielsen, 1965; Konigsmark and Murphy, 1972), but the functional significance of these changes is unclear. When special audiological tests thought to be specific for "central auditory processing disorders" have been administered to old subjects, one study suggested that perhaps 20 percent of these subjects had poorer brain function than younger subjects with the equivalent degree of audiometric threshold shift (Cooper and Gates, 1991). Others (e.g., Kelly-Ballweber and Dobie, 1984) have found no differences in performance on central auditory tests between elderly subjects and audiometrically matched young controls.

CAUSES

An old person may have hearing loss caused by one or more identifiable causes: occupational noise exposure, non-occupational noise exposure, or other otologic disorders (e.g., ear infections, otosclerosis, Ménière's disease). More often, hearing loss in old age has no such identifiable cause; the label *presbycusis* is then commonly applied. Surveys of hearing loss in advancing age usually have one of two different goals. They may wish to simply describe how well or how poorly individuals in a particular age-group hear, in which case it is appropriate to include all comers, regardless of the causes of hearing loss. However, if the intent is to specifically describe the magnitude of presbycusis, it is essential to screen out subjects who are known to have other otologic disorders. Most such studies have excluded subjects who worked in noisy jobs, but many failed to identify and exclude those who had had significant nonoccupational noise exposure. Glorig and Nixon (1962) recognized this failing and pointed out that such studies were really studying "presbycusis" plus "socioacusis," a term they coined to refer to the damaging effects of nonoccupational noise in modern society (for example, hunting).

Ward (1977) later pointed out that even the best available otologic screening may fail to screen out persons whose hearing loss is caused wholly or in part by some unrecognized otologic disorder. For example, diabetes and hypertension are increasingly prevalent in old age and may or may not cause significant inner ear damage and hearing loss, but no study of presbycusis has eliminated diabetic or hypertensive individuals. For Ward, even the best-designed study could not exclude the effects of *nosoacusis*, his term for otologic disease or injury (*other* than due to noise or to "pure aging").

Combining Ward's with Glorig and Nixon's terminology, presbycusis can now be quite narrowly defined as a degenerative process confined to the inner ear, independent of environmental influence, intrinsic and inexorable. In this usage, presbycusis is by definition a genetic disorder. This does not exclude a genetic role for socioacusis and nosoacusis—one could inherit susceptibility to damage by noise, drug, or cholesterol—but presbycusis would be the *purely* genetically determined loss of hearing with age.

Like humans, mice lose hair cells and spiral ganglion cells as they age, and many genetically distinct strains of mice lose these cells much more rapidly than wild-type mice (e.g., McFadden et al., 1999; Willott and Erway, 1998). Genetic effects in aging humans have been demonstrated by comparing identical versus fraternal twins (Karlsson et al., 1997) and related versus spousal pairs (Gates et al., 1999). These studies show that the more closely related two people are, the more similar their hearing thresholds are likely to be, even taking into account shared environmental influences.

Unfortunately, different authors use these words differently. Table 6–1 shows some of the variability. This author finds much merit in the Glorig-Nixon-Ward nomenclature; however, in discussing data from specific studies, we will just refer to age-related hearing loss (ARHL) or age-related permanent threshold shift (ARPTS), which will always include presbycusis and some nosoacusis, and often socioacusis.

Is presbycusis a disease? As we have defined the term, presbycusis has some of the features of a disease: It is associated with progressive, autonomous inner ear pathological changes and significant dysfunction. On the other hand, it is universal (although with variable severity), has no specific etiology other than genetic variability, and its pathological changes are

TABLE 6–1
Terminology in Age-Related Hearing Loss

Cause	Ward	Glorig and Nixon	Conventional
Genetic	presbycusis ⎱		
"Other otologic" disease	nosoacusis ⎰	presbycusis ⎱	presbycusis
Nonoccupational noise	socioacusis	socioacusis ⎰	
Occupational noise	NIHL	NIHL	NIHL

neither homogeneous nor specific. This is essentially a semantic problem, but one that may have legal ramifications in jurisdictions where aggravations of an existing disease is a factor to be weighed.

HEARING HANDICAP IN ARHL

Gates et al. (1990) studied 1,662 subjects between the ages of 63 and 95. Fifty-five percent had worse ear pure-tone averages (PTA-5123) for 0.5, 1, 2, and 3 kHz (kilohertz) $\geq$ 25 dB HL (hearing level), that is, hearing handicap (HH) $\geq$ 0 percent by the American Academy of Otolaryngology (AAO) 1979 rule, but only 41 percent admitted a "hearing problem." Coincidentally, the same percentage (41 percent—but not necessarily the same 41 percent) had HH > 10 percent. These data suggest that most subjects in this age range complain of hearing problems when their PTA-5123 exceeds about 32 dB HL (10 percent HH). Salomon, Vesterager, and Jagd (1988) found similar results for a group of 70-to-75-year-old subjects: 30 dB HL for PTA-5124 divided those who complained of problems with conversation (in quiet or noise) from those who did not admit to problems. Ventry and Weinstein (1983) found that thresholds exceeding 40 dB for either 1 or 2 kHz best predicted self-report of handicap on the Hearing Handicap Inventory for the Elderly (HHIE), while Bess et al. (1989) found that PTA-512 was superior to PTA-124, speech reception threshold (SRT), or the Ventry and Weinstein criteria in predicting handicap on the HHIE. Taken together, these studies, along with Matthews et al. (1990), who found 1 kHz to be the best single-frequency predictor of HHIE scores, suggest that the AAO-1979 rule overestimates self-perceived hearing handicap in the elderly, at least at the low fence. Most older persons have lost hearing very gradually and to some degree imperceptibly. For many, this process coincides with a less active and less communicatively demanding lifestyle, so it's not too surprising that the threshold for noticing (or admitting) handicap is higher.

Speech Discrimination in ARHL

Since Gaeth's (1948) description of "phonemic regression," it has been clear that many older persons have difficulties understanding speech. Schuknecht (1964) believed these individuals had a disproportionate degree of *neural* cell loss, compared to the more common *sensory* (hair cell) atrophy. In recent studies, however, most of the speech discrimination difficulties of hearing-impaired older subjects have been predictable based on their pure-tone audiograms, that is, by the *audibility* of different speech sounds (e.g., Humes and Roberts, 1990; Humes and Christopherson, 1991; Humes et al., 1994; Souza and Turner, 1994). Other investigators have found that speech discrimination in noise *is* worse than would be predicted by audibility in older subjects (e.g., Dubno, Dirks, and Morgan, 1984; Schum, Matthews, and Lee, 1991), especially after age 80 (Studebaker et al., 1997).

Functional Impact

The Sickness Impact Profile (SIP) has become popular as a measure of overall functioning, with scales for such things as mobility, self-care, communication, sleep, eating, and work. Normal unimpaired adults typically score between 2 and 3, while patients with advanced lung disease or terminal cancer might score 25 or 35, respectively. Bess et al. (1989) have reported strong effects of hearing loss on the SIP in elderly subjects after controlling for age, other medical illnesses, vision, and mental status. For pure-tone losses exceeding 40 dB, the mean SIP score was 17.1 (cf. 5.3 for loss < 17 dB). Surprisingly, nearly all scales were affected—not only those dealing explicitly with communication and emotion.

The association between hearing loss and depression (and probably psychosis) in the elderly has been mentioned in Chapter 5. There may also be a significant link with cognitive function and dementia (Uhlmann et al., 1989), but this is controversial (Thomas et al., 1983; Eastwood et al., 1985). The apparent correlation could be caused by a shared risk factor for both hearing loss and dementia or by either hearing loss or depression interfering with cognitive function testing.

EPIDEMIOLOGY

The general relationships between aging and pure-tone thresholds are well known. In all populations studied (and in almost all individuals), the highest frequencies are first and most severely affected. Men usually show more severe losses than women, at least above 1 kHz. For a given frequency, the threshold shifts *accelerate* over time; the older the subject, the greater the amount of additional threshold shift expected over a given interval.

The U.S. Public Health Service (USPHS) conducted an important survey of hearing thresholds at different ages in 1960–1962 (Glorig and Roberts, 1965). This study was designed to be truly representative of the U.S. population and was therefore *unscreened;* it must, therefore, have included subjects with occupational and nonoccupational noise exposure. While the inclusion of such individuals probably increased threshold levels, only better-ear data were reported, which had the opposite effect. These data were reanalyzed and smoothed by Johnson (1978), and eventually incorporated into an international standard (ISO-1999, 1990) to be discussed later in this chapter. Figure 6–1 shows the median, tenth, and ninetieth percentile

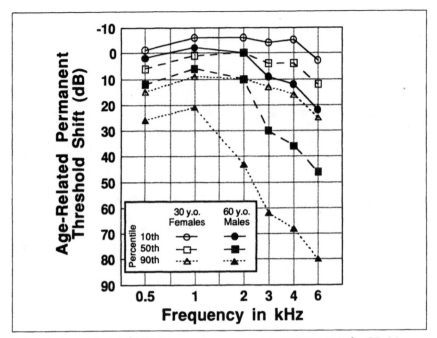

Figure 6–1. U.S. Public Health Service survey data (1960–1962) for 25–34-year old women and 55–64-year old men. Median (50th percentile) and extreme (10th and 90th percentile) audiograms are shown.

audiograms for 30-year-old women and 60-year-old men (actually, the age groups of 25–34 and 55–64 are represented). The vertical axis represents ARPTS, while frequency is on the horizontal axis. The degree of variability is obvious: The best 10 percent of the older men hear better than the worst 10 percent of the young women. Figure 6–2 shows median curves only, for both genders and four age groups; all the expected features—acceleration, greater losses for high frequencies and for men—are obvious. Medians as well as tenth and ninetieth percentile values for ARPTS are also presented in Table 6–2.

The 1960–1962 USPHS survey, using Ward's (1977) terminology, includes presbycusis, nosoacusis, and socioacusis, and some occupational NIHL. More recent population-based audiometric surveys (e.g., Cruickshanks et al., 1998) offer no evidence that hearing levels have changed in the United States, although they do provide data at more advanced ages.

Many other, mostly smaller, surveys have screened out occupationally and nonoccupationally noise-exposed subjects and can thus claim to represent presbycusis plus some nosoacusis. Robinson and Sutton (1979) combined the data from several such studies and found that they could fit the data quite well

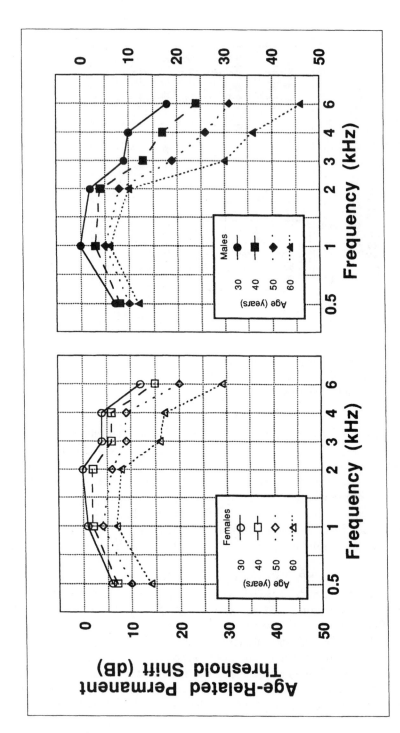

Figure 6–2. Median audiograms from 1960–1962 USPHS survey are shown for men and women of different age groups.

TABLE 6–2
Age-Related Permanent Threshold Shift

Frequency (Hz)	Hearing Threshold Level (dB)											
	Age (years)											
	30			40			50			60		
	Percentiles											
	10	50	90	10	50	90	10	50	90	10	50	90
Males												
500	−1	7	15	0	8	19	1	10	21	2	12	26
1,000	−5	0	10	−4	3	15	−3	5	16	−2	6	21
2,000	−4	2	13	−3	4	19	−2	8	28	0	10	43
3,000	−1	9	30	2	13	41	5	19	51	9	30	62
4,000	−1	10	38	4	17	50	8	26	54	12	36	68
6,000	8	18	48	11	24	62	17	31	62	22	46	80
Females												
500	−1	6	15	0	7	19	1	10	23	4	14	29
1,000	−6	1	9	−5	2	13	−4	4	16	−2	7	21
2,000	−6	0	10	−4	2	13	−2	6	23	0	8	29
3,000	−4	4	13	−2	6	18	0	9	26	6	16	37
4,000	−5	4	16	−4	6	18	−1	9	26	4	17	43
6,000	3	12	25	5	15	31	8	20	45	15	29	57

Sources: USPHS, 1960–1962 and Clark and Bohl, 1992.

by a series of quadratic equations, that is, ARPTS increased in proportion to the *square* of increasing age (over age 18). Figure 6–3 shows the median ARPTS for the Robinson and Sutton formulae, in a form comparable to Figure 6–2. Median, tenth, and ninetieth percentile ARPTS values are also shown in Table 6–3, rounded to the nearest decibel. Robinson and Sutton's data show, as expected, less ARPTS throughout than the USPHS data. Data from the Baltimore Longitudinal Study of Aging (Pearson et al., 1995; Morrell and Gordon-Salant, 1996) generally agree quite well with Robinson and Sutton's cross-sectional data. The Baltimore subjects were very highly screened (audiograms with notches or asymmetry were removed) and were of generally high educational level and socioeconomic status (SES).

Since the most widely used formula for estimating HH uses PTA-5123, we can conveniently use this average to compare the Robinson and Sutton and USPHS data; this is shown in Figure 6–4. Note that male and female curves from both data sets show acceleration over time. The Robinson and Sutton curve for men is about 3 dB better than the USPHS curve at age 20; this difference stays about the same through age 60, suggesting that most of the socioacusis and nosoacusis in unscreened American population samples is

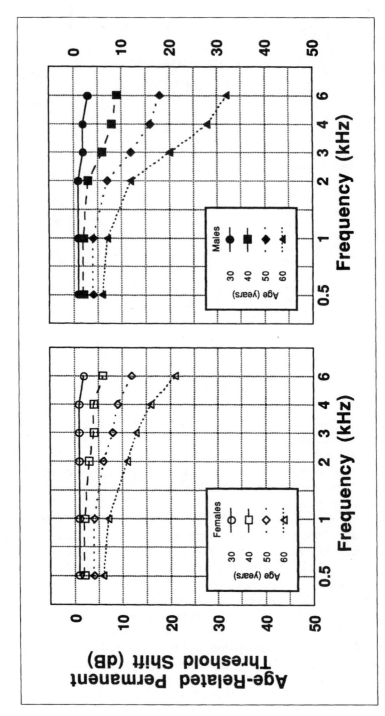

Figure 6–3. Median audiograms for "highly screened" subjects (Robinson and Sutton, 1979); men and women of different age groups.

TABLE 6–3
Age-Related Permanent Threshold Shift

Frequency (Hz)	Hearing Threshold Level (dB)											
	Age (years)											
	30			40			50			60		
	Percentiles											
	10	50	90	10	50	90	10	50	90	10	50	90
Males												
500	−6	1	9	−5	2	11	−4	4	14	−3	6	18
1,000	−6	1	9	−5	2	11	−4	4	14	−2	7	19
2,000	−7	1	11	−6	3	15	−4	7	21	−1	12	29
3,000	−7	2	13	−5	6	19	−2	12	29	3	20	42
4,000	−7	2	14	−4	8	23	0	16	37	7	28	55
6,000	−8	3	16	−5	9	26	0	18	41	8	32	62
Females												
500	−6	1	9	−5	2	11	−4	4	14	−3	6	18
1,000	−6	1	9	−5	2	11	−4	4	14	−2	7	19
2,000	−6	1	10	−5	3	13	−3	6	18	−1	11	25
3,000	−7	1	11	−5	4	15	−3	8	21	0	13	30
4,000	−7	1	12	−6	4	17	−3	9	25	1	16	35
6,000	−8	2	14	−6	6	21	−2	12	31	2	21	45

Source: Robinson and Sutton, 1979.

present by early adulthood. As we will see in Chapter 8, the most important source of nonoccupational NIHL is recreational shooting; most participants begin in adolescence.

Lutman and Davis (1994) and Sixt and Rosenthall (1997) have shown low SES to be an independent risk factor for hearing loss, even after controlling for noise exposure. Davis (1989) found that effects of low SES were greater than the effects of 50-year career exposure at 81–90 dBA. These effects could be genetic, environmental, or both.

Rosen et al. (1962) reported a hearing survey of Mabaan tribesmen from Africa, purporting to show much less ARPTS than had ever been found in studies of aging people in Western civilization; in addition, there were no significant male-female differences. Kryter (1983) considered that these data best represented "true presbycusis," since these people had lived in a very quiet environment (free of socioacusis); since their hearing was better than even women's in well screened Western studies, he believed that they were also much less prone to nosoacusis—perhaps because of better diet, lower stress, and thus less cardiovascular disease. However, the validity of the Mabaan data has been questioned in two important ways. First, when compared to well-

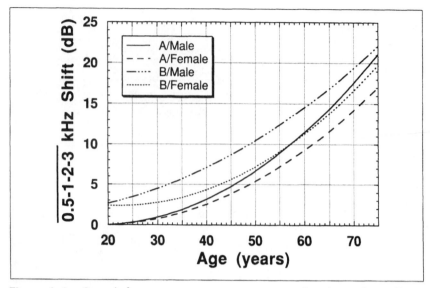

Figure 6–4. Speech frequency pure-tone averages as functions of age. Databases A and B (ISO-1999) are identical to Robinson and Sutton (1979) and USPHS (1960–1962), respectively.

screened data from Western countries, the Mabaans hear better only for males over 60, in the high frequencies (Bergman, 1966). Second, the subjects' ages were undocumented—many old Mabaan tribesmen simply did not know their true ages. Even if the data were valid, we could not confidently conclude that the differences seen were entirely caused by the absence of socioacusis and nosoacusis since the genetic properties of this population were very different from those of any Western population that has been studied. If these people did indeed have remarkably good hearing in old age, it could very well have been because of a fortunate genetic heritage, rather than freedom from noise and "diseases of civilization." Goycoolea et al. (1986) have presented data showing that Easter Islanders, a genetically homogeneous Polynesian group, have more hearing loss in middle and old age if they have spent substantial periods of their lives off the island in "civilization" (usually in Chile, which owns Easter Island). However, the periods spent off the island typically involved military service and factory jobs, neither of which existed on the island, so the hearing differences seen could have been entirely attributable to occupational NIHL. There are still insufficient data to conclude that "Western Civilization" is bad for your hearing, with the obvious exception of exposure to the hazardous noise levels that will be described in Chapters 7 and 8. Chapter 10 discusses possible effects of cardiovascular and other systemic diseases on hearing.

ISO-1999 AND ANSI S3.44

In 1990, the International Organization for Standardization (ISO) published a method for estimating hearing levels in noise-exposed and non-noise-exposed populations. ISO-1999 recommends the use of Robinson and Sutton's (1979) formulae for predicting ARPTS in populations screened for noise exposure and ear disease—this is "database A" in ISO-1999 (these data should probably not be used for populations of low SES). For unscreened populations "database B" is recommended; this can be any unscreened data-set believed to be appropriate to the group under study, but ISO-1999 gives the 1960–1962 USPHS data as the sole example of database B.

In 1996, the American National Standards Institute published a standard nearly identical to ISO-1999, but added as "Annex C" (Table 6–4) a new database for populations screened only for occupational noise exposure (ANSI S3.44-1996). The Annex C thresholds were obtained using self-recording (Békésy) audiometry and therefore are probably about 2–3 dB better than would have been expected with manual audiometry (see Chapter 3). In general, the Annex C data (binaural averages) are similar to the 1960–1962 USPHS data (better ears), although a marked racial difference is apparent: blacks of either sex hear better than whites of either sex. A recent British report (Smith et al., 1999) suggests that even highly screened young adults have hearing that is closer to the USPHS and Annex C values than to those of Robinson and Sutton (database A).

In Chapter 7, we will see the data-sets recommended by ISO-1999 for noise-induced permanent threshold shift (NIPTS), and in Chapter 13 we will see how the ARPTS and NIPTS data can be used together to arrive at reasonable estimates of the relative contributions of noise and aging in individual cases of hearing loss.

Prevalence of ARHL

Since hearing threshold levels represent a continuum, with no obvious dividing line beyond which abnormality or handicap exists, the prevalence (percent of population affected) of ARHL will depend on the definition of ARHL. The National Health Interview Survey periodically asks whether subjects are "deaf in one or both ears" or have "any other trouble hearing with one or both ears." Since 1979, the percentage of Americans responding positively has varied between 8.0 and 9.4 percent (8.3 percent in the most recent survey), but is much higher (30 percent) in those over 65 (Anonymous, 1999). Since this survey did not include elderly persons in nursing homes and other institutions, the real prevalence rates are probably somewhat

TABLE 6–4
Age-Related Permanent Threshold Shift

	Hearing Threshold Level (dB)											
	Age (years)											
	30			40			50			60		
	Percentiles											
Frequency (Hz)	10	50	90	10	50	90	10	50	90	10	50	90
White Males												
500	3	9	17	4	10	19	5	11	21	6	13	24
1,000	−1	5	13	0	6	17	1	8	20	2	10	24
2,000	−4	3	14	−1	6	20	1	10	29	3	15	41
3,000	−1	6	27	3	12	38	6	20	48	9	31	56
4,000	1	12	37	6	21	50	11	30	58	16	41	63
6,000	4	17	43	10	26	58	15	36	67	20	47	71
Black Males												
500	−1	6	14	−2	5	13	−4	6	16	−6	9	24
1,000	−4	1	7	−4	2	9	−6	3	16	−9	6	28
2,000	−6	0	5	−5	1	8	−6	4	16	−7	7	30
3,000	−5	3	13	−4	5	19	−2	9	28	0	16	41
4,000	−3	3	15	−3	7	22	−2	14	34	−3	25	50
6,000	−4	5	17	−3	9	25	1	14	36	7	21	51
White Females												
500	2	9	16	3	11	19	5	13	24	7	16	33
1,000	−1	5	11	0	7	16	0	10	23	1	14	32
2,000	−5	2	9	−3	5	14	0	8	25	3	13	39
3,000	−5	3	10	−3	6	16	0	12	27	3	20	42
4,000	−2	5	14	1	10	22	3	17	34	6	26	50
6,000	−1	7	15	2	13	25	7	22	39	13	33	58
Black Females												
500	4	10	18	4	10	18	2	10	20	0	11	26
1,000	−1	4	14	−1	5	17	−1	6	18	−1	7	19
2,000	−5	2	13	−4	3	16	−3	5	18	−3	8	20
3,000	−4	1	12	−3	2	15	−2	6	19	−2	11	24
4,000	−3	4	14	−1	6	17	−1	8	20	−1	11	24
6,000	−1	6	19	2	9	24	3	15	29	2	21	35

Source: Annex C, ANSI S3.44.

TABLE 6–5
Prevalence of Problems and Threshold Elevations

Age	In Noise	In Quiet	PTA-5124 ≥ 25 (worse ear)
17–30	14%	8%	6%
51–60	31%	22%	34%
71–80	44%	38%	72%

higher. A large British national study (Davis, 1989) showed how reported difficulties and audiometric thresholds (pure-tone average, 0.5, 1, 2, and 4 kHz) increased with age (Table 6–5).

Tinnitus can accompany any type of hearing loss and is of no diagnostic value in determining the cause of hearing loss. Axelsson and Ringdahl (1987) have shown that, as the prevalence of hearing impairment increases with age, so does tinnitus. In their survey of over 2,000 Swedish adults, 20 percent of those over 50 years of age complained of tinnitus "often" or "always." Three percent of Danish men between ages 53 and 75 reported tinnitus that interfered with sleep, reading, or concentration (Parving et al., 1993).

REFERENCES

American Academy of Otolaryngology–Committee on Hearing and Equilibrium and the American Council of Otolaryngology–Committee on the Medical Aspects of Noise. 1979. Guide for the evaluation of hearing handicap. *JAMA* 241(19):2055–2059.

American National Standards Institute. 1996. *Determination of Occupational Noise Exposure and Estimation of Noise-Induced Hearing Impairment, ANSI S3.44-1996.* New York: Acoustical Society of America.

Anonymous. 1999. Current estimates from the National Health Interview Survey, 1996. *Vital and Health Stat. Series* 10 (200).

Axelsson, A. and A. Ringdahl. 1987. The occurrence and severity of tinnitus: A prevalence study. In *Proceedings of the Third International Tinnitus Seminar,* ed. Harald Feldmann. Karlsruhe, Federal Republic of Germany: Harsch Verlag.

Bergman, Moe. 1966. Hearing in the Mabaans: A critical review of related literature. *Arch. Otolaryngol.* 84(4):411–415.

Bess, Fred H., Michael J. Lichtenstein, Susan A. Logan, and M. Candice Burger. 1989. Comparing criteria of hearing impairment in the elderly: A functional approach. *J. Speech Hear. Res.* 32(4):795–802.

Clark, William W. and Carl D. Bohl. 1992. Corrected values for Annex B of ISO 1999. *J. Acoust. Soc. Am.* 91(5):3064–3065.

Cooper, John C., Jr. and George A. Gates. 1991. Hearing in the elderly—The Framingham Cohort, 1983–1985: Part II. Prevalence of central auditory processing disorders. *Ear & Hearing* 12(5):304–311.

Cruickshanks, K. J., T. L. Wiley, T. S. Tweed, B. E. Klein, R. Klein, J. A. Mares-Perlman, and D. M. Nondahl. 1998. Prevalence of hearing loss in older subjects in Beaver Dam, Wisconsin: The Epidemiology of Hearing Loss Study. *Am. J. Epidemiol.* 148:879–886.

Davis, Adrian C. 1989. The prevalence of hearing impairment and reported hearing disability among adults in Great Britain. *Intl. J. Epidemiol.* 18:911–917.

Dubno, Judy R., Donald D. Dirks, and Donald E. Morgan. 1984. Effects of age and mild hearing loss on speech recognition in noise. *J. Acoust. Soc. Am.* 76(1):87–96.

Eastwood, M. R., S. L. Corbin, M. Reed, H. Nobbs, and H. B. Kedward. 1985. Acquired hearing loss and psychiatric illness: An estimate of prevalence and co-morbidity in a geriatric setting. *Br. J. Psychiatry* 147(11):552–556.

Gaeth, J. H. 1948. *A study of phonemic regression in relation to hearing loss.* Unpublished doctoral diss., Northwestern University, Evanston, IL.

Gates, George A., John C. Cooper Jr., William B. Kannel, and Nancy J. Miller. 1990. Hearing in the elderly—The Framingham Cohort, 1983–1985: Part I. Basic audiometric test results. *Ear & Hearing* 11(4):247–256.

Gates, George A., N. N. Couropmitree and R. H. Myers. 1999. Genetic assocations in age-related hearing thresholds. *Arch. Otolaryngol. Head Neck Surg.* 125:654–659.

Glorig, Aram and James Nixon. 1962. Hearing loss as a function of age. *Laryngoscope* 72(11):1596–1610.

Glorig, Aram and J. Roberts. 1965. *Hearing Levels of Adults by Age and Sex: United States, 1960–1962 (DHEWPUB-1000-SER-11-11).* Washington, DC: U.S. Department of Health, Education and Welfare–National Center for Health Services Research and Development.

Goycoolea, Marcos V., Hortensia G. Goycoolea, Corina R. Farfan, Leonardo G. Rodriguez, Gumaro C. Martinez, and Ricardo Vidal. 1986. Effect of life in industrialized societies on hearing in natives of Easter Island. *Laryngoscope* 96(12):1391–1396.

Gratton, Michael D. and Bradley A. Schulte. 1995. Alterations in microvasculature are associated with atrophy of the stria vascularis in quiet-aged gerbils. *Hearing Res.* 82:44–52.

Hansen, C. C. and Edith Reske-Nielsen. 1965. Pathological studies in presbycusis. *Arch. Otolaryngol.* 82(2):115–132.

Hinchcliffe, Ronald. 1958. The pattern of the threshold of perception for hearing and other special senses as a function of age. *Gerontologia* 2(6):311–320.

Humes, Larry E. and Laurel Christopherson. 1991. Speech identification difficulties of hearing-impaired elderly persons: The contributions of auditory processing deficits. *J. Speech Hear. Res.* 34(3):686–693.

Humes, Larry E. and Lisa Roberts. 1990. Speech-recognition difficulties of the hearing-impaired elderly: The contributions of audibility. *J. Speech Hear. Res.* 33(4):726–735.

Humes, Larry E., B. U. Watson, L. A. Christensen, C. G. Cokely, D. C. Halling, and L. Lee. 1994. Factors associated with individual differences in clinical measures of speech recognition among the elderly. *J. Speech Hear. Res.* 37:465–474.

International Organization for Standardization. 1990. *Acoustics: Determination of Occupational Noise Exposure and Estimation of Noise-Induced Hearing Impairment, ISO-1999.* Geneva: International Organization for Standardization.

Johnson, Daniel L. 1978. *Derivation of Presbycusis and Noise Induced Permanent Threshold Shift (NIPTS) to be Used for the Basis of a Standard on the Effects of Noise on Hearing (AMRL-TR-78-128).* Wright-Patterson Air Force Base, Dayton, OH: Aerospace Medical Research Laboratory.

Johnsson, Lars-Goran and Joseph E. Hawkins, Jr. 1972a. Sensory and neural degeneration with aging, as seen in microdissections of the human inner ear. *Ann. Otol. Rhinol. Laryngol.* 81(2):179–193.

———. 1972b. Vascular changes in the human inner ear associated with aging. *Ann. Otol. Rhinol. Laryngol.* 81(3):364–376.

Karlsson, K. K., J. R. Harris, and M. Svartengren. 1997. Description and primary results from an audiometric study of male twins. *Ear & Hearing* 18: 114–120.

Katsarkas, A. and H. Ayukawa. 1986. Hearing loss due to aging (presbycusis). *J. Otolaryngol.* 15(4):239–244.

Kelly-Ballweber, Denise and Robert A. Dobie. 1984. Binaural interaction measured behaviorally and electrophysiologically in young and old adults. *Audiology* 23(2):181–194.

Kirikae, Ichiro, Tsunemasa Sato, and Tetsuya Shitara. 1964. A study of hearing in advanced age. *Laryngoscope* 74(2):205–220.

Konigsmark, Bruce W. and Edmond A. Murphy. 1972. Volume of the ventral cochlear nucleus in man: Its relationship to neural population and age. *J. Neuropathol. Exp. Neurol.* 31(2):304–316.

Kryter, Karl D. 1983. Presbycusis, sociocusis and nosocusis. *J. Acoust. Soc. Am.* 73(6):1897–1917.

Lutman, M. E. and A. C. Davis. 1994. The distribution of hearing threshold levels in the general population aged 18–30 years. *Audiology* 33:327–350.

Marshall, Lynne, Serge Martinez, and Mary E. Schlaman. 1983. Reassessment of high-frequency air-bone gaps in older adults. *Arch. Otolaryngol.* 109(9):601–606.

Matthews, Lois J., Fu-Shing Lee, John H. Mills, and Donald J. Schum. 1990. Audiometric and subjective assessment of hearing handicap. *Arch. Otolaryngol. Head Neck Surg.* 116(11):1325–1330.

McFadden, S. L., D. Ding, A. G. Reaume, D. G. Flood, and R. J. Salvi. 1999. Age-related cochlear hair cell loss is enhanced in mice lacking copper/zinc superoxide dismutase. *Neurobiol. Aging* 20:1–8.

Morrell, C. H. and S. Gordon-Salant. 1996. Age- and gender-specific reference ranges for hearing level and longitudinal changes in hearing level. *J. Acoust. Soc. Am.* 100:1949–1967.

Parving, A., H. O. Hein, P. Suadicani, B. Ostri, and F. Gyntelberg. 1993. Epidemiology of hearing disorders. *Scand. Audiol.* 22:101–107.

Pearson, J. D., C. H. Morrell, S. Gordon-Salant, L. J. Brant, E. J. Metter, L. L. Klein, and J. L. Fozard. 1995. Gender differences in a longitudinal study of age-associated hearing loss. *J. Acoust. Soc. Am.* 97:1196–1205.

Randolph, Loren J. and Ronald L. Schow. 1983. Threshold inaccuracies in an elderly clinical population: Ear canal collapse as a possible cause. *J. Speech Hear. Res.* 26(1):54–58.

Robinson, D. W. and G. J. Sutton. 1979. Age effect in hearing: A comparative analysis of published threshold data. *Audiology* 18(4):320–334.

Rosen, Samuel, Moe Bergman, Dietrich Plester, Aly El-Mofty, and Mohamed Hamad Satti. 1962. Presbycusis: Study of a relatively noise-free population in the Sudan. *Ann. Otol. Rhinol. Laryngol.* 71(3):727–743.

Salomon, Gerald, Vibeke Vesterager, and Marianne Jagd. 1988. Age-related hearing difficulties: I. Hearing impairment, disability, and handicap—a controlled study. *Audiology* 27(3):164–178.

Schmiedt, R. A., J. H. Mills, and J. C. Adams. 1987. Endocochlear potential decrease with age in gerbils. *Soc. Neurosci. (Abstr.)* 13:1260.

Schuknecht, Harold F. 1964. Further observations on the pathology of presbycusis. *Arch. Otolaryngol.* 80(4):369–382.

Schuknecht, Harold F. and M. R. Gacek. 1993. Cochlear pathology in presbycusis. *Ann. Otol. Rhinol. Laryngol.* 102:1–6.

Schum, Donald J., Lois J. Matthews, and Fu-Shing Lee. 1991. Actual and predicted word-recognition performance of elderly hearing-impaired listeners. *J. Speech Hear. Res.* 34(3):636–642.

Sixt, E. and U. Rosenthall. 1997. Presbyacusis related to socioeconomic factors and state of health *Scand. Audiol.* 126:133–140.

Smith, P., A. Davis, M. Ferguson, and M. Lutman. 1999. Hearing in young adults. *Noise and Health* 4:1–10.

Soucek, Sava, L. Michaels, and A. Frohlich. 1986. Evidence for hair cell degeneration as the primary lesion in hearing loss of the elderly. *J. Otolaryngol.* 15(3):175–183.

Souza, P. E. and C. W. Turner. 1994. Masking of speech in young and elderly listeners with hearing loss. *J. Speech Hear. Res.* 37:655–661.

Studebaker, G. A., R. L. Sherbecoe, and D. M. McDaniel. 1997. Age-related changes in monosyllabic word recognition performance when audibility is held constant. *J. Am. Acad. Audiol.* 8(3):150–162.

Suga, Fumiro and John R. Lindsay. 1976. Histopathological observations of presbycusis. *Ann. Otol. Rhinol. Laryngol.* 85(2):169–184.

Thomas, Paula D., William C. Hunt, Philip A. Garry, Richard B. Hood, Jean M. Goodwin, and James S. Goodwin. 1983. Hearing acuity in a healthy elderly population: Effects on emotional, cognitive, and social status. *J. Gerontol.* 38(3):321–325.

Uhlmann, Richard F., Eric B. Larson, Thomas S. Rees, Thomas D. Koepsell, and Larry G. Duckert. 1989. Relationship of hearing impairment to dementia and cognitive dysfunction in older adults. *JAMA* 261(13):1916–1919.

Ventry, Ira M. and Barbara E. Weinstein. 1983. Identification of elderly people with hearing problems. *ASHA* 25(7):37–42.

Ward, W. Dixon. 1977. Effects of noise exposure on auditory sensitivity. In *Handbook of Physiology, Section 9: Reactions to Environmental Agents,* ed. Douglas Harry Kedgwin Lee, pp. 1–15. Bethesda, MD: American Physiological Society.

Willott, J. F. and L. C. Erway. 1998. Genetics of age-related hearing loss in mice. IV. Cochlear pathology and hearing loss in 25 B×D recombinant inbred mouse strains. *J. Speech Hear. Res.* 119:27–36.

Chapter 7

Noise-Induced Hearing Loss and Acoustic Trauma

Excessive noise exposure causes hearing loss; this is now common knowledge, and was recognized in otologic treatises in the eighteenth century, according to Chadwick (1971). However, it was not until the development of the electric audiometer that Bunch (1937) was able to describe the typical high-frequency loss. This chapter will discuss noise-induced hearing loss (NIHL) from the pathological, clinical, and epidemiologic points of view. NIHL is the product of *repeated* exposures to sounds that are too intense and too long in duration. There are initial temporary hearing changes that are reversible, but eventually permanent loss occurs. We will also discuss *acoustic trauma*—single exposure to intense noise leading to permanent hearing loss. We will focus especially on occupational NIHL—hearing loss from nonoccupational exposures is the subject of Chapter 8.

TYPES OF NOISE

Noise is often defined as "unwanted sound," but the ability of a sound to damage the inner ear is unrelated to its desirability or unpleasantness. A Bach fugue, played loud enough and long enough, can be as hazardous to the ear as a chainsaw. Noises differ in several ways that are important in assessing hazard. High-frequency sounds (up to about 5,000 Hz) are more hazardous than low-frequency sounds; the use of A-weighted sound levels (see Chapter 2) cancels these effects, so that two sounds with the same dBA level have approximately the same hazard, even though one may contain predominantly high-frequency energy and the other low-frequency energy. Very narrow-band sounds such as pure tones are more hazardous than broad-spectrum sounds of the same A-weighted sound level. The International Organization for Standardization (ISO-1999, 1990) and the American National Standards Institute (ANSI S3.44, 1996) state that "some users may" wish to add 5 dB to sound level measurements for such sounds to obtain estimates of equivalent hazard.

Noises are classified in the temporal dimension as *continuous, fluctuating, intermittent, impact*, and *impulse*. *Intermittent* noises have periods of relative quiet interspersed with periods of continuous noise. *Impact* noise is created by collision of objects (e.g., hammer and anvil), with a resultant high-intensity peak (which decays as the struck object "rings"). *Impulse* noise is created by a sudden release of energy into the air, usually by an explosion (e,g., gunfire). Impact noise is common in industry and usually produces less than 140 dB peak pressure (Hamernik and Hsueh, 1991), while impulses from weapons typically exceed 140 dB peak pressure at the ear of the user.

THE NOISE-DAMAGED EAR

The otologist can directly examine only the outer ear and, to a limited extent, the middle ear. Inner ear damage can be inferred from audiometric data (see Chapter 3), but is invisible to the otologist. X-rays and other imaging methods have (so far) been unable to demonstrate noise-induced inner ear damage.

Middle ear injury from noise is rare and can occur only with extremely high levels. Human cadaver tympanic membranes (TMs) may perforate when subjected to over 10 lb/in.^{2} peak overpressure (Garth, 1994), but some patients have apparently sustained perforations from explosions with as little as 2–3 lb/in.^{2} peak overpressure, equivalent to about 180 dB SPL (Hirsch, 1968). Ossicular injury has not been reported with noise or blast injury at less than 190 dB SPL in guinea pigs and rabbits (Akiyoshi et al., 1966). Ossicular injury was never seen in 120 patients who suffered TM perforations from nonexplosive blast injury (e.g., a slap to the ear that seals the ear canal), although 25 percent had at least temporary sensorineural hearing loss, indicating inner ear injury (Berger et al., 1997). In experimental animals, when impulse levels are sufficient to rupture the TM, *less* cochlear damage is seen; that is, there is a protective effect (Eames et al. 1975). However, clinical studies of bomb blast victims suggest that TM perforation does not prevent sensorineural hearing loss (Kerr and Byrne, 1975; Pahor, 1981). TM perforations with conductive and sensorineural hearing loss are part of the clinical picture of *acoustic trauma* but not of *NIHL* per se.

Inner ear injury from noise has been well characterized by postmortem studies in both humans and experimental animals. The most vulnerable structures in the cochlea are the outer hair cells. Initially, their stereocilia lose their stiffness and hence their ability to vibrate in response to sound; this causes a reversible hearing loss (temporary threshold shift, or TTS). After repeated hazardous exposures, the stereocilia become permanently damaged, the hair cell dies, and permanent threshold shift (PTS) occurs (Liberman and Mulroy, 1982). The more intense and prolonged the exposures, the greater the degree of outer hair cell loss. Eventually, inner hair cells and auditory nerve fibers will be lost as well. This pattern of progressive hair cell loss is commonly believed to be caused by metabolic phenomena (Saunders, Dear, and Schneider, 1985), rather than direct mechanical trauma to the hair cells, at least for typical NIHL.

As described in Chapter 3, the cochlea is tonotopically organized, with the lowest frequencies preferentially transduced at the apex and the highest frequencies at the base. For any given frequency, there is a point along the cochlear spiral where response is maximal, and conversely, every cochlear place has a corresponding best frequency to which it responds maximally. One might expect an intense pure tone to damage the cochlear region that best transduces that tone and to cause a hearing loss for the frequency of the stimulating tone. This is almost true, but the maximum loss from pure-tone exposure is usually at about a half-octave *above* the offending frequency. For example, a 1 kHz (kilohertz) tone would cause a hearing loss greatest at about 1.5 kHz. Low-frequency sounds can also damage the high-frequency part of the cochlea. Interestingly, when the low-frequency sounds are made intermittent, but with the same total sound energy, there is considerably less hair cell damage than would be expected in the cochlear apex (low-frequency region); intermittency is much less protective for the basal region (Bohne, Zahn, and Bozzay, 1985). Broad-spectrum sounds can cause widespread damage, but the basal part of the cochlea shows the greatest changes, especially the 3 to 6 kHz region. Saunders, Dear, and Schneider (1985) and Saunders, Cohen, and Szymko (1991) have summarized the research data on the pathological anatomy of the cochlea in NIHL.

Noise-Induced Vestibular Injury

Ylikoski (1987) has shown that *acoustic trauma* from impulses can damage both the auditory and vestibular parts of the inner ear of experimental animals, but it is doubtful that exposures causing NIHL (as opposed to acoustic trauma) can cause vestibular system injury. Endolymphatic hydrops in the cochlea can be seen after almost any type of insult (drug, infection, head trauma, acoustic trauma) in guinea pigs (Kimura, 1982); humans with Ménière's disease (see Chapter 10) are typically found at postmortem examination to have endolymphatic hydrops, but this connection is nonspecific (Rauch, Merchant, and Thedinger, 1989). Several papers have reported an association between NIHL and Ménière's disease in humans, but even the better-documented articles (Paparella and Mancini, 1983; Ylikoski, 1988) are weak in clinical criteria for Ménière's disease, in documentation of noise exposure, or both; also, neither NIHL nor Ménière's disease is rare, and many cases of association would occur by chance. It seems likely that acoustic trauma, not NIHL, can cause vestibular injury in animals, but human cases seem to be rare (Kerr and Byrne, 1975; Pahor, 1981). Probably, most noise-exposed patients with vertigo or disequilibrium have other, coincidental causes for their vestibular dysfunction, if any. A British Inter-Society working group (Hinchcliffe et al., 1992) reached a similar conclusion.

TTS AND PTS

Most hazardous noise exposures initially produce TTS, which recovers between exposures. Eventually, PTS occurs. TTS is often noticeable to workers as a dull or muffled quality to sounds at the end of a shift. The worker who has to turn the car radio up after work, then finds it too loud in the morning, may be experiencing TTS. The Occupational Safety and Health Administration (OSHA) requires that baseline audiometry for hearing conservation programs be performed after at least 14 hours freedom from significant noise exposure, to avoid superimposing TTS on a worker's "true" hearing levels.

Since there is great variability in degree of hearing loss among workers with similar noise exposures, there has been considerable interest in measuring *susceptibility* to NIHL. It seemed logical that TTS would provide such a measure: A worker who experienced an unusually large TTS after a day's work should be more likely to experience a large PTS after 10 years, compared to a worker who demonstrated a small TTS. Unfortunately, this logical theory has never been proven to accurately predict susceptibility to NIHL. However, a daily exposure that does not cause TTS will not cause PTS over a working lifetime (Ward, Cushing, and Burns, 1976).

PTS and TTS both vary with the frequency, intensity, and temporal properties of the noise exposure, just as the hair cell loss previously discussed. For broad-spectrum noises, the earliest (and largest) threshold shifts are in the 3 to 6 kHz region, with better thresholds at 8 kHz (this is an audiometric "notch," as seen in Figure 4–7). Several reasons for this 3 to 6 kHz predilection have been advanced. For example, the blood supply may be more tenuous in this part of the cochlea, or the shearing forces somewhat greater because of the cochlear geometry. The simplest and probably strongest reasons are two. First, the ear canal and middle ear resonances combine to enhance sounds in the 1 to 4 kHz region (Rosowski, 1991). in fact, people with smaller ear canals and thus higher resonant frequencies also have notches at higher frequencies (Pierson et al., 1994). Second, the acoustic reflex attenuates the transmission of loud sounds below about 2 kHz (Borg, 1968). Against these simple arguments is the fact that closed head injury and other causes (see Chapter 10) can give rise to an identical notch at 3, 4, or 6 kHz—neither acoustic reflex nor outer/middle ear resonance are relevant in these cases, so there must be some special vulnerability to the 4 kHz region of the cochlea. Indeed, many patients with high-frequency notches deny any recollection of significant noise expo-sure, head injury, or other otologic disorder (Mostafapour et al., 1998); in fact, some notches are probably artefactual (Williams, 1996).

The acoustic reflex clearly plays a partially protective role in NIHL. Zakris-son (1975), Zakrisson et al. (1980), and Borg, Nilsson, and Engstrom (1983) have shown in both human and experimental animal studies that unilateral stapedial muscle paralysis results in greater noise-induced TTS and PTS, espe-cially for lower frequencies (2 kHz and below). Some of the variability seen in susceptibility to NIHL may be caused by variability in reflex strength.

Hamernik et al. (1989) correlated PTS with hair cell loss in over 400 noise-exposed chinchillas. Outer hair cell loss began at 0 to 10 dB PTS and was nearly total at about 45 dB PTS. Inner hair cell loss began at about 25 dB PTS and was never total: About 10 percent of inner hair cells remained when PTS reached its maximum of about 65 dB. It must be emphasized that, as in all such studies, there was considerable variability; one cannot precisely predict hair cell loss from PTS, or vice versa.

Both TTS and PTS are commonly accompanied by tinnitus. Temporary tinnitus after noise exposure is a useful warning sign that TTS has occurred and that PTS will occur if exposure continues without hearing protection.

Otoacoustic emissions (OAEs), discussed in Chapters 3 and 4, are sensi-tive, objective indicators of inner ear health, and some have speculated that OAEs might be useful for detecting early NIHL. However, experience to date (e.g., Kvaerner et al., 1995) has failed to demonstrate that OAEs were better suited for this role than pure-tone audiometry.

ACOUSTIC TRAUMA

Early models of cordless telephones had no separate ringer—the phone rang through the earpiece, and if the user forgot to switch from "ring" mode to "talk" mode before answering the phone, a 140 dB SPL ring at 750 Hz (hertz) would be delivered directly to the ear. Dozens of unfortunate consumers suffered per-manent hearing loss (usually the largest threshold shifts were at 1 kHz) from a single ring of this type (Singleton et al., 1984, and personal experience). This is acoustic trauma: permanent loss from a single event or exposure without inter-vening TTS. The cordless telephone example is unusual—most cases of acoustic trauma are caused by impulses from explosions (bombs, industrial blasting, firearms and other weapons). Whereas NIHL progresses through stages of loss of stereociliary stiffness (and TTS) to hair cell loss (and PTS), acoustic trauma probably involves direct mechanical injury to the organ of Corti. As previously mentioned, this can also involve tympanic membrane perforations.

Pure-tone audiograms after acoustic trauma may show PTS similar to what is seen in NIHL, that is, notches at 3 to 6 kHz. However, a variety of other audiogram shapes can be seen (Teter, Newell, and Aspinall, 1970); of these, down-sloping and flat audiograms are most common (Salmivalli, 1967; Pahor, 1981). Hearing loss from acoustic trauma may improve over four to six months (Pahor, 1981; Segal et al., 1988).

It is difficult to specify the minimum levels at which acoustic trauma can occur. The cordless phone cases suggest that pure tones above 135 dB SPL can cause almost instantaneous damage, sometimes severe, at least in some susceptible individuals. (Remember that both ISO and ANSI suggest possibly adding 5 dB to pure-tone levels to estimate equivalent-risk broad spectrum levels.) The level at which a few seconds of broad-band noise can cause acoustic trauma in the most susceptible individuals probably lies somewhere between 130 and 140 dBA. Single exposures of minutes or hours leading to acoustic trauma are even more difficult to estimate, although studies of human TTS give some guidance. Miller (1971) summarized the TTS data of Ward, Glorig, and Sklar (1959) and other investigators; based on the assumption that TTS_2 (two minutes after cessation of exposure) in excess of 40 dB constituted a "region of possible acoustic trauma," and relying on extrapolation from animal TTS data, he proposed the following approximate risk levels for 4 kHz, the most susceptible frequency for humans:

Level (dB SPL)	Exposure Time (minutes)
130	5
120	8
110	20
100	80

The A-weighted levels for these 2400 to 4800 Hz exposures were probably 1 to 2 dB higher than the SPLs shown above. Ahaus and Ward (1975) showed that average TTS_2 after 15 minutes *continuous exposure* to 700 to 2,800 Hz noise at 114 dB SPL was only 25 dB at 2 to 4 kHz, and that interrupted exposures of the same total duration produced much less TTS_2, especially if the noise bursts were long enough (about one second) to activate the acoustic reflex. Thus, the values tabulated above are probably overly protective, at least for intermittent exposure and ears of *average* susceptibility. They are also quite speculative, being based on TTS (not PTS) data, some from animals.

Ward (1991a) has reviewed the few reported cases of acoustic trauma following tonal or noise exposure (including the cordless phone cases) and suggests that the *most susceptible* ears may experience PTS for exposures exceeding:

Level (dB SPL)	Exposure Time (minutes)
140	$\frac{1}{30}$
130	1
120	15
110	220

More recently, Hunter et al. (1999) described two cases of acoustic trauma from audiometric reflex decay testing; both patients were exposed at about 130 dB SPL for 10 seconds (at 1 and 2 kHz, respectively). Tens, perhaps hundreds, of thousands of patients have had reflex decay testing, so the risk of acoustic trauma for this intensity/duration combination must be quite small.

Based on extrapolation from cat data, Price (1983) suggests that the "critical" level for acoustic trauma from rifle fire (50–100 rounds) for median human ears is in the 155 to 160 dB peak level range, but that some ears may be susceptible at levels above 140 dB peak. These suggestions would be overprotective for impulses with less hazardous spectra, and for smaller numbers of impulses. Single impulses above 160 dB peak level, from automobile airbag deployment, have caused dozens of cases of acoustic trauma (Yaremchuk and Dobie, 1999).

HEARING LOSS FROM IMPULSE AND IMPACT NOISE EXPOSURE

As mentioned above, impulse noise and continuous noise can both cause acoustic trauma. Both can also cause NIHL, hearing loss that accrues gradually over months and years. Estimating risk for impulse exposure has proved more difficult than for continuous noise for at *least* four reasons. First, it is more difficult to measure impulses accurately. Second, the description of a given exposure is multidimensional, requiring specification of peak sound pressure level, two kinds of duration (A-duration is the duration of the initial or principal pressure pulse; B-duration is the 20-dB decay time), number of impulses, and temporal spacing of impulses (this parameter is by itself multidimensional unless the impulses are evenly spaced in time). Third, cochlear damage from impulses may be inherently less predictable than from continuous noise, because of qualitatively different damage mechanisms and greater individual variation in susceptibility. Finally, most NIHL from impulses is recreational rather than occupational, so large field studies of persons with known exposure are not available.

The Committee on Hearing, Bioacoustics, and Biomechanics (CHABA) recommended damage-risk criteria for impulses in 1968 (Ward, 1968a). The CHABA criteria assume that risk increases with increasing peak level and with increasing B-duration, which seems logical since both level and duration are related to total sound energy. However, Price (1983) has shown that *pulse* duration (A-duration) is *inversely* related to risk in the 0.07 to 4.0 msec range; the longer pulses have more energy but are concentrated in the low-frequency part of the spectrum where hazard is low because the outer and middle ear filter out most of the energy. Price (1974) has also pointed out that intense low-frequency sounds (including impulses) probably drive the stapes to its point of maximum displacement, further limiting the amount of energy that enters the cochlea by a process called peak-clipping. The most hazardous impulses are probably those with A-durations between 0.1 and 1 msec, based on TTS studies (Loeb and Fletcher, 1968), chinchilla behavioral studies (Hamernik, Ahroon, Hsueh, 1991), and Price's previously cited work in cats.

The 1968 CHABA criteria also assume that a tenfold change in the number of impulses per day is equivalent (in risk) to a 5 dB change in peak intensity. Further, temporal spacing is not considered at all, although there is ample evidence that this is important (Henderson and Hamernik, 1986; Danielson et al., 1991). In general, inter-pulse intervals of 1 to 10 sec are most hazardous: Shorter intervals permit the acoustic reflex from one impulse to reduce the effective intensity of the next impulse, while longer intervals probably permit cochlear recovery processes to mitigate damaging effects.

The 1968 CHABA criteria have not been adopted by any governmental body, probably because of the uncertainties described above (and acknowledged in the 1968 report). The most important problem with these criteria is their failure to incorporate impulse spectrum, either directly or indirectly (through A-duration); the wording of the criteria, perhaps inadvertently, mandates the use of the longer duration, which is nearly always B-duration. The net result is probably appropriately protective for short impulses such as rifle fire (A-duration = 0.2–0.4 msec) and overprotective for longer impulses such as cannon fire (A-duration = 3–4 msec; B-durations would be about an order of magnitude larger; Ward, personal communication). With this caveat, some typical permissible exposure levels from the 1968 CHABA document are shown in Table 7–1. Included are the number/level trade previously mentioned and a 5 dB correction for grazing incidence versus normal incidence (that is, sound from the front versus from the side of the head).

A CHABA working group again chaired by Ward has recently endorsed the 1968 criteria with certain limitations (CHABA, 1992):

TABLE 7–1
Permissible Impulse Exposures in Peak SPL[a] (CHABA)

B-duration (msec)	NORMAL			GRAZING		
	10,000/day	100/day	1/day	10,000/day	100/day	1/day
0.3	(147)	157	167	(152)	162	172
3	(140)	150	160	(145)	155	165
20	(135)	145	155	(140)	150	160
≥ 200	(128)	(138)	148	(133)	143	153

[a]Values in parentheses to be interpreted with caution (see text).
Source: Ward, 1968a.

1. Application only for small arms fire with peak levels > 140 dB SPL;
2. Cautious application of impulse number/level trading above 100 impulses/day;
3. Nonapplication for low-frequency impulses such as sonic booms and heavy weapons (the CHABA criteria would be *over*protective in these instances);
4. Nonapplication for small arms fire impulses under hearing protectors (which usually remove high-frequency energy selectively and are thus more protective for impulses than for steady-state noise exposure).

Table 7–1 recognizes cautions 1 and 2 by placing appropriate entries in parentheses.

OSHA (1971) set a limit of 140 dB peak sound pressure level for occupational exposures to impacts and impulses, regardless of the number or duration. While this is almost certainly overprotective for many exposures to gunfire and other impulses, it could be underprotective for exposures that do rarely occur in industry, for example, impact noise at 140 dB peak level, with frequent peaks added to a background of continuous noise. Particularly for frequencies above 2 kHz, noise with very high impulse content (such as a car body shop where peak levels within two-minute intervals typically exceeded average levels by 27 dB) may be more hazardous than steady-state noise (Theiry and Meyer-Bisch, 1988). As for pure-tone exposures, ISO and ANSI state that some users may wish to add 5 dB in order to estimate hazard in such cases.

CLINICAL AND FIELD STUDIES

NIHL was called "boilermaker's deafness" in the early twentieth century, and the literature is replete with papers reporting NIHL in various occupations. These include

- bell-ringers (Bruusgaard, 1962)
- divers (Molvaer and Lehmann, 1985)
- truck drivers (Dufresne, Alleyne, and Reesal, 1988)

and others too numerous to list. Most of these studies are essentially anecdotal and lack careful exposure histories and control groups, making it difficult to know whether the reported loss is really caused by occupational exposure. Those that include sound level measurements are included in Appendix A, which lists typical levels for various types of equipment and work environments. However, the post–World War II period saw several large and well controlled studies permitting the separation of occupational noise induced PTS from age-related hearing loss (ARHL). Some of the results of these studies are described below; clinical and field studies of nonoccupational NIHL (including the effects of shooting) are described in Chapter 8.

Noise-Induced Permanent Threshold Shift

To determine the effects of occupational noise exposure on pure-tone thresholds over a 40-year career, it is necessary to test 60-year-old (or older) workers. At age 60, we expect elevated thresholds even in the absence of significant occupational or recreational noise exposure (see Chapter 6); these must be taken into account. The usual strategy has been to assemble a control group with no history of occupational noise exposure, but otherwise as similar as possible to the noise-exposed group in every respect (age, gender, nonoccupational exposure, etc.). The *difference* between the thresholds of the two groups represents the effects of the noise exposure in question: This is called noise-induced permanent threshold shift (NIPTS).

A classic study by Taylor et al. (1965) illustrates this method. Figure 7–1 shows median audiograms for a group of retired female jute weavers and for

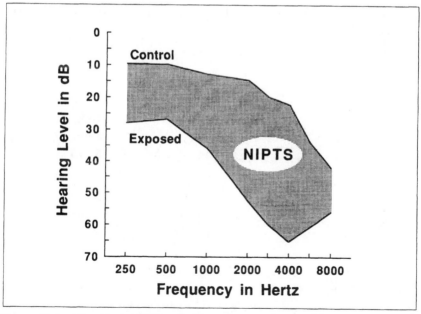

Figure 7–1. The upper ("control") curve shows the median audiogram of a group of non-noise-exposed women age-matched to a group of retired jute weavers (lower curve). The difference between the two curves is the noise-induced permanent threshold shift (NIPTS) for this extreme (> 100 dBA) exposure (Source: Taylor, 1965).

a control group of women the same ages who had never had noisy employ-ment. The weavers had been exposed for many years to levels above 100 dBA and clearly had much higher hearing levels than the control subjects. The dif-ference between the groups—shaded in Figure 7–1—is the NIPTS. Figure 7–2 shows NIPTS for different lengths of employment in the jute mill. In the early years, there is rapid growth of NIPTS in the high frequencies, especially 4 kHz (while this is true on the average, individual cases often show maxi-mum loss at 3 to 6 kHz). After about 10 years, high-frequency loss deceler-ates, but continues at a slow pace, while loss at lower frequencies continues, and even seems to accelerate at 2 kHz in this data set.

Large studies involving thousands of workers with different exposure lev-els and durations have been reviewed by ISO (1990), ANSI (1996), and the U.S. Occupational Safety and Health Administration (OSHA 1981), based in part on the intergroup comparisons and analyses of Johnson (1978). All these groups have found the data generally in good agreement and have published detailed (and very similar) tables of NIPTS that best fit the mass of published data, as a function of exposure level, exposure duration, and audiometric fre-quency. Representative NIPTS values from the ISO-1999 (1990) document are shown in Figures 7–3 to 7–5 (the values in ANSI S3.44 are identical).

Figure 7–3 shows median and extreme (tenth and ninetieth percentile) val-ues for NIPTS for workers exposed for 40 years at 90 and 100 dBA. The

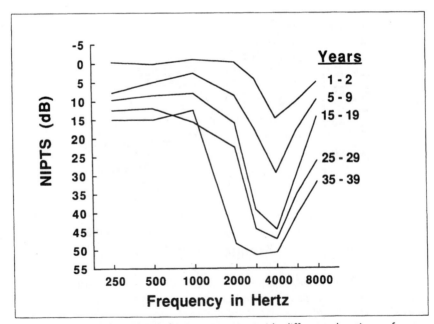

Figure 7–2. Median NIPTS for jute weavers with different durations of expo-sures, as a function of frequency (Source: Taylor, 1965).

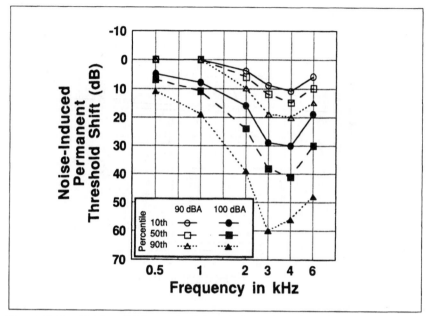

Figure 7–3. Median (50th percentile) and extreme (10th and 90th percentiles) NIPTS after 40 years of workplace exposure at 90 and 100 dBA (Source: ISO-1999, 1990).

effect of increasing exposure level is large and obvious: The least susceptible (tenth percentile) workers exposed at 100 dBA accrue more NIPTS than the most susceptible (ninetieth percentile) workers exposed at 90 dBA. Figure 7–4 shows the progression of NIPTS over time for these same two exposure levels, plotting only the median values. At all frequencies, changes are most rapid in the first 10 years, then decelerate, but this trend is strongest for the highest frequencies. At 4 and 6 kHz, for example, about 75 percent of the eventual 40-year NIPTS is present at 10 years.

Figure 7–5 shows median growth curves for pure tone averages at 0.5, 1, 2, and 3 kHz (PTA-5123) for exposure levels from 85 to 100 dBA. All curves show marked deceleration: 40-year NIPTS for 85 dBA in the speech frequencies is barely measurable even in large population studies. While levels around 80 dBA don't cause detectable NIPTS, they may delay recovery of TTS from exposure to higher-intensity sounds. Levels below 76 to 78 dBA have been considered to be "effective quiet," because they neither cause TTS nor retard recovery of TTS (Melnick, 1991).

It is important to remember that the curves shown in Figures 7–3 and 7–4 are not audiograms—they are plots of NIPTS values derived by subtracting thresholds of control subjects from those of noise-exposed subjects. To predict the median expected hearing threshold level for a population of given

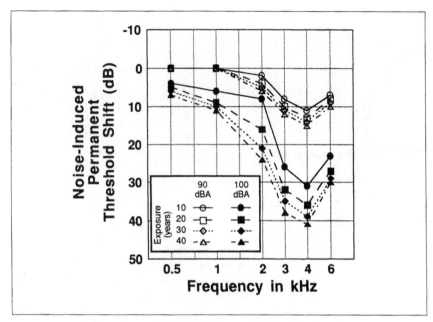

Figure 7–4. Progression of NIPTS for 90 and 100 dBA (median data; source: ISO-1999, 1990).

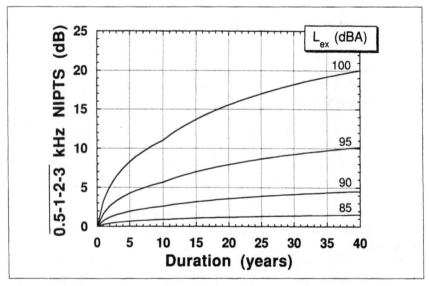

Figure 7–5. Speech-frequency average NIPTS as a function of years of exposure; the parameter is exposure level (Source: ISO-1999, 1990).

age, gender, exposure level, and exposure duration, the median NIPTS values must be added to appropriate age-related permanent threshold shift (ARPTS) values (see Chapter 6).

The NIPTS values used to construct Figures 7–3 to 7–5 are shown (rounded to the nearest decibel) in Table 7–2. "$L_{ex,8hr}$" is the noise level that, if steadily present for eight hours, would deliver the same amount of sound energy as a particular intermittent or fluctuating noise exposure; it is thus similar to the time-weighted average defined in Chapter 2, except that ISO-1999 uses a 3-dB rule, instead of the 5-dB rule required by OSHA. Clearly, the accuracy of these NIPTS values depends on the selection of appropriate control groups. As mentioned in Chapter 6, socioeconomic status (SES) has only

TABLE 7–2
Noise-Induced Permanent Threshold Shift (dB)

		NIPTS (dB)										
		Years of Exposure										
		10			20			30			40		
$L_{ex,8hr}$ dBA	Freq. (Hz)	Percentiles										
		10	50	90	10	50	90	10	50	90	10	50	90
85	500	0	0	0	0	0	0	0	0	0	0	0	0
	1,000	0	0	0	0	0	0	0	0	0	0	0	0
	2,000	0	1	1	1	1	2	1	1	2	1	2	2
	3,000	2	3	5	3	4	6	3	4	7	3	5	7
	4,000	3	5	7	4	6	8	5	6	9	5	7	9
	6,000	1	3	4	2	3	5	2	3	6	2	4	6
90	500	0	0	0	0	0	0	0	0	0	0	0	0
	1,000	0	0	0	0	0	0	0	0	0	0	0	0
	2,000	0	2	6	2	4	8	3	5	9	4	6	10
	3,000	4	8	13	7	10	16	8	11	18	9	12	19
	4,000	7	11	15	9	13	18	10	14	19	11	15	20
	6,000	3	7	12	4	8	14	5	9	15	6	10	15
95	500	0	0	1	0	0	1	0	1	1	0	1	1
	1,000	1	2	4	2	3	5	2	3	5	2	3	6
	2,000	0	5	13	5	9	17	7	12	20	9	14	22
	3,000	8	16	25	13	19	31	16	22	34	18	23	37
	4,000	13	20	27	16	23	32	18	25	34	19	26	36
	6,000	5	14	23	8	16	26	10	18	28	12	19	29
100	500	2	4	8	3	5	9	4	6	11	5	7	11
	1,000	3	6	12	6	9	15	7	10	17	8	11	19
	2,000	0	8	23	8	16	31	13	21	35	16	24	39
	3,000	13	26	41	21	32	51	26	35	56	29	38	60
	4,000	20	31	42	25	36	49	28	39	53	30	41	56
	6,000	9	23	37	14	27	42	17	29	46	19	30	48

Source: ISO-1999, 1990.

recently been well recognized as a factor in age-related hearing loss. Analyses of the British National Study of Hearing have not only shown the importance of SES, but have also suggested that the older studies summarized in ISO-1999 and ANSI S3.44 used inappropriate controls, comparing noise-exposed manual workers (lower SES) to nonnoise-exposed nonmanual workers (higher SES); the effect would be an overestimation of noise effects (Lutman and Davis, 1996). Specifically, their estimates for speech-frequency NIPTS after 50 years of workplace exposure between 90 and 100 dBA is only 6 dB (Lutman and Spencer, 1991); exposures between 80 and 90 dBA had no significant effect on frequencies other than 3 and 4 kHz.

The ISO and ANSI standards don't show thresholds for 8 kHz, because of missing data for some of the underlying studies. Thus, it is sometimes unclear whether a 3 to 6 kHz notch is to be expected for workers of a particular age, gender, and noise exposure. However, some of the studies did report 8 kHz data. Taylor et al. (1965) found that the median audiogram of their retirees (mean age = 69, mean exposure = 46 years above 100 dBA) still showed a notch. Similarly, Passchier-Vermeer's (1974) model showed notches, at both the 50th and 90th percentile, for 60-year-old workers with 40-year exposures at 90 dBA. Notches typically persist into middle age or later, depending on the degree of exposure, despite the progression of age-related changes that tend to efface them.

INTERMITTENCY

The NIPTS curves in Figures 7–3 to 7–5 are based entirely on studies of workers who had essentially continuous workday noise exposure (other than lunch and breaks). Exposures for less than eight hours a day are of course less hazardous, but how *much* less hazardous? ISO-1999 accepts what has been called the "equal-energy principle": exposures that deliver equal acoustic energy to the listener's ear are equally hazardous. Since a 3-dB change in intensity corresponds to a doubling (or halving) of the rate of sound energy flow (Chapter 2), an eight-hour exposure at 90 dBA delivers as much energy as four hours at 93 dBA, or two hours at 96 dBA. The equal-energy principle predicts that each of these exposures carries equal risk.

Relating hazard to total acoustic energy is an attractive simplification, but it has clearly been shown to be incorrect in many experiments. Perhaps most dramatically, the amount of hearing loss from a very intense exposure can be reduced by prior exposure to moderate-level sound; this is called "conditioning" the ear (Canlon et al., 1988; Henderson et al., 1992). In other words, more energy leads to less damage. Conditioning exposures apparently elicit changes in the physiology of the cochlea (Yamasoba et al., 1999a; Kujawa and Liberman, 1999), including the activation of natural antioxidant systems to combat oxidative stress (Jacono et al., 1998). In addition, there is considerable evidence that brief exposures, when made intermittent, are less hazardous than longer exposures of equal energy, probably because some recovery occurs in the "noise-off" periods (reviewed by Clark, 1991; Ward, 1991b). These relationships are complex and it is difficult to generalize how much less hazardous intermittent exposures are. Many real-world industrial exposures to very high levels are intermittent (although the noise-off periods may not be quiet enough to permit inner ear recovery processes to work optimally), and OSHA (1983) has attempted to correct for this by using a 5-dB rule instead of the 3-dB rule recommended by ISO-1999.

OSHA regulations forbid unprotected exposures exceeding 90 dBA "time-weighted average" (TWA) (As will be discussed in Chapter 9, hearing conservation programs are required for exposures exceeding 85 dBA-TWA). Using a 5-dB rule, the permissible exposures at different levels are as shown below (note that each of these exposures equals 90 dBA-TWA):

Level (dBA)	Duration (hours)	TWA (dBA)
90	8	90
95	4	90
100	2	90
105	1	90
110	½	90
115	¼	90

This is a controversial area and probably will remain so. Just as with impulse noise exposures, hazard depends on the exact temporal spacing of noise bursts (Ward, 1991b), and it is unrealistic to expect that a simple 3-, 4-, or 5-dB rule will accurately estimate hazard for all possible exposures.

Based on his chinchilla studies, Ward (1991b) thought the best estimate of hazard for a time-varying noise exposure was somewhere between the "equal-energy" estimate (3-dB rule) and a simple average of the dB levels (the latter method gives results similar to the 5-dB rule in many cases). Unfortunately, there appear to be no published studies of human NIPTS that include sufficient numbers of workers with well-described intermittent exposures to permit a definitive determination of the best rule.

Although the 5-dB rule incorporates the protective effects of intermittency, it is inadequate at the highest levels. For example, we have noted earlier that exposures of a few seconds can cause acoustic trauma at levels above 130 dB SPL, yet the 5-dB rule, in conjunction with a 90 dBA-TWA standard, would permit exposures of up to 112 seconds at 130 dBA. For this reason, OSHA applies the 5-dB rule only up to 115 dBA, where up to 15 minutes is allowed without ear protection. Only impulses and impacts less than one second in duration are permitted at higher levels, up to 140 dB peak level, the absolute OSHA ceiling.

Sataloff et al. (1983) have suggested, based on comparisons between groups of workers exposed to both continuous and intermittent noise, that intermittency is more protective for low frequencies than high frequencies. This agrees with the results in noise-damaged animals cited earlier (Bohne, Zahn, and Bozzay, 1985).

INTERACTIONS

Several other agents (age, drugs, vibration) may accompany hazardous noise in or out of the workplace. As we will see, the resultant hearing loss is often greater than would be expected for either agent alone. However, none of these other agents has been shown to lower the levels and durations of noise at which hazard begins. Stated differently, noise exposures that do not cause TTS or PTS alone do not interact with other agents to cause TTS or PTS.

Age

Aging and noise are the two main causes of hearing loss in the United States of America. (Chapter 10 discusses the many other causes.) They frequently coexist; in fact, most workers claiming compensation for NIHL have signifi-cant ARHL as well. How do different agents—such as aging and noise—act together? How will the effects on the ear and on hearing differ from those seen when these agents act separately? Specifically, we will limit our dis-cussion to pure-tone thresholds and consider the different possibilities for interaction.

The simplest case is the combination of a sensorineural hearing loss and a conductive hearing loss. If a sensorineural loss results in a 20 dB hearing level (HL), this means sound intensity must be increased 100-fold (compared to nor-mal young adults) to be audible. An earplug that blocks 99.9 percent of incom-ing sound energy causes a 30 dB conductive hearing loss (see Chapter 2). In a perfectly normal ear, the HL will now be 30 dB. In an ear with preexistent 20 dB hearing level from a sensorineural cause, the resultant HL with the earplug will be 50 dB. Conductive and sensorineural losses show *decibel additivity*.

When both agents cause sensorineural loss, there are more possibilities. Decibel additivity is a natural assumption that has been used by virtually all field studies of NIHL (HL = ARPTS + NIPTS). Decibel additivity would predict that ARPTS would progress at the expected rate in individuals who have sustained NIHL early in life; Macrae (1971, 1991) has shown just that to be true. It would also predict that noise exposure begun late in life in subjects with preexistent ARPTS would cause as much NIPTS as in younger subjects; Welleschik and Raber (1978) have confirmed this in a massive study. There are some contrary data (Novotny, 1975) based on a much smaller study, but it seems likely that decibel additivity describes the interaction of ARPTS and NIPTS well, at least when the total HL is 40 dB or less. Mills' (1992) study in aging, noise-exposed gerbils supported additivity of ARPTS and NIPTS; the decibel differences between average audiograms of elderly noise-exposed and nonnoise-exposed animals was similar to the asymptotic threshold shift seen in noise-exposed younger animals.

ISO-1999 and ANSI S3.44 suggest the use of decibel additivity, with a compression term to be subtracted from the predicted threshold shift when the sum exceeds 40 dB. The ISO-1999 formula for predicting HL from ARPTS and NIPTS is:

$$HL = ARPTS + NIPTS - \frac{(ARPTS)(NIPTS)}{120}$$

For example, if ARPTS and NIPTS were each 60 dB, HL would be 60 + 60 − (3600 ÷ 120) = 90 dB (not 120 dB). The rationale for this compression is that the effects of noise and aging overlap in the cochlea; both damage hair cells, for example. When many or most of these have been damaged by one agent, there is simply less opportunity for the other agent to cause damage. The ISO-1999 compression constant of 120 dB may not be optimal, especially for different animal species; for example, the gerbil data of Mills et al. (1997) would have required a lower compression constant to fit the additivity model well.

Other forms of interaction are possible. One agent could protect the cochlea from damage caused by the other, resulting in much less hearing loss than would be predicted by decibel additivity. The two agents could potentiate one another, resulting in much more loss than the decibel sum of the two agents acting independently. Bies and Hansen (1990) have postulated that ARPTS and NIPTS add as sound levels do in acoustics, that is, 30 dB + 30 dB = 33 dB (see Chapter 2), but there is no theoretical basis, nor are there experimental or epidemiological data to support this idea. Humes and Jesteadt (1991) suggested a power-law transformation to better fit data for growth of TIFS and masking; for both of these, decibel additivity works well only for small values, beyond which the net effect of two "doses" of the agent in question approaches a limiting value. While modified decibel additivity with a compression term (as in ISO-1999) would probably have worked just as well, the power-law approach is reasonable. However, there are no data to support its use for combining NIPTS and ARPTS; in the hypothetical example shown by Humes and Jesteadt, the derived NIPTS curve has the implausible feature of showing deceleration in the second decade, then acceleration in the third decade of noise exposure.

Gates et al. (2000) have suggested that threshold shifts at 2 kHz, in older men with NIHL, *after* cessation of noise exposure, were in excess of normal age-related shifts. This is contrary to the findings of other authors (e.g., Corso, 1980; Rosenthall et al., 1990; Rosler, 1994). Gates et al. assumed (but could not confirm) that their "NIHL" subjects had had no significant noise exposure after their first audiogram, when their average age was 64. Further, since the groups were defined by audiometric shape rather than by noise exposure history, the differences seen in progression of hearing loss cannot be attributed to prior noise exposure with confidence.

Drugs and Chemicals

Humes (1984) and Boettcher et al. (1987) have reviewed the extensive literature regarding drugs and noise exposure. Several ototoxic drugs, including cisplatin (an anticancer drug) and the arninoglycoside antibiotics (gentamicin, neomycin, and many others) can cause hearing loss alone; when combined with simultaneous noise exposure, hearing losses may occur that are greater than occur with either agent alone. Brown et al. (1978) found that guinea pigs receiving both noise and neomycin suffered more hearing loss than the decibel sum of losses seen with neomycin alone and noise alone. Boettcher et al. (1987) have shown that cisplatin doses that cause no significant threshold shifts by themselves in chinchillas can more than double the TTS when combined with noise. However, most studies have shown *less* loss than would be expected from an additive model (Humes, 1984). Normally, people receiving these drugs are too sick to work, so simultaneous ototoxic drug and noise exposure is, practically speaking, rare (nevertheless, patients who have received ototoxic drugs should avoid potentially hazardous noise exposure for two weeks after their last dose, even if there has been no drug-related threshold shift). Two potential exceptions, commonly used by outpatients who may receive occupational noise exposure, are aspirin and furosemide (a diuretic); both cause only transient hearing loss and neither has been shown to potentiate NIPTS. However, the studies of McFadden and Plattsmier (1983) and Lindgren and Axelsson (1985) suggest that, while 1 g aspirin daily (three tablets) does not increase noise-induced TTS, daily doses of 1.9 g (six tablets) or more may cause increased magnitude and slower recovery of TTS. Thus, it is probably wise to avoid combining hazardous noise exposure and high-dose aspirin therapy. Furosemide is probably of less concern, because only *intravenous* doses of this drug cause transient hearing loss in persons with normal kidney function, and occupationally noise-exposed workers would usually be taking the drug orally, if at all.

Several organic solvents (e.g., toluene, xylene, carbon disulfide) and other industrial chemicals (lead, mercury, carbon monoxide) have been suspected of causing hearing loss, both alone and in combination with noise exposure (Fechter, 1989; see also the section, Acquired Hearing Loss [Toxic], in Chapter 10). Morata et al. (1991) report that Brazilian printers habitually exposed to toluene at 78-390 ppm and to noise (above 85 dBA) developed more NIHL than printers with similar noise exposure, but no toluene exposure.

Fortunately, it appears that these effects occur only at exposure levels (for both noise and the chemicals in question) that are above those already prohibited by British (Cary et al., 1997) and American (Clansky, 1991) occupational safety regulations.

Vibration

Vibration is common in the workplace and often coexists with potentially hazardous noise exposure. Vibration alone does not cause hearing loss (Boettcher et al., 1987), but there continues to be concern and controversy regarding possible interactive effects for simultaneous exposures to noise and vibration. Boettcher et al. (1989) found that chinchillas exposed to vibration at their body resonant frequency (about 75 Hz) suffered more TTS, PTS, and hair cell loss from noise exposure than chinchillas given noise exposure without vibration. Manninen (1983) has shown that human subjects also show greater noise-induced TTS if subjected to whole-body vibration, and that this effect is greatest for vibration at body resonant frequency (about 5 Hz for humans). Finally, Pyykko et al. (1981) and Iki et al. (1985) have both shown increased PTS in forestry workers who develop "vibration-induced white finger," presumably because of a noise/vibration interaction (or perhaps because people who are susceptible to "white finger" are also susceptible to NIHL). Szanto and Ligia (1999) have replicated this finding in miners. Most of the effects found in these studies were small, and the data are too scanty to permit estimations of either the threshold or magnitude of hazard.

VASCULAR EFFECTS

No organ can survive without adequate blood supply, so it is only natural that investigators have wondered whether blood flow changes play a role in NIHL. On one hand, noise might cause a decrease in cochlear blood flow even in healthy individuals; this could be one of the mechanisms of NIHL. On the other hand, persons with vascular disease—for example, diabetes or hypertension—might be more prone to NIHL because of preexisting poor blood flow to the cochlea. (Possible effects of vascular disease on hearing in the absence of noise exposure will be discussed in Chapter 10.)

Axelsson and Vertes (1982) have reviewed the copious and confusing literature on vascular changes in healthy animal cochleas exposed to noise. Some studies show increased blood flow, some show decreased flow, and some show no change. Saunders, Dear, and Schneider (1985) felt that the preponderance of evidence supported an overall decrease in blood flow, but pointed out that the effects seen were quite small.

The literature on vascular disease and NIHL is equally inconclusive. Borg (1982b) showed that spontaneously hypertensive rats developed more ARHL than normotensive controls; he also (1982c) demonstrated that these rats were unusually susceptible to NIHL. While this could mean that hypertension causes hearing loss by itself and interacts with NIHL, it could equally mean that these genetically abnormal rats shared genes for both hypertension and hearing loss. This explanation seems most likely since rats with renal (non-genetic) hypertension did not show unusual susceptibility to hearing loss (Borg, 1982a). Pillsbury (1986) replicated some of Borg's earlier studies and extended them by feeding some rats atherogenic diets (leading to severe hypertriglyceridemia). While this diet appeared to exacerbate the hearing loss and hair cell loss seen in spontaneously hypertensive/noise-exposed rats, the effects were very small. Genetically normal rats on the atherogenic diet showed no increased hair cell loss; in fact, the diet appeared to have a *protective* effect with respect to hearing loss in noise-exposed rats.

Some human studies have suggested correlations between vascular disease and NIHL, but there is no consensus in this area. Gold et al. (1989) reviewed some of this literature and found in 800 noise-exposed military personnel that there were no correlations between NIHL and cardiovascular risk factors (glucose, cholesterol, blood pressure, obesity, smoking). Negative studies have also been reported showing no association between NIHL and blood pressure (Lees and Roberts, 1979) and cholesterol (Axelsson and Lindgren, 1985). Green et al. (1991) even found that NIHL was *negatively* correlated with blood pressure in 220 noise-exposed workers. Dengerink et al. (1987) reported an equally paradoxical result: Smokers had *less* TTS (from brief noise exposure) than nonsmokers.

If there are significant relationships between vascular disease and hearing loss (especially NIHL), they are hard to find, perhaps in part because otologists have no way to assess blood flow in the cochlea in humans. At this writing, however, Saunders, Dear, and Schneider's (1985) conclusion still seems apt:

> It seems to us that the extensive vascular literature with its confusing or contradictory findings, its relatively mild effects, and its inability to draw a clear relation between vascular damage and hair cell loss is telling us something. It is not farfetched to consider that the vascular hypothesis is wrong, and that there is no meaningful vascular pathology that contributes to hair cell damage along the organ of Corti.

SUSCEPTIBILITY

A group of factory workers with identical age, seniority, and occupational noise exposures will demonstrate highly variable degrees of hearing loss, even after the best efforts to eliminate differences in non-occupational exposure and otologic disease. Many investigators have sought to identify factors such as gender, race, or vascular disease (see previous section) that could possibly predict susceptibility to NIHL and thus reduce the variability seen in field studies.

Humes (1984) reviewed the literature in these areas and concluded only that animal studies demonstrated greater susceptibility for immature animals (compared to adults). Many studies have suggested more NIHL in men than in women, and more NIHL in whites than in blacks. However, effects of gender and race on susceptibility to NIHL have not been demonstrated to be independent of nonoccupational exposure; Royster and Royster (1982), for example, found that with careful control of nonoccupational exposures and ear disease, black and white workers had equivalent degrees of NIHL. ISO-1999 includes only one set of NIPTS values (see Figures 7–3 to 7–5), to be used regardless of gender or race. Most authorities would agree that the evidence simply does not yet permit prediction of susceptibility in humans based on preexposure factors.

For a given daily noise exposure in a group of subjects, TTS (two minutes after cessation of exposure) is about the same magnitude as the PTS seen in a group of workers similarly exposed for 10 years. This generalization was essential to the CHABA damage risk criteria for intermittent and steady-state noise (Kryter et al., 1966) and impulse noise (Ward, 1968a). Since both TTS and PTS display great variability, many investigators have speculated that TTS could measure susceptibility to PTS, that is, to separate "tough" from "tender" ears (use of these labels is not intended to imply that there are two kinds of ears; there is a spectrum of susceptibility to noise, and "tough" and "tender" are simply convenient ways to describe the two ends of the continuum). Unfortunately, even within TTS studies, susceptibility varies according to the details (spectrum, intensity, time) of the exposure, and Ward (1965, 1968b) was pessimistic about the prospects of developing a general susceptibility test based on TTS. In a more recent review, Melnick (1991) concurred.

The 1990 National Institutes of Health Consensus Conference report on "Noise and Hearing Loss" (NIH 1990) concluded that "scientific knowledge is currently inadequate to predict that any individual will be safe in noise that exceeds established damage-risk criteria or that specific individuals will show greater-than-average hearing loss following a given exposure."

Three exceptions seem essential. Conductive hearing loss of substantial degree (say $\geq$ 30 dB air-bone gaps from 500–4,000 Hz) *must* be protective; sound input to the cochlea will be reduced at least as effectively as with very well-fit hearing protective devices. Less firmly, we can predict that individuals with absent acoustic reflexes, but no conductive hearing loss—for example, after a severe Bell's palsy—will have *increased* susceptibility to NIHL. Common sense dictates a third exception: If an individual has already demonstrated an unexpectedly large threshold shift after noise exposure, even though there may be other (unidentified) causes, it is prudent to treat this person as if more susceptible. In fact, the hearing conservation programs mandated by OSHA require just such an approach.

Underwater noise exposure is a special case. A fetus or a scuba diver hears because sound waves cause the entire skull to vibrate, that is, by bone conduction—remember that the middle ear is adapted to deliver airborne sound to the inner ear, and it works poorly underwater. This means hearing will be much poorer than in air, especially in the speech frequency range where the ear canal and middle ear normally enhance hearing. The American Conference of Governmental Industrial Hygienists has expressed concern that maternal exposures above 115 dB (time-weighted average on the C scale, which attenuates less than 5 dB from 25 Hz to 10 kHz) may be hazardous to the fetus after the fifth month of gestation (Daniel Johnson, personal communication). Hazard assessment for noise-exposed divers is also is also in flux (e.g., Al-Masri and Martin, 1996; Kirkland et al., 1990). Low-frequency sounds are the main concern for both the fetus and the diver for two reasons: they are less attenuated underwater than are high-frequency sounds; and the acoustic reflex, which normally attenuates loud low-frequency sounds, has little effect underwater.

Genetic research in mice has shown that susceptibility to NIHL is inherited, and is correlated with susceptibility to ARHL (Davis et al., 1999; Ohlemiller et al., 2000a, 2000b). Otoacoustic emission tests (Chapter 3) can separate "tough-eared" guinea pigs from those with "tender ears" (Maison and Liberman, 2000). These findings suggest that it may one day be possible to predict NIHL (and ARHL) susceptibility in humans as well.

CRITERIA FOR DIAGNOSIS

Chapter 13 considers the process of diagnosis in detail, but it is useful to summarize the typical features of NIHL here. The American College of Occupational Medicine (ACOM, 1989) has done this for us in a recent position paper, which is quoted here in its entirety:

Definition

Occupational noise-induced hearing loss, as opposed to occupational acoustic trauma, is a slowly developing hearing loss over a long period (several years) as the result of exposure to continuous or intermittent loud noise. Occupational acoustic trauma is a sudden change in hearing as a result of a single exposure to a sudden burst of sound, such as an explosive blast. The diagnosis of noise-induced hearing loss is made clinically by a physician and should include a study of the noise exposure history.

Characteristics

The principal characteristics of occupational noise-induced hearing loss are as follows:

1. It is always sensorineural affecting the hair cells in the inner ear.
2. It is almost always bilateral. Audiometric patterns are usually similar bilaterally.
3. It almost never produces a profound hearing loss. Usually, low-frequency limits are about 40 dB and high-frequency limits about 75 dB.
4. Once the exposure to noise is discontinued, there is no significant further progression of hearing loss as a result of the noise exposure.
5. Previous noise-induced hearing loss does not make the ear more sensitive to future noise exposure. As the hearing threshold increases, the rate of loss decreases.
6. The earliest damage to the inner ears reflects a loss at 3000, 4000, and 6000 Hz. There is always far more loss at 3000, 4000, and 6000 Hz than at 500, 1000, and 2000 Hz. The greatest loss usually occurs at 4000 Hz. The higher and lower frequencies take longer to be affected than the 3000 to 6000 Hz range.
7. Given stable exposure conditions, losses at 3000, 4000, and 6000 Hz will usually reach a maximal level in about 10 to 15 years.
8. Continuous noise exposure over the years is more damaging than interrupted exposure to noise, which permits the ear to have a rest period.

Most of the ACOM statement simply restates what we have covered so far in this chapter, but a few points deserve comment. As we have seen earlier, NIHL *can* begin in frequencies other than the 3 to 6 kHz region, but this is rare and should only be accepted when there has been a documented exposure to an intense narrow-band low-frequency sound (the cordless telephone cases are the only ones this author has seen). Asymmetric losses ($\geq$ 15 dB for PTA) are fairly frequent in noise-exposed workers (Alberti, Symons, and Hyde, 1979), but it is usually possible to identify the causes, which include asymmetric exposures (especially gunfire, as we will see in Chapter 8) and otologic diseases. The epidemiologic data embodied in ISO-1999 suggest that even at 3 to 6 kHz, PTS does not completely stop after 10 to 15 years, but rather continues to grow at a very much reduced rate (see Figures 7–4 and 7–5). ISO-1999 models also predict that, after 40 years of exposure at 90 dBA, or 20 years at 100 dBA, 95 percent confidence limits for 3 to 6 kHz exceed the 75 dB HL limits suggested by the ACOM statement (see Figures 13–1 and 13–2).

CLINICAL MANAGEMENT

Unfortunately, the physician really has nothing of proven benefit to offer for medical or surgical treatment of NIHL or acoustic trauma. Some (Kellerhals, 1972, for example) have endorsed treatment to dilate blood vessels after acoustic trauma, but the best evidence is that these treatments result in no better recovery than occurs without treatment (Tschopp and Probst, 1989; Probst et al., 1992).

Based on animal studies showing that magnesium deficiency increased the effects of acoustic trauma (Ising et al., 1982), Attias et al. (1994) gave magnesium supplements or placebo to army recruits. Those given placebo had worse hearing than those given magnesium, 7–10 days after firearm training, but it was unclear whether threshold shifts (before vs. after) were different between the two groups. A U.S. Army study of soldiers with extensive noise exposure showed no correlation between audiometry and magnesium levels (Walden et al., 2000).

Oxidative stress (damage triggered by reactive oxygen species or free radicals) has already been mentioned (see the section on Intermittency) as part of the process of hair cell death after noise exposure, and is beginning to be familiar to the general public as an important factor in aging, heart disease, cancer, and other diseases. Sha et al. (2000) found that outer hair cells at the base of the cochlea—the very cells that are most susceptible to age, noise, and drugs—are also more susceptible to free radical damage than other cochlear cells. Several antioxidants and similar agents (allopurinol, glutathione, iron chelators, vitamins A, C, and E, etc.) have shown promise in reducing noise-induced hair loss in animals (Seidman et al., 1993; Shoji et al., 2000; Yamasoba et al., 1998, 1999b), but all these studies involved drug treatment before and/or during noise exposure.

Hearing aids can be of significant benefit, but do not completely correct the hearing handicap of NIHL (or of sensorineural hearing loss in general).

Prevention of NIHL through occupational hearing conservation programs (HCPs) is discussed in Chapter 9. However, many patients have either non-occupational-related NIHL, or are employed by companies that can't or won't support HCPs. Physicians and audiologists must provide counseling, protectors, and audiometric follow-up for such individuals.

NONAUDITORY EFFECTS

Although our primary interest is in NIHL, we have already discussed the possibility that noise may damage the vestibular organs in the inner ear. There is also a large literature on "nonauditory" effects of noise, referring to the following areas:

1. Speech interference
2. Performance
3. Annoyance
4. Sleep interference
5. Physiological effects

The first of these, *speech interference*, is easiest to understand. As background noise levels rise, listeners have increasing difficulty understanding speech; first consonants then vowels are masked and become inaudible. Speakers automatically compensate by raising their voices in levels above about 55 dBA (Kryter, 1985). At a one-meter conversational distance, shouting is necessary in background levels above 80 to 85 dBA, and even shouted conversations are inadequate above 95 to 100 dBA (Webster, 1978; these figures are extrapolated from a figure relating distance to *speech interference level* [SIL], an average of octave band levels from 0.5 to 4 kHz; SIL is usually about 10 dB less than dBA). These correlations between noise level and vocal effort can be useful in medical-legal assessment of occupational NIHL when workplace noise-exposure measurements are unavailable. In general, a worker who has not had to shout at normal conversational distances on the job has not had hazardous exposures (impulse noises would provide one obvious exception to this rule). A reported need to shout to converse suggests a possibly hazardous exposure, although hazard is negligible in the 80 to 85 dBA range. When valid sound-level measurements or dosimetry are available, these should be given much greater weight than reports of vocal effort, however.

Performance of mental tasks can be disrupted by loud noise, but this is harder to predict from noise levels than speech interference or risk of NIHL. *Annoyance* and *sleep interference* are even more tenuously related to level; everyone has had the experience that very soft sounds (a dripping faucet) can be quite annoying in a quiet background. Many factors that increase annoyance are either irrelevant or even protective with respect to risk of NIHL. For example, intermittent sounds are more annoying than continuous noise—but less hazardous to hearing. Time of day, subject attitude about the noise source, predictability, and perceived control are all important for annoyance and are irrelevant for NIHL.

A voluminous literature has grown up around the question of whether noise can cause adverse *physiological effects* in body systems other than the inner ear. Everyday experience tells us that a child's scream, the screech of brakes, or a police siren can trigger a sudden tensing of muscles and rapid heartbeat; one would expect a rise in blood pressure as well. Can chronic exposure to noise cause permanent adverse effects in this way? A priori, there is good reason to doubt it. These acute effects are directly related to the unexpectedness and especially the *meaning* of these sounds, not to their intensity. Chronic exposure would be expected to cause progressively weaker reactions.

Most of the human and animal studies on non-auditory health effects have focused on hypertension, that is, chronic elevation of blood pressure, and other cardiovascular effects. The literature has been reviewed by Kryter (1980), CHABA (1981), DeJoy (1984), van Dijk, Ettema, and Zielhuis (1987), and Suter (1992), among others. For every putative effect, there are as many negative studies as there are those showing associations between noise and adverse health effects. Considering that even positive studies nearly always show very small effects and that some negative studies probably are not published (publication bias), it is difficult to conclude that there are clinically significant non-auditory health effects of chronic noise exposure per se. Most "positive" studies have not controlled for other stressors that frequently accompany noisy jobs: dirt, dust, stench, smoke, strenuous and physically hazardous activities, vibration, heat, shiftwork, and low socioeconomic status, to name a few. Thus, health differences (e.g., increased blood pressure) between noise-exposed and nonnoise-exposed groups, when found, could have myriad causes. One large study that did control for these confounding variables (van Dijk, Souman, and deVries, 1987) found no association between noise and blood pressure. Obviously, noise can be unpleasant; when it is resented by a highly reactive individual, it is conceivable that chronic occupational noise exposure could act as a stressor—probably in concert with others—to cause or exacerbate hypertension. Kryter's (1980) comment is apt:

> [I]t appears not likely that noise in industry can be a direct cause of general health problems (setting aside damage to the ear), except that the noise can create conditions of psychological stress . . . [which] can, in turn, cause physiological stress reactions that can be detrimental to physical and psychological health.

However, such effects are probably neither frequent nor large. The conclusion of the CHABA working group in 1981 is probably still valid: "Evidence from available research reports is suggestive, but it does not provide definitive answers to the question of health effects, other than to the auditory system, of long-term exposure to noise."

REFERENCES

Ahaus, William H. and W. Dixon Ward. 1975. Temporary threshold shift from short-duration noise bursts. *J. Am. Aud. Soc.* 1(1):4–10.

Akiyoshi, Masatoyo, Akira Amemiya, Kiichi Sato, Takami Takeda, and Tadashi Shoji. 1966. On the pathogenesis of acoustic trauma of the cochlea in rabbits and guinea pigs due to explosion. *Int'l. Audiology* 5:270–271.

Alberti, P. W., F. Symons, and M. L. Hyde. 1979. Occupational hearing loss: The significance of asymmetrical hearing thresholds. *Acta Otolaryngol. (Stockh.)* 87(3–4):255–263.

Al-Masri, M. and A. Martin. 1996. Underwater Hearing and Occupational Noise Exposure. In *Scientific Basis of Noise-Induced Hearing Loss,* ed. A. Axelsson et al. New York: Thieme.

American College of Occupational Medicine–Noise and Hearing Conservation Committee. 1989. Occupational noise-induced hearing loss. *J. Occup. Med.* 31(12):996.

American National Standards Institute. 1996. *Determination of Occupational Noise Exposure and Estimation of Noise-Induced Hearing Impairment.* New York: Acoustical Society of America, ANSI S3.44-1996.

Attias, J., G. Weisz, S. Almog, A. Shahar, M. Wiener, Z. Joachims, A. Netzer, H. Ising, E. Rebentisch, and T. Geunther. 1994. Oral magnesium intake reduces permanent hearing loss induced by noise exposure. *Am. J. Otolaryngol.* 15:26–32.

Axelsson, Alf and Fredrik Lindgren. 1985. Is there a relationship between hypercholesterolaernia and noise-induced hearing loss? *Acta Otolaryngol. (Stockh.)* 100(5–6):379–386.

Axelsson, Alf and Dianne Vertes. 1982. Histological findings in cochlear vessels after noise. In *New Perspectives on Noise-Induced Hearing Loss*, eds. Roger P. Hamernik, Donald Henderson, and Richard Salvi, pp. 49–68. New York: Raven Press.

Berger, G., Y. Finkelstein, S. Avraham, and M. Himmelfarb. 1997. Patterns of hearing loss in non-explosive blast injury of the ear. *Laryngol. and Otol.* 111:1137–1141.

Bies, David A. and Colin H. Hansen. 1990. An alternative mathematical description of the relationship between noise exposure and hearing loss. *J. Acoust. Soc. Am.* 88(6):2743–2754.

Boettcher, Flint A., Donald Henderson, Michael Anne Gratton, Clyde Byrne, and B. Bancroft. 1989. Recent advances in the understanding of noise interactions. *Arch. Complex. Environ. Studies* 1:15–21.

Boettcher, Flint A., Donald Henderson, Michael Anne Gratton, Richard W. Danielson, and Clyde D. Byrne. 1987. Synergistic interactions of noise and other ototraurnatic agents. *Ear & Hearing* 8(4):192–212.

Bohne, Barbara A., Shirley J. Zahn, and Denyse G. Bozzay. 1985. Damage of the cochlea following interrupted exposure to low frequency noise. *Ann. Otol. Rhinol. Laryngol.* 94(2 Pt. 1):122–128.

Borg, E. 1968. A quantitative study of the effect of the acoustic stapedius reflex on sound transmission through the middle ear of man. *Acta Otolaryngol. (Stockh.)* 66(6):461–472.

———. 1982a. Noise-induced hearing loss in rats with renal hypertension. *Hear. Res.* 8(1):93–99.

———. 1982b. Auditory thresholds in rats of different age and strain: A behavioral and electrophysiological study. *Hear. Res.* 8(2):101–115.

———. 1982c. Noise-induced hearing loss in normotensive and spontaneously hypertensive rats. *Hear. Res.* 8(2):117–130.

Borg, Erik, R. Nilsson, and B. Engstrom. 1983. Effect of the acoustic reflex on inner ear damage induced by industrial noise. *Acta Otolaryngol. (Stockh.)* 96(5–6):361–369.

Brown, Jeffrey J., Robert E. Brummett, Mary B. Meikle, and Jack Vernon. 1978. Combined effects of noise and neomycin: Cochlear changes in the guinea pig. *Acta Otolaryngol. (Stockh.)* 86(5–6):394–400.

Bruusgaard, A. 1962. *T'norske Laegeforen* 82:1285.

Bunch, C. C. 1937. Symposium: The Neural Mechanisms of Hearing. B. "Nerve deafness" of known pathology or etiology: The diagnosis of occupational or traumatic deafness; a historical and audiometric study. *Laryngoscope* 47(9):615–691.

Canlon, Barbara, Erik Borg, and Ake Flock. 1988. Protection against noise trauma by pre-exposure to a low level acoustic stimuli. *Hear. Res.* 34(2):197–200.

Cary, R., S. Clarke, and J. Delic. 1997. Effects of combined exposure to noise and toxic substances—critical review of the literature. *Ann. Occup. Hygiene* 41:455–465.

Chadwick, Denis. 1971. Noise and the ear. In *Scott-Brown's Diseases of the Ear, Nose and Throat: Volume 2—The Ear,* 3rd ed., ed. John Ballantyne and John Groves, pp. 475–539. Philadelphia: J. B. Lippincott.

Clansky, K. B. 1991. *Chemical Guide to the OSHA Hazard Communication Standard.* Bethesda, MD: Roytech Publishers.

Clark, William W. 1991. Recent studies of temporary threshold shift (TTS) and permanent threshold shift (PTS) in animals. *J. Acoust. Soc. Am.* 90(1):155–163.

Committee on Hearing, Bioacoustics, and Biomechanics. 1981. *The Effects of Human Health from Long-Term Exposures to Noise: Report of Working Group 81.* Washington, DC: National Academy Press.

Committee on Hearing, Bioacoustics, and Biomechanics, the Commission on Behavioral and Social Sciences and Education, and the National Research Council—Working Group on Hazardous Exposure to Impulse Noise. 1992. *Hazardous Exposure to Impulse Noise.* Washington, DC: National Academy Press.

Corso, John F. 1980. Age correction factor in noise-induced hearing loss: A quantitative model. *Audiology* 19:221–232.

Danielson, R., D. Henderson, M. A. Gratton, L. Bianchi, and R. Salvi. 1991. The importance of "temporal pattern" in traumatic impulse noise exposures. *J. Acoust. Soc. Am.* 90(1):209–218.

Davis, R., M. Cheever, E. Krieg, and L. Erway. 1999. Quantitative measure of genetic differences in susceptibility to noise-induced hearing loss in two strains of mice. *Hearing Res.* 134:9–15.

DeJoy, David M. 1984. A report on the status of research on the cardiovascular effects of noise. *Noise Control Eng. J.* 23(1):32–39.

Dengerink, H. A., F. Lindgren, A. Axelsson, and J. E. Dengerink. 1987. The effects of smoking and physical exercise on temporary threshold shifts. *Scand. Audiol.* 16(3):131–136.

Dufresne, Ronald M., Brian C. Alleyne, and Michael R. Reesal. 1988. Asymmetric hearing loss in truck drivers. *Ear & Hearing* 9(1):41–42.

Eames, B. L., R. P. Hamernik, D. Henderson, and A. Feldman. 1975. The role of the middle ear in acoustic trauma from impulses. *Laryngoscope* 85(9):1582–1592.

Fechter, Lawrence D. 1989. A mechanistic basis for interactions between noise and chemical exposure. *Arch. Complex. Environ. Studies* 1:23–28.

Galland, L. 1992. Magnesium, stress and neuropschiatric disorders. *Magnes. Trace Elem.* 10:287–301.

Garth, R. 1994. Blast injury of the auditory system: A review of the mechanisms and pathology. *J. Laryngol. Otol.* 108:925–929.

Gates, G., P. Schmid, S. Kujawa, B. Nam, and R. D'Agostino. 2000. Longitudinal threshold changes in older men with audiometric notches. *Hearing Res.* 141:220–228.

Gold, Shlomit, Ildit Haran, Joseph Attias, Itzhak Shapira, and Amnon Shahar. 1989. Biochemical and cardiovascular measures in subjects with noise-induced hearing loss. *J. Occup. Med.* 31(11):933–937.

Green, Manfred S., Kalman Schwartz, Gil Harari, and Theodore Najenson. 1991. Industrial noise exposure and ambulatory blood pressure and heart rate. *J. Occup. Med.* 33(8):879–883.

Hamernik, Roger P., William A. Ahroon, and Keng D. Hsueh. 1991. The energy spectrum of an impulse: Its relation to hearing loss. *J. Acoust. Soc. Am.* 90(1):197–204.

Hamernik, Roger P. and Keng D. Hsueh. 1991. Impulse noise: Some definitions, physical acoustics and other considerations. *J. Acoust. Soc. Am.* 90(1): 189–196.

Hamernik, Roger P., James H. Patterson, George A. Turrentine, and William A. Ahroon. 1989. The quantitative relation between sensory cell loss and hearing thresholds. *Hear. Res.* 38(3):199– 211.

Henderson, Donald, Pierre Campo, Malini Subrarnaniam, and Francesco Fiorino. 1992. Development of resistance to noise. In *Noise-Induced Hearing Loss*, ed. Armand L. Dancer, pp. 476–488. Philadelphia: B. C. Decker.

Henderson, Donald and Roger P. Hamernik. 1986. Impulse noise: Critical review. *J. Acoust. Soc. Am.* 80(2):569–584.

Hinchcliffe, R., R. Coles, and P. King. 1992. Occupational noise induced vestibular malfunction. *Br. J. Ind. Med.* 49:63–65.

Hirsch, F. Effects of overpressure on the ear—a review. 1968. *Ann. NY Acad. Sci.* 152:147–162.

Humes, Larry E. 1984. Noise-induced hearing loss as influenced by other agents and by some physical characteristics of the individual. *J. Acoust. Soc. Am.* 76(5):1318–1329.

Humes, Larry E. and Walt Jesteadt. 1991. Modeling the interactions between noise exposure and other variables. *J. Acoust. Soc. Am.* 90(1):182–188.

Hunter, L., D. Ries, R. Schlauch, S. Levine, and W. Ward. 1999. Safety and clinical performance of acoustic reflex tests. *Ear & Hearing* 20:506–514.

Iki, Masayuki, Norio Kurumatani, Kuniaki Hirata, and Tadashige Moriyama. 1985. An association between Raynaud's phenomenon and hearing loss in forestry workers. *Am. Ind. Hyg. Assoc. J.* 46(9):509–513.

International Organization for Standardization. 1990. *Acoustics: Determination of Occupational Noise Exposure and Estimation of Noise-Induced Hearing Impairment, ISO-1999.* Geneva: International Organization for Standardization.

Ising, H., M. Handrock, T. Gunther, R. Fisher, and M. Dombrowski. 1982. Increased noise trauma in guinea pigs through magnesium deficiency. *Arch. Otorhinolaryngol.* 236(2):139–146.

Jacono, A., R. Kopke, D. Henderson, T. Van de Water, and H. Steinman. 1998. Changes in cochlear antioxidant enzyme activity after sound conditioning and noise exposure in the chinchilla. *Hearing Res.* 117:31–38.

Johnson, Daniel L. 1978. *Derivation of Presbycusis and Noise Induced Permanent Threshold Shift (NIPTS) to Be Used for the Basis of a Standard on the Effects of Noise on Hearing (AMRL-TR-78-128).* Wright-Patterson Air Force Base, Dayton, OH: Aerospace Medical Research Laboratory.

Kellerhals, B. 1972. Acoustic trauma and cochlear microcirculation: An experimental and clinical study on pathogenesis and treatment of inner ear lesions after acute noise exposure. In *Advances in Oto-Rhino-Laryngology,* Vol. 18, ed. C. R. Pfaltz, pp. 91–168. Basel, Switzerland: S. Karger.

Kerr, A. G. and J. E. T. Byrne. 1975. Concussive effects of bomb blast on the ear. *J. Laryngol. Otol.* 89(2):131–143.

Kimura, Robert S. 1982. Animal models of endolymphatic hydrops. *Am. J. Otolaryngol.* 3(6):447–451.

Kirkland, Paul C., Elbert A. Pence, Robert A. Dobie, and Phillip A. Yantis. 1990. *Underwater noise exposure and the conservation of divers' hearing: A review.* Washington, DC: U.S. Naval Sea Systems Command.

Kryter, Karl D. 1980. Physiological acoustics and health. *J. Acoust. Soc. Am.* 68(1):10–14.

———. 1985. *The Effects of Noise on Man,* 2nd ed. New York: Academic Press.

Kryter, Karl D., W. Dixon Ward, James D. Miller, and Donald H. Eldredge. 1966. Hazardous exposure to intermittent and steady-state noise. *J. Acoust. Soc. Am.* 39(3):451–464.

Kujawa, S. and M. Liberman. 1999. Long-term sound conditioning enhances cochlear sensitivity. *J. Neurophysiol.* 82:863–873.

Kvaener, K., B. Engdahl, A. Arnesen, and I. Mair. 1995. Temporary threshold shift and otoacoustic emissions after industrial noise exposure. *Scand. Audiol.* 24:137–141.

Lees, R. E. M. and J. Hatcher Roberts. 1979. Noise-induced hearing loss and blood pressure. *CMAJ* 120(9):1082–1084.

Liberman, M. Charles and Michael J. Mulroy. 1982. Acute and chronic effects of acoustic trauma: Cochlear pathology and auditory nerve pathophysiology. In *New Perspectives on Noise-Induced Hearing Loss,* ed. Roger P.

Hamernik, Donald Henderson, and Richard Salvi, pp. 105–135. New York: Raven Press.

Lindgren, Frederik and Alf Axelsson. 1985. Temporary threshold shift induced by noise exposure and moderate salicylate intake. *Scand. Audiol. Suppl.* 26:41–44.

Loeb, Michel and John L. Fletcher. 1968. Impulse duration and temporary threshold shift. *J. Acoust. Soc. Am.* 44(6):1524–1528.

Lutman, Mark, and Adrian Davis. 1996. Distributions of hearing threshold levels in populations exposed to noise. In *Scientific Basis of Noise-Induced Hearing Loss,* ed. A. Axelsson et al. New York: Thieme.

Lutman, Mark and H. Spencer. 1991. Occupational noise and demographic factors in hearing. *Acta Otolaryngol. Suppl. (Stockh.)* 476:74–87.

Macrae, J. H. 1971. Noise-induced hearing loss and presbyacusis. *Audiology* 10(5):323–333.

Macrae, J. H. 1991. Presbycusis and noise-induced permanent threshold shift. *J. Acoust. Soc. Am.* 90:2513–2516.

Maison, S. and M. Liberman. 2000. Predicting vulnerability to acoustic injury with a non-invasive assay of olivocochlear reflex strength. *J. Neurosci.* 20:4701–4707.

Manninen, O. 1983. Studies of combined effects of sinusoidal whole body vibrations and noise of varying bandwidths and intensities on TTS_2 in men. *Int. Arch. Occup. Environ. Health* 51(3):273–288.

McFadden, Dennis and H. S. Plattsmier. 1983. Aspirin can potentiate the temporary hearing loss induced by intense sounds. *Hear. Res.* 9(3):295–316.

Melnick, William. 1991. Human temporary threshold shift (TTS) and damage risk. *J. Acoust. Soc. Am.* 90(1):147–154.

Miller, James D. 1971. *Effects of Noise on People (Contract 68-01-05000).* Washington, DC: U.S. Environmental Protection Agency.

Mills, John H. 1992. Noise-induced hearing loss: Effects of age and existing hearing loss. In *Noise-Induced Hearing Loss*, ed. Armand L. Dancer, pp. 237–245. Philadelphia: B. C. Decker.

Mills, John H., Flint A. Boettcher, and Judy R. Dubno. 1997. Interaction of noise-induced permanent threshold shift and age-related threshold shift. *J. Acoust. Soc. Am.* 101:1681–1686.

Molvaer, O. I. and E. H. Lehmann. 1985. Hearing acuity in professional divers. *Undersea Biomed. Res.* 12(3):333–349.

Morata, T. C., D. E. Dunn, L. W. Kretschmer, G. K. Lemasters, and U. P. Santos. 1991. Effects of simultaneous exposure to noise and Toluene on workers' hearing and balance. In *Proceedings of the Fourth International Conference on the Combined Environmental Factors*, ed. Laurence D. Fechter, pp. 81–86. Baltimore: Johns Hopkins University.

Mostafapour, S. P., K. Lahargoue, and G. A. Gates. 1998. Noise-induced hearing loss in young adults: The role of personal listening devices and other sources of leisure noise. *Laryngoscope* 108:1832–1839.

National Institutes of Health–Office of Medical Applications of Research. 1990. Consensus Conference: Noise and hearing loss. *JAMA* 263(23):3185–3190.

Novotny, Z. 1975. Development of occupational deafness after entering a noisy employment in older age. *Cesk Otolaryngol.* 24(3):151–154.

Ohlemiller, K., J. S. Wright, and A. F. Heidbecker. 2000a. Vulnerability to noise-induced hearing loss in "middle-aged" and young adult mice: A dose response approach in CBA, C57BL, and BALB inbred strains. *Hear. Res.* 149(1–2):239–247.

Ohlemiller, K., P. Lear, and Y. Ho. 2000b. Deficiency of cellular glutathione peroxidase increases noise-induced hearing loss in young adult mice. *ARO Abstracts* 23:219.

Pahor, Ahmes L. 1981. The ENT problems following the Birmingham bombings. *J. Laryngol. Otol.* 95(4):399–406.

Paparella, Michael M. and Fernando Mancini. 1983. Trauma and Meniere's syndrome. *Laryngoscope* 93(8):1004–1012.

Passchier-Vermeer, W. 1974. Hearing loss due to continuous exposure to steady-state broad-band noise. *J. Acoust. Soc. Am.* 56:1583–1593.

Pierson, L. L., K. J. Gerhardt, G. P. Rodriguez, and R. B. Yanke. 1994. Relationship between outer ear resonance and permanent noise-induced hearing loss. *Am. J. Otolaryngol.* 15:37–40.

Pillsbury, Harold C. 1986. Hypertension, hyperhypoproteinemia, chronic noise exposure: Is there synergism in cochlear pathology? *Laryngoscope* 96(10): 1112–1138.

Price, G. Richard. 1974. Transformation function of the external ear in response to impulsive stimulation. *J. Acoust. Soc. Am.* 56(1):190–194.

———. 1983. Relative hazard of weapons impulses. *J. Acoust. Soc. Am.* 73(2):556–566.

Probst, R., K. Tschopp, E. Ludin, B. Kellerhals, M. Podvinec, and C. R. Pfaltz. 1992. A randomized, double-blind, placebo-controlled study of dextran/pentoxifylline medication in acute acoustic trauma and sudden hearing loss. *Acta. Otolaryngol.* 112:435–443.

Pyykko, I., J. Starck, M. Farkkila, M. Hoikkala, O. Korhonen, and M. Nurminen. 1981. Hand-arm vibration in the aetiology of hearing loss in lumberjacks. *Br. J. Ind. Med.* 38(3):281–289.

Rauch, Steven D., Saumil N. Merchant, and Britt A. Thedinger. 1989. Meniere's syndrome and endolymphatic hydrops: Double-blind temporal bone study. *Ann. Otol. Rhinol. Laryngol.* 98(11):873–883.

Rosenhall, U., K. Pederson, and A. Svanborg. 1990. Presbycusis and noise-induced hearing loss. *Ear & Hearing* 11:257–263.

Rosler, G. 1994. Progression of hearing loss caused by occupational noise. *Scandinavian Audiology* 23:13–37.

Rosowski, John J. 1991. The effects of extenal- and middle-ear filtering on auditory threshold and noise-induced hearing loss. *J. Acoust. Soc. Am.* 90(1): 124–135.

Royster, Larry H. and Julia D. Royster. 1982. Methods of evaluating hearing conservation program audiometric data bases. In *Personal Hearing Protection in Industry*, ed. Peter W. Alberti, pp. 511–540. New York: Raven Press.

Salmivalli, Altti. 1967. Acoustic trauma in regular army personnel: Clinical audiologic study. *Acta Otolaryngol. Suppl. (Stockh.)* 222:1–85.

Sataloff, Joseph, Robert T. Sataloff, Hyman Menduke, Raymond A. Yerg, and Robert P. Gore. 1983. Intermittent exposure to noise: Effects on hearing. *Ann. Otol. Rhinol. Laryngol.* 92(6 Pt. 1):623–628.

Saunders, James C., Yale E. Cohen, and Yvonne M. Szymko. 1991. The structural and functional consequences of acoustic injury in the cochlea and peripheral auditory system: A five year update. *J. Acoust. Soc. Am.* 90(1):136–146.

Saunders, James C., Steven P. Dear, and Mark E. Schneider. 1985. The anatomical consequences of acoustic injury: A review and tutorial. *J. Acoust. Soc. Am.* 78(3):833–860.

Segal, S., M. Harell, A. Shahar, and M. Englender. 1988. Acute acoustic trauma: Dynamics of hearing loss following cessation of exposure. *Am. J. Otol.* 9(4):293–298.

Seidman, M. D., B. G. Shivapuja, and W. S. Quirk. 1993. The protective effects of allopurinol and superoxide dismatuse on noise-induced cochlear damage. *Otolaryngol. Head Neck Surg.* 109:1052–1056.

Sha, S., R. Taylor, A. Forge, and J. Schacht. 2000. Differential vulnerability of basal and apical hair cells is based on intrinsic susceptibility to free radicals. *ARO Abstracts* 23:42–43.

Shoji, F., T. Yamasoba, E. Magal, D. F. Dolan, R. A. Altschuler, and J. M. Miller. 2000. Glial cell line-derived neurotrophic factor has a dose dependent influence on noise-induced hearing loss in the guinea pig cochlea. *Hear. Res.* 142:41–55.

Singleton, George T., David L. Whitaker, Robert J. Keim, and F. J. Kemker. 1984. Cordless telephones: A threat to hearing. *Ann. Otol. Rhinol. Laryngol.* 93(6 Pt. 1):565–568.

Suter, Alice H. 1992. Noise sources and effects: A new look. *Sound and Vibration* 26(1):18–34.

Szanto, C. S. and S. Ligia. 1999. Correlation between vibration induced white finger and hearing loss in miners. *J. Occup. Health* 41:222–237.

Taylor, W., J. Pearson, A. Mair, and W. Burns. 1965. Study of noise and hearing in jute weaving. *J. Acoust. Soc. Am.* 38(1):113–120.

Teter, Darrel I., Robert C. Newell, and Kenneth B. Aspinall. 1970. Audiometric configurations associated with blast trauma. *Laryngoscope* 80(7):1122–1132.

Theiry, L. and C. Meyer-Bisch. 1988. Hearing loss due to partly impulsive industrial noise exposure at levels between 87 and 90 dB. *J. Acoust. Soc. Am.* 84:651–659.

Tschopp, Kurt and Rudolf Probst. 1989. Acute acoustic trauma: A retrospective study of influencing factors and different therapies in 268 patients. *Acta Otolaryngol. (Stockh.)* 108(5–6):378–384.

U.S. Department of Labor–Occupational Safety and Health Administration. 1971. Occupational Safety and Health Standards, National Consensus Standards and Established Federal Standards. *Federal Register* 36(105; May 29, 1971):10518.

———. 1981. Occupational Noise Exposure: Hearing Conservation Amendment. *Federal Register* 46(11; January 16, 1981):4078–4179.

———. 1983. Occupational Noise Exposure: Hearing Conservation Amendment; Final Rule. *Federal Register* 48(46):9738–9784.

van Dijk, F. J. H., J. H. Ettema, and R. L. Zielhuis. 1987. Non-auditory effects of noise in industry. VII. Evaluation, conclusions and recommendations. *Int. Arch. Occup. Environ. Health* 59(2):147–152.

van Dijk, F. J. H., A. M. Souman, and F. F. deVries. 1987. Non-auditory effects of noise in industry. VI. A final field study in industry. *Int. Arch. Occup. Environ. Health* 59(2):133–145.

Walden, B. E., L. W. Henselman, and E. R. Morris. 2000. The role of magnesium in the susceptibility of soldiers to noise-induced hearing loss. *J. Acoust. Soc. Am.* 108:453–456.

Ward, W. Dixon. 1965. The concept of susceptibility to hearing loss. *J. Occup. Med.* 7(12):595–607.

———. 1968a. *Proposed Damage-Risk Criterion for Noise (Gunfire): Report of Working Group 57.* Washington, DC: NAS-NRC Committee on Hearing, Bioacoustics, and Biomechanics.

———. 1968b. Susceptibility to auditory fatigue. In *Contributions to Sensory Physiology,* Vol. 3, ed. William D. Neff, pp. 191–226. New York: Academic Press.

———. 1970. Temporary threshold shift and damage-risk criteria for intermittent noise exposures. *J. Acoust. Soc. Am.* 48(2):561– 574.

———. 1991a. *Hearing Loss from Noise and Music.* Paper read at the 91st Convention of the Audio Engineering Society, 4–8 October, New York.

———. 1991b. The role of intermittence in PTS. *J. Acoust. Soc. Am.* 90(1):164–169.

Ward, W. Dixon, E. Marion Cushing, and Edward M. Burns. 1976. Effective quiet and moderate TTS: Implications for noise exposure standards. *J. Acoust. Soc. Am.* 59(1):160–165.

Ward, W. Dixon, Aram Glorig, and D. L. Sklar. 1959. Temporary threshold shift from octave-band noise: Applications to damage-risk criteria. *J. Acoust. Soc. Am.* 31(4):522–528.

Webster, John C. 1978. Speech interference aspects of noise. In *Noise and Audiology,* ed. David M. Lipscomb, pp. 193–228. Baltimore: University Park Press.

Welleschik, B. and A. Raber. 1978. Einfluss von expositionszeit und alter auf den iarmbedingten horverlust [Influence of exposure time and age on noise-induced hearing loss: Observations of 25,544 industrial workers (author's trans.)]. *Laryngol. Rhinol. Otol.* 57(12):1037–1048.

Williams, R. G. 1996. Review paper: The diagnosis of noise-induced hearing loss. *J. Audiol. Med.* 6:45–58.

Yamasoba, T., A. L. Nuttall, C. Harris, Y. Raphael, and J. M. Miller. 1998. Role of glutathione in protection against noise-induced hearing loss. *Brain Res.* 784:82–90.

Yamasoba, T., D. F. Dolan, and J. M. Miller. 1999a. Acquired resistance to acoustic trauma by sound conditioning is primarily mediated by changes restricted to the cochlea, not by systematic responses. *Hear. Res.* 127: 31–40.

Yamasoba, T., J. Schacht, F. Shoji, and J. M. Miller. 1999b. Attenuation of cochlear damage from noise trauma by an iron chelator, a free radical scavenger and glial cell line-derived neurotrophic factor in vivo. *Brain Res.* 815:317–325.

Yaremchuck, Kathleen and Robert Dobie. 1999. The otologic effects of airbag deployment. *J. Occup. Hearing Loss* 2:67–72.

Ylikoski, Jukka. 1987. Impulse noise induced damage in the vestibular end organs of the guinea pig: A light microscopic study. *Acta Otolaryngol. (Stockh.)* 103(5–6):415–421.

———. 1988. Delayed endolymphatic hydrops syndrome after heavy exposure to impulse noise. *Am. J. Otol.* 9(4):282–285.

Zakrisson, John-Erik. 1975. The role of the stapedius reflex in poststimulatory auditory fatigue. *Acta Otolaryngol. (Stockh.)* 79(1–2):1–10.

Zakrisson, John-Erik, Erik Borg, Gunnar Liden, and Roland Nilsson. 1980. Stapedius reflex in industrial noise: Fatigability and role for temporary threshold shift (TTS). *Scand. Audiol. Suppl.* 12:326–334.

Chapter 8

Nonoccupational NIHL

SOCIOACUSIS

As pointed out by Glorig and Nixon (1962; see Chapter 6), many—perhaps most—surveys of hearing in populations are contaminated by what they called socioacusis. Even when people with a history of noisy jobs are excluded, many subjects will have had damaging exposures to noises of everyday life. Careful screening out of subjects with substantial exposure to shooting, power tools, motorcycles, and the like permits a better measurement of the effects of presbycusis ("pure" aging) and nosoacusis (undiagnosed ear disease), but it is a rare person who has never had a potentially hazardous noise exposure. Socioacusis and nonoccupational noise-induced hearing loss (NIHL) are really synonymous, but we will generally use the former to refer to populations and large studies, and the latter to refer to individuals. The biology of NIHL and acoustic trauma described in Chapter 7—types of inner ear damage, interactions, growth patterns, and so on—is as relevant for non-occupational as for occupational exposures. Lindgren and Axelsson (1983) have shown that some subjects have less temporary threshold shift (TTS) after loud music exposure than after noise exposure of equivalent intensity, frequency, and temporal pattern. Notwithstanding this isolated finding, most authorities still consider that risk for NIHL is based on intensity (dBA), duration, and individual susceptibility rather than the perceptual or esthetic properties of the sound in question. Annoyance and sleep disturbance, conversely, are more correlated with these psychological factors than with intensity (Chapter 7), but these will not be further discussed here.

174

NONOCCUPATIONAL NOISE SOURCES

Separation of occupational from nonoccupational noise sources is somewhat artificial. Truck cab noise, gunfire, and rock music are all occupational for some people, recreational for others. Personal stereo systems (e.g., the Walkman) are normally nonoccupational, but workers who are permitted to wear them on the job in noisy environments may substantially increase their noise exposures. Noise exposure off the job, even if safe by itself, can add to occupational exposure, increasing total risk. Schori and McGatha (1978) found average daily exposures, in an urban sample of adults without occupational noise exposure, in the 73 to 76 dBA range. Many occupationally exposed persons may have higher off-the-job exposures, which could retard recovery of TTS and accelerate the development of NIHL.

Appendix A presents an extensive list of exposure levels (dBA) for different types of tools, equipment, jobs, et cetera. In many cases, ranges rather than specific figures are given, because a given type of tool may produce very different levels depending on size, style, state of repair, mode of use, and other factors. The levels in Appendix A—or better, direct measurements of the tools or environments in question—plus consideration of temporal patterns, permit estimation of hazard. In this chapter, we will discuss only some of the more notorious causes of non-occupational NIHL: shooting, loud music, other recreational sources, household appliances, and transportation. We will see that some are far more important than others.

Shooting

Guns are the main source of hazardous impulse noise. Although .22 caliber weapons usually deliver less than 140 dB peak sound pressure to the shooter's ears, shotguns, pistols, and rifles of larger caliber frequently deliver up to 170 dB (Odess, 1972). These impulses can cause either acoustic trauma (sudden and permanent threshold shift) or NIHL (with TTS that initially recovers, and eventually becomes permanent after repeated exposures). Rifles and shotguns are usually placed on the right shoulder (for a right-handed person); the left ear then receives the brunt of the noise, while the right ear is protected by "head shadow."

Many studies (reviewed by Phaneuf and Hetu, 1990; see also Nondahl et al., 2000) have shown that subjects with recreational exposure to gunfire have increased high-frequency hearing loss (compared to control subjects with equivalent occupational exposure). Johnson and Riffle (1982) found significant differences for both right and left ears (with only small average inter-ear asymmetry) for men, but no significant differences for women; they believed this was because most of the women fired only .22 caliber weapons, while

90 percent of the men used larger guns. The effects of gunfire were about the same in groups with exposures ranging from below 75 to above 84 dBA; in all groups, these effects were equivalent to a 20-year occupational exposure at 89 dBA. Updike and Kramer (1990) found gun club members' hearing *much* worse than expected; the effects were approximately equivalent to 40 years of occupational exposure at 95 dBA.

Prosser, Tartari, and Arslan (1988) found hunters had worse hearing only in their left ears, compared to nonhunting coworkers. Although this study was weakened by highly variable and undocumented occupational exposures, Prosser, Tartari, and Arslan could show that hearing asymmetries were (as expected) related to the *amount* of gunfire experienced: Below 2,000 shots, most workers had symmetrical hearing at 4 kHz; above 2,000 shots, most had asymmetrical hearing. Chung et al. (1981) also showed a correlation of asymmetry with total exposure, measured in years of hunting, but took the indefensible position that shooting could *only* cause unilateral NIHL (left ear in right-shouldered shooters). It would be convenient if this were true: One could then separate an individual's NIHL into occupational and hunting-related components by simply subtracting right ear from left ear thresholds. Most studies, though, suggest that both ears are involved (e.g., Taylor and Williams, 1966; Updike and Kramer, 1990; Clark, 1991). In the medical-legal setting, asymmetry argues in favor of a contribution of gunfire to an individual's NIHL, and lack of asymmetry argues against such a contribution, but neither of these is absolute. Job et al. (1998) found that even left-handed shooters had more loss in their left ears than in their right ears, suggesting an innately greater susceptibility for left ears.

Some authors (e.g., Keim, 1969; Ylikoski, 1989) have reported maximum NIPTS at 6 kHz in shooters, in contrast to the 4 kHz notch usually seen with occupational NIHL. However, other authors have found no audiometric differences (e.g., Gupta and Vishwakarma, 1989; Ward, Fleer, and Glorig, 1961).

Shooting is clearly the most important nonoccupational cause of NIHL (or of acoustic trauma). While many other nonoccupational sounds are intense enough to cause NIHL, *durations* of exposure are usually too brief to be hazardous. In fact, with the exception of gunfire and other noises capable of causing acoustic trauma—for example, firecrackers—the only nonoccupational noise exposure that has been shown to cause permanent hearing loss is motorcycling. While the epidemiological data are insufficient to develop the type of dose-response curves that relate NIHL to occupational noise exposure (ISO-1999, 1990), it seems likely that for many workers in industry, hunting and target shooting are more important causes of hearing loss than their work environments. In the U.S. population as a whole, recreational shooting may be as important a cause of hearing loss as occupational noise exposure. Far more Americans shoot (42 million, according to the National Rifle Association; personal communication 1990) than work in noisy jobs (probably about 5–10 million, based on various estimates), and most occupational exposure is at levels below 90 dBA, the approximate equivalent risk level for the average recreational shooter (Johnson and Riffle, 1982). Kramer (1990) estimates that only 1 percent use personal hearing protective devices while hunting. Shooters interviewed at a sporting goods store had shot since age 14, on the average; 42% had noisy jobs as well (Stewart et al., 1998).

Military service exposes many people to firearm noise. Service in infantry, artillery, or armor is especially hazardous (Henselman et al., 1995; Eisen et al., 1991), but even basic training frequently results in hearing loss (Kiukaanniemi et al., 1992).

Loud Music

While symphony orchestras and big bands can be loud, it was not until rock 'n' roll emerged, after the invention of the electric guitar, that people began to worry about possible hearing loss from music. Clark (1991) comments that "attendees at rock concerts or noisy discotheques are routinely exposed to sound levels above 100 dBA." This may or may not be higher than it was 30 years ago: Rintelmarm and Borus (1968) found levels of 91 to 114 dB SPL (sound pressure level) at distances 11 to 60 feet from center stage when recording from "hard rock" bands (since spectra were dominated by energy below 1,000 Hz, A-weighted levels would probably have been about 5 dB less).

The Occupational Safety and Health Administration (OSHA) permits daily exposures of two hours at 100 dBA; obviously, musicians and fans alike exceed this exposure routinely. However, the OSHA criteria are intended to protect against NIHL over a 40-hour work week, 50 weeks a year, for 40 years. Single exposures of this type will cause substantial TTS, but no permanent threshold shift (Clark and Bohne, 1986); even the TTS may be less than expected because of the intermittency that characterizes musical exposures,

Rintelmann and Borus (1968) found typical NIHL in only one out of 42 rock musicians tested; they reported exposures to amplified music averaging 11 hours per week for 3 years. Many professional musicians exceed these exposures. Some have reported their hearing losses in the popular press, but there has been no well-documented study of the prevalence or severity of NIHL in rock musicians.

Very few music fans accumulate the *durations* of exposure necessary to be truly hazardous, and there are no convincing data that concert or discotheque exposure alone causes permanent NIHL (excluding musicians and others for whom the exposure is *occupational* and regular). However, there are probably isolated cases where very frequent loud music exposure adds substantially to exposures received on the job and in other nonoccupational pursuits (especially shooting) to cause NIHL.

Personal stereo systems, such as the Walkman, provide additional opportunities for hazardous noise exposure, producing as much as 110 to 120 dBA at maximum output. Clark (1991) reviewed several studies showing that most listeners chose volume levels producing less than 90 dBA, although some do choose levels above 100 dBA, and also listen for prolonged periods. Personal stereo systems are certainly capable of causing permanent NIHL, although they have not been shown to do so (Mostafapour et al., 1998). Skrainar et al. (1987) point out what is probably their greatest hazard: Some occupationally exposed workers use them to "drown out" factory noise, thereby increasing their overall exposure and risk of NIHL.

Loud music, whether experienced live or by earphones, is relatively unimportant as a cause of *nonoccupational* NIHL. Curiously, this good news is unwelcome to many people. Reporters love to write stories about a generation of young people with rock-ravaged ears, and parents love to seize on what they believe is self-destructive behavior by "kids nowadays" (even though many of these parents also grew up with rock music). There is no evidence that today's schoolchildren have poorer hearing than those of 30 years ago (e.g., Lundeen, 1991; Axelsson et al., 1994). While many adolescents have high-frequency hearing loss (Lipscomb, 1969), this affects mainly boys (Axelsson, Aniansson, and Costa, 1987) and is probably due primarily to recreational shooting.

Other Recreational Sources

Firecrackers and other fireworks can produce peak levels at the ear well in excess of 150 dB; thus they pose the same type of hazard as gunfire. Well-documented cases of permanent hearing loss from firecrackers have been reported by Ward and Glorig (1961) and Gupta and Vishwakarma (1989), among others. Some toy guns and horns can also produce hazardous impulse noise (Gjaevenes, 1966; McMillan and Kileny, 1994).

Appendix A lists typical sound levels for several noisy hobbies. As with loud music, very few people accumulate truly hazardous exposures. While leaf blowers (up to 110 dBA), chain saws (up to 115 dBA), and small-plane cockpits (up to 107 dBA) are all potentially hazardous, they are far more likely to cause NIHL in those who have occupational—that is, prolonged and regular—exposure than in the occasional user.

Motorcycles and snowmobiles (up to 110 dBA) may be significantly hazardous for real enthusiasts; in such cases, it is useful to determine the total miles or hours of experience. Motorcycle exposure is unusual; above 40 mph, wind noise predominates over engine noise, so that regardless of the type of motorcycle, levels under helmets range from about 90 dBA at 40 mph to 107 dBA at 80 mph (McCombe et al., 1994). Without helmets, levels are about 18 dB worse (Binnington et al., 1993). "Leisure riders" with an average of over 100,000 miles on motorcycles had worse hearing than expected, especially at 500 and 1,000 Hz (McCombe et al., 1995).

Household Appliances

Some garbage disposals can produce over 90 dBA, but with negligible duration and thus negligible risk. Most other appliances produce nonhazardous levels, with the exception of home stereo systems (loud music has already been discussed).

As mentioned in Chapter 7, early models of cordless telephones were capable of delivering a ringing tone to the ear at about 140 dB SPL, causing instant and permanent hearing loss in at least several dozen individuals (Orchik et al., 1987).

With these exceptions, household appliances do not appear to pose a significant risk to hearing.

Transportation

Subway passengers are exposed to varying levels above 80 dBA, with occasional brake screeches above 110 dBA. A worker with hazardous occupational noise exposure can substantially increase the risk of NIHL by adding an hour or two of subway noise to on-the-job exposure. Bus and private car noise levels are usually much lower, assuming personal and vehicular stereo systems are not in use (some "boom cars" can reproduce music at over 140 dB SPL, according to Suter, 1992).

Airplane cabin noise levels are typically in the 75 to 85 dBA range throughout the flight, enough to require increased vocal effort or even shouting at a normal conversational distance, but not significantly hazardous for passengers.

Residents of neighborhoods near the runways of major airports often find takeoff and landing noise annoying and disruptive of sleep and concentration. However, there is little basis for concern regarding risk of NIHL from these exposures; although peak levels can be up to 115 dBA outside and above 90 dBA inside, they are brief and intermittent, rarely exceeding 20 seconds above 80 dBA per 3 minutes. Ward, Cushing, and Burns (1976) showed that six hours of exposure to a "worst-case" simulation of *outdoors* exposure (111 dBA peaks, 40 takeoffs/landings per hour) produced negligible TTS, far less than would have been predicted by the "equal-energy rule" or even by a 5-dB trading ratio (see Chapter 7).

REGULATION

Prior to the 1960s, many communities had regulations restricting excessively noisy activities, but these were generally vague and erratically enforced. Around 1970, several states passed more specific laws limiting noise emissions from various sources, for example, heavy trucks. In 1968, Congress directed the Federal Aviation Administration to devise regulations for airport noise, and in 1972, the Noise Control Act was passed, directing the Environmental Protection Agency (EPA) to embark on an ambitious program regulating nonoccupational noise exposure. This history has been extensively reviewed by Shapiro (1991).

The Office of Noise Abatement and Control (ONAC) within EPA was charged with several tasks:

1. Regulate noise emissions of products in interstate commerce.
2. Require informative labeling of products that emit or attenuate noise.
3. Coordinate noise-control activities of all federal agencies, including mandated purchase of quieter products when economically feasible.
4. Sponsor research and disseminate information to the public, as well as to states and municipalities, regarding noise hazards and control.

During its decade of bureaucratic life, ONAC produced a report setting a goal of exposures no more than the equivalent of 75 dBA per eight-hour day to protect against NIHL and no more than 55 dBA to prevent interference with various activities. ONAC also identified several noisy products felt to contribute in major ways to negative effects on public health and welfare:

1. Air compressors
2. Motorcycles
3. Trucks
4. Truck-mounted waste compactors
5. Buses
6. Tractors
7. Pavement breakers
8. Power lawn mowers
9. Rock drills
10. Truck-mounted refrigeration units

Emissions standards were actually promulgated for the first four products on this list, although the garbage truck standard was later withdrawn and the other three are not subject to any ongoing federal enforcement activity.

ONAC did promulgate a standard for the uniform labeling of personal hearing protective devices, for example, earplugs and earmuffs, requiring that each such device be given a "noise reduction rating" (NRR), the number of dB of attenuation of noise to be expected with proper use (see Chapter 9). Although NRRs routinely overstate "real world" attenuation, manufacturers continue to use this method of labeling. No standards for labeling of noise-emitting products were imposed.

In 1981, the Office of Management and Budget terminated ONAC's funding, and Congress acquiesced. Oddly, EPA remains responsible for enforcing the regulations promulgated by ONAC prior to its demise, but without staff or funding to do so.

State and local governments' efforts in environmental (nonoccupational) noise abatement also dwindled during the 1980s, partly because of the lack of leadership from the now-defunct ONAC (Shapiro, 1991), and perhaps partly because of the antiregulatory tenor of the times. Civil suits remain an option that has not been widely used. However, a recent rash of "third-party" suits by workers against the manufacturers of the noisy equipment they used in their jobs (not against employers, who are protected from suit by state workers' compensation laws) suggests that similar strategies could be used by consumers who have been damaged by non-occupational use of noisy equipment (especially guns).

REFERENCES

Axelsson, A., G. Aniansson, and O. Costa. 1987. Hearing loss in school children: A longitudinal study of sensorineural hearing impairment. *Scand. Audiol.* 16(3):137–143.

Axelsson, A., U. Rosenhall, and G. Zachau. 1994. Hearing in 18-year-old Swedish males. *Scand. Audiol.* 23:129–134.

Binnington, J., A. McCombe, and M. Harris. 1993. Warning signal detection and the acoustic environment of the motorcyclist. *Br. J. Audiol.* 27:415–422.

Chung, David Y., R. Patrick Gannon, Glenn N. Willson, and Keith Mason. 1981. Shooting, sensorineural hearing loss, and workers' compensation. *J. Occup. Med.* 23(7):481–484.

Clark, William W. 1991. Noise exposure from leisure activities: A review. *J. Acoust. Soc. Am.* 90(1):175–181.

Clark, William W. and Barbara A. Bohne. 1986. Temporary hearing losses following attendance at a rock concert. *J. Acoust. Soc. Am. Suppl.* 79(1):S48–S49.

Eisen, S. A., J. Goldberg, W. R. True, and W. G. Henderson. 1991. A co-twin control study of the effects of the Vietnam War on the self-reported physical health of veterans. *Am. J. Epidemiol.* 134:49–58.

Gjaevenes, Kjell. 1966. Measurements on the impulsive noise from crackers and toy firearms. *J. Acoust. Soc. Am.* 39(2):403–404.

Glorig, Aram and James Nixon. 1962. Hearing loss as a function of age. *Laryngoscope* 72(11):1596–1610.

Gupta, Deepak and S. K. Vishwakarma. 1989. Toy weapons and firecrackers: A source of hearing loss. *Laryngoscope* 99(3):330–334.

Henselman, L. W., D. Henderson, and J. Shadoan. 1995. Effects of noise exposure, race, and years of service on hearing in U.S. Army soldiers. *Ear & Hearing* 16:382–391.

International Organization for Standardization. 1990. *Acoustics: Determination of Occupational Noise Exposure and Estimation of Noise-Induced Hearing Impairment, ISO-1999.* Geneva: International Organization for Standardization.

Job, A., P. Grateau, and J. Picard. 1998. Intrinsic differences in hearing performances between ears revealed by the asymmetrical shooting posture in the army. *Hearing Res.* 122:119–124.

Johnson, Daniel L. and Carol Riffle. 1982. Effects of gunfire on hearing level for selected individuals of the Inter-Industry Noise Study. *J. Acoust. Soc. Am.* 72(4):1311–1314.

Keim, Robert J. 1969. Sensorineural hearing loss associated with firearms. *Arch. Otolaryngol.* 90(11):581–584.

Kiukaanniemi, H., H. Lopponen, and M. Sorri. 1992. Noise-induced low- and high-frequency hearing losses in Finnish conscripts. *Military Medicine.* 157:480–482.

Kramer, W. L. 1990. Gunfire noise and its effect on hearing. *Hearing Instruments* 41(10):26–28.

Lindgren, Fredrik and Alf Axelsson. 1983. Temporary threshold shift after exposure to noise and music of equal energy. *Ear & Hearing* 4(4):197–201.

Lipscomb, David M. 1969. Ear damage from exposure to rock and roll music. *Arch. Otolaryngol.* 90(5):545–555.

Lundeen, Conrad. 1991. Prevalence of hearing impairment among school children. *LSHSS* 22(1):269–271.

McCombe, A., J. Binnington, and D. Nash. 1994. Two solutions to the problem of noise exposure for motorcyclists. *Occup. Med.* 44:239–242.

McCombe, A., J. Binnington, A. Davis, and H. Spencer. 1995. Hearing loss and motorcyclists. *J. Laryngol. Otol.* 109:599–604.

McMillan, P. and P. Kileny. 1994. Hearing loss from a bicycle horn. *J. Am. Acad. Audiol.* 5:7–9.

Mostafapour, S., M. Lahargoue, and G. Gates. 1998. Noise-induced hearing loss in young adults: The role of personal listening devices and other sources of leisure noise. *Laryngoscope.* 108:1832–1839.

Nondahl, D. M., K. J. Cruickshanks, T. L. Wiley, R. Klein, B. E. Klein, and T. S. Tweed. 2000. Recreational firearm use and hearing loss. *Arch. Fam. Med.* 9:352–357.

Odess, John S. 1972. Acoustic trauma of sportsman hunter due to gun firing. *Laryngoscope* 82(11):1971–1989.

Orchik, Daniel J., Daniel R. Schmaier, John J. Shea Jr., John R. Emmett, William H. Moretz Jr., and John J. Shea III. 1987. Sensorineural hearing loss in cordless telephone injury. *Otolaryngol. Head Neck Surg.* 96(1):30–33.

Phaneuf, Richard and Raymond Hetu. 1990. An epidemiological perspective of the causes of hearing loss among industrial workers. *J. Otolaryngol.* 19(1):31–40.

Prosser, S., M. C. Tartari, and E. Arslan. 1988. Hearing loss in sports hunters exposed to occupational noise. *Br. J. Audiol.* 22(2):85–91.

Rintelmann, William F. and Judith F. Borus. 1968. Noise-induced hearing loss and rock and roll music. *Arch. Otolaryngol.* 88(4):377–385.

Schori, Thomas R. and Edward A. McGatha. 1978. A real-world assessment of noise exposure. *Sound and Vibration* 12(9):24–30.

Shapiro, Sidney A. 1991. *Administrative Conference of the United States: The Dormant Noise Control Act and Options to Abate Noise Pollution.*

Skrainar, Stephen F., Larry H. Royster, E. H. Berger, and Richard G. Pearson. 1987. The contribution of personal radios to the noise exposure of employees at one industrial facility. *Am. Ind. Hyg. Assoc. J.* 48(4):390–395.

Stewart, M., L. M. Ball, and T. H. Simpson. 1998. *Shooting habits and demographic risk patterns for recreational firearm users.* Presented to National Hearing Conservation Association, Albuquerque, NM, Feb. 21, 1998.

Suter, Alice H. 1992. Noise sources and effects: A new look. *Sound and Vibration* 26(1):18–34.

Taylor, G. Dekle and Everett Williams. 1966. Acoustic trauma in the sports hunter. *Laryngoscope* 76(5):863–879.

Updike, Claudia D. and William L. Kramer. 1990. Hearing loss in recreational shooters. *Hearing J.* 43(1):22–24.

Ward, W. Dixon, E. Marion Cushing, and Edward M. Burns. 1976. TTS from neighborhood aircraft noise. *J. Acoust. Soc. Am.* 60(1):182–185.

Ward, W. Dixon, Robert E. Fleer, and Aram Glorig. 1961. Characteristics of hearing losses produced by gunfire and by steady noise. *J. Aud. Res.* 1:325–356.

Ward, W. Dixon and Aram Glorig. 1961. A case of firecracker-induced hearing loss. *Laryngoscope* 71(12):1590–1596.

Ylikoski, J. 1989. Acute acoustic trauma in Finnish conscripts: Etiological factors and characteristics of hearing impairment. *Scand. Audiol.* 18(3):161–165.

Chapter 9

Hearing Conservation

Howard K. Pelton

INTRODUCTION

Noise is one of the most pervasive occupational health problems. It is a by-product of many industrial processes. Exposure to high levels of noise causes temporary and permanent hearing loss and may cause other harmful health effects as well. The extent of damage depends primarily on the intensity of the noise and the duration of the exposure. (OSHA, 1981)

This is the opening paragraph of the preamble to the Occupational Safety and Health Administration (OSHA) Noise Standard. Noise-induced hearing loss (NIHL) occurs not only in the workplace, but also in many recreational activities, for example, when using guns, snowmobiles, and motorcycles; and from noisy equipment found around the house, for example, power saws and small-engine driven equipment. This chapter will provide a basis for understanding the hearing conservation process and the role of noise control in effective hearing conservation programs (HCPs).

History of Federal and State Regulations

There has been an awareness of the connection between noise and hearing loss for a long time. Suter (1986) cites cases of gunfire noise causing hearing loss aboard ship in the late 1800s, as well as hearing loss caused by blacksmithing. The advent of the Industrial Revolution brought more machinery and equipment that made noise. An example is the steam engine, used for primary power. In addition, the construction of the steam engine's boiler required riveting which was indeed quite loud; most people have heard the expression "boilermaker's ears."

Soon after World War I, histological studies were done on animal and human organs of Corti to determine the effect of noise (Guild, 1919). However, it was not until World War II that NIHL (mostly military-related) was recognized as a serious problem and a serious effort was made by medical researchers to study the connection between hearing loss and noise exposure (Gasaway, 1985).

One of the earliest HCPs was developed by the Air Force in 1948, with the other branches of service following by 1950. During the 1950s and into the 1960s, it was recognized, documented, and defined by scientific studies that hearing loss was caused by excessive exposure to high levels of noise and that comprehensive HCPs were required to reduce the impact of hearing loss.

Until World War II, the workers' compensation statutes in various states did not cover hearing loss since it was not considered an accident and did not result in lost wages (AMIA, 1964). This all changed in 1948 when the New York Court of Appeals awarded a claim to an employee for NIHL that did not result in a loss in wages. From 1948 to 1959, Wisconsin, Missouri, Maryland, and Georgia all awarded hearing loss claims under workers' compensation. The other precedent-setting case was under the United States Longshoremen's and Harbor Worker's Compensation Act, in which the court ordered an insurance company to pay for NIHL (AMIA, 1964).

In 1971, North Carolina passed an advanced law for hearing loss compensation that had advantages for both management and labor. It was considered a model law at the time (Sataloff and Michael, 1973), defining "harmful noise" and "occupational loss of hearing." There would be no compensation payments for temporary hearing loss, tinnitus, or psychogenic hearing loss. The company was only liable for the loss occurring during employment at that particular company. A claim period was provided, as well as a statute of limitations, after exposure to harmful noise. Further, the use of employer-furnished hearing protectors constituted removal from harmful noise; if the employee did not use the hearing protectors, compensation would be denied.

By 1977, all states except two compensated workers for all occupational diseases, including NIHL. Following an OSHA Commission on State Workers' Compensation Acts, all states have now modified their workers' compensation laws to include NIHL or acoustic trauma (Cudworth, 1991).

The hearing loss cases brought from 1948 to 1959 influenced the development of hearing conservation, as did research that investigated the relationship between hearing loss, noise level, frequency content, and duration of the noise. Studies by Kryter, Baughn, Rosenblith and Stevens; Burns and Robinson; and Passchier-Vermeer produced a body of evidence that had a considerable influence on the government and consensus on noise standards in the United States and overseas. Even with this evidence, few employers had established any type of HCP; one notable exception was DuPont, which set up a program in 1956 (Suter, 1986). The companies served by Employers Mutual Liability Insurance Company of Wausau were required to implement HCPs as a condition of insurance coverage in the 1950s and 1960s (Suter, 1986).

In 1969, the U.S. government published the first noise regulations, incorporated in the Department of Labor's (DOL) Walsh-Healy Public Contracts Act. This regulation applied to companies that had contracts with the government of over $10,000 and set a permissible exposure level (PEL) of 90 dBA for an eight-hour work shift. If the duration was halved, the allowed noise exposure was 95 dBA. Thus, for every halving of time the noise exposure was allowed to be increased by 5 dBA up to a limit of 115 dBA. There was a ceiling on peak sound pressure level of 140 dB. If the levels were exceeded, personal hearing protection devices (PHPDs) were to be provided or the noise reduced by feasible engineering controls. The standard also included language about providing "continuing effective hearing conservation programs" (Sataloff and Michael, 1973).

The Walsh-Healy Act (DOL, 1969) became applicable to all industries with enactment of the Occupational Safety and Health (OSH) Act in 1970 (OSHA, 1970). Detailed hearing conservation program requirements were added in 1983 (OSHA, 1983) after a very long process of hearings and studies. The final rules issued in 1983 amended the regulation to set the "action level" for implementation of this program at 85 dBA time-weighted average (TWA; see Chapter 2), while leaving the PEL at 90 dBA-TWA.

Engineering controls remain in the current regulation; however, through OSHA's administrative process (at least through the late 1980s and 1990s), there is usually no citation issued for failure to implement engineering controls unless the noise exposure (not level) is over 100 dBA-TWA.

The hearings that OSHA conducted prior to issuing the final Hearing Conservation Amendment in 1983 brought together all of the best thinking in the area of hearing conservation. A summary of these hearings (OSHA, 1981) provides the evidence for the need for hearing conservation programs in industry to protect the noise-exposed population. Table 9–1 shows the percent excess risk for "material impairment" (compared to what would be expected from aging alone) at various levels of noise for over 40 years, as estimated by three different agencies. Material impairment was defined as average threshold exceeding 25 dB hearing level (HL) at frequencies of 0.5, 1, and 2 kHz. At 90 dBA, the estimated excess risk of material impairment was 21 to 29 percent which OSHA thought was substantial. The risk of material impairment for 85 dBA for 40 years was 10 to 15 percent (OSHA, 1981). Estimates based on more recent standards (ISO-1999 and ANSI S3.44-1996) yield excess risk values of less than 1 percent for 80 dBA, 3 percent for 85 dBA, and 8–11 percent for 90 dBA (see Chapter 11).

The hearings also presented data about the economic feasibility of controlling noise to 85 dBA and 90 dBA. These noise-control studies found that

TABLE 9–1
Percentage Risk of Impairment

Organization	Noise Exposure (dBA)	Excess Risk (%)
ISO	90	21
	85	10
	80	0
EPA	90	22
	85	12
	80	5
NIOSH	90	29
	85	15
	80	3

Source: OSHA, 1981.

there were no feasible engineering controls to reduce some noise sources, and that the cost to reach 85 dBA for some industries would be prohibitive. However, even a modest reduction in noise levels can be helpful. For example, if the noise exposure levels could be reduced to the 90 to 95 dBA-TWA range, then hearing protectors would be more effective at reducing noise at the ear canal below hazardous levels.

The 1983 OSHA Hearing Conservation Amendment covers most noise-exposed American workers, but there are several exceptions. Miners and some railroad workers are covered by different federal agencies, while construction, agricultural, and oil and gas workers are not covered by any detailed federal hearing conservation regulations.

ELEMENTS OF A HEARING CONSERVATION PROGRAM

Measurement of Noise Exposure

There may be several reasons why a noise hazard or exposure study is required. Some are as follows:

- Estimate the potential noise hazard
- OSHA regulation or investigation
- Data required for a hearing conservation program
- Workers' compensation for hearing loss
- Hearing loss litigation
- Safety program
- Individual employee request

In order to define which individuals or job classifications must be included in the hearing conservation program, an evaluation of the noise exposure must be carried out. The OSHA Noise Exposure Regulation (CFR 1910.95) gives a very simple equation to calculate the mixed exposure values, or Noise Dose, as follows:

$$Percent\ Dose \quad = \quad 100 \left\{ \frac{C_1}{T_1} + \frac{C_2}{T_2} + \cdots \frac{C_n}{T_n} \right\}$$

where

C_n = Total time of exposure at specified noise level

T_n = Total time of exposure permitted at that level.

Table 9–2 (OSHA, 1983) shows a portion of Table G–16a from the OSHA standard. This specifies the permissible noise exposures for the specified amounts of time.

It is well known that most industrial noise is not steady, and that employees are constantly moving about, being exposed to a variety of noise levels. Use of the above equations is not very practical to determine the employee noise exposure, allowable Noise Dose, or TWA over an 8- 10-, or 12-hour work shift. In order to conduct this type of evaluation, a noise dosimeter is placed on the employee for the entire work shift. This electronic instrument samples the noise several times a second and stores the result. At the end of the day, the data can be retrieved and the exposure automatically calculated along with other statistical data that can assist in evaluating which noise sources influence the exposure.

TABLE 9–2
OSHA Noise Standard Permissible Noise Exposure

Duration per Day (hours)	Sound Level dBA Slow Response
32	80
16	85
8	90
6	92
4	95
3	97
2	100
1.5	102
1	105
0.5	110
0.25 or less	115

Source: OSHA, 1983.

The following equation can be used to calculate the eight-hour TWA from the Dose:

$$TWA = 16.61 \, log_{10} \left(\frac{D}{100}\right) + 90 \, dBA$$

where

D = Dose

Table 9–3 (OSHA, 1983) shows a tabulation of this equation. Table A–1 in the standard provides the equivalent TWA for measured dosages from 10 to 99 percent noise exposure.

Several references (Gasaway, 1985; Royster, Berger, and Royster, 1986; Royster and Royster, 1990) provide detailed procedures for conducting a noise dosimetry survey. In particular, Royster, Berger, and Royster (1986) provides a detailed plan for conducting and documenting the data for evaluation. The six basic steps are as follows:

1. Define the purpose of the survey.
2. Walk through and alert employees to be surveyed.
3. Calibrate all the dosimeters and place on employees.
4. Monitor the employees' movements and take sound-level measurements in case the dosimeter fails.
5. Retrieve the dosimeters and print out the data.
6. Recalibrate the dosimeters as a final check.

The great advantage of dosimeters over sound level meters is that they automatically include all of an individual's exposures over a single measurement period. There are pitfalls as well (Earshen, 1986; Royster et al., 1986). A dosimeter attached to a jacket that is left in an employee's locker will fail to record actual exposure. A jacket placed over a dosimeter may produce a rubbing noise far in excess of actual exposure. Inadvertent or deliberate shouting into or tapping the dosimeter can produce readings of 140 dB or

TABLE 9–3
Conversion from "Percent Noise Exposure" or "Dose" to Time-Weighted Average Sound Level

% Noise Exposure	TWA (dBA)	% Noise Exposure	TWA (dBA)	% Noise Exposure	TWA (dBA)
10	73.4	200	95.0	700	104.0
50	85.0	300	97.9	800	105.0
70	87.4	400	100.0	900	105.8
90	89.2	500	101.6	999	106.6
100	90.0	600	102.9		

Source: OSHA, 1983.

more. Microphone placement variations can cause 5–7 dBA errors. Even if all these pitfalls are avoided, dosimeters tend to produce TWA levels that are 2–3 dB higher than those taken from sound level meters, both because of reflections from the worker's head and body, and because dosimeters more faithfully capture brief periods of high-intensity noise. Overall, however, they do provide efficiencies in gathering more data than can be obtained with a sound level meter. It is important to understand that several TWAs may be required for reliability.

In addition to the noise monitoring using dosimeters, it is important to conduct a sound level survey at the employee's work station or in the general area. The purpose of this is to determine if there are levels over 85 dBA and how these noise sources might influence the TWAs that are being monitored with the dosimeter. Also, some description of the type of noise source should be recorded, such as steady, fluctuating, transient, or impulsive.

The result of the survey should present visualization of the noise environment. The survey should be done in specific areas of the plant, at the operator's work station, at individual pieces of equipment if the employee is a mobile operator as in a process plant, and at plant column lines. This can help define the hazardous noise areas above 90 dBA, and high noise areas between 85 and 90 dBA where PHPDs may be required. Figure 9–1 illustrates this type of presentation. To provide the visual image over the area, a noise contour map can be drawn from this data, shown in Figure 9–2 (Pelton, 1992). It should be remembered that all of these represent approximations of the noise levels; they should be used as general guidelines for hearing conservation programs.

Another type of visualization is to locate the employees who have confirmed significant threshold shifts (STS) on a plant layout. This will provide the following benefits:

1. Allow some correlation with noise sources.
2. Assist in monitoring changes in hearing.
3. Determine if the HCP needs tightening up or if engineering controls should be installed to lower the level.
4. Monitor the effectiveness of the PHPDs.

The monitoring of employee noise exposures should be done on an annual basis as part of the HCP. In addition, monitoring is required if there is a change in production, processes, or equipment modifications. Any of these could change noise exposure. The employees should be properly notified and allowed to observe the monitoring (OSHA, 1983).

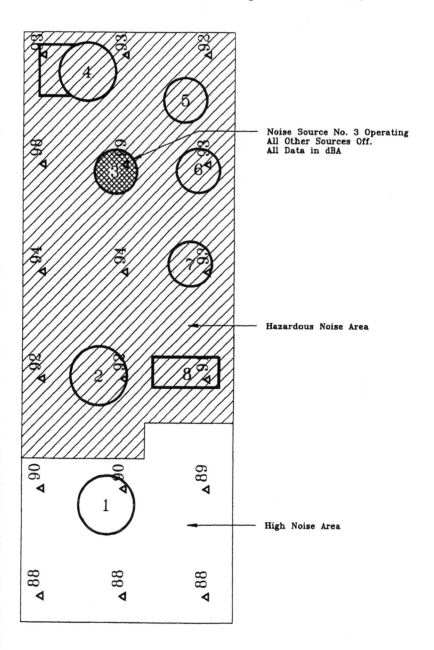

Figure 9–1. High- and hazardous-noise areas.

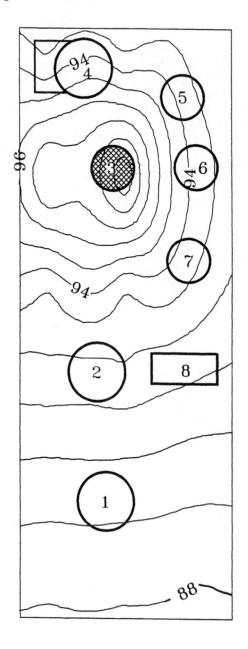

Figure 9–2.   Noise contours.

Reduction of Noise Exposure

Engineering (Source-Path-Receiver)

Any noise control problem can be divided into three parts: *SOURCE-PATH-RECEIVER*. The first step is to determine which of these should be treated based on an engineering study. The following outline highlights examples of several different approaches to engineering controls for each of these three areas.

Noise Source

1. *Maintenance*—Replacement or adjustment of worn and loose or unbalanced parts of machines
2. *Substitution of machines*—Larger, slower machines instead of smaller, faster ones
3. *Substitution of processes*—Pressing instead of forging

Noise Path

1. Reduce noise by reducing its transmission through air by

    a. Barriers
    b. Silencers
    c. Enclosures for individual machines
    d. Acoustical absorbing materials
    e. Confining high-noise machines to insulated rooms

Noise Receiver

1. Isolate the operator in a personnel shelter or control room
2. Use hearing protection

Management should take into consideration the existing technology, economic factors, benefit, maintenance, production, and practicality when evaluating the design and implementation of engineering controls. Any project, whether new or as additions to existing facilities, should include noise control at the planning stage. Purchase orders should include noise specifications to obtain quiet equipment and systems. Vendors supplying machinery and equipment must be advised that specified low noise levels will be a factor in the selection process. Suppliers should be asked to provide information on the noise levels of their equipment. Noise control feasibility requires careful, objective analysis from a practical and economic standpoint.

Administrative Control

An employee's noise exposure can also be reduced through administrative measures:

1. Rearrange work schedules so employees will work a major portion of the shift at levels that will not overexpose them for the total shift.
2. Rotate employees and job scheduling to keep individual noise exposure within permissible time limits.
3. Rearrange production schedules to run portions of noisy jobs each day rather than all day to introduce intermittency.
4. Operate very noisy equipment at night when a minimum number of employees will be exposed.

While these controls will reduce noise exposure, they are not usually workable for a variety of reasons (cross-training, union rules, plant environment, etc.). In the past 20 years, the author has seen only two occasions when this really worked as it was designed.

Personal Hearing Protective Devices

OSHA requires that PHPDs be made available for employees exposed above the action level (TWA = 85 dBA). They are mandatory for all employees above 90 dBA-TWA and for those above 85 dBA-TWA who have experienced an STS. The employer may elect, as a matter of policy, to require PHPDs for all employees exposed to noise above the action level or whatever levels below that he deems suitable to protect the employees. PHPDs should also be required for workers exposed to high noise levels that have not yet been measured (e.g., temporary construction and maintenance projects).

PHPDs should be replaced when necessary and (within reason) at no direct cost to the employee. Employees should have available "a variety, two or more," (OSHA, 1974) of models of PHPDs when making their selection. However, the employees are not permitted to select the size of PHPD they desire. PHPDs must be properly fit by an appropriately trained individual (e.g., nurse, physician, or occupational hearing conservationist). Employees should be trained in the use and care of their PHPDs. For a hearing conservation program to be effective, workers should be supervised on the job to ensure that they continue to wear their PHPDs correctly.

It is management's responsibility to ensure that all areas requiring the use of PHPDs are properly designated with signs. The following wording is recommended: "HIGH NOISE AREA, HEARING PROTECTION REQUIRED." These signs are available from safety equipment suppliers and are usually black letters on a yellow background.

In an effective HCP, management will require that PHPDs not only be worn, but be worn properly. Management can set an example by wearing

PHPDs in designated areas even though they may not be overexposed during their short visits.

Most PHPD choices will be conventional earplugs or earmuffs. The National Hearing Conservation Association (NHCA) recommends that the key criterion for selection should be "a comfortable, noise-blocking seal which can consistently be maintained," but other important considerations are as follows:

Noise exposure

Noise reduction

Variations in noise level

User preference

Communication needs

Hearing ability

Other safety equipment

Physical limitations

Climate, other working conditions

Replacement, care, and use

Noise reduction (attenuation) should be sufficient to reduce effective exposures to 85 dBA-TWA or less. In 1979, the Environmental Protection Agency (EPA) published labeling requirements for PHPDs that are still in force, although they are increasingly viewed as inadequate. The EPA noise reduction rating (NRR) estimates the amount of attenuation achieved by 98 percent of subjects when the PHPD has been fitted in the laboratory by the experimenter; it grossly overstates the attenuation to be expected in real-world settings (Berger et al., 1996). OSHA recommends that NRRs should be divided by two to estimate real-world performance.

An NHCA task force, supported by almost all of the relevant professional organizations, has recommended to EPA that they adopt a new "subject-fit" (SF) method described in ANSI S12.6-1997, because attenuation values obtained by naive subjects fitting their own PHPDs correlate much better with real-world data than do those obtained with the old EPA method (Berger and Royster, 1996). The new NRR-SF can be used directly with A-weighted sound levels, whereas the old NRR is intended for use with C-weighted levels. A foam earplug whose old NRR was 29 dB has an NRR-SF of 16 dB, meaning that 84 percent of subjects who followed directions would be expected to experience A-weighted level reductions of 16 dB or more.

Berger (2000) points out that "avoidance of overprotection must also be a consideration, especially in marginal noise environments such as those less than or equal to 90 dBA." The secondary label proposed by NHCA would give the range of attenuation that two thirds of persons could expect; for the foam plug example, that range would be 16–30 dB. Thus, about 16 percent of users would get 30 dB or more attenuation, which could create problems hearing speech or other important sounds, especially for hearing-impaired persons or those working in highly variable noise levels. Solutions to the overprotection problem include selecting PHPDs with less attenuation (especially so-called "flat" attenuation devices that—unlike conventional plugs and muffs—attenuate all frequencies more or less equally), selecting muffs rather than plugs when easy removal in quieter settings is desired, and use of radio communication headsets. Hearing-impaired workers can sometimes safely use hearing aids under earmuffs, but this is a choice best left to an audiologist or physician.

Average attenuation for the foam plug mentioned above would be about 23 dB, based on the SF method, but even this overstates real-world average performance. Berger et al. (1996) showed that mean real-world octave-band attenuation for PHPDs in common use was 6–35 dB (always lowest for the 125 Hz band, never below 10 dB for 500 Hz and above). King et al. (1992) estimate real-world average attenuation of A-weighted levels to be 10 dB for premolded plugs, 15 dB for formable plugs, and 20 dB for muffs. Double protection (muffs over plugs) adds about 5 dB to the attenuation value of the higher-rated PHPD (NHCA, 1996). However, PHPDs must be worn regularly to obtain substantial benefit; in a constant-level environment, a PHPD worn only 50 percent of the shift can provide no more than 5 dB reduction in TWA exposure.

Neither NRR nor NRR-SF should be used to estimate protection from impulse noise. Ordinary earplugs are more protective against gunfire than predicted from their attenuation of steady-state noise (Patterson and Johnson, 1996). Perforated "nonlinear" earplugs (offering more opposition to very high levels of sound than to lower levels) are also effective against impulses, despite very low attenuation of steady-state noise (Dancer et al., 1992). Electronic PHPDs are particularly useful for people intermittently exposed to impulses or other high-level noise. These devices include an external microphone to pick up sound and deliver it to a speaker close to the ear (under the PHPD), as long as the sound level is below a cut-off level, typically about 85 dBA. Above that level, the electronic circuit works like an ordinary PHPD.

Electronic "noise cancellation" devices attempt to reduce the noise reaching the ear by introducing another noise of equal intensity but opposite polarity, that is, a positive pressure to cancel a negative pressure and vice versa. These devices offer practical levels of attenuation only for low frequencies, up to about 500 Hz, and are of little value in most HCPs. They have been useful in a few environments characterized by low-frequency noise and the need to communicate using headsets, such as general (private) aviation and military armored vehicles.

Education and Motivation

In today's work environment, employee training is an ongoing function, necessary just to keep up with new technology. The OSHA noise regulation requires hearing conservation training to be repeated annually as part of the HCP. This should also cover noisy off-job activities. Most people are subjected to high noise around the house from power tools, lawn mowers, and engine-powered grass trimmers, for example. They should be encouraged to take PHPDs home and use them there.

The minimum topics required for a training session are as follows:

1. The effects of noise on hearing
2. The purpose of PHPDs
3. The advantages, disadvantages, and attenuations of various types of PHPDs
4. Instructions on the selection, use, care, and fitting of PHPDs
5. The purpose of audiometric testing, and an explanation of the test procedure and results

Feedback from employees will keep them involved in all aspects of the HCP. They may have suggestions for improved engineering controls, maintenance procedures, or anything else that will be beneficial in reducing noise. The program must be short, tailored to employee needs, simple and without a lot of technical jargon, and motivating.

Failures in the HCP can often be traced to a lack of training. Many companies provide the required variety of PHPDs, but do little else, then wonder why threshold shifts occur when comparing serial audiograms. Management involvement in presentations sends a clear, strong message that this is an important issue (Gasaway, 1985). Lack of an effective and comprehensive program will result in hearing-loss compensation claims and perhaps litigation for hearing loss.

The supervisors are the first line of defense and must enforce the proper wearing of PHPDs. Walking through work areas to observe is effective, but supervisors and all others entering the area must wear PHPDs, too! This sends a clear message to the employees and is a continuing means of motivation.

Audiometry

Audiometry—the measurement of an individual's hearing thresholds (see Chapter 3)—is carried out in a quiet environment using an instrument that presents tones of decreasing level to determine the threshold of hearing at specified frequencies (0.5, 1, 2, 3, 4, and 6 kHz are required by OSHA). This test, given on an annual basis, tracks an individual's hearing level (HL) and provides a method of evaluating the HCP. Audiometry can be performed by a technician—preferably an occupational hearing conservationist certified by the Council on Accreditation in Occupational Hearing Conservation—or by an audiologist or physician.

If the average HL has changed by 10 dB or more at 2, 3, and 4 kHz in either ear from the baseline audiogram (age correction is optional), a standard threshold shift (STS) is said to occur, and action is required. The action might involve the individual, the HCP as a whole, and/or reports to the employee and government authorities.

The OSHA noise standard includes sections that discuss the following major points:

- Audiometric testing program
- Baseline audiogram
- Annual audiogram
- Evaluation of audiogram
- Follow-up procedures
- Revised baseline audiogram
- Standard threshold shifts
- Audiometric test requirements
- Audiometer calibration

Other references (Gasaway, 1985; Morrill, 1986; Royster and Royster, 1990) provide a variety of views on audiometry, evaluation of the data, and how it fits in the HCP.

Since the objective of the HCP is to prevent occupational hearing loss, the only mechanism available for measuring its success is to conduct annual audiograms and analyze the results. Analysis of this data provides several checks for HCP effectiveness:

1. Detecting work-related STSs in employees' hearing levels
2. Providing a record of an employee's hearing level on an annual basis
3. Strengthening the hearing protection program by identifying weaknesses such as inadequate PHPD use and/or ineffective education and training of employees
4. Identifying plant areas requiring an engineering noise control study
5. Evaluating the effectiveness of engineering noise control measures by measuring the hearing threshold of employees working near the treated equipment
6. Helping to provide justification for noise-control expenditures

The following are recommendations for periodic audiometric testing (more detailed information is found in the OSHA regulation):

1. All employees included in the HCP exposed to noise at or above 50 percent of the PEL should have a baseline audiometric test, against which future hearing tests will be compared for hearing conservation purposes.
2. All employees included in the HCP should have a periodic test at least annually after obtaining a baseline audiogram.
3. All employees should be away from the workplace noise for at least 14 hours prior to their baseline audiometric test. OSHA does not require either a 14-hour noise-free period or use of PHPDs prior to annual audiograms. Indeed, many authorities recommend that annual tests occur during the work shift, with no special precautions to reduce noise exposure, so that temporary threshold shifts can be detected. Thus, any suspected STS may require a retest after a quiet period.
4. The medical or audiological professional responsible for the supervision of the audiometric testing program determines the follow-up procedures necessary whenever an individual employee shows an STS.
5. When deemed practical, all employees included in the HCP should have an audiometric examination prior to leaving the company, if their last audiometric test preceded the departure date by more than six months.

Audiometric measurements should be made with an audiometer that conforms to the requirements for wide-range, pure tone, discrete frequency audiometers prescribed by the American National Standard Specification for Audiometers, ANSI S3.6-1989. If a pulsed tone audiometer is used, the "on" time of the tone should be at least 200 milliseconds. The instrument used should be either a manual audiometer or any other audiometer testing system of equal or greater accuracy and effectiveness.

Audiometer calibration should be checked acoustically at least annually by a properly trained and equipped individual. The local representative for the audiometer manufacturer can provide this calibration service.

A biological calibration should be made prior to each day's use of the audiometer:

1. Testing at least one person having a known stable audiometric curve that does not exceed 10 dB hearing threshold level at any frequency and comparing the test results with the known curve;
2. Registering the subject's response to distortions and/or unwanted sounds from the audiometer.

If the audiometer does not pass the biological calibration (whenever the results of the "daily use" biological calibration indicate hearing level differences greater than ± 5 dB at any frequency), it should be removed from service and sent out for an acoustical calibration prior to further testing. Other problems include signal distortion and attenuator or tone switch transients (e.g., clicks, noises, hums). Only after the problem with the audiometer is corrected to within permitted tolerances can it be put back into service.

The area designated for audiometric testing must meet the ambient noise criteria required by the OSHA regulation. The sound pressure level in any octave band when measured in the audiometric booth, or test room where subjects are actually tested, should not exceed the values in Table 9–4.

Audiometer calibration records and background noise levels in test booths or rooms should be maintained with the audiometric test results. When contract services are used, these records must be provided by them and kept on file.

Notification and Counseling

Any opportunity to motivate employees in relation to the HCP cannot be overlooked. For example, audiometric database analysis might point to ineffective wearing of PHPDs. Personal counseling sessions should be conducted for those identified employees. This can be done after the training sessions to insure that this subject is brought to the attention of the employee on a regular basis. The effectiveness of the counseling session can be evaluated by the employee's supervisor on a daily basis.

This also provides a good opportunity to notify the employees of the results of the hearing tests as required by the standard. This can be done with a single memo provided by the medical department or the provider used to monitor the hearing levels.

Every opportunity must be used to remind employees of the importance of the HCP (Royster and Royster, 1990). This is especially true when the audiometric tests are given. Supplementary materials should be made available to read and take home in addition to the annual safety training. If the employee does not obtain the required information they feel is necessary they would be encouraged to go up the management chain until their concerns are addressed (Royster and Royster, 1990).

TABLE 9–4
Maximum Allowable Background Noise Levels in Audiometric Rooms

Octave Band Center Frequency (Hz)	Sound Pressure Level (dB SPL)[a]
500	40
1,000	40
2,000	47
4,000	57
8,000	62

[a] = re: 20 μPa.
Source: OSHA, 1983.

Referral

In any comprehensive HCP there will be a need to refer employees for further evaluation to outside otological and audiological clinics. This should be done when there is substantial loss or asymmetry on baseline testing, when large or repeated threshold shifts are seen on periodic audiometry, and when otologic symptoms such as vertigo or ear pain are noted (Dobie and Archer, 1981; Dobie, 1982). The referral criteria must be set by the professional supervisor of the HCP. A good set of referral criteria has been established by the American Academy of Otolaryngology–Head and Neck Surgery Foundation (AAO–HNS, 1983). Briefly, referral is recommended when there have been significant ear symptoms in the past year (such as vertigo or ear pain), or when certain audiometric findings are present:

1. Baseline hearing level in either ear, averaged over 0.5, 1, 2, and 3 kHz, exceeding 25 dB HL;
2. Baseline threshold asymmetry, averaged over 0.5, 1, and 2 kHz, exceeding 15 dB HL;
3. Baseline threshold asymmetry, averaged over 3, 4, and 6 kHz, exceeding 30 dB HL;
4. Shifts from baseline, averaged over 0.5, 1, and 2 kHz, exceeding 15 dB; or
5. Shifts from baseline, averaged over 3, 4 and 6 kHz, exceeding 20 dB.

Simpson et al. (1995) applied the audiometric criteria to data from several HCPs and estimated that good HCPs would experience about 7 percent baseline referrals and 1–2 percent annual referrals.

Some reasons for referral are as follows:

1. Determine cause(s) of observed hearing loss.
2. Determine why proper PHPD cannot be worn.
3. Seek medical and/or surgical treatment that affects the employee's ability to wear PHPD.
4. Obtain a professional opinion about the disposition of an employee who has an apparent problem that is getting worse.

Recordkeeping

Recordkeeping for the HCP requires the same diligence that is applied to payroll records, tax records, and so forth. When an OSHA inspection occurs, the only means of demonstrating that a comprehensive HCP is in place is to have the proper documentation. The OSHA regulation requires the following information:

1. Noise exposure measurements
2. Audiometric records

   a. Name and job classification
   b. Date of audiogram
   c. The examiner's name
   d. Date of last acoustic calibration
   e. Employee's most recent noise exposure assessment
   f. Accurate record of background sound pressure levels in audiometric test rooms

The record must be retained as follows:

1. Noise exposure records—2 years
2. Audiometric test records—duration of employee's employment

The records must be available upon request to employees, former employees, representatives designated by the individual employees, and the OSHA officials. If the employer ceases to do business, it must transfer all records required to be maintained to successor employers. An employee is well advised to take any records to the next employer when he leaves employment (OSHA, 1983). In some states, the current employer is only responsible for the hearing loss incurred while employed.

The following is a more detailed list of records and documentation that should be gathered and retained (Royster and Royster, 1990). The employer should tailor the amount and type of records to suit the need of the specific facility.

1. Noise exposure, survey measurements, noise maps of facility
2. Noise control engineering and/or administrative controls
3. Annual training and education programs
4. Hearing protection devices used, training, NRR calculation
5. Audiometric records
6. Technician training, audiometer, calibration data
7. Audiogram follow-up and review
8. Medical history related to the HCP
9. Pre- and postemployment audiogram

OSHA Log 200

As part of the recordkeeping requirement of the OSHA Act two forms are required to record injuries and illnesses. OSHA Form 200 serves two purposes:

1. As the Log of Occupational Injuries and Illnesses on which the occurrence, extent, and outcome of cases are recorded during the year
2. As the Summary of Occupational Injuries and Illnesses, which is used to summarize the log at the end of the year to satisfy the employer posting obligation

The other form, the Supplementary Record of Occupational Injuries and Illnesses, OSHA No. 101, provides additional information on each of the cases that have been recorded on the log (DOL, 1986).

Recording an injury or illness under the OSHA system does not necessarily mean the management or worker was at fault, that an OSHA violation occurred, or that an injury or illness is compensable under workers' compensation or another system. It is simply a means of reporting in a very specific manner. In addition, the OSHA Act provides a basic description of which cases are to be recorded (in 29 CFR Part 1904) that also expands on the definitions of recordability.

Under the OSHA Act all work-related illnesses must be recorded, while only injuries that require medical attention must be recorded. Injuries are defined as caused by instantaneous events in the work environment. Cases resulting from anything other than instantaneous events are considered illnesses. NIHL is thus defined as an occupational illness caused by repeated exposure to the work environment with the causal agent being excessive noise (DOL, 1986). The definition of what constitutes a *recordable* illness in relation to hearing loss has been the subject of some discussion since the standard was issued.

A shift in hearing level of $\geq$ 25 dB (averaged across 2, 3, and 4 kHz) should be recorded as an occupational illness (although, for the purposes of the standard, OSHA has not issued any recordability guidelines, current enforcement policy requires recording at this degree of threshold shift). There has been some effort to use the 10-dB STS as the criterion for recording NIHL on OSHA Form 200. Several professional organizations such as the American Industrial Hygiene Association (AIHA), American Speech-Language-Hearing Association, and NHCA have supported such a change (Driscoll and Morrill, 1987), arguing that relatively few recordable STSs would exist by incorporating proper procedures, that is, having an effective HCP. Thus, recordkeeping for OSHA Form 200 would be minimal. On the other hand, Sataloff et al. (1998) have shown that men who had annual audiometry but little or no noise exposure above 85 dBA had a high incidence of STS, presumably caused by aging. For example, one third of men aged 40–49 with 15–19 years of hearing tests had demonstrated STS. These rates would of course have been lower with age correction.

EFFICACY

ANSI Standard

An HCP can produce the required effects if properly administered. A method of making this determination is found in Draft ANSI S12.13-1991 standard *Evaluating the Effectiveness of Hearing Conservation Programs*. The efficacy of a program is determined by examining serial audiograms of the employees over a period of several years. This approach is referred to as audiometric database analysis (ADBA; ANSI S12.13, 1991). This is a cost-effective tool that management can use to determine the effectiveness of the program and help avoid OSHA citations.

The ADBA is a statistically based evaluation that operates on a population of workers in the facility. Comparison of the serial audiograms for several years can be evaluated against a criterion that will determine the efficacy of the program. This methodology uses the total variability in the employees' hearing threshold on a year-to-year basis.

Variability in hearing threshold comes from

1. Normal fluctuation in how the individual takes the audiometric test
2. Changes in true threshold caused by temporary or permanent hearing loss when inadequate hearing protection has been provided (Royster and Royster, 1990)
3. Background noise
4. Other factors (see Chapter 3)

If the variability is low (compared to values published in the standard) then the program is judged successful. If the variability is too high, then the HCP must be evaluated to determine the cause of the high variability, such as inadequate test procedures, and hearing loss. The two basic variability procedures recommended by the ANSI S12-13 Working Group are based on determining the percent of employees showing hearing level changes of 15 dB or more between sequential tests (Royster and Royster, 1990).

Critics have pointed out that both age (Arlinger and Ivarsson, 1999) and preexisting hearing loss (Simpson et al., 1998) affect the variability metrics in ANSI S12.13, and Simpson et al. (1994) argue that OSHA-defined STS, even without age correction, works as well as audiometric variability as an index of HCP performance.

Another standard that will be of assistance to the serious student of HCPs is International Standards Organization (ISO) 1999:1990(E), *Acoustics-Determination of Occupational Noise Exposure and Estimation of Noise-Induced Hearing Impairment*. This includes references for the past 20 years of development of the field of NIHL. This standard (and its American counterpart, ANSI S3.44-1996) are discussed in more detail in Chapters 6, 7, and 13.

ROLE IN HEARING LOSS CLAIMS

The noise levels and individual employee noise-exposure levels within a plant determine the need for an HCP. In the last few years, claims for hearing loss compensation have grown because of class action litigation brought against both employers and the companies that supplied the equipment installed in the plants alleged to have caused hearing loss. The best defense against future claims is to have a continuing and effective HCP that can be monitored for individual employee hearing loss. Conversely, the lack of an effective HCP, or records showing excessive hearing loss growth without appropriate action, can strongly support claimants in their case.

As the legal profession deals with more and more hearing-loss cases, it is beginning to rely on noise control engineers to interpret various types of noise data relevant to the case. These data can be pivotal in determining whether, and to what extent, occupational noise contributed to an individual's hearing loss (see Chapters 12–14).

The acoustical—or noise control—engineer must make accurate measurements that are appropriate to the case at hand. The necessary time must be spent working with attorneys to develop a verbal description that will allow individuals to vicariously experience the event and place it in proper and accurate perspective (Fann, 1990). It is important that the judge and jury have the most accurate and objective facts available to make their decision.

REFERENCES

[Several chapters from the American Industrial Hygiene Association's *Noise and Hearing Conservation Manual* (4th ed., 1986) are listed below. The 5th edition, retitled *The Noise Manual,* Elliott H. Berger, Larry H. Royster, Julia D. Royster, Dennis P. Driscoll, and Martha Layne (Eds.), 2000, AIHA, Fairfax, VA, has just been published and will be a valuable reference.]

American Academy of Otolaryngology–Head and Neck Surgery–Medical Aspects of Noise Subcommittee. 1983. *Otologic Referral Criteria for Occupational Hearing Conservation Programs.* Washington, DC: American Academy of Otolaryngology–Head and Neck Surgery Foundation, Inc.

American Mutual Insurance Alliance. 1964. *Background for Loss of Hearing Claims.* Chicago: American Mutual Insurance Alliance.

American National Standards Institute. 1989. *American National Standard Specification for Audiometers, ANSI S3.6-1989.* New York: Acoustical Society of America.

———. 1991. *Evaluating the Effectiveness of Hearing Conservation Programs, Draft ANSI S12.13-1991.* New York: Acoustical Society of America.

———. 1996. *American National Standard Determination of Occupational Noise Exposure and Estimation of Noise-Induced Hearing Impairment,* ANSI S3.44-1996. New York: Acoustical Society of America.

Arlinger, S. and U. Ivarsson. 1999. On quality assurance in occupational hearing conservation programs: An evaluation based on ANSI S12.13-1999. *Noise and Health* 2:73–77.

Berger, Elliott H., John R. Franks, and Fredrik Lindgren. 1996. International review of field studies of hearing protector attenuation. In *Scientific Basis of Noise Induced Hearing Loss,* ed. A. Axelsson, New York: Thieme.

Berger, Elliott H. 2000. *Hearing Protector Testing—Let's Get Real.* Ear Log #21. Indianapolis: Aearo Company.

Berger, Elliott H., and Larry H. Royster. 1996. In search of meaningful measures of hearing protector effectiveness. *Spectrum* (Suppl. #1) 13:29ff.

Cudworth, Allen L. 1991. Hearing loss: Legal liability. In *Handbook of Acoustical Measurements and Noise Control,* 3rd ed., ed. Cyril M. Harris, pp. 20.4–20.6. New York: McGraw-Hill.

Dancer, A., P. Grateau, and A. Cabanis. 1992. Effectiveness of earplugs in high-intensity impulse noise. *J. Acoust. Soc. Am.* 91(3):1677–1689.

Dobie, Robert A. 1982. Otologic referral criteria. *Otolaryngol. Head Neck Surg.* 90(5):598–601.

Dobie, Robert A. and Robert J. Archer. 1981. Otologic referral in industrial hearing conservation programs. *J. Occup. Med.* 23(11):755–761.

Driscoll, Dennis P. and Jeffrey C. Morrill. 1987. A position paper on a recommended criterion for recording occupational hearing loss on the OSHA Form 200, Noise Committee of the American Industrial Hygiene Association. *Am. Ind. Hyg. Assoc. J.* 48(11):A714–A716.

Earshen, John J. 1986. Sound measurement: Instrumentation and noise descriptors. In *Noise and Hearing Conservation Manual,* ed. Elliot H. Berger, W. Dixon Ward, Jeffrey C. Morrill, Larry H. Royster, Akron, OH: American Industrial Hygiene Association.

Fann, Michael, 1990. Cutting through the clutter. *Experts-at-Law* (Sept.–Oct.): 60–61.

Gasaway, Donald C. 1985. *Hearing Conservation.* Englewood Cliffs, NJ: Prentice Hall.

Guild, S. R. 1919. War deafness and its prevention: Report of the labyrinths of the animals used in testing of preventive measures. *J. Lab. Clin. Med.* 4:153–180.

International Organization for Standardization. 1990. *Acoustics: Determination of Occupational Noise Exposure and Estimation of Noise-Induced Hearing Impairment, ISO-1999.* Geneva: International Organization for Standardization.

King, P. F., R. R. A. Coles, M. E. Lutman, and D. W. Robinson. 1992. *Assessment of Hearing Disability: Guidelines for Medicolegal Practice.* London: Whurr Publishers.

Morrill, Jeffrey C. 1986. Hearing measurements. In *Noise and Hearing Conservation Manual,* ed. Elliott H. Berger, W. Dixon Ward, Jeffrey C. Morrill, and Larry H. Royster, pp. 233–292. Akron, OH: American Industrial Hygiene Association.

National Hearing Conservation Association. 1996. *Selecting Hearing Protection.* Milwaukee: NHCA.

Patterson, J. H. and D. L. Johnson. 1996. Protection of hearing against high-intensity impulse noise. *J. Acoust. Soc. Am.* 99(1):23.

Pelton, Howard. 1992. *Noise Control Management.* New York: Van Nostrand Reinhold.

Royster, Julia Doswell and Larry H. Royster. 1990. *Hearing Conservation Program.* Chelsea, MI: Lewis Publishers, Inc.

Royster, Larry H., Elliott H. Berger, and Julia Doswell Royster. 1986. *Noise survey and data analysis.* In *Noise and Hearing Conservation Manual,* ed. Elliott H. Berger, W. Dixon Ward, Jeffrey C. Morrill, and Larry H. Royster, pp. 100–111. Akron, OH: American Industrial Hygiene Association.

Sataloff, Joseph and Paul L. Michael. 1973. *Hearing Conservation.* Springfield, IL: Charles C. Thomas.

Sataloff, Joseph, R. T. Sataloff, H. Menduke, and J. Robb. 1998. Standard threshold shift in non-noise-exposed men. *J. Occup. Hear. Loss* 1(3):173–178.

Simpson, T. H., M. Steward, and J. A. Kaltenbach. 1994. Early indicators of hearing conservation program performance. *J. Am. Acad. Audiol.* 5:300–306.

Simpson, T. H., M. Stewart, and B. W. Blakley. 1995. Audiometric referral criteria for industrial hearing conservation programs. *Arch. Otolaryngol. Head Neck Surg.* 121:407–411.

Simpson, T. H., N. Amos, and W. F. Rintelmann. 1998. Effects of pre-existing hearing loss on proposed ANSI S12.13 outcomes for characterizing hearing conservation program effectiveness. *J. Am. Acad. Audiol.* 9(2):112–120.

Suter, Alice H. 1986. Hearing conservation. In *Noise and Hearing Conservation Manual,* ed. Elliott H. Berger, W. Dixon Ward, Jeffrey C. Morrill, and Larry H. Royster, pp. 1–18. Akron, OH: American Industrial Hygiene Association.

U.S. Department of Labor. 1969. Walsh-Healy Noise Regulation. *Federal Register* 34(May 20, 1969):7946–7949.

U.S. Department of Labor–Bureau of Labor Statistics. 1986. *Recordkeeping Guidelines for Occupational Injuries and Illnesses, O.M.B. No. 1220-0029* (Effective September 1986). Washington, DC: U.S. Government Printing Office.

U.S. Department of Labor–Occupational Safety and Health Administration. 1970. *The William Steiger Occupational Safety and Health Act of 1970.*

———. 1974. Occupational Noise Exposure: Proposed Requirements and Procedures. *Federal Register* 39(207; October 24, 1974):37773–37784.

———. 1981. Occupational Noise Exposure: Hearing Conservation Amendment. *Federal Register* 46(11; January 16, 1981):4078–4179.

———. 1983. Occupational Noise Exposure: Hearing Conservation Amendment; Final Rule. *Federal Register* 48(46):9738–9784.

Chapter 10

Other Otologic Disorders

Chapters 6, 7, and 8 have discussed hearing loss associated with aging and excessive noise exposure in some detail; these two factors account for more hearing loss (in adults) than all others put together. Of course, the ear is subject to many disorders, ranging from infections to tumors to intoxications, and it is impossible to give even an exhaustive *listing* of all of these in a single chapter. The intent here is rather to present a superficial outline of the types of causes of hearing loss, with discussion of the more common disorders in some detail, depending particularly on the level of medical-legal importance. As elsewhere in the book, there is a dual goal: nonotologist readers will acquire a better understanding of the types of disease processes that cause hearing loss, and will thus find otologic reports more useful; we hope otologists will find a useful collection of facts and analyses in controversial areas such as head and neck injury and ischemic hearing loss. Since many disorders cause both conductive and sensorineural hearing loss (see Chapter 3 if unfamiliar with these concepts), the chapter is organized into sections on *congenital* and *acquired* disorders, with conductive and sensorineural loss treated together. Chapter 7 discusses the interactions between noise-induced hearing loss (NIHL) and other disorders, including the protective effects of conductive losses.

CONGENITAL HEARING LOSS

A *congenital* hearing loss is present at birth; all other cases are acquired. A congenital disorder may be *hereditary*, that is, caused by an inherited genetic abnormality, or may be caused by some environmental agent acting prior to birth, for example, maternal rubella infection. Similarly, acquired hearing losses *can* be hereditary, if the inherited trait does not express itself until later in life.

About one child in one thousand is born deaf or with severe hearing loss (Martin, 1982); about 50–60 percent of these cases are hereditary (Marazita et al., 1993). However, this figure probably includes both congenital cases and cases acquired in infancy but without identifiable cause, because hearing loss is usually not identified before six months of age. For this reason, we will discuss some perinatal causes of hearing loss in this section, although they are really cases of early acquired hearing loss.

Hereditary

Ear anomalies can be inherited as isolated defects or in combination with other anomalies. The combination of hereditary hearing loss with other anomalies defines a *syndrome*. Most of us remember from biology class that the nucleus of every cell contains genes arranged in chromosomes, and that each person receives two copies of each gene, one from each parent (one exception: males receive only one X chromosome and also receive a Y chromosome). If a defective gene produces a harmful protein, the hereditary disorder will be *dominant:* If either copy is defective, the disorder will manifest itself, and the affected individual has a 50:50 chance to pass the defective gene to his or her offspring. If the defective gene produces no protein or an ineffective protein, the disorder is *recessive:* It will not be apparent unless both copies are defective, and all offspring of affected persons will carry the defective gene (but usually only one copy). These simple principles of Mendelian genetics apply to most types of hereditary hearing loss, although we will note in passing some complexities that are beyond the scope of this book. Most of our genes are in the cell nucleus, but a few of them are in the mitrochondria, tiny intracellular organelles that provide energy for the cell. Mitochondrial genes are inherited only from the mother.

Syndromic

Table 10–1 shows a few of the more common hereditary syndromic causes of hearing loss. Several different organ systems can be affected along with the ear. As a general rule, sensorineural losses are more often associated with recessive inheritance and conductive losses with dominant transmission. Many dominantly transmitted disorders have variable penetrance, that is, not all affected individuals have the same degree of hearing loss. Dominant sensorineural loss tends to be milder (but more likely to progress) than recessive sensorineural loss. Deafness has also been associated with chromosomal anomalies. For example, extra copies of chromosome numbers 13, 15, or 18 (so-called trisomy) cause multiple organ system anomalies, including deafness. Although these chromosome anomalies arise *in utero* and are not really inherited from the parents, they are mentioned here because they do represent alterations of genetic material.

TABLE 10–1
Selected Hereditary Hearing Loss Syndromes

Syndrome	Mode of Inheritance	Type of Hearing Loss	Other Involved Organ Systems
Pendred	Recessive	Sensorineural	Thyroid
Waardenburg	Dominant	Sensorineural	Skin, hair, iris
Usher	Recessive	Sensorineural	Retina
Jervell	Recessive	Sensorineural	Heart
Alport[a]	X-linked	Sensorineural	Kidney
Crouzon	Dominant	Conductive	Skull, face
Treacher-Collins	Dominant	Conductive	Face

[a]Delayed onset, i.e., acquired.

Nonsyndromic

Hereditary hearing loss without other anomalies is much more common than syndromic deafness (Bieber and Nance, 1979). Several different types have been identified and classified according to mode of inheritance, chromosomal locus, severity, natural history, and frequencies primarily involved. However, even the most common form, recessive congenital severe deafness, can be caused by abnormalities at any of several different genes; in other words, several different genetic disorders can give rise to identical clinical manifestations. It seems likely that advances in molecular genetics will eventually allow these disorders to be more precisely identified in the clinic, including carrier states, so that physicians can give more accurate genetic counseling to prospective parents.

Infections

Intrauterine infection with various viruses or other microorganisms can cause congenital deafness. *Rubella* (German measles) was formerly responsible for many cases of deafness, but is now less common, partly because of widespread immunization. *Cytomegalovirus* is now the most common infectious cause of congenital hearing loss and may account for as much as 12 percent of congenital deafness (Peckham et al., 1987). Other intrauterine infections occasionally associated with congenital hearing loss include toxoplasmosis, syphilis, and herpes virus.

Toxic

Certain drugs taken early in pregnancy can be teratogenic—prone to cause developmental anomalies. Thalidomide, the best-known of these before being removed from the market, caused mainly limb and gut anomalies. Ear anomalies resulting in conductive hearing loss were also frequent, especially when the drug was taken in the fourth week of pregnancy (Shepard, 1986). More recently, birth defects including ear, craniofacial, central nervous system, and heart were reported in association with isotretinoin (Accutane), an anti-acne product (Marwick, 1984). The 12 cases of ear anomalies (involving the external and middle ear) occurred in children whose mothers had taken the drug for varying periods of time (up to the eighteenth week of pregnancy), but always including the fourth week.

Shepard (1986) has listed definite, possible, and unlikely teratogens (Table 10–2). In general, these physical, chemical, and biological agents can cause developmental anomalies in different organ systems, depending on the timing of the exposure during embryonic and fetal life. However, there are agent-specific effects as well: Viruses are far more likely to cause inner ear than outer or middle ear anomalies, while the opposite is true for teratogenic drugs.

Ionizing radiation in excess of 10 to 20 rad during pregnancy is considered teratogenic, but microwave radiation is probably not teratogenic at dose levels below those ($30 \, mW/cm^2$) that cause heating of tissue, that is, far beyond normal home or occupational exposure. Ultrasound is commonly used for imaging during pregnancy and has raised concerns regarding possible ear damage, but no increases in anomalies or deafness have been documented. Noise and vibration have not been shown to be teratogenic (U.S. Congress—Office of Technology Assessment, 1985).

Most birth defects are *not* associated with an identifiable teratogenic agent. Congenital ear anomalies occur in about 5 of every 10,000 births in the United States (U.S. Dept. …Centers for Disease Control, 1982). Most of these are external ear anomalies without associated hearing loss. About 0.6 per 10,000 births result in an anomaly with hearing loss; unilateral ear canal atresia (a combined external and middle ear anomaly) is the most common.

Ammoglycoside antibiotics and other drugs that are toxic to the developed ear will be discussed later in this chapter; most of these cross the placenta easily and maternal use could therefore injure the fetal ear. Little is known about susceptibility to ototoxic drugs at different developmental stages, but it is obviously wise to avoid their use during pregnancy. Excessive accumulation of bilirubin can occur in infants who have immature liver function or who suffer from maternal-fetal blood group incompatibility which causes hemolysis (breakdown of blood cells). Elevated bilirubin levels can be toxic to the brain, causing multiple neurological problems; hearing loss usually reflects cochlear nucleus involvement (Volpe, 1987). This disorder, called *kernicterus*, is actually perinatal rather than congenital, but is mentioned here because it is often difficult to separate intrauterine events from those occurring in the first days of extrauterine life. Based on a large prospective study, Newman and Klebanoff (1993) state that elevated bilirubin levels pose little risk to full-term babies who do not have hemolysis.

TABLE 10–2
Teratogenic Agents in Human Beings

RADIATION	DRUGS AND ENVIRONMENTAL
Therapeutic	CHEMICALS
Radioiodine	Androgenic hormones
Atomic weapons	Aminopterin and methylaminopterin
	Cyclophosphamide
INFECTIONS	Busulfan
Rubella virus	Thalidomide
Cytomegalovirus	Mercury, organic
Herpes simplex virus I and II	Chlorobiphenyls, e.g., PCBs
Toxoplasmosis	Diethylstilbestrol
Venezuelan equine encephalitis	Diphenylhydantoin
virus	Trimethadione and paramethadione
Syphilis	Coumarin anticoagulatns
	Valproic acid
MATERNAL METABOLIC	Goitrogens and antithyroid drugs
IMBALANCE	Tetracyclines
Endemic cretinism	13-cis-retinoic acid (isotretinoin, Accutane)
Diabetes	Lithium
Phenylketonuria	Methimazole
Virilizing tumors and metabolic	
conditions	
Alcoholism	
Hyperthermia	
Rheumatic disease and	
congential heart block	

POSSIBLE TERATOGENS	UNLIKELY TERATOGENS
Cigarette smoking	Aspirin
Diazepam (Valium)	Birth control pills
Zinc deficiency	Ultrasound
High vitamin A	Spermicides
Varicella	Bendectin (antinauseant)
Binge drinking	Illicit drugs (marijuana, LSD, cocaine)
Organic solvents (laboratory	Videodisplay terminals
workers)	Aspartame
Penicillamine	Anesthetics
	Rubella vaccine
	Metronidazole
	Agent Orange

Neoplastic

Congenital tumors affecting the ear are quite rare. *Teratomas* and *dermoids* are not true neoplasms, but rather developmental errors in which normal tissues and organs grow in inappropriate anatomical locations. Either of these congenital tumors can occur (rarely) in proximity to the auricle, middle ear, or eustachian tube and cause hearing loss. However, there are invariably other signs and symptoms that lead to diagnosis.

Ischemic and Hypoxic

Inadequate blood flow (ischemia) or oxygenation (hypoxia) can injure any organ; the inner ear is more susceptible to ischemia than the outer and middle ear. During difficult deliveries, and especially during prolonged periods of neonatal intensive care and assisted ventilation, there may be periods of inadequate blood flow to the head. Hearing loss in these cases is often associated with other problems such as brain damage, and may be progressive (Borg, 1997; Marlow et al., 2000)

ACQUIRED HEARING LOSS

Hereditary

Many hereditary characteristics are not apparent at birth, and may manifest themselves only in adulthood; male-pattern baldness is one common example. In Chapter 6, we discussed age-related hearing loss (ARHL) and its three components (according to Ward): presbycusis, nosoacusis, and socioacusis. Using this schema, presbycusis is by definition the hereditary component of ARHL. It is important to recognize that while presbycusis can be conceptualized as a purely genetic sensorineural loss becoming manifest during aging, virtually any disorder could have a genetic component. For example, there is marked variability in susceptibility to NIHL; "tough ears" and "tender ears" may well be inherited as is true in experimental animals (see Chapter 7). The effects of vascular disease on hearing are still controversial (and are discussed later in this chapter), but if such effects exist, they probably have a genetic component, as is true for coronary artery disease and diabetes. These are examples where genetic and environmental influences interact to produce clinical disease.

Genetic contributions to ARHL, NIHL, and other otologic disorders are likely, but are difficult to measure, partly because of the confounding effects of environment, but also because they probably reflect the contributions of many different genes. There are also a few purely genetic otologic disorders in which there is no hearing loss at birth. For example, in *Alport's disease,* a (usually) X-linked disorder that includes hearing loss and kidney disease, affected individuals begin in childhood and adolescence to experience a progressive sensorineural hearing loss.

Paget's disease is an autosomal dominant disease (with variable penetrance) that does not become clinically apparent until middle age or later, characterized by increased bone metabolism. Patients with skull disease are likely to have conductive, sensorineural, or mixed hearing loss (Walker et al., 1979), caused by bone overgrowth affecting the ear canal, ossicles, and internal auditory canal.

Otosclerosis

Based on temporal bone postmortem studies, about 10 percent of the Caucasian population has otosclerosis (also called *otospongiosis*), a disorder of bone growth limited to the otic capsule (the bone surrounding the inner ear fluid spaces). Most affected individuals suffer no hearing loss from the disease and indeed cannot reliably be identified as otoselerotics during life. Less than 1 percent of the Caucasian population develops *clinical* otosclerosis (Hinchcliffe, 1961; Hall, 1974), in which the abnormal bone growth interferes with the movement of the stapes in the oval window. The result is a progressive *conductive* hearing loss beginning in youth or middle age, usually bilateral, affecting low frequencies first. The disease may also affect inner ear function, resulting in a mixed hearing loss, that is, with both conductive and sensorineural components. Typically, the bone conduction curve shows a dip at 2 kHz (the Carhart notch). Many otologists believe that otosclerosis can cause pure sensorineural loss and that the disease can be diagnosed by computerized tomography (a type of X-ray) in the *absence* of conductive loss, but these are controversial propositions. The diagnosis is usually made based on the combination of conductive hearing loss and the absence of other causes such as head injury or chronic otitis media. Family history is helpful, because otosclerosis is inherited in an autosomal dominant fashion; however, as noted above, there is variable penetrance, with *most* otosclerotics being free of hearing loss from the disease, so a negative family history doesn't rule out otosclerosis. When the hearing loss becomes handicapping, patients can choose between hearing aids and surgery, with excellent results in most cases from either approach. Only the conductive component is correctable with surgery, so patients with severe mixed losses may require both surgery and hearing aids.

Infections

Infections of the outer ear, middle ear, and inner ear (Chapter 3) can all cause hearing loss.

Otitis Externa

Bacteria and fungal infections of the skin of the ear canal are common, especially in susceptible individuals: swimmers and persons exposed to high humidity, persons with skin disorders, and those who traumatize their ear canals with Q-tips and other foreign objects. Earplugs used to prevent NIHL may trigger otitis extema (OE) by interfering with the normal process of skin migration by which dead canal skin and cerumen (earwax) is removed from the ear canal. OE causes little or no hearing loss unless the swelling of the canal skin and/or accumulated debris and secretions block the ear canal. Treatment is usually simple, consisting of cleaning followed by the use of antibiotic ear drops. Elderly diabetics are prone to a very serious disorder called *necrotizing* (or "malignant") OE, in which the usual canal skin infection spreads to the underlying bone; aggressive intravenous antibiotic treatment is needed to prevent cranial nerve damage or even death.

Otitis Media

Middle ear infections form a spectrum of disease ranging from mild and self-limiting to life-threatening. Almost every child has at least one episode of *acute otitis media* (AOM), infection of the middle ear mucous membrane with the same viruses and bacteria that cause other upper respiratory infections such as sinusitis and tonsillitis. Children with AOM have pain, fever, and a mild conductive hearing loss due to fluid filling the middle ear space. Oral antibiotics hasten the resolution of the infection and probably reduce the risk of complications.

Children with poor eustachian tube function are subject to repeated bouts of AOM and to *otitis media with effusion* (OME), in which a thin or mucoid fluid (and hearing loss) persist after the acute infection, fever, and pain have resolved. In the cleft palate deformity, for example, the muscles that open the eustachian tubes are not properly connected to one another; even after successful surgical repair of the cleft, eustachian tube function remains abnormal. However, OME and recurrent AOM are quite common; very few affected children have cleft palates or other identifiable congenital anomalies. Bacterial colonization of the adenoids is another probable cause of repeated middle ear infections. Treatment of OME and recurrent AOM may involve prolonged use of antibiotics, incision of the eardrum (myringotomy) and placement of ventilating tubes, and/or adenoidectomy. Removal of middle ear fluid corrects the conductive loss unless chronic changes have occurred.

Chronic otitis media (COM) also involves a spectrum of changes in the middle ear. Perforations of the eardrum may be small and cause only negligible hearing loss, while larger perforations may cause substantial conductive losses. The eardrum may also be thinned (atrophy) or thickened (myringosclerosis) by chronic infections; either change can reduce vibratory function and contribute to hearing loss. Conductive losses larger than 30 dB in COM usually indicate erosive damage to the ossicles; the incus is most vulnerable. Patients with COM are subject to frequent infections with ear drainage (otorrhea) often triggered by colds or by getting water in the ear (carrying ear canal bacteria through a perforation into the middle ear). Reconstructive surgery (tympanoplasty) may be necessary to remove infected tissue, close the eardrum, and/or rebuild the ossicular chain, with the goals of a dry ear and better hearing.

Sometimes skin from the ear canal or the outer lining of the eardrum migrates into the middle ear through a perforation, or is sucked into the middle ear by chronic negative pressure from eustachian tube dysfunction. The result can be an accumulation of dead skin inside a narrow-necked sac of skin, that is unable to cleanse itself and, as a result, repeatedly becomes infected. This condition is called *cholesteatoma* (or sometimes *keratoma*) and can be quite dangerous, expanding and eroding adjacent structures with resultant conductive loss (ossicular erosion), sensorineural loss and vertigo (erosion of labyrinthine bone), facial paralysis (facial nerve compression or destruction), and even intracranial complications, such as brain abscess in some cases. While these complications are uncommon, they can be handicapping, disfiguring, or life-threatening, so surgery is almost always recommended for patients with cholesteatoma.

Labyrinthitis (Including Sudden Hearing Loss)
Inner ear infection, or labyrinthitis, can follow erosion of a cholesteatoma (or rarely, COM without cholesteatoma) into the cochlea or one of the semicircular canals. Meningitis, an infection of the brain-lining membranes, can also spread to the inner ear to cause labyrinthitis. In either case, the typical result is a sudden, total, and permanent sensorineural hearing loss. It has recently been shown (Lebel et al., 1988) that adding steroids to the usual antibiotic regimen for meningitis reduces the risk of labyrinthitis. Vaccines against some bacteria (*Hemophilus influenzae*, type B) causing meningitis are now available and have already been shown to prevent what is presently the predominant cause of acquired deafness in childhood.

Labyrinthitis secondary to cholesteatoma or meningitis is usually bacterial, but viral diseases such as mumps and measles can also cause labyrinthitis and deafness (rubella and cytomegalovirus have already been mentioned as causes of congenital inner ear infection). Sudden unilateral sensorineural hearing loss without identifiable cause is relatively common and many authorities believe it is usually due to a viral labyrinthitis. While 4 kHz notches like those seen in noise-induced hearing loss have been reported in cases of idiopathic sudden loss (Simmons, 1968), unilaterality and the typical history will usually make differential diagnosis easy. Syphilis may also cause a distinct type of labyrinthitis, with progressive, sometimes fluctuant, and usually bilateral sensorineural loss. Steroids may be helpful in syphilitic and sudden loss cases.

Toxic

Scores of drugs and chemicals have been reported to cause inner ear injury and sensorineural hearing loss. Table 10–3 offers a somewhat selective list, mostly culled from the *CRC Handbook of Ototoxicity* (Miller, 1985) by eliminating those that seemed especially poorly documented. However, a strong *caveat* is still in order: Many of the drugs listed in Table 10–3 can only be considered suspects for possible ototoxicity. Single case reports, even when well documented, can represent association by coincidence; the disease being treated (e.g., meningitis) may be more likely to cause hearing loss than the drug; and many of the agents listed (e.g., mercury) have been reported to cause hearing loss only at doses causing very widespread toxicity including nervous system, kidney, and liver damage. Many animal studies have used doses not really comparable to those experienced in human exposures. Two drug groups are responsible for almost all documented cases of permanent human ototoxicity: the aminoglycoside antibiotics and the platinum-based anticancer drugs, cisplatin and carboplatin. Fortunately, other drugs have been identified that *prevent* ototoxicity from these two drug groups and may soon become part of clinical practice (Schacht, 1998; Muldoon et al., 2000). Reversible hearing loss is fairly common with anti-inflammatory drugs, especially aspirin, and occasionally with the loop diuretics and quinine derivatives. Ototoxicity from other agents is rare and should, when alleged, be examined with a critical eye. Rybak (1992) has recently reviewed reports of ototoxicity from "environmental" sources, specifically organic solvents and heavy metals. Many of these agents, when present at toxic levels, affect primarily the brain rather than the ear (see discussion in Chapter 7).

Radiation therapy for tumors can damage the middle ear and inner ear, causing both conductive and sensorineural hearing loss. These effects are unusual with total doses less than 5000 rad, and they may be progressive (Sataloff and Rosen, 1994).

Aminoglycosides

The ototoxicity of aminoglycosides includes both hearing loss and vestibular dysfunction and has been recognized since streptomycin began to be used against tuberculosis in the 1940s. More recent members of this drug family, including gentamicin and tobramycin, remain useful for the treatment of serious infections; they are virtually always given by injection (intravenous or intramuscular) or as eye or ear drops. In evaluating a patient with unexplained bilateral sensorineural hearing loss, one can essentially rule out aminoglycoside ototoxicity if the patient denies having had a series of antibiotic injections, usually in a hospital. This is fortunate, because patients frequently can't remember the names of antibiotics they have received. Aminoglycosides also can cause kidney damage. Aminoglycoside ototoxicity cannot be treated, but effective

TABLE 10–3
Drugs and Chemicals Reported to Cause Human Ototoxicity with Systemic Use

AMINOGLYCOSIDE ANTIBIOTICS
Amikacin
Dihydrostrptomycin
Gentamicin
Kanamycin
Neomycin
Netilmicin
Streptomycin
Tobramycin

OTHER ANTIBIOTICS AND
ANTIMICROBIAL DRUGS
Capreomycin
Chloramphenicol
Eflornithine (DFMO)[a]
Erythromycin[b]
Polymyxin
Rifampin
Ristocetin
Vancomycin
Viomycin

LOOP DIURETICS
Ethacrynic acid[b]
Furosemide[b]

ANTICANCER DRUGS
Cisplatin, carboplatin
Nitrogen mustard
Vincristine[b]
6-aminonicotinamide

MISCELLANEOUS
Oral contraceptives
Practolol (beta-blocker)
Vaccines (pertussis, rabies, smallpox, tetanus)
Hydrocodone[c]

ANTIMALARIALS AND
DERIVATIVES
Chloroquine[b]
Quinidine[b]
Quinine[b]

ORGANIC SOLVENTS
Carbon disulfide
Carbon monoxide
Methanol
Toluene
Trichloroethylene

INORGANIC CHEMICALS
Arsenic
Bromate
Cobalt
Gallium
Lead
Manganese
Mercury
Thorium

ANTI-INFLAMMATORY DRUGS
Aspirin[b]
Benorylate[b]
Indomethacin[b]
Naproxen[b]
Sodium salicylate[b]

[a]Croghan, Aickin, and Meyskens, 1991.
[b]Usually reversible.
[c]Friedman et al., 2000.

prevention demands that these drugs only be used when necessary—not for minor infections—and that blood levels and/or renal function be monitored to ensure that the drug is not accumulating excessively and to permit dose adjustment if levels rise too high (Matz and Lerner, 1981). Some patients (especially Asians) are unusually susceptible to aminoglycosides because of a mitochondrial mutation transmitted in the maternal line (Fischel-Ghodsian et al., 1997).

Anticancer Drugs

Cisplatin is a highly effective intravenous drug for patients with some types of cancer. In cumulative doses, it begins to cause high-frequency permanent sensorineural hearing loss, rarely involving frequencies below 2 kHz (kilohertz). Obviously, this is usually a small price to pay if there is no equally effective and less toxic drug available to fight the cancer. Carboplatin is a closely related drug.

Aspirin, Quinine, Diuretics

Orally administered drugs rarely if ever cause permanent hearing loss. Transient loss, reversible upon cessation of the drug, is frequent with high-dose aspirin therapy (in excess of eight five-grain tablets per day for most people), usually accompanied by tinnitus. Other anti-inflammatory drugs have also been implicated in reversible hearing loss, as have quinine and its derivatives (Table 10–3).

The loop diuretics, ethacrynic acid and furosemide, can cause severe but reversible sensorineural loss with intravenous use. However, they may also interact with other drugs and with disease states in a dangerous fashion. Patients with kidney failure have sustained permanent hearing loss from loop diuretics. Ethacrynic acid combined with kanamycin (an aminoglycoside) causes irreversible total deafness in guinea pigs, in doses that would be much less toxic for either drug given alone.

Topical Ototoxicity

The discussion to this point has been limited to systemic ototoxicity, where the drug enters the bloodstream after oral, intramuscular, or intravenous administration. *Topical* administration of drugs directly to the ear, usually in the form of drops, can also damage the inner ear if there is a perforation of the tympanic membrane that permits the drops to enter the middle ear and to contact the round window membrane. Indeed, neomycin, a highly ototoxic aminoglycoside, is an ingredient in several types of ear drops used to treat ear infections. Most otolaryngologists use these drops routinely in cases of COM with perforation, yet well documented sensorineural loss caused by such use is exceedingly rare (Roland, 1994; Marais and Rutka, 1998). Two possible explanations for this surprising *lack* of ototoxicity of neomycin drops have been offered: First, the round window membrane is thickened in COM and doesn't allow the drug to pass into the cochlea; and second, the COM itself may have injured the very high-frequency hair cells, nearest the round window, which the drug would be most likely to affect. On the other hand, aminoglycosides delivered to an uninfected middle ear can certainly cause inner ear damage, with both hearing loss and dizziness. In fact, middle ear injection of gentamicin has become a popular treatment for intractable Ménière's disease; the goal is to destroy all or part of the balance organ without causing substantial hearing loss (gentamicin is much more toxic to the vestibular system than to the cochlea).

Trauma

NIHL and acoustic trauma were discussed in Chapters 7 and 8. This section will cover head injury, neck injury, and barotrauma.

Head Injury

Blunt or penetrating trauma to the head can fracture the temporal bone, which houses the middle ear and inner ear. *Transverse fractures* are the most severe, passing through both middle ear and inner ear, with tearing of the labyrinthine membranes. Usually, there is severe to profound sensorineural hearing loss, with vertigo, and often with associated facial nerve disruption. *Longitudinal fractures* pass through the middle ear, but do not enter the labyrinth. Conductive losses predominate, often from fracture or dislocation of the incus and/or stapes. However, longitudinal fractures may also cause sensorineural losses, usually mild and primarily high frequency; these losses are believed to be caused by "labyrinthine concussion" and can mimic NIHL very closely, complete with a 4 kHz notch (Schuknecht and Davison, 1956).

Less severe trauma can cause unconsciousness without temporal bone fracture. Here, too, a labyrinthine concussion can cause a sensorineural loss, usually mild (Barber, 1969). In epidemiological studies, a history of head injury with loss of consciousness is strongly correlated with risk of hearing loss at all frequencies from 0.5 to 6 kHz. (Bauer et al., 1991; Neuberger et al., 1992). Injuries too mild to cause loss of consciousness will rarely, if ever, cause permanent hearing loss (Schuknecht and Davison, 1956; Kerr and Smyth, 1987). Head injury can also cause *perilymph fistula* (discussed later under *Barotrauma*) and perhaps delayed *endolymphatic hydrops* (discussed under *Ménière's Disease*).

Patients struck by lightning can display ear injuries of variable severity, including tympanic membrane perforation, ossicular injury, perilymph fistula, and inner ear damage (Jones et al., 1991). Complete bilateral deafness with atrophy of the organ of Corti may result (Youngs et al., 1988).

Surgery in and around the ear and auditory nerve naturally carries risk for hearing loss. Even removal of cerumen (earwax) can cause perforation of the eardrum in rare instances. Surgical operations with substantial risk of hearing loss include stapes operations for otosclerosis, correction of congenital middle ear anomalies, and intracranial operations involving the VIIIth nerve.

Neck Injury

Patients often complain of dizziness after whiplash injuries, but there is no good evidence that this is caused by inner ear injury per se. Similarly, although there have been papers reporting hearing loss after whiplash (Toglia, Rosenberg, and Ronis, 1970; Shapiro, 1972; Rubin, 1973), these data are essentially anecdotal, with no evidence that patients had losses unexplained by other causes. Tjell et al. (1999) showed in a large study that hearing thresholds were essentially normal in patients with whiplash. Brownson et al. (1986) described two patients who had severe unilateral hearing loss and vertigo after therapeutic manipulation of the cervical spine. Their suggestion that this was caused by compression of the vertebral artery by extreme neck rotation seems plausible, given the known association between chiropractic manipulation and stroke (Hufnagel et al., 1999), but this must be a rare event.

Barotrauma

As discussed briefly in Chapter 3, the eustachian tube provides the middle ear with a supply of air from the nasopharynx to replace gases absorbed by the mucous membranes of the middle ear. The eustachian tube is normally closed, opening with each swallow to permit air flow and equalization of pressure. When the tube fails to open adequately (e.g., because of allergic or infectious swelling of the tube's lining membrane), the middle ear mucosa continues to absorb air and a partial vacuum results. If the tube remains closed, the negative pressure will draw fluid from the mucosa, filling the middle ear and causing a conductive hearing loss. Otitis media may result, or the effusion may remain sterile, resolving spontaneously or with treatment.

The above sequence of events is not traumatic unless the ambient pressure changes rapidly. For example, when an airplane descends, air pressure in the ear canal and nasopharynx rises with cabin pressure. If the eustachian tube fails to open, a relative vacuum develops quickly in the middle ear, and the mucosa may bleed. During scuba or free dive descent, pressure changes even more rapidly; if pressure is not equalized, the tympanic membrane may rupture. Barotrauma is virtually always caused by rapid *descent*, with ambient pressure exceeding middle ear pressure, because the eustachian tube passes air freely from middle ear to nasopharynx, but not vice versa.

Barotrauma may also cause tears in inner ear membranes, including the round and/or oval window membranes, with a resultant *perilymph fistula* (PLF). A patient with inner ear barotrauma may experience dizziness and progressive or fluctuating sensorineural hearing loss; audiometric contour may occasionally mimic noise-induced hearing loss, with a 4 kHz notch (Freeman and Edmonds, 1972). PLF may also be caused by very sudden *increases* in middle ear pressure from vigorous nose-blowing or the "modified Valsalva" maneuver used by many divers to drive air into the middle ear during descent. Rapid changes in spinal fluid pressure from lifting and straining are also capable of causing PLF in some individuals.

Scuba diving is associated with two other potential causes of sensorineural hearing loss (Weisskopf, 1981). *Bends,* or decompression sickness, occurs when a diver has stayed too long at depths greater than 60 feet without gradual decompression; dissolved nitrogen in body tissues literally boils as ambient pressure drops, and the nitrogen bubbles can injure the inner ear along with other organs. *Air embolism* is caused by breath-holding during scuba ascent; the air in the lungs expands and ruptures the alveoli, allowing air bubbles to travel through the bloodstream, blocking small blood vessels downstream. Some studies (e.g., Haraguchi et al., 1999) suggest that long-term scuba diving is associated with increased hearing loss, even in the absence of reported episodes of barotrauma, bends, or sudden hearing loss.

Neoplastic

Outer Ear
The skin lining the auricle and ear canal is subject to the same common types of skin cancer found throughout the body, but especially on sun-exposed areas: basal cell carcinoma, squamous cell carcinoma, and melanoma. Hearing loss occurs only when the ear canal is totally blocked by tumor.

Middle Ear
In rare instances, squamous cell carcinoma originates in or grows into the middle ear. Tumors of the other middle ear tissues are even rarer, with the exception of the *glomus tumor,* which develops from nerves on the inner wall of the middle ear or in the jugular bulb, just below the floor of the middle ear. Any middle ear tumor can cause a conductive hearing loss.

Inner Ear
The tissues of the inner ear are unique in that they rarely give rise to tumors. Endolymphatic sac tumors are seen in patients with von Hippel-Lindau syndrome, a hereditary disease also involving tumors of the retina, brain, and abdomen. Rarely, cancers metastasize to the inner ear from primary sites elsewhere (e.g., breast, kidney, lung), and tumors of the auditory and vestibular nerves, usually found in the internal auditory canal, rarely originate from the nerve endings in the inner ear. However, tumors of the organ of Corti, stria vascularis, or vestibular labyrinth have not been described.

Internal Auditory Canal

Slowly growing tumors of the lining tissue of the vestibular nerve are fairly common. Because unilateral sensorineural hearing loss is usually the earliest symptom, these tumors were called (and continue to be called) *acoustic neuromas*, although they are more properly called *vestibular schwannomas* (they originate from Schwann cells). These benign tumors eventually grow out of the internal auditory canal and enlarge in the posterior fossa of the intracranial cavity, compressing the cerebellum and brainstem. They can reach considerable size (4–5 cm) and age (10–20 years) prior to diagnosis. Untreated, they are eventually life-threatening, and surgical removal carries serious risks, which increase with the size of the tumor.

Ischemic

Ischemia—lack of adequate blood flow—caused by vascular disease is the primary cause of most heart attacks and strokes and an important cause of kidney failure, vision loss, and amputations. Obviously, vascular disease is common in our society and potentially can affect any organ, including the inner ear. Many investigators have attempted to establish and measure the relationships between vascular disease and hearing loss, with highly variable results. Positive effects, when found, are invariably small when compared to (for example) age effects. We will briefly review some selected evidence for and against the vascular hypothesis; one could (and someone probably should) write a book about this subject alone.

Vascular disease could be an important component of nosoacusis (see Chapter 6), the part of ARHL caused by undiagnosed ear disease in epidemiological survey subjects. If this were true, one would expect a substantial amount of ARHL to be sudden; in other organ systems, vascular disease causes both gradual loss of function and sudden events. Sudden unexplained sensorineural hearing losses do occur, but more commonly in young, healthy people; this is one of the reasons many otologists suspect they are usually caused by viruses rather than vascular occlusion (sudden hearing loss does rarely occur after cardiac bypass surgery, possibly caused by vascular occlusion; Millen et al., 1982). Elderly people almost always report that their hearing has declined gradually, and longitudinal studies have offered no evidence for stepwise progression of hearing loss with age (such evidence would be supportive of, but not proof of, the vascular hypothesis). The symmetry usually seen in ARHL also argues against stepwise progression.

One major problem in studying the putative effects of vascular disease on hearing is that we have no way to measure blood flow in the human inner car. Laser Doppler methods have shown promise in animal models, but have not been successfully adapted for clinical use. Instead of correlating cochlear blood flow with hearing loss, investigators are forced to use weaker indirect methods, assessing hearing in populations believed likely to have cochlear ischemia. We will review a few such clinical studies and some related animal research in the areas of established cardiovascular disease, diabetes, hypertension, hyperlipidemia, smoking, and blood viscosity.

Established Cardiovascular Disease

Rubinstein et al. (1977) selected 46 nursing home residents for two age- and gender-matched groups (most were in their seventies). The group without any evidence of cardiovascular disease had significantly better hearing levels (34 dB average) than those with "appreciable cardiovascular disturbances with signs of impaired peripheral circulation" (42 dB average). A large middle group had some evidence of cardiovascular disease and was not studied audiometrically. However, the criteria for selection were vague; "about 200" subjects were screened to obtain the 46 subjects. Drugs, depression, and/or dementia could have interfered with accurate audiometry; all would be expected to be more prevalent in the "cardiovascular" group.

The Framingham Heart Study is a well known longitudinal study of heart disease and risk factors, and has been active since 1948. Audiometry was added in 1978 to the periodic examinations of the subjects. Moscicki and Kannel (1984), in an unpublished report, found that, at a given age (from 57 to 89 years), subjects with pure-tone averages (1, 2, 3 kHz) greater than 40 dB were almost twice as likely to have had a heart attack or stroke as subjects with better hearing. A major weakness of the Moscicki and Kannel report is the apparent failure to include noise exposure history in their analysis of relative risk for cardiovascular events. Occupational noise exposure probably correlates with several stressors predictive of cardiovascular disease, for example, smoking and low socioeconomic status. Gates et al. (1993) have reanalyzed the Framingham data, confirming an association between cardiovascular disease (coronary artery disease, stroke) and hearing loss, more marked in women than in men; however, risk factors such as smoking, hypertension, hyperlipidemia, and diabetes did not predict hearing loss, and noise exposure, as before, was uncontrolled.

Parving et al. (1993) studied over 5,000 subjects and found no association between hearing loss and coronary artery disease.

Diabetes Mellitus

Diabetes ought to offer a nearly ideal test of the vascular hypothesis. Compared to nondiabetic subjects, diabetics have much higher prevalences of heart disease, stroke, kidney failure, blindness, and peripheral vascular disease. However, the literature does not offer conclusive evidence that diabetes is associated with hearing loss, with the exception of rare hereditary diseases in which both conditions coexist, usually with other manifestations (Tanaka et al., 2000; Fuqua, 2000).

Axelsson, Sigroth, and Vertes (1978) reviewed the prior literature and concluded that postmortem histological changes had been demonstrated in diabetics throughout the inner ear, but that audiological studies had been conflicting and inconclusive. Their study of 205 adult diabetics showed hearing a little worse than expected from published age norms, but there was no control group and many of their diabetic subjects had had occupational noise exposure. They could establish no relationship between duration or severity of disease and hearing loss.

Taylor and Irwin (1978) found mean differences up to 9 dB between diabetic subjects and controls, but their age-matching was not well described. Similar findings were reported from India by Kurien, Thomas, and Bhanu (1989). Very small effects of diabetes on hearing (in very large studies) were found by Ma et al. (1998) and Dalton et al. (1998). However, most other authors have found no significant differences in hearing levels between diabetics and published age norms (Harner, 1981) or matched control groups (Gibben and Davis, 1981; Miller et al., 1983; Sieger et al., 1983; Parving et al., 1990; Gates et al., 1993).

Hypertension

Like diabetes, hypertension is an important risk factor for cardiovascular disease, and here, too, substantial evidence for association with hearing loss is lacking. Drettner et al. (1975) studied 1,000 50-year-old men and found that noise exposure and socioeconomic class were the only significant predictors of hearing loss. Hypertension (along with smoking, triglycerides, and glucose tolerance) was not correlated with hearing loss. Hansen (1968) also found no correlation between blood pressure and hearing level, and large-scale studies in the British National Study of Hearing (Davis, 1987) confirm this lack of association. More recent studies have been both positive (Brant et al., 1996) and negative (Parving et al., 1993; Gates et al., 1993).

Hyperlipidemia

Animal studies (Saito, Sato, and Saito, 1986; Sikora et al., 1986) have shown that diets made extremely high in cholesterol can cause slight hearing loss compared to normal controls. The relevance of these studies to clinical disease is questionable because of the "dose" of dietary lipid. Cunningham and Goetzinger (1974) found no differences between normal and hypercholesterolemic subjects in the conventional audiometric range (up to 8 kHz), but there were differences at higher frequencies. Lowry and Isaacson (1978) noted *lower* serum lipids in patients with ARHL than expected for their ages and genders. Drettner et al. (1975), Jones and Davis (1999), and Gates (1993) all reported negative results.

The most intriguing results in this area are those of Rosen and Olin (1965) and Rosen, Olin, and Rosen (1970), who subjected the inmates of two Finnish psychiatric hospitals to a nine-year crossover study in which first one, then the other, hospital had its diet modified from the "normal" high-fat Scandinavian diet to one low in saturated fats. The results suggested small but significant advantages for the low-fat diet in each hospital at most frequencies. However, the largest differences seen, at 4 kHz, were almost entirely caused by a *conductive* component in the high-fat diet group, raising the possibility of audiometric artifacts from ear-canal collapse during testing. In addition, there was no baseline testing. The first tests were done after several years of diet modification and found better hearing in the low-fat group. The second set of tests was performed after the crossover, with only 60 percent of the original subjects available (and able to cooperate), and no intergroup differences were found. Moreover, there was no statistical analysis of audiometric changes across subjects, so their results do not establish that diet affects hearing.

Smoking

As mentioned in Chapter 7, smoking appears to have a paradoxical protective effect in experiments designed to produce temporary noise-induced hearing loss, but notwithstanding one weakly positive study (Cruickshanks et al., 1998) there is little evidence of any effect of smoking on permanent NIHL or ARHL (Drettner et al., 1975; Gates et al., 1993; Brant et al., 1996).

Viscosity

Studies from Scotland (Browning, Gatehouse, and Lowe, 1986), Wales (Gatehouse et al., 1989), and Israel (Hildesheimer et al., 1990) have found associations between whole-blood viscosity and sensorineural hearing loss. Browning et al. speculate that more rigid, less deformable red blood cells account for this viscosity difference, and that these rigid cells move poorly through the capillaries of the inner ear, leading to ischemia. Plasma viscosity has not yet been accepted as an independent predictor of cardiovascular disease in general. Since it correlates with other known risk factors (obesity, smoking, hyperlipidemia), increased viscosity could be an intermediate mechanism by which these risk factors promote thrombosis and clinical cardiovascular disease (Lowe et al., 1991).

Metabolic

Extreme levels of hypothyroidism, rarely seen in the United States, are said to cause a flat or sloping hearing loss (conductive or sensorineural), but thyroid disease is not ordinarily associated with hearing loss. Meyerhoff

(1985) reviewed this literature and concluded that the evidence linking hypothyroidism to hearing loss of any kind was weak. Disorders of adrenal, parathyroid, pituitary, or gonadal function have not conclusively demonstrated any association with hearing loss. Diabetes mellitus has been discussed above, under *ischemia*. Its specifically metabolic effects (hyperglycemia, etc.) have not been associated with hearing loss.

Inflammatory

Sensorineural hearing loss is occasionally seen with autoimmune and inflammatory diseases such as polyarteritis nodosa, rheumatoid arthritis, sarcoidosis, and Cogan's disease, and sometimes responds to steroid treatment. Rapidly progressive, steroid-responsive hearing losses are seen in the absence of documented autoimmune disease, and many otologists believe these cases represent an isolated "autoimmune inner ear disease." However, no well accepted tests exist to prove the existence of inner ear autoimmunity, and this disorder remains an enigma.

Miscellaneous

Ménière's Disease

Ménière's disease is a relatively common disorder characterized by spontaneous episodes of whirling vertigo (often with nausea and vomiting), fluctuating sensorineural hearing loss (affecting mainly the low frequencies at first), tinnitus, and ear fullness or pressure. Unilateral at the outset, many or most cases become bilateral, although the hearing is almost always asymmetrical. Some otologists believe that allergy, hypothyroidism, hyperlipidemia, NIHL, and diabetes are common causes of Ménière's disease, but there is no good evidence that any of these disorders are more prevalent in Ménière's patients than in the general population. Several case reports indicate that patients who have suffered severe head injury with unilateral deafness may later develop episodic vertigo similar to that seen in Ménière's disease (Schuknecht, 1978), but it has not been established that head injury and Ménière's disease coexist more often than would be expected by coincidence alone. Ménière's disease is probably best regarded as an idiopathic disorder, that is, its cause is unknown. Temporal bone studies document an association between Ménière's disease and endolymphatic hydrops, a dilation of the endolymphatic space, perhaps because of reduced absorptive capacity of the endolymphatic sac. However, this association, too, has been questioned (Rauch, Merchant, and Thedinger, 1989). Most patients do well with medical treatment designed to reduce endolymph volume—usually, a diuretic and salt restriction. Some patients require surgery or aminoglycoside treatment (see section on topical ototoxicity) to achieve vertigo control; neither surgical nor medical treatment seems to have any beneficial effect on hearing in Ménière's disease. Fortunately, the disease very rarely progresses to total deafness.

Cerumen Impaction

This humble condition is not really a disease, but certainly causes considerable hearing loss. Normally, dead canal skin combines with the oily secretions of the cerumen glands to produce earwax, which is then transported to the outer portion of the ear canal by skin migration, and falls out. This orderly sequence can be interrupted by narrowing of the ear canal; by age-related changes in cerumen production and migration; by excessive ear canal hair; by ill-advised use of Q-tips (which only serve to pack the earwax more firmly into the deeper recesses of the ear canal); and by unknown factors. When the canal becomes completely blocked, a substantial conductive hearing loss may result, along with fullness and discomfort. Irrigation or removal with instruments restores the hearing to preimpaction levels. Hearing aids and earplugs can interfere with normal cerumen migration and lead to cerumen impaction.

REFERENCES

Axelsson, Alf, Kjell Sigroth, and Dianne Vertes. 1978. Hearing in diabetics. *Acta Otolaryngol. Suppl. (Stockh.)* 356:1–23.

Barber, Hugh O. 1969. Head injury: Audiological and vestibular findings. *Ann. Otol. Rhinol. Laryngol.* 78(2):239–252.

Bauer, Peter, Karl Korpert, Manfred Neuberger, Alfred Raber, and Friedrich Schwetz. 1991. Risk factors for hearing loss at different frequencies in a population of 47,388 noise-exposed workers. *J. Acoust. Soc. Am.* 90(6):3086–3098.

Bieber, Frederick R. and Walter E. Nance. 1979. Hereditary hearing loss. In *Clinical Genetics: A Sourcebook for Physicians*, ed. Laird G. Jackson and R. Neil Schimke, pp. 443–461. New York: John Wiley & Sons.

Borg, Erik. 1997. Perinatal asphysia, hypoxia, ischemia and hearing loss. *Scand. Audiol.* 16:77–91.

Brant, L. J., S. Gordon-Salant, J. D. Pearson, L. L. Klein, C. H. Morrell, E. J. Metter, and J. L. Fozard. 1996. Risk factors related to age-associated hearing loss in the speech frequencies. *J. Am. Acad. Audiol.* 7:152–160.

Browning, G. G., S. Gatehouse, and G. D. O. Lowe. 1986. Blood viscosity as a factor in sensorineural hearing impairment. *Lancet* 1(8473):121–123.

Brownson, Richmond Jay, William K. Zollinger, Tony Madeira, and David Fell. 1986. Sudden sensorineural hearing loss following manipulation of the cervical spine. *Laryngoscope* 96(2):166–170.

Croghan, Marilyn K., Mikel G. Aickin, and Frank L. Meyskens. 1991. Dose-related α-difluoromethylornithine ototoxicity. *Am. J. Clin. Oncol.* 14(4):331–335.

Cruickshanks, K. J., R. Klein, B. E. Klein, T. L. Wiley, D. M. Nondahl, and T. S. Tweed. 1998. Cigarette smoking and hearing loss. *JAMA* 279:1715–1719.

Cunningham, David R. and Cornelius P. Goetzinger. 1974. Extra-high frequency hearing loss and hyperlipidemia. *Audiology* 13(6):470–484.

Dalton, D. S., K. J. Cruickshanks, R. Klein, B. E. Klein, and T. L. Wiley. 1998. Association of NIDDM and hearing loss. *Diabetes Care* 21:1540–1544.

Davis, Adrian C. 1987. Epidemiology of hearing disorders. In *Scott-Brown's Oto-laryngology: Volume 2—Adult Audiology*, 5th ed., ed. Dafydd Stephens, pp. 90–126. London: Butterworths.

Drettner, B., H. Hedstrand, I. Klockhoff, and A. Svedberg. 1975. Cardiovascular risk factors and hearing loss: A study of 1,000 fifty-year-old men. *Acta Oto-laryngol. (Stockh.)* 79(5–6):366–371.

Fischel-Ghodsian, N., T. R. Prezant, W. E. Chaltraw, K. A. Wendt, R. A. Nelson, K. S. Arnos, and R. E. Falk. 1997. Mitochondrial gene mutation is a significant predisposing factor in aminoglycoside ototoxicity. *Am. J. Otoloaryngol.* 18:173–178.

Freeman, Peter and Carl Edmonds. 1972. Inner ear barotrauma. *Arch. Otolaryngol.* 95(6):556–563.

Friedman, R. A., J. W. House, W. M. Luxford, S. Gherini, and D. Mills. 2000. Profound hearing loss associated with hydrocodone/acetaminophen abuse. *Am. J. Otol.* 21:188–191.

Fuqua, J. S. 2000. Wolfram syndrome: Clinical and genetic aspects. *Endocrinologist* 10:51–59.

Gatehouse, S., E. J. Gallacher, G. D. O. Lowe, J. W. G. Yarnell, R. D. Hutton, and I. Ising. 1989. Blood viscosity and hearing levels in the Caerphilly Collaborative Heart Disease Study. *Arch. Otolaryngol. Head Neck Surg.* 115(10):1227–1230.

Gates, George A., Janet L. Cobb, Ralph B. D'Agostino, and Philip A. Wolf. 1993. The relation of hearing in the elderly to the presence of cardiovascular disease and cardiovascular risk factors. *Arch. Otolaryngol. Head Neck Surg.* 119(2):156–161.

Gibben, K. P. and C. G. Davis. 1981. A hearing survey in diabetes mellitus. *Clin. Otolaryngol.* 6(5):345–350.

Hall, Jens G. 1974. Otosclerosis in Norway: Geographic and genetical study. *Acta Otolaryngol. Suppl. (Stockh.)* 324:1–20.

Hansen, Carl Christian. 1968. Perceptive hearing loss and arterial hypertension. *Arch. Otolaryngol.* 87(2):119–122.

Haraguchi, H., T. Ohgaki, J. Okubo, Y. Noguchi, T. Sugimoto, and A. Komatsuzaki. 1999. Progressive sensorineural hearing impairment in professional fishery divers. *Ann. Otol. Rhinol. Laryngol.* 108:1165–1169.

Harner, Stephen G. 1981. Hearing in adult-onset diabetes mellitus. *Otolaryngol. Head Neck Surg.* 89(2):322–327.

Hildesheimer, Minka, Fani Bloch, Chava Muchnik, and Moshe Rubinstein. 1990. Blood viscosity and sensorineural hearing loss. *Arch. Otolaryngol. Head Neck Surg.* 116(7):820–823.

Hinchcliffe, Ronald. 1961. Prevalence of the commoner ear, nose, and throat conditions in the adult rural population of Great Britain: A study by direct examination of two random samples. *Brit. J. Prev. Soc. Med.* 15(3): 128–139.

Hufnagel, A., A. Hammers, P. W. Schonle, K. D. Bohn, and G. Leonhardt. 1999. Stroke following chiropractic manipulation of the cervical spine. *J. Neurol.* 246:683–688.

Jones, Dwight T., Frederic P. Ogren, Lynn H. Roh, and Gary F. Moore. 1991. Lightning and its effects on the auditory system. *Laryngoscope* 101(8):830–834.

Jones, N. S. and A. Davis. 1999. A prospective case-control study of patients presenting with idiopathic SNHL to examine the relationship between hyperlipidemia and SNHL. *Clin. Otolaryngol.* 24:531–536.

Kerr, Alan G. and Gordon D. L. Smyth. 1987. Ear trauma. In *Scott-Brown's Otolaryngology: Volume 3—Otology*, 5th ed., ed. John B. Booth, pp. 172–184. London: Butterworths.

Kurien, M., K. Thomas, and T. S. Bhanu. 1989. Hearing threshold in patients with diabetes mellitus. *J. Laryngol. Otol.* 103(2):164–168.

Lebel, Marc H., Bishara J. Freij, George A. Syrogiannopoulos, Dale F. Chrane, M. Jean Hoyt, Sunita M. Stewart, Betsy D. Kennard, Kurt D. Olsen, and George H. McCracken, Jr. 1988. Dexamethasone therapy for bacterial meningitis. *N. Engl. J. Med.* 319(15):964–971.

Lowe, G. D. O., D. A. Wood, J. T. Douglas, R. A. Riemersma, C. C. A. Macintyre, T. Takase, E. G. D. Tuddenham, C. D. Forbes, R. A. Elton, and M. F. Oliver. 1991. Relationships of plasma viscosity, coagulation and fibrinolysis to coronary risk factors and angina. *Thromb. Haemost.* 65(4): 339–343.

Lowry, Louis D. and Steven R. Issacson. 1978. Study of 100 patients with bilateral sensorineural hearing loss for lipid abnormalities. *Ann. Otol. Rhinol. Laryngol.* 87(3):404–408.

Ma, F., O. Gomez-Marin, D. J. Lee, and T. Balkany. 1998. Diabetes and hearing impairment in Mexican-American adults: A population-based study. *J. Laryngol. Otol.* 112:835–839.

Marais, J., and J. A. Rutga. 1998. Ototoxicity and topical eardrops. *Clin. Otolaryngology* 23:360–367.

Marazita, M. L., L. M. Ploughman, R. Rawlings, E. Remington, K. S. Arnos, and W. E. Nance. 1993. Genetic epidemiological studies of early-onset deafness in the U.S. school-age population. *Am. J. Med. Genet.* 46:486–491.

Marlow, E. S., L. P. Hunt, and N. Marlow. 2000. Sensorineural hearing loss and prematurity. *Arch. Dis. Childhood* 82:141–144.

Martin, J. A. M. 1982. Aetiological factors relating to childhood deafness in the European community. *Audiology* 21(2):149–158.

Marwick, Charles. 1984. More cautionary labeling appears on isotretinoin. *JAMA* 251(24):3208–3209.

Matz, Gregory J. and Stephen A. Lerner. 1981. Prospective studies of aminoglycoside ototoxicity in adults. In *Aminoglycoside Ototoxicity*, ed. Stephen A. Lerner, Gregory J. Matz, and Joseph E. Hawkins, pp. 327–339. Boston: Little, Brown and Company.

Meyerhoff, William L. 1985. Endocrine disorders and hearing loss. In *Advances in Audiology:* Vol. 3, ed. V. Colletti and S. D. G. Stephens, pp. 98–105. Basel, Switzerland: S. Karger.

Millen, S. J., R. J. Toolhill, and R. H. Lehman. 1982. Sudden sensorineural hearing loss: Operative complications in non-otologic surgery. *Laryngoscope* 92:613–617.

Miller, Julian J. 1985. *CRC Handbook of Ototoxicity*. Boca Raton, FL: CRC Press, Inc.

Miller, Julian J., Lynne Beck, Adrian Davis, Diane E. Jones, and Alun B. Thomas. 1983. Hearing loss in patients with diabetic retinopathy. *Am. J. Otolaryngol.* 4(5):342–346.

Moscicki, Eve K. and William B. Kannel. 1984. *Cardiovascular Disease and Hearing Loss: The Framingham Heart Study Cohort.* Paper read at the Annual Meeting of the American Speech-Language-Hearing Association, November 1984.

Muldoon, L. L., M. D. Pagel, R. A. Kroll, R. E. Brummett, N. D. Doolittle, E. G. Zuhowski, M. J. Egorin, and E. A. Neuwelt. 2000. Delayed administration of sodium thiosulfate in animal models reduces platinum ototoxicity without reduction of antitumor activity. *Clin. Cancer Res.* 6:309–315.

Neuberger, Manfred, Karl Korpert, Alfred Raber, Friedrich Schwetz, and Peter Bauer. 1992. Hearing loss from industrial noise, head injury and ear disease: A multivariate analysis on audiometric examinations of 110,647 workers. *Audiology* 31(1):45–57.

Newman, T. B. and M. A. Klebanoff. 1993. Neonatal hyperbilirubinemia and long-term outcome: Another look at the Collaborative Perinatal Project. *Pediatrics* 92:651–657.

Parving, A., C. Elberling, V. Balle, J. Parbo, A. Dejgaard, and H-H. Parving. 1990. Hearing disorders in patients with insulin-dependent diabetes mellitus. *Audiology* 29(3):113–121.

Parving, A., H. O. Hein, P. Suadicani, B. Ostri, and F. Gyntelberg. 1993. Epidemiology of hearing disorders. *Scand. Audiol.* 22:101–107.

Peckham, C. S., O. Stark, J. A. Dudgeon, J. A. M. Martin, and G. Hawkins. 1987. Congenital cytomegalovirus infection: A cause of sensorineural hearing loss. *Arch. Dis. Child.* 62(12):1233–1237.

Rauch, Steven D., Saumil N. Merchant, and Britt A. Thedinger. 1989. Ménière's syndrome and endolymphatic hydrops: Double-blind temporal bone study. *Ann. Otol. Rhinol. Laryngol.* 98(11):873–883.

Roland, Peter S. 1994. Clinical ototoxicity of topical antibiotic drops. *Otolaryn-gol. Head Neck Surg.* 110:598–602.

Rosen, Samuel and Pekka Olin. 1965. Hearing loss and coronary heart disease. *Arch. Otolaryngol.* 82(9):236–243.

Rosen, Samuel, Pekka Olin, and Helen V. Rosen. 1970. Dietary prevention of hearing loss. *Acta Otolaryngol.* 70:242–247.

Rubin, Wallace. 1973. Whiplash with vestibular involvement. *Arch. Otolaryngol.* 97(1):85–87.

Rubinstein, M., M. Hildesheimer, S. Zohar, and T. Chilarovitz. 1977. Chronic cardiovascular pathology and hearing loss in the aged. *Gerontology* 23(1): 4–9.

Rybak, Leonard P. 1992. Hearing: The effects of chemicals. *Otolaryngol. Head Neck Surg.* 106(6):677–686.

Saito, T., K. Sato, and H. Saito. 1986. An experimental study of auditory dys-function associated with hyperlipoproteinernia. *Arch. Otorhinolaryngol.* 243(4):242–245.

Sataloff, R. T. and D. C. Rosen. 1994. Effects of cranial irradiation on hearing acuity: A review of the literature. *Am. J. Otology* 15:772–780.

Schacht, Jochen. 1998. Aminoglycoside ototoxicity: Prevention in sight? *Oto-laryngol. Head Neck Surg.* 118:674–677.

Schuknecht, Harold F. 1978. Delayed endolymphatic hydrops. *Ann. Otol. Rhinol. Laryngol.* 87(3):743–748.

Schuknecht, Harold F. and Roderick C. Davison. 1956. Deafness and vertigo from head injury. *Arch. Otolaryngol.* 63(5):513–528.

Shapiro, S. L. 1972. The otologic symptoms of cervical whiplash injuries. *EENT Monthly* 51(7):259–263.

Shepard, Thomas H. 1986. *Catalog of Teratogenic Agents*, 5th ed. Baltimore: Johns Hopkins University Press.

Sieger, Ann, Neil H. White, Margaret W. Skinner, and Gershon J. Spector. 1983. Auditory function in children with diabetes mellitus. *Ann. Otol. Rhinol. Laryngol.* 92(3 Pt. 1):237–241.

Sikora, Michael A., Tetsuo Morizono, W. Dixon Ward, Michael M. Paparella, and Kimberly Leslie. 1986. Dietinduced hyperlipidemia and auditory dysfunc-tion. *Acta Otolaryngol. (Stockh.)* 102(5–6):372–381.

Simmons, F. Blair. 1968. Theory of membrane breaks in sudden hearing loss. *Arch. Otolaryngol.* 88(1):41–48.

Tanaka, K., Y. Takada, T. Matsunaka, S. Yuyama, S. Fujino, M. Maguchi, S. Ya-mashita, and I. Yuba. 2000. Diabetes mellitus, deafness, muscle weakness and hypocalcemia in a patient with an A3243G mutation of the mitochon-drial DNA. *Int. Med.* 39:249–52.

Taylor, I. G. and J. Irwin. 1978. Some audiological aspects of diabetes mellitus. *J. Laryngol. Otol.* 92(2):99–113.

Tjell, C., A. Tenenbaum, and V. Rosenhall. 1999. Auditory function in whiplash-associated disorders. *Scand. Audiol.* 28:203–209.

Toglia, Joseph U., Philip E. Rosenberg, and Max L. Ronis. 1970. Posttraumatic dizziness; vestibular, audiologic, and medicolegal. *Arch. Otolaryngol.* 92(5):485–492.

U.S. Congress—Office of Technology Assessment. December 1985. *Reproductive Health Hazards in the Workplace (OTA-BA-266)*. Washington, DC: U.S. Government Printing Office.

U.S. Department of Health and Human Services—Centers for Disease Control. 1982. *Congenital Malformations Surveillance*. Washington, DC: U.S. Government Printing Office.

Volpe, Joseph J. 1987. *Neurology of the Newborn*, 2nd ed. Philadelphia: W.B. Saunders Company.

Walker, G. S., J.M. Evanson, D. P. Canty, and N. W. Gall. 1979. Effect of calcitonin on deafness due to Paget's disease of the skull. *Br. Med. J.* 2(6186):364–365.

Weisskopf, Alex. 1981. *Diving Medicine*. Rochester, MN: American Academy of Otolaryngology–Head and Neck Surgery.

Youngs, Robin, John Deck, Peter Kwok, and Michael Hawke. 1988. Severe sensorineural hearing loss caused by lightning. *Arch. Otolaryngol. Head Neck Surg.* 114(10):1184–1187.

Chapter 11

Legal Remedies for Hearing Loss

Thomas R. Jayne

For many years, the injuries that came before American courts were the result of a single accident or trauma, and our judicial system has long provided remedies for those so damaged by the negligence or fault of others. It is not surprising, therefore, that when faced with claims for damages from diseases or conditions caused by long-term exposures, our courts would tailor remedies to fit these claims, concluding that "damage is damage whether it arises from disease or injury" (*Triff* v. *National Bronze & Aluminum Foundry Co.*, 20 N.E.2d 232 [Ohio 1939]). This process of legal evolution began in the early part of this century and there are now well established legal remedies for "occupational injuries," such as hearing loss resulting from long-term noise exposure, where the exposure was caused by the negligence or fault of others.

As will be explained in Chapter 15, the elements of a tort claim include a legal duty owed by defendant to plaintiff, a breach of that duty, a causal relation between the breach of duty and an injury or condition, and damages as a result of the injury or condition. These elements are typically supplied by a combination of legal presumptions (statutory or common law) and evidence. The evidence is usually both fact and opinion testimony, through lay and expert witnesses. The purpose of this chapter is to provide a brief overview of the major legal avenues of relief likely to confront hearing professionals, and highlight how the elements of various remedies may affect their roles as treating, consulting, or testifying experts. Because federal noise regulations play a major role in litigation, a section of this chapter is devoted to a brief history and outline of those regulations. Finally, the standards governing the admissibility of expert testimony are discussed.

235

WORKERS' COMPENSATION

At the start of the Industrial Revolution, an employee's only recourse for a job-related injury was a negligence suit. Under the common law, an employer had a duty to furnish a "reasonably safe" place to work, and an injured employee could seek damages in a jury trial for breach of that duty. Several legal doctrines made recovery difficult, however. If the employee's negligence was a partial cause of the injury, or if the employee was aware of a dangerous condition and "chose" to work in that condition, defenses known as contributory negligence and assumption of the risk were a complete bar to recovery. If the injury was caused in part by the negligence of a coworker with similar job duties, as opposed to some omission or fault of management, the fellow servant rule prevented recovery. These defenses, along with the tendency of juries to award inconsistent and unpredictable amounts, led to efforts to find a more satisfactory system.

Workers' compensation plans, which date back to the early part of the 20th century, were the result of these efforts. Such plans were created by legislation to avoid common law obstacles facing a worker who sought compensation for a job-related injury, to simplify the recovery process, and to make awards more uniform. Workers' compensation laws were *designed* to provide an exclusive remedy against the employer; that is, the employee cannot elect to file suit on another theory, such as negligence. However, several states permit other actions under special circumstances.

Workers' compensation laws exist in all 50 states and for most federal workers. Unfortunately, these laws are not uniform, particularly with respect to hearing-loss claims, and employ a bewildering array of widely differing schemes to determine whether compensation is appropriate and, if so, how much is due (Fodor and Oleinick, 1986; see also Appendix B). To make matters worse, some states apparently administer their systems in ways that are not entirely consistent with their "governing" legislation (ASHA, 1992). In 1992, the American Speech-Language-Hearing Association (ASHA) reported that workers in the same state offices have provided different interpretations of the same rule. Before becoming involved with a workers' compensation case, the professional should obtain a copy of the appropriate state statute *and* seek advice from another professional experienced with the system. The professional should also be aware that such statutes are frequently amended.

Workers' compensation schemes share common characteristics, however. All are essentially "no-fault," creating a presumption that supplies the elements of duty owed by employer to employee and breach of that duty, in every case where there is a work-related injury. Also, the amount of compensation, if appropriate, is set (and limited) by schedule. This is the trade-off fundamental to workers' compensation: The employee need not show fault of the employer; however, the recovery will be fixed by schedule, governed for the most part by objective measures, not subjective descriptions of complaints. Beyond these basic characteristics numerous other factors must be addressed.

Assessment of Impairment

Workers' compensation systems typically provide for payment based on a weekly rate of pay, and the severity of an injury is translated into a number of weeks of payment. The weekly rate is usually determined by taking a percentage (usually two thirds) of the employee's pay record for the last year, subject to maximum and minimum reference rates. These reference rates are adjusted at least annually based on average wages for the state.

If the hearing loss causes a complete disability in fact, that is—if the employee cannot continue to work—the claim is "rated" like any other injury that creates total permanent disability. This typically results in payment of weekly benefits over the remaining work life of the worker. More often, there is no actual disability, and the rating is based on a percentage assessment of handicap that is applied to the scheduled value set for "loss of hearing" as a presumed permanent partial disability. There is no real agreement as to the formula used to calculate handicap. While a majority of states use either the methods recommended in 1959 by the American Academy of Ophthalmology and Otolaryngology (AAOO-1959), later adopted by the American Medical Association (AMA, 1961); or those defined by the American Academy of Otolaryngology (AAO, 1979; see Chapter 5), application of a formula is often supplemented by adjustments for preexisting loss, tinnitus, assumed presbycusis, or "self-assessment." In addition, some states reduce the award if improvement from the use of hearing aids is demonstrated. A loss or impairment not considered material is not compensable.

Although it is not necessary to show fault on the part of the employer, some states reduce or eliminate recovery based upon "fault" of the employee in failing to utilize hearing protection devices. A few states have set minimum noise exposure requirements, generally 90 dBA, in order to authorize an award, (e.g., Ill. Rev. Stat. Ch. 40, §138.8). Because all workers' compensation systems require a showing that the hearing loss was caused by workplace exposure, it is obvious that competent professionals will require an adequate noise-exposure history, making such a significant occupational history an implicit requirement. Because of the debate and uncertainty concerning the damage risk criteria, statutory exposure requirements are more an expression of policy than a statement of scientific principle.

Some states further complicate the issue by adjusting a worker's audiogram for nonwork-related causes. This adjustment may be based upon the opinion of an expert, or it may be statutorily presumed, and derived from a table. A majority of states reduce compensation if there is a preemployment audiogram demonstrating loss. A few states reduce compensation for presumed presbycusis, by reference to a table that reduces the percentage of handicap for the age of the worker. Ironically, common law tort principles usually permit *less* mitigation of an award because of a preexisting injury than for an injury resulting from concurrent causes, such as noise and age, if the evidence is sufficient to establish the causal relationship.

The following is an example of how one workers' compensation system, the Longshore and Harbor Workers' Compensation Act, would treat the claim of an individual with hearing levels shown in Chapter 5 at Figure 5–4. This Act covers workers who load, unload, build, repair, or disassemble vessels upon navigable waters, and uses AAO-1979 to assess a percentage handicap (33 U.S.C. §903). Our example case has hearing levels (HL) in the right ear of 15 dB at 0.5 kilohertz (kHz), 25 dB HL at 1 kHz, 35 dB HL at 2 kHz, and 45 dB HL at 3 kHz, and hearing levels in the left ear of 20 dB HL at 0.5 kHz, 40 dB HL at 1 kHz, 60 dB HL at 2 kHz, and 80 dB HL at 3 kHz, for an AAO-1979 hearing handicap of 12.5 percent. If this worker earned $600 per week he would receive about $400 (two-thirds his actual weekly earnings history) for 25 weeks (200 weeks for "loss of hearing" × 12.5 percent) or a total of $10,000.

By contrast, the state of Illinois uses a three-frequency average of 1, 2, and 3 kHz, with a 30 dB "low fence." Above the low fence, handicap is assumed at the rate of 1.82 percent for each 1 dB (Occupation Disease Act, Ill. Rev. Stat., Ch. 40, §138.8). There is no "weighting" for the better ear; in this example, a handicap of 9.1 percent in the right ear and 54.6 percent in the left ear are each applied to a 100-week maximum. Assuming the same weekly rate of pay as above, this claimant would be awarded 63.7 weeks, or $25,480.

Under workers' compensation statutes, the expert's role is somewhat limited. Opinion testimony is needed to assess the extent of the hearing loss and to determine if the loss was caused by workplace noise.

PRODUCT LIABILITY CLAIMS

Product liability law is a collection of legal theories that enables one who claims injury or damage as the result of use of a product to seek compensation from the manufacturer or supplier of the product. This area of law has received a great deal of recent publicity, much of it negative. Physicians are particularly familiar with claims involving drugs and surgical implants, which have been credited with driving up the price of medical care and actually discouraging research or release of new products. Huber (1991) reports one case where a "psychic" alleged that a CT scan caused her to lose her powers, and persuaded a jury to return a one-million-dollar verdict in her favor. This case, which suggested theories of both product liability law and malpractice, is clearly the extreme of potential legal abuse, and the verdict was ultimately set aside. The underlying theories of product liability law are not particularly revolutionary, however, and are firmly established by decades of American jurisprudence.

Cases against manufacturers of cordless telephones alleged to have caused traumatic hearing loss were common several years ago. Recently, there has been an effort to extend product liability law to the workplace, allowing the employee who claims an occupational hearing loss to seek recovery from another "deep pocket," this time without the limitation on damages imposed by workers' compensation systems. The theory behind this effort is simple, and fits fairly easily into existing legal doctrines. Once an employee identifies an alleged occupational hearing loss, in addition to the workers' compensation claim asserted, a common law action is filed against the manufacturers of tools, machinery, and equipment that generated the workplace noise. The actions are typically filed on behalf of large groups of workers, usually after they have been identified by a union screening. To date, the success of these efforts has not been established. The manufacturers are charged with failing to design quieter products and failing to warn of the need for proper hearing protection.

A triad of legal theories often raised in a single suit makes up what is described as product liability law. These theories, which have slightly different requirements and limitations, are briefly discussed below to give the reader a general understanding of the significant issues in such cases.

Negligence

A manufacturer of a product must take reasonable precautions to avoid injury to consumers or users of its products. This theory implies a "reasonable man" standard, requiring a manufacturer to exercise ordinary, prudent care in the design, manufacture, and inspection of its product, and in providing instructions to the consumer in its use. In the case of an employee suing a tool maker, for example, it may be reasonable to assume that a large employer will implement an effective hearing conservation program, which would include education about potential noise sources. Contributory or comparative negligence, such as misuse of the product, is a defense in most states, usually operating to reduce, not eliminate, recovery. Further, under this theory a manufacturer is not held to a standard of care that has not yet evolved, even though it may have been "knowable." It is no longer required that the plaintiff have a direct buyer-seller relationship with the defendant.

Breach of Warranty

The emergence of product liability law as an important doctrine in the early part of the twentieth century was largely the result of the expansion of what is essentially contract law. For many years courts have held that a manufacturer or seller gives an implied warranty with each product, promising that the product will be reasonably fit for its intended use. If the product in ordinary use causes injury or death, it typically has not met this warranty. Because this theory evolved primarily from contract and not tort law, most courts require a true buyer-seller relationship, or "privity" of contract. Further, economic losses may be recovered, although tort theories do not permit such recovery. This is a form of strict liability, which applies even to latent defects in a product that could not be prevented by reasonable design, manufacture, or inspection practices.

Strict Liability

The third theory that makes up product liability law is based upon a publication of the American Law Institute, section 402A of the Restatement of Torts. The restatement suggested liability be imposed for the sale of a product in a "defective" condition. A defect may consist of a manufacturing flaw or an unsafe design. Also, if a product is unreasonably dangerous when used in its intended manner, the failure to warn of the danger (or properly instruct on the use of the product) may make the product defective. Privity between the buyer and seller is not required.

The nuances of defining "defective" are beyond the scope of this chapter. However, the focus of the inquiry is on the product and the reasonable expectations of the consumer, including whether a known danger would be appreciated by an ordinary individual. Typically, the contributory fault of the plaintiff will operate to reduce—but not eliminate—a recovery, unless the fault is a misuse of the product that was not reasonably anticipated by the manufacturer. In most states, assumption of the risk—the voluntary exposure of oneself to a known danger—is a complete defense. In others, it is only evidence of contributory fault. In hearing loss cases, the focus of the dispute is likely to be whether effective noise abatement measures were feasible and whether warnings should have accompanied the product.

RAILROAD AND MARITIME WORKERS

In 1908, many of the common law principles of employer-employee negligence law were incorporated into the Federal Employers Liability Act (FELA; 45 U.S.C. §§51–60), which now governs the rights of all railway workers in interstate commerce. The FELA, as first enacted, abolished the fellow servant doctrine and provided that the contributory negligence of the employee would not bar recovery, but would operate only to reduce recovery by the percentage of fault attributed to the employee. Later amendments eliminated the defense of assumption of the risk and provided strict liability barring any consideration of negligence of the employee for injuries caused by violations of federal laws regulating railroad equipment. When applicable, the FELA is the exclusive remedy for injured railroad workers, although usually not the only *benefit* available,

In 1920, the Jones Act (46 U.S.C. §688) extended the essential provisions of the FELA to crew members of vessels operating in navigable waters, commonly known as seamen. An injured seaman previously had a common law remedy for work-related injury, under federal common law known as the general maritime law. Unlike the FELA, the Jones Act permitted seamen to retain their common law remedy.

The only significant legal distinction between the rights of seamen and railroad workers is that the general maritime law provides strict liability for injuries caused by the "unseaworthiness" of the vessel. A "seaworthy" vessel is one where the vessel, appurtenances, and crew are reasonably fit for their intended purposes. As a practical matter, and for purposes of this chapter, the remedies available to railroad and maritime workers are identical.

Both FELA and Jones Act claims are governed by federal, not state law. Liberal venue provisions allow these claims to be brought in state or federal court in any judicial district in which the defendant does business. This permits a practice known as forum shopping. As will be shown below, the various characteristics of these remedies *encourage* that practice.

Standard of Liability and Causation

To prevail in a FELA action, the employee must prove an injury was caused, in whole or in part, by employer negligence. Negligence is defined as the failure to use the degree of care that an ordinary, careful, and prudent person would use under the same or similar circumstances. In a case alleging occupational hearing loss, this typically means showing that the employer failed to provide part or all of an effective hearing conservation program to an employee who worked in a noise environment that required such a program. There is no binding reference standard for determining what an effective hearing conservation program is, or the noise environment that requires a program. If a violation of Federal Railroad Administration (FRA) regulations can be shown, however, a per se negligence rule is applied, imposing strict liability without regard to actual negligence of either party. Opinions about these questions are typically provided by expert witnesses, and the issues are ultimately decided by a jury.

The FELA provides a liberal test of whether an injury was caused by employer negligence. The test permits recovery for an injury if the evidence demonstrates "that employer negligence played any part, even the slightest" in producing the injury (*Rogers* v. *Missouri Pacific Railroad*, 352 U.S. 500, 506 [1957]). This means that if an employee's work-related hearing loss is caused by a combination of employee negligence in wearing nonapproved hearing protection devices, manufacturer negligence in failing to properly label the hearing protective devices, and employer negligence in failing to monitor the plaintiff and observe that he was wearing inappropriate protection, the employer will be liable for some part of the damages. If, for example, a jury determined the injury was caused by employee negligence (25 percent), manufacturer negligence (70 percent), and employer negligence (5 percent), the employer would be required to pay 5 percent of the damages and could be required to pay 75 percent if the manufacturer was insolvent.

The in whole or in part language does *not* mean that employers may be liable for that part of an employee's hearing loss not caused by the job. In cases where a gradual hearing loss results from a combination of aging, disease, work, and recreational noise exposure, the employee may only recover damages for the loss sustained as a direct result of the occupational noise exposure. Thus, where an employee's nonwork-related asthma was the cause of the worker's total inability to work, and workplace asbestos exposure caused only mild changes in pulmonary function, the employer was liable for the mild changes caused, in whole or in part, by asbestos exposure, but was *not* liable for the asthma-related disability (*Dale* v. *Baltimore & Ohio R.R.*, 552 A.2d 1037 (PA 1989)).

Assessment of Damages

Because of the lack of standards governing liability and damage assessment, FELA hearing-loss cases present issues appropriate for expert evaluation and testimony that are not typically presented by workers' compensation cases. Other common law hearing loss claims such as product liability suits (e.g., cordless telephones), medical malpractice cases, or even business invitee claims (e.g., attendees at rock concerts) present similar issues. There is no "low fence" for determining whether an individual has "an impairment sufficient to affect a person's efficiency in the activities of daily living" (AAO, 1979). Testimony concerning subjective symptoms and complaints, including complaints of tinnitus, is nearly always received in evidence. There is no agreement as to what hearing levels are considered within the range of normal, or which frequencies are important to understanding speech. This leads to inconsistent and unpredictable results with respect to identifying "compensable" injuries.

The author is familiar, for example, with two cases tried in separate courts that presented nearly identical audiograms, from two workers in their mid-forties. One case resulted in a defense verdict because the jury believed the plaintiff's hearing was typical for his age, even had he never been exposed to noise, and did not create a handicapping loss. The other case resulted in a substantial verdict, despite evidence that the hearing loss was not considered handicapping under AAO-1979. The expert witness in such cases must, therefore, assess not only the hearing levels of the plaintiff, but whether his complaints are the result of impaired hearing or the prospect of receiving a large verdict.

Tinnitus Claims

The problem of assessing injury and damages without the assistance of objective standards is particularly acute where claims of tinnitus are included. The lack of reliability of measurement of loudness and pitch by matching techniques and the prevalence of tinnitus in the population compounds the problem. Glorig (1987) described a guideline used by the Veterans Administration that may be useful to experts in forming opinions as to the validity of tinnitus complaints. This guideline lists six criteria to be met before a tinnitus complaint may be considered valid:

1. The complaint (or claim) that tinnitus was present and disabling must have been unsolicited. If the complaint was not present in the medical records prior to the claim, it seemed reasonable to assume that it arose as a consequence of the interview and medical history process.
2. The tinnitus must accompany a compensable level of hearing loss.
3. The treatment history must include one or more attempts to alleviate the perceived disturbance by medication, prosthetic management, or psychiatric intervention.
4. There must be evidence to support the idea of personality change or sleep disorders.
5. There must be no contributory history of substance abuse.
6. The complaint of tinnitus must be supported by statements from family or significant others.

The ultimate assessment is, of course, made by the jury.

Statute of Limitations

The statute of limitations for FELA cases requires that suit be filed within three years of the date the cause of action "accrues." In the event of a traumatic injury, accrual is obviously the date of the accident. In cases alleging occupational disease or injury, however, no single day or event during exposure or in the process of pathology acts alone to cause the damage. Therefore, courts look to the manifestation of symptoms as the triggering event. A rule has evolved that requires the exercise of diligence by an employee, but does not unfairly bar a claim before the employee has a reasonable opportunity to identify it. In cases of occupational hearing loss, the cause of action accrues when the plaintiff is armed with such facts that he knows, or in the exercise of reasonable care should have known, that he has suffered an injury caused by his employment (*Fries* v. *Chicago & Northwestern Transportation Co.*, 909 F.2d 1092 [7th Cir. 1990]).

While this is an objective standard, it depends on the plaintiff's recognition of subjective symptoms and level of knowledge. For example, an individual working in an extremely loud environment, who is aware of the availability of hearing protection and its purpose and who experiences symptoms of hearing loss (even temporary symptoms) will likely be required to assert a claim within three years of the appearance of the first symptoms. This individual *should have known* that symptoms were caused by the job, regardless of actual knowledge. However, an individual who works in a moderate noise environment—and who is completely inexperienced in the use of hearing protection and unaware of a need for it—presents a different case. Without evidence that this individual had reason to associate his slowly developing problems with his job and not simply advancing age, his cause of action might not be deemed to accrue until he recognizes a problem in normal functioning or receives a diagnosis of hearing loss.

The combination of liberal venue rules, lack of recognized standards, and inconsistent jury determination of highly technical issues makes the FELA an antiquated and unsatisfactory vehicle for dispute resolution, particularly in hearing-loss cases. Brummer (1984) relates a history of similar criticism dating back more than 60 years. Railroads have sought reform or repeal, but trial lawyers, who benefit from contingent fee arrangements, have defended the Act under the guise of its purported role as a "safety" statute. Unless and until this reform effort is successful, the FELA will continue to bring challenges and opportunities to experts in noise and hearing.

IMPORTANCE OF FEDERAL NOISE REGULATION IN INJURY LITIGATION

As explained above, in common law actions the questions of whether a workplace is reasonably safe and whether a noise-exposure history caused a particular hearing loss are resolved by a jury. Experts often use federal regulations and their accompanying comments to support opinions on these important issues, even if the regulations do not apply to the facts of the case and are not admitted in evidence at trial. These regulations also form the basis for what constitutes standard practice in the industry, influencing both corporate conduct and the perception of what is "ordinary care." Legal rules concerning admissibility of regulations and their effect if admissible are discussed in more detail below. As a practical matter, if admitted in evidence, regulations effectively provide a "minimum" standard of conduct, regardless of their legal effect, because most jurors perceive them that way. The Department of Labor took months of testimony and years of deliberation to endorse an occupational noise standard designed to "furnish to . . . employees . . . a place of employment . . . free from recognized hazards . . ." (29 U.S.C. §654 [1970]). Yet a jury may decide compliance with that standard was not sufficient, effectively "overruling" this determination.

A Brief History of Federal Occupational Noise Regulations

Government regulation of occupational noise exposure roughly paralleled the development of damage risk criteria. In 1964, efforts by the Department of Labor to regulate occupational noise exposure led to the formation of the Intersociety Committee on Guidelines for Noise Exposure Control, a panel of distinguished experts representing the American Conference of Governmental Industrial Hygienists (ACGIH), the AAOO, the American Academy of Occupational Medicine, the American Industrial Hygiene Association, and the Industrial Medical Association. The committee reviewed and evaluated existing literature and studies, all of which reviewed the hearing levels of workers and evaluated their noise exposure history by octave band analysis. The major studies reviewed included Glorig and Nixon (1960), Glorig, Ward, and Nixon (1961), and Gallo and Glorig (1964). The committee studied the percentage of noise-exposed persons found to suffer significant hearing loss as defined by AAOO-1959, compared to the percentage of nonnoise-exposed persons who suffered similar loss.

The Intersociety Committee (1967) concluded that the percentage of workers exposed to 85 dB octave band noise (approximately 92 dBA) with significant hearing loss exceeded the percentage found in the control population by 8 percent. However, this difference was just at the limits of the precision of the data. At exposure to 88 dB octave band noise levels (approximately 95 dBA), an excess percentage of workers with significant loss was found that clearly reached the level of statistical meaning. At exposures to 78 dB octave band noise levels (approximately 85 dBA), the rate of significant hearing loss was essentially identical to the control population.

Based in large part upon the efforts of the Intersociety Committee, the ACGIH proposed a limit of four to eight hours per day of 92 dBA (Jones, 1968). According to Jones (1984), the initial noise regulations adopted by the Secretary of Labor under the Walsh-Healy Act chose essentially the midpoint of this recommendation, and six hours per day at 92 dBA became eight hours per day at 90 dBA (U.S. Dept. of Labor . . . OSHA, 1969). Thus, the first federal occupational noise regulation was slightly more conservative than suggested by existing studies.

The Occupational Safety and Health Act was adopted in 1970, and in 1972 the National Institute for Occupational Safety and Health issued its "criteria document" (U.S. Dept. of Health . . . NIOSH, 1972). In response, the Secretary of Labor appointed a standards advisory committee to review the data and, if appropriate, revise and supplement the Walsh-Healy standard that had been adopted as an Occupational Safety and Health Administration (OSHA) regulation in 1971. This committee, under the leadership of Dr. Floyd A. Van Atta, held meetings and public hearings and reviewed written submissions, including the Environmental Protection Agency's so-called levels document (U.S. EPA,

1974). Both the criteria document and the levels document concluded that a risk of significant hearing loss at exposures above 80 dBA was established by the data, and that a much higher risk of significant loss existed at exposure levels of 90 dBA and greater. There was pressure to adopt exposure limits of 85 dBA or lower, particularly from the EPA.

After careful review of the new and old studies, the standards committee, however, rejected this suggestion and recommended keeping the 90 dBA eight-hour standard, while using 85 dBA as a "surveillance level." The scientific representative of the committee, Dr. Joseph Sataloff (1973), concluded that "we can protect practically all of our population by effective standards at 90 dBA." Based on the committee's recommendation, a proposed regulation was published in the Federal Register (U.S. Dept. of Labor . . . OSHA, 1974), which recommended retaining the 90 dBA eight-hour time-weighted exposure limit, and requiring a hearing conservation program for exposures exceeding 85 dBA on an eight-hour time-weighted basis.

The EPA filed formal exceptions to the OSHA proposal, claiming that the standard did not sufficiently protect workers. OSHA (U.S. Dept. of Labor . . . 1975) responded by reviewing the credible data establishing damage risk criteria and discussing the EPA objections. Because of criticism of the definition of handicap, OSHA also considered the impact of assessing handicap using the four-frequency formula that was later adopted as AAO-1979. OSHA concluded that it was "clear that the risk of impairment is minimal under either an 85 dBA or 90 dBA standard, being limited to the most sensitive 2 percent of the population at risk." Table 11–1 shows the risk assessment figures cited by OSHA using both AAOO-1959 and a predecessor to AAO-1979. In reaching this conclusion, OSHA expressly rejected the report of Baughn (1973), which suggested a higher incidence of hearing handicap in workers in the 85 to 90 dBA environment, because of the many flaws of the study. Conclusions of NIOSH and EPA that 85 to 90 dBA posed a higher risk of loss were implicitly rejected.

The Inter Industry Noise Study (Yerg et al., 1978) was designed to address weaknesses of previous studies and provide a critical analysis of the effect of working in steady-state noise of 82 to 92 dBA. This report, which included longitudinal data for exposures from 1974 to 1978, concluded that there was no statistically significant difference in the speech-frequency hearing levels of noise-exposed workers as compared to a control population exposed to less than 75 dBA. The report also concluded that there were no statistically significant differences at any frequency in the hearing levels of workers within the noise-exposed population, that is, between those exposed to 82 dBA and those exposed to 92 dBA. This report seemed to validate OSHA's 1975 conclusions, and carried the additional credibility of coauthors Glorig and Sataloff.

However, in 1981 OSHA published its final rule, accompanied by extensive comments (U.S. Dept. of Labor . . . OSHA, 1981). While the substance of the rule was not materially different from the 1974 proposal, the conclusions of the comments were materially changed, dramatically affecting how the

TABLE 11–1
**Estimated Hearing Impairment Expected in Sensitive Individuals
Because of Occupational Noise Exposure**

Level (dBA)	Duration (years)	Percent of Population	Hearing Level (dB)				Impairment (%)[c]	
			500	1,000	2,000	3,000	AAOO[a]	AAO[b]
90	30	2	20	25	30	42	0	6.4
90	30	10	12	16	23	31	0	0
85	30	2	15	18	26	34	0	0
85	30	10	10	12	17	22	0	0

[a]AAOO-1959 (AMA, 1961).
[b]AAO-1979.
[c]Impairment figures (percent) have been recalculated using the tabled hearing level values, and are corrected from the incorrect impairment figures in the source document.
Source: OSHA, 1975.

rule was and is perceived by many professionals, many of whom are unfamiliar with the underlying studies. A contributing author on the OSHA staff in 1981 was on the staff of EPA at the time of the publication of its levels document, perhaps coloring the tone of the new comments.

Specifically, the comments state that the work of the EPA, NIOSH, and the International Organization for Standardization (ISO-1999, 1975; a draft standard derived primarily from data of Baughn), "provide reliable and consistent estimates of the percentages of the population at risk of developing material impairment due to exposure to daily average noise levels of 80, 85, and 90 dBA for a working lifetime" (U.S. Dept. of Labor . . . OSHA, 1981). OSHA's summary of these reports suggested that up to 29 percent of the population exposed to noise levels of 85 to 90 dBA for a working lifetime suffer a material impairment in hearing. The summary also suggested some workers in 80 to 85 dBA would suffer material impairment as a result of their jobs. Table 9–1 shows the risk assessment figures published with these comments. A regulation that failed to protect such an important percentage of workers would certainly not meet OSHA's mandate to "furnish to . . . employees . . . a place of employment . . . free from recognized hazards . . ." (29 U.S.C. §654 [1970]). Accompanied with these comments, many people concluded the OSHA regulations were a "compromise," clearly a "minimum" standard in the context of litigation.

In 1990, following years of additional research and analysis, ISO published ISO-1999-E (1990). ANSI S3.44 (American National Standards Institute, 1996) is nearly identical to ISO-1999. Like the previous version, the new standard provides algorithms that predict the percentage of "excess" hearing loss that can be expected in a population with a given noise exposure. Using the same assumptions about noise exposure and material impairment used by the Intersociety Committee (AIHA, 1967) and OSHA, it predicts no statistically significant risk of material impairment at exposures of 85 dBA (Clark, 1992). Even substituting the modern definition of material impairment, AAO-1979, only slightly increases the predicted excess loss at exposures of 85 and 90 dBA. Table 11–2 and Figure 11–1 show those risk estimates as predicted by ANSI S3.44 for ISO-1999 (calculated by Dobie using Annexes A, B, and E of ANSI S3.44-1996). The method in Annex E assumes that an individual's hearing levels are perfectly correlated; in other words, that an individual with hearing levels in the 90th percentile at 1,000 Hz will have hearing levels in that percentile at all other frequencies. This likely overstates the percentage of people impaired at noise levels at or below 90 dBA and may understate the percentage impaired at higher levels.

NIOSH (1998) has recently published a revised "criteria" document on occupational noise. Using "new scientific information," NIOSH reanalyzed the same data studied and reported in its original Criteria Document. Its findings were consistent with the predictions of ISO-1999-E (1990) and ANSI S3.44-1996. However, NIOSH changed its definition of hearing impairment, omitting 500 Hz and including 4,000 Hz, based on a 1981 task force report (ASHA, 1981). By changing the definition of the level of hearing deserving protection, NIOSH was able to maintain its position that a 90 dBA time weighted average is not sufficiently protective. Absent a medical consensus based on empirical data and peer-reviewed publications, it is difficult to justify adopting a new definition of hearing handicap. By reference to more widely accepted definitions, this recent work of NIOSH essentially confirms the validity of the OSHA standard.

Thus, after almost 30 years of debate, it appears that 90 dBA is "a highly satisfactory criterion to determine the need for a hearing conservation program" (Glorig, 1980), and that the existing OSHA regulations are much more protective than many believe. The 85 dBA eight-hour exposure level is now well accepted as appropriate as an action level for hearing conservation, and

TABLE 11–2
Calculation of Percentage of Population at Risk of Hearing Loss, Assuming Male Workers, 60 Years of Age, with 40 Years of Exposure, Using Highly Screened and Unscreened Populations

Exposure	% Impaired		% Excess Risk	
	Annex A	*Annex B*	*Annex A*	*Annex B*
No noise	13.2%	28.3%		
80 dBA	13.6%	28.7%	<1%	<1%
85 dBA	16%	31%	3%	3%
90 dBA	24%	36%	11%	8%
95 dBA	38%	46%	25%	18%
100 dBA	65%	72%	52%	44%

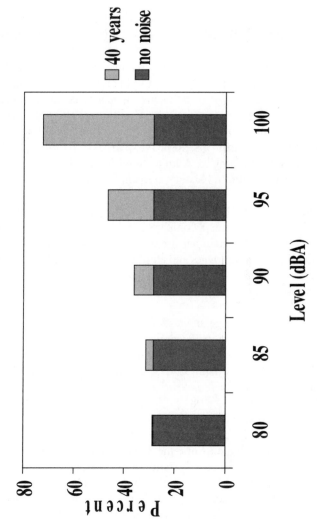

Figure 11–1. Excess risk of hearing handicap as a function of exposure level (Annexes A, B, and E).

there is no rational reason to consider a higher or lower level. Clearly, efforts at proper enforcement of the present standard are more important in ensuring a safe workplace. The above history does make it clear, however, that in the context of litigation, our occupational noise standard should be viewed as highly effective, not a compromise.

Use of Regulations and Alleged Violations as Evidence

The legislative history of the Occupational Safety and Health Act reflects the intention of Congress to limit its use in civil suits. A Senate report states that the act was not designed to "in any manner affect any Federal or state workmen's compensation laws, or the rights, duties, or liabilities of employers and employees under them," or to "modify other Federal laws prescribing safety and health standards" (S. Rep. No. 1282, 91st Cong. [1970]), reprinted in 1970 U.S. Code Cong. & Admin. News 5177, 5199).

Consistent with this history, Section 653(b)(4) of the Act states:

Nothing in [OSHA] shall be construed to supersede or in any manner affect any workmen's compensation law or to enlarge or diminish or affect in any other manner the common law or statutory rights, duties, or liabilities of employers and employees under any law with respect to injuries, diseases, or death of employees arising out of, or in the course of, employment.

This clear language suggests that evidence of the regulations or violations should have no effect in any civil suit, and should not even be mentioned in evidence. The better reasoned cases follow this logic, but other cases have not.

Most civil cases using OSHA regulations have failed to address the language of the Act. In *Industrial Tile* v. *Stewart* (388 So. 2d 171 [Ala. 1980], *cert. denied*, 499 U.S. 1081 [1981]), plaintiff sued for injuries sustained while attempting to aid an imperiled employee of Industrial Tile. The trial court admitted evidence that Industrial Tile had been cited for violating OSHA regulations. The Alabama Supreme Court referred to previous cases admitting regulations as evidence of a standard of care, and reasoned that "[i]f the regulations are admissible as going to show a standard of care, then it seems only reasonable that evidence of violation of the standards would also be admissible as evidence that the defendant failed to meet the standards that it should have followed" (388 So. 2d at 174).

In *Melerine* v. *Avondale Shipyards, Inc.* (659 F.2d 706 [5th Cir. 1981]), the employee of a contractor sued the employer of a crane operator for injuries sustained while assisting the crane operator, arguing that violation of an OSHA regulation established negligence per se. The court held that, in order to establish negligence per se, a plaintiff must prove "th[e] violation of a statute which is intended to protect the class of persons to which the plaintiff belongs against the risk of the type of harm which has in fact occurred." If negligence per se is so proved then the plaintiff bears the burden of proving that the violation was the proximate cause of his injury. The court held that the plaintiff fell outside the protected class of persons under OSHA, but nonetheless held that the plaintiff could offer the OSHA regulations as evidence of the defendant's negligence even though the regulations could not be used to establish negligence per se. Finally, *Pratico* v. *Portland Terminal Co.* (783 F.2d 255 [1st Cir. 1985]), a FELA case, held that violation of an OSHA regulation constitutes negligence per se, arguing this did not "affect" liability.

Those cases that refuse to admit OSHA regulations in evidence, or those that permit their admissibility but refuse to allow evidence of a violation to show per se fault, simply acknowledge the plain language of 29 U.S.C. §653(b)(4). If the Act is not permitted to "enlarge or diminish or affect" any civil action, evidence of OSHA regulations is, at best, superfluous and, at worst, highly prejudicial. A recent FELA opinion (*Ries* v. *National RR Passenger Corp.*, 960 F.2d 1156, 1162 [3rd Cir. 1992]) provides a good example:

> If a violation of an OSHA regulation could constitute negligence per se and bar contributory negligence under the FELA, it would be almost axiomatic that the effect would be to "enlarge or diminish or affect" the statutory duty or liability of employer.

In *Otto* v. *Specialties, Inc.* (386 F. Supp. 1240 [N. D. Miss. 1974]), plaintiff sued for injuries sustained when he fell from a ladder while performing work for the defendant. Defendant moved to prevent the plaintiff from introducing OSHA regulations at trial. The defendant argued that because OSHA does not create a private civil remedy, none should be implied, and plaintiff should not refer to the Act during trial. The plaintiff, on the other hand, maintained that even if OSHA created no private remedy, its standards could still be used under the common law as evidence of the defendant's negligence.

The court stated that "[n]owhere in the Act or in its legislative history can be found any indication that Congress intended to allow additional civil actions instituted by aggrieved employees injured through violations of OSHA standards." The court found that the penalties set forth under OSHA's provisions provided sufficient enforcement mechanisms and that "[n]o useful purpose related to Congressional policy goals would be served by tacking on yet another enforcement vehicle." Thus, the court held that "OSHA regulations may not be used as conclusive proof or evidence of negligence" (386 F. Supp. at 1245).

Where OSHA regulations are preempted by another agency, such as the FRA, additional policy reasons favor exclusion from evidence. Where another agency exclusively governs the activity at issue, even if it has chosen not to issue specific regulations, evidence of OSHA regulations or violations should not be admitted as evidence.

Litigants have also attempted to use OSHA regulations in product liability cases to show that certain products are unreasonably dangerous. In *Minichello* v. *U.S. Industries* (756 F.2d 26 [6th Cir. 1985]), plaintiff appealed from a verdict in favor of defendant, arguing that it was an error for the court to admit evidence showing that the product in question did not violate OSHA regulations. The appellate court agreed and reversed, holding that it was improper to use OSHA regulations to establish whether a product is unreasonably dangerous.

The court based its decision on the language of Section 653(b)(4), reasoning that:

> If knowledge of the regulations leads the trier of fact to find a product defective, the effect is to impermissibly alter the civil standard of liability. If, on the other hand, knowledge of the regulations does not affect a result the trier of fact would have reached even without the knowledge, the regulations serve no purpose and their discussion is simply a waste of time (756 F.2d at 29).

In another product liability case, *McKinnon* v. *Skil Corp.* (638 F.2d 270 [1st Cir. 1981]), the court refused to admit OSHA regulations in evidence, holding that such regulations were not relevant in a product liability action against a manufacturer. (See *Bailey* v. *V & O Press Co.*, 770 F.2d 601 [6th Cir. 1985]) where court held that testimony regarding OSHA standards was irrelevant to manufacturer's obligation to make a safe product; and *Murphy* v. *L & J Press Corp.*, 558 F.2d 407 (8th Cir. 1977) finding OSHA regulations inadmissible in strict liability action).

Regulations Often Encountered in Civil Litigation

The following is a brief description of those regulations most likely to affect cases alleging noise-induced hearing loss. The OSHA regulations are discussed first because they are best known and govern the working conditions of the largest number of workers. The major provisions are mentioned to provide a framework of comparison with other regulatory schemes. A detailed discussion of these regulations is found in Chapter 9.

OSHA: 29 C.F.R. §1910.95

The OSHA regulations regarding exposure limits and hearing conservation cover most American workers. Construction and the oil and gas drilling and servicing industries are not covered by the OSHA Hearing Conservation

Amendment; OSHA has informally stated its intent to revise its rules to cover those workers more completely. In general, all employers are covered, except for industries regulated by other agencies. The agriculture industry is the only major industry specifically excluded by OSHA (29 C.F.R. §1928.21).

Two concepts provide the foundation for the OSHA occupational noise regulations. The first is that workplace exposure must be limited to a time-weighted average of 90 dBA or less, on an eight-hour basis [29 C.F.R. §1910.95(a)]. Measurement procedures require integrating measurements from noise sources of 90 dBA and above (a 90 dBA "threshold") using a 5 dB exchange rate. To meet this permissible exposure limit (PEL), an employer may be required to implement engineering or administrative controls, or impose mandatory hearing protection, depending on the circumstances.

The second concept underlying the OSHA regulations is that an effective hearing conservation program must be implemented for employees who are exposed to time-weighted averages of 85 dBA on an eight-hour basis. This exposure is also measured using a 5 dB exchange rate, but integrates measurements from additional noise sources by employing an 80 dBA threshold. The Hearing Conservation Amendment was published as a final rule on March 8, 1983, and initially required compliance before March 1, 1984. However, the regulations were stayed by court action until early in 1985 (*Forging Industries Association* v. *Secretary of Labor*, 773 F.2d 1436 [4th Cir. en banc. 1985]).

OSHA Construction Standards: 29 C.F.R. §1926.52

These regulations apply to workers in the construction industry. They impose a PEL of 90 dBA on an eight-hour time-weighted basis, measured with a 90 dBA threshold and a 5 dB exchange rate. However, hearing conservation measures are not specified. Amendment of this standard is likely within the next few years.

Mine Safety and Health Administration (MSHA): 30 C.F.R. §62.100

In September 1999 the Mine Safety and Health Administration announced a final rule (MSHA, 1999) effective in September of 2000, providing uniform regulation for all types of mines. The regulation is similar to the OSHA Hearing Conservation Amendment, with a few modifications. MSHA added a "dual hearing protection level," at a time-weighted eight-hour exposure of 105 dBA. At and above those levels, MSHA requires double hearing protection, although its rule also prohibits any exposure over 115 dBA (slow response), determined without reference to hearing protection. MSHA requires that mine operators use "all feasible engineering and administrative controls to reduce the miner's noise exposure to the permissible exposure level" and to "as low a level as is feasible" (30 C.F.R. §62.130). This is similar to the language of the OSHA regulation. OSHA typically assumes that noise control measures are not "feasible" below about 105 dBA.

Federal Railroad Administration: 49 C.F.R. §229.115

These regulations apply to most railroad employees with the exception of shop workers. Where they apply, they preempt OSHA standards. FRA imposes a PEL of 90 dBA on an eight-hour time-weighted basis. However, because of extended work duty cycles, the PEL is extended to 12 hours, permitting a maximum time-weighted exposure of 87 dBA, to be measured with an 87 dBA threshold. No hearing conservation requirement is specified. It is anticipated that FRA will also adopt an OSHA-based hearing conservation requirement in the near future.

Numerous other government publications and regulations, while perhaps not directly regulating workplace exposures, may affect litigation. One such example is the United States Coast Guard Navigation and Vessel Inspection Circular No. 12-82, *Recommendations on Control of Excessive Noise*, June 2, 1982. Other examples include 49 C.F.R. §325.7, concerning motor vehicle noise emissions, 49 C.F.R. §393.94, regulating vehicle interior noise levels, 40 C.F.R. §204, concerning construction equipment noise emissions, 49 C.F.R. §201, regulating railroad equipment noise emissions (excluding horns and other warning devices), and 40 C.F.R. §211, requiring certain products to have noise labels. These latter regulations are not well known, perhaps because of the absence of an enforcement mechanism at the EPA.

ADMISSIBILITY OF EXPERT OPINION TESTIMONY

Expert testimony is permitted as an exception to general principles of evidence which prohibit opinion testimony. The exception is based on the assumption that the subject of the testimony is beyond the knowledge of the typical juror, and the expert is qualified to discuss it. Until recent years there was little court oversight of expert testimony, beyond determining whether the expert's education, training, or experience provided a sufficient basis for the opinions offered. The result was some testimony which had little foundation in science or medicine, and was at best, speculation or theory. Thousands of cases involving silicone gel filled breast implants are a poignant example (Angell, 1996).

In science and medicine new discoveries are not always widely anticipated or immediately accepted. While "junk scientists" often cite examples of how important discoveries were initially derided and rejected, most new theories are wrong, and are not *ever* confirmed. Confirmation using the scientific method requires that findings be replicated and that theories pass peer review. In short, "discoveries" should be made outside of the courtroom, and verdicts based on real science, not theory or speculation. It is beyond debate that juries are not well equipped to decide between competing theories of science, or even decide if they are "junk science" or worthy of true debate (Huber, 1991). Experienced trial lawyers would be able to convince many juries that "cold fusion" was a good source of energy!

How do courts distinguish opinion testimony based on real science from that based on "courtroom science"? Prior to the adoption of the Federal Rules of Evidence, all federal and most state courts followed the *Frye* test. *Frye* v. *United States,* 293 F. 1013 (D.C. Cir. 1923). *Frye* involved a criminal defendant's offer of testimony that he had passed a lie detector test. The testimony was excluded as unreliable. Under the *Frye* test "novel" scientific evidence was admissible only if the principle upon which it was based was "sufficiently established to have gained general acceptance in the particular field in which it belongs." *Id.* at 1014. Following the adoption of the Federal Rules of Evidence, however, many courts focused only on the qualifications of the expert, and left the "substance" of the testimony to the cross-examination process. This system left experts free to use one standard to reach conclusions in the courtroom and another in the scientific community.

In *Daubert* v. *Merrill Dow Pharmaceuticals, Inc.,* 509 U.S. 579, 113 S. Ct. 2786 (1993), the United States Supreme Court held that the Federal Rules of Evidence, and in particular Fed. R. Evid. 702, superseded *Frye*'s "general acceptance" test. *Daubert* introduced a "new era" in the scrutiny of expert testimony. Faced with a proffer of expert scientific evidence, the trial court must act as "gatekeeper" and scrutinize the proposed testimony. *Daubert* is now followed by numerous state courts, in part because many states adopted the Federal Rules of Evidence almost verbatim. In order to prepare an opinion which will be admissible, the expert needs a general understanding of *Daubert*.

Daubert established two requirements. First, the evidence must be reliable, or in other words, trustworthy. *Daubert,* 509 U.S. at 590 n.9, 113 S. Ct. at 2795 n.9. Trustworthiness requires that the information be supported by scientific methods and procedures. *Id.* at 590, 113 S. Ct. at 2795. Second, the evidence must be relevant. *Id.* at 591, 113 S. Ct. at 2795–96. The criterion of relevance is one of "fit." *Id.* In other words, the proffered testimony or evidence must be sufficiently tied to the facts of the case that it will help the jury in resolving a factual dispute. *Id.*

The Supreme Court discussed four factors that help determine whether an opinion is reliable or trustworthy. The first factor is whether the theory or technique can be and has been tested. *Id.* at 593, 113 S. Ct. at 2796. The second is whether the theory or technique has been subjected to peer review and publication. *Id.* at 593, 113 S. Ct. at 2797. The third factor is the known or potential rate of error. *Id.* at 594, 113 S. Ct. at 2797. The final factor, as required by *Frye,* is whether the theory has been generally accepted by the scientific community. *Id.* Many courts now also consider whether the expert's proffered testimony "grew naturally and directly" from research conducted independent of litigation and was thereby trustworthy, or whether the expert formed his opinion in the context of litigation, rendering the testimony suspect. *Daubert v. Merrill Dow Pharmaceuticals, Inc.*, 35 F.3d 1131, 1317 (9th Cir. 1995) (opinion on remand from the Supreme Court).

How does a physician or other expert prepare for a *Daubert* review? A typical case requires a good understanding of the history and findings, a knowledge of the appropriate diagnostic criteria, and a logical explanation of the application of the latter to the former. In a "novel" case, it may be necessary to review the epidemiology of the adverse health outcome, and to be prepared to explain how the studies meet the criteria suggested by Sir Bradford Hill for determining causation (1965). For further discussion of these issues the reader is referred to books by the Federal Judicial Center (1994), and by Foster and Huber (1997).

REFERENCES

American Academy of Otolaryngology–Committee on Hearing and Equilibrium and the American Council of Otolaryngology–Committee on the Medical Aspects of Noise. 1979. Guide for the evaluation of hearing handicap. *JAMA* 241(19):2055–2059.

American Medical Association–Committee on Medical Rating of Physical Impairment. 1961. Guide to the evaluation for permanent impairment: Ear, nose, throat, and related structures. *JAMA* 177(7):489–501.

American National Standards Institute. 1996. Determination of Occupational Noise Exposure and Estimation of Noise-Induced Hearing Impairment. ANSI S3.44-1996. New York: Acoustical Society of America.

American Speech-Language-Hearing Association (ASHA). 1992. A survey of states' workers' compensation practices for occupational hearing loss. *ASHA Suppl.* 34(Suppl. 8):2–8.

American Speech-Language-Hearing Association(ASHA), Task Force on the Definition of Hearing Handicap. 1981. On the definition of hearing handicap. *ASHA* 23:293–297.

Angell, M. 1996. *Science on Trial: The Clash of Medical Evidence and the Law in the Breast Implant Case*. London and New York: W. W. Norton & Company.

Baughn, W. L. 1973. *Relation Between Daily Noise Exposure and Hearing Loss Based on the Evaluation of 6,835 Industrial Noise Exposure Cases (AMRL-TR-83-53)*. Wright-Patterson Air Force Base, Dayton, OH: Aerospace Medical Research Laboratory.

Brummer, C. 1984. Occupational disease litigation under the Federal Employers' Liability Act. *The Forum* XIX(2):205–232.

Clark, William W. 1992. Hearing: The effects of noise. *Otolaryngol. Head Neck Surg.* 106(6):669–676.

Federal Judicial Center. 1994. *Reference Manual on Scientific Evidence*. St. Paul, MN: West Publishing Co.

Fodor, W. J. and A. Oleinick. 1986. Workers' compensation for occupational noise-induced hearing loss: A review of science and the law, and proposed reforms. *St. Louis University Law Journal* 30:703–804.

Foster, K. R. and P. W. Huber. 1997. *Judging Science: Scientific Knowledge and the Federal Laws*. Cambridge, MA: MIT Press.

Gallo, Ronald and Aram Glorig. 1964. Permanent threshold shift changes produced by noise exposure and aging. *Am. Ind. Hyg. Assoc. J.* 25(3):237–245.

Glorig, Aram. 1980. Noise: Past, present and future. *Ear & Hearing.* 1(1):4–18.

———. 1987. *Tinnitus: Suggested Guidelines for Determining Impairment, Handicap and Disability*. Paper read at the Annual Meeting of the American Academy of Otolaryngology–Head and Neck Surgery, September 1987, Chicago.

Glorig, Aram and James Nixon. 1960. Distribution of hearing loss in various populations. *Ann. Otol. Laryngol. Rhinol.* 69(2):497–516.

Glorig, Aram, W. Dixon Ward, and James Nixon. 1961. Damage risk criteria and noise induced hearing loss. *Arch. Otolaryngol.* 74(10):413–423,

Hill, A. B. 1965. The environment and disease: association or causation? *Proc. Roy. Soc. Med.* 59:295–300.

Huber, Peter W. 1991. *Galileo's Revenge: Junk Science in the Court Room*. New York: Basic Books, Inc.

International Organization for Standardization. 1975. *Assessment of Occupational Noise Exposure for Hearing Conservation Purposes, ISO-1999*. Geneva: International Organization for Standardization.

International Organization for Standardization. 1990. Acoustics: *Determination of Occupational Noise Exposure and Estimation of Noise-Induced Hearing Impairment, ISO-1999*. Geneva: International Organization for Standardization.

Intersociety Committee on Guidelines for Noise Exposure Control. 1967. Guidelines for noise exposure control. *Am. Ind. Hyg. Assoc. J.* 28(5):418–424.

Jones, Herbert H. 1968. American conference of governmental industrial hygienists' proposed threshold limit value for noise. *Am. Ind. Hyg. Assoc. J.* 29(6):537–540.

———. 1984. Historical development of the Walsh-Healy noise regulations. In *Annals of the American Conference of Governmental Industrial Hygienists: Volume 9—Threshold Limit Values: Discussion and Thirty-Five Year Index With Recommendations*, ed. Marshall E. LaNier, pp. 187–191. Cincinnati: American Conference of Governmental Industrial Hygienists.

Mine Safety and Health Administration (MSHA). 1999. Mine Safety and Health Administration—Notice of Proposed Rulemaking. *Federal Register* 64(176), Sept. 13, 1999: 49548–49634.

Sataloff, Joseph. 1973. *Meeting of the Standard Advisory Committee on Noise*. Paper read at the U.S. Department of Labor—Occupational Health and Safety Administration, August 11, 1973, Waterville, Maine.

U.S. Department of Health, Education and Welfare—National Institute for Occupational Safety and Health. 1972. *Criteria for a Recommended Standard: Occupational Exposure to Noise (HSM 73, 11001)*. Washington, DC: U.S. Government Printing Office.

U.S. Department of Health and Human Services—National Institute for Occupational Safety and Health. 1998. *Criteria for a Recommended Standard: Occupational Exposure to Noise, Revised Criteria*. Washington, DC: U.S. Government Printing Office.

U.S. Department of Labor. 1969. Walsh-Healy Noise Regulation. *Federal Register* 34(May 20, 1969):7946–7949.

U.S. Department of Labor—Occupational Safety and Health Administration. 1971. Occupational Safety and Health Standards, National Consensus Standards and Established Federal Standards. *Federal Register* 36(105; May 29, 1971):10518.

———. 1974. Occupational Noise Exposure: Proposed Requirements and Procedures. *Federal Register* 39(207; October 24, 1974):37773–37784.

———. 1975. Occupational Noise Exposure: Review and Report Requested by EPA. *Federal Register* 40(53; March 18, 1975):12336–12339.

———. 1981. Occupational Noise Exposure: Hearing Conservation Amendment. *Federal Register* 46(11; January 16, 1981):4078–4179.

U.S. Environmental Protection Agency. 1974. *Information on Levels of Environmental Noise Requisite to Protect Public Health and Welfare with an Adequate Margin of Safety—550/9-74-004*. Washington, DC: U.S. Government Printing Office.

Yerg, Raymond A., Joseph Sataloff, Aram Glorig, and Hyman Menduke. 1978. Inter Industry Noise Study: The effects upon hearing of steady state noise between 82 and 92 dBA. *J. Occup. Med.* 20(5):351–358.

Chapter 12

Otologic Evaluation

BEFORE THE VISIT

This chapter will describe what actually happens during otologic evaluation (including the audiometric examination that usually accompanies it). However, it is essential to first discuss some types of information that are best obtained before the patient's visit to the otologist's or otolaryngologist's office.

Reasons for Referral

Preemployment

Employers may want complete otologic evaluation on prospective employees for any of several reasons. First, they may need to know whether the worker's hearing is adequate for the communicative demands of the job. As indicated in Chapter 5, some workers (e.g., airline pilots, railroad engineers, and interstate truckers) are covered by statutory hearing requirements; in other cases, the determination of job fitness, with respect to hearing abilities, is extremely difficult. More often, the prospective employee is referred for the purpose of verifying abnormalities detected on baseline audiometric testing in the hearing conservation program. Dobie and Archer (1981) have shown that otologic referrals based on baseline audiometric abnormalities have a fairly high yield for detection of significant otologic disease, especially when significant asymmetries are present. In these cases, diagnosis and treatment can be initiated. Even when no treatable otological disorder is uncovered, the preemployment evaluation establishes the degree of prior loss, which may limit any damages for which the prospective employer might be responsible in the future.

During Employment

Hearing conservation programs (HCPs) for workers whose time-weighted average exposures exceed 85 dBA must include annual audiometry, with professional supervision (physician or audiologist). The Occupational Safety and Health Administration (OSHA) does not specify otologic referral criteria, but virtually all HCPs have some system by which workers with otologic complaints or large changes in hearing are referred for evaluation. Chapter 9 discusses criteria for otologic referral. The otologist's role is to determine whether the hearing changes detected in the HCP are real, whether they are work-related, and whether there are any serious or treatable otologic conditions. The otologist can also reinforce the counseling of the HCP regarding reduction of noise exposure, including the use of personal hearing protective devices.

Compensation Claim

Usually, workers file for workers' compensation near the end of their careers, although midcareer filings are also permitted. It is essential that the otologist be informed whether a particular patient referral is part of a workers' compensation claim or not. The need for careful evaluation and differential diagnosis is the same as for an HCP referral, but there is a greater emphasis on a valid and quantitative estimate of hearing handicap.

Lawsuit

Although most occupational hearing loss claims come through the workers' compensation systems of the state and federal governments, certain classes of workers (for example, railroad trainmen) are permitted to sue their employers for noise-induced hearing loss (NIHL). In addition, individuals may suffer hearing loss from head injuries, ototoxic drugs, surgical misfortunes, and other acts or omissions for which they may wish to sue. The otologist's role in these cases is to provide diagnosis and sometimes treatment, and to assess the magnitude of the hearing loss, if any, and the handicap associated with it.

Obviously, the otologist can do a better job if the purpose of the referral is made clear.

It is not always necessary for the otologist to physically see and examine a patient to render a valid medical-legal opinion. In some cases, multiple recent otologic examinations have already been performed with no dispute regarding the facts of the history, physical findings, audiological data, and so on. In such cases, one can often counsel the attorney or insurance company requesting consultation without actually seeing the patient. However, when deposition or court testimony is likely to be required, many attorneys will request a complete examination, if only to add credibility to the otologic consultant's testimony.

OUTSIDE RECORDS

In many cases prior hearing tests, especially if done before the event or exposure alleged to have caused hearing loss, can be crucial to the decision-making process. When occupational noise exposure is in question, workplace sound level measurements or dosimeter readings indicate whether the exposure was indeed potentially hazardous and, if so, gives some indication of the magnitude of loss to be expected after a given period of exposure. The methods and examples in Chapter 13 show how important an audiometric history and noise exposure measurements can be, especially when allocating the hearing loss between different causes, for example, noise and aging. When exposure measurements are unavailable, approximate figures can often be obtained from published measures made for similar jobs and workplaces (see Appendix A).

When some other form of injury is at question, accident reports, medical records and test results can be important to the otologist. It is far preferable to obtain these materials prior to the patient's visit rather than after, because the information contained therein may influence the course of the evaluation visit. For example, previous records may show inconsistencies that can be resolved by additional history-taking.

HISTORY

The elements of a complete history (not always necessary) are as follows:

1. Chief complaint
2. Present illness
3. Review of systems
4. Medical-surgical history, allergies, drugs
5. Current medications
6. Social history (habits, socioeconomic, occupational, marital)
7. Family history

Usually hearing loss is the chief complaint, within the context of this book. However, it is often important to ask the patient what really bothers him the most—it may be tinnitus, or vertigo, or something totally unrelated. For the chief complaint and other significant symptoms, it is helpful to document the following:

1. The *nature* of the complaint (qualitative)
2. Its *severity* (quantified if possible)
3. Its *chronology* (date of onset, changes over time, frequency and duration of episodes, if episodic)

4. Factors making it better or worse, or triggering episodes
5. How it affects the patient in daily life, that is, perceived disability

If an injury is claimed, it is essential to determine its date of occurrence, its nature and severity, as well as any apparent temporal relationship between the injury and the patient's symptoms. When chronic occupational noise exposure is at issue, the dates, durations, and severity of exposures should be documented; as we will see later, a detailed questionnaire can be very helpful.

The history is especially important for persons claiming substantial problems with tinnitus. The impact of tinnitus on everyday life can only be assessed through self-report, which is of course susceptible to exaggeration. The physician should look for consistency, plausibility, and credibility (for example, is there evidence for exaggerated hearing loss?). Glorig's criteria (cited in Chapter 11) emphasize early unsolicited reports, care-seeking, and corroborated evidence for interference with activities of daily life. Coles (2000) has noted that "whatever caused the hearing loss, most probably caused the tinnitus too," and "Usually a diagnosis of noise-induced tinnitus cannot be made in the absence of a diagnosis of noise-induced hearing loss." However, both Coles (2000) and Kerr and Smyth (1987) recognized that the onset of tinnitus can be associated with events that could not themselves damage the ear or central auditory system, such as moderate noise episodes, minor head trauma, or even emotional shocks. Levine (1999) has documented that most tinnitus patients can modulate their tinnitus by isometric muscle contraction (due to brain connections between somatosensory nuclei and auditory nuclei); this provides a plausible basis for stress-induced unmasking of latent or previously ignored tinnitus related to preexisting hearing loss. Once unmasked, tinnitus may persist due to vicious cycles involving both muscle tension and attention, as frequently occurs after minor whiplash injuries (Ferrari and Russell, 1999).

ASSISTANTS

Many physicians ask a nurse, physician's assistant, or resident to obtain a history prior to examining the patient themselves. In the medical-legal setting, it is essential for the reporting physician to take responsibility for the entire evaluation, including history and physical examination. This responsibility does not exclude the use of assistants, as long as the assistant recites the patient's history to the physician in the patient's presence and the patient is given the opportunity to correct or add to that history, and the assistant's participation is documented. The physician must resolve inconsistencies, fill in gaps, and follow leads suggested by the assistant's preliminary history. Use of an assistant in this fashion can add efficiency and reliability to the evaluation process.

ACCOMPANYING PERSONS

Occasionally, a patient may wish to bring a family member, friend, or even an attorney into the examining room. Usually, this poses no real problem, as long as that person's identity, role, and relation to the patient are made known, and the accompanying person agrees to remain silent and not interfere with the examination. Ordinarily, the accompanying person will be simply an observer. If the patient is a competent adult, accompanying persons should be firmly instructed not to answer questions for the patient or to volunteer information. Transgressions should be documented and repeatedly discouraged. For a child or an incompetent adult, a parent or caretaker may be the primary source of the history; in these situations, it is important to document who said what. If the patient does not speak English well, it is best not to rely on a spouse or other accompanying person for translation. A member of the physician's staff or other third party can translate the questions and answers with less risk of editing. Normally, no more than one or two accompanying persons should be admitted for practical reasons.

QUESTIONNAIRES

While certainly not essential, printed questionnaires can be quite helpful in taking a good otologic history in legal cases, ensuring that important questions are not omitted. The physician must review the questionnaire responses with the patient and attempt to resolve inconsistencies and fill in gaps. However, this is still far less time-consuming than asking all the questions directly. The patient can be asked to date and sign the questionnaire; corrections and additions by the physician can be entered as marginal notes which are then initialed at the end. A questionnaire used in cases involving occupational noise exposure is presented at the end of the chapter. The questions are organized so the first part of the otologic report (see Chapter 14) can be dictated directly from the questionnaire.

The first section covers issues of hearing loss and other otologic symptoms, as well as history. The physician should also, of course, record the patient's own description of his hearing loss and how it bothers him, but the questionnaire provides some useful benchmarks such as telephone use. The questions about temporary hearing loss and tinnitus can be helpful in determining whether a particular occupational exposure was hazardous or not.

The questions about prior medical examinations and hearing tests often disclose the existence of information that may not have been provided to the physician in advance of the visit. As previously mentioned, old hearing tests in particular can be quite valuable in establishing causation.

The remainder of this section focuses on past history. Most ototoxic hearing loss is caused by aminoglycoside antibiotics and cisplatin, given by injection. Hearing loss caused by cisplatin, an anticancer drug, will be associated with hospitalization. Thus, rather than a laundry list of drugs that patients would probably neither remember nor recognize, we simply ask whether they have received antibiotic injections, paying special attention to patients' surgical and hospitalization histories.

The next section of the questionnaire elicits an employment history. As indicated in Chapter 7, hazard to hearing begins at approximately the same level where individuals have to shout to communicate at arm's length. Of course, workplace noise-level measurements should be given precedence, but in a surprisingly large number of cases no such measurements are available. Thus, a patient's report regarding communicative difficulties in the workplace can be useful in determining whether the noise level was likely to have been hazardous. A history of personal hearing protection is also important.

A history of military service, with specific attention to actual noise exposure, is followed by a checklist of potentially hazardous nonoccupational noise exposures. It is wise to specifically question workers about hunting and target shooting regardless of their questionnaire answers. If they've answered "no," be sure that this is accurate; if they've answered "yes," find out what types of weapons were used and how often.

The final portion of the questionnaire determines whether the individual may have had hazardous noise exposure recently enough to contaminate the audiogram with unrecovered temporary threshold shift (TTS; see Chapter 7). TTS usually recovers nearly completely within hours, but small shifts (usually less than 5 dB) can persist for days, depending on the nature of the noise exposure and the magnitude of the TTS. Threshold shifts associated with acoustic trauma or head injury are especially likely to demonstrate prolonged recovery. Alberti (1987) recommends minimum noise-free intervals of *72 hours* for cases involving NIHL and *3 months* for acoustic trauma or head injury. However, based on evidence presented in Chapter 7 (see the section Acoustic Trauma), it is probably wise to double these limits.

The patient's signature documents his or her participation and consent for a report to be sent, and may encourage truthful answers. If the patient declines to consent to a report, the physician may choose to decline to proceed with the examination.

EXAMINATION

Behavior

While taking the history, the physician can observe whether the patient is cooperative or obstructive, direct or evasive, appropriate or inappropriate.

Inappropriate behavior should be recorded in a factual manner, as should inconsistencies in the history. The otologist may, on occasion, question the truthfulness of the history; one railroad engineer who wore a National Rifle Association belt buckle to the examination claimed that he had worn earplugs on every occasion that he shot a firearm during the past 30 years, but never wore one on the job because the employer did not provide them. While these suspicions may lead the otologist and audiologist to be especially vigilant during the remainder of the evaluation process, only the facts (including the patient's statements) should be recorded.

Communicative Ability

The interview process also affords the otologist an opportunity to assess the patient's speech reception abilities in an informal way. Examining rooms are usually quiet and well lit, although some have undesirable reverberation characteristics. Face-to-face spoken communication is usually relatively easy in such a setting, even for patients with mild to moderate hearing losses. It is rather rare to encounter a young or middle-aged patient with NIHL who is unable to converse easily in a well lit examination room. Leaning forward, cupping the ears, or asking for questions to be repeated may be signs either that there is a severe hearing loss or that the patient is exaggerating his difficulties. Sometimes these behaviors are themselves obviously exaggerated, even compared to those displayed by individuals with severe hearing loss, and such histrionic displays should be noted. During the interview and the physical examination, the examiner can unobtrusively vary the difficulty of the communicative milieu to determine whether the individual's responses are appropriate. For example, he may walk behind the patient or cover his mouth to eliminate the possibility of lip reading; he may vary the intensity and difficulty of his speech message as well. Occasionally, it will be possible, by comparing these observations to the audiogram, to conclude that there is gross inconsistency. More often, suspicions are raised that lead to greater vigilance during the audiometric testing.

Otoscopy

Chapter 10 describes the causes of conductive hearing loss; most of these are associated with otoscopic abnormalities. Ear canal blockages can not only be diagnosed, but often treated at the initial office visit. Both active middle ear infections and the sequelae of old middle ear infections can be detected by otoscopy as well. Particularly when there is conductive hearing loss present, a binocular operating microscope is often used in place of the otoscope. Isolated ossicular fixations and discontinuities, such as occur with otosclerosis and after head trauma, cause conductive hearing loss, but are usually not visible with either the otoscope or with the operating microscope. Diseases causing pure sensorineural hearing loss rarely display any otoscopic abnormalities. During *pneumatic otoscopy*, the ear canal is sealed by a tight-fitting speculum, with positive or negative pressure introduced to move the eardrum back and forth. The mobility of the eardrum offers valuable clues to the presence of fluid in the middle ear, retraction pockets, and other abnormalities.

Tuning Fork Tests

Prior to electronic audiometry, otologists used tuning forks of different frequencies to conduct crude assessments of hearing ability. Nowadays, these tests are used primarily as a cross-check on the audiogram. When an audiogram has been competently performed with a properly calibrated instrument and a cooperative subject, the tuning fork tests add nothing to the diagnostic assessment. However, when tuning forks and audiometry disagree, this raises a red flag, suggesting that the hearing test may be inaccurate for any of the multiple reasons discussed in Chapter 3.

Two tuning fork tests are widely used nowadays, most often with the 512 Hz (hertz) tuning fork. The *Weber* test is conducted with the fork placed firmly against the forehead. This stimulates both ears by bone conduction; if the two ears hear equally well the sound will seem to be in the middle of the head. If the patient hears the tone primarily in one ear or the other this points to at least minor hearing asymmetry. If the loss is purely conductive, the tone will usually be heard in the *worse* ear while a purely sensorineural loss will lead to the tone being heard in the *better* ear. In the *Rinne* test, the tuning fork is placed first behind the ear, pressed against the mastoid bone, and then in the air just in front of the ear canal. The patient is asked to judge which of the two tones is louder. Normal subjects, subjects with sensorineural hearing losses and subjects with mild conductive losses will hear the second tone (air conduction) more loudly than the first (bone conduction). With conductive losses exceeding about 25 dB (for the 512 Hz fork), the bone-conducted tone will be heard more loudly than the air-conducted tone; this is called a *negative* Rinne test.

Head and Neck Examination

In the presence of chronic otitis media, especially if unilateral, the nasopharynx should be examined; rarely, tumors block the eustachian tube causing secondary middle ear problems. Palpation of the neck may detect metastasis from tumors in the nasopharynx. More often, nasal examination may disclose the presence of chronic allergic or infectious conditions that contribute to eustachian tube dysfunction and middle ear disease. Palatal clefts, even if incomplete or repaired, can contribute to eustachian tube dysfunction as well. However, oral, pharyngeal, and laryngeal examinations rarely contribute to the diagnosis of conductive hearing loss. Acquired sensorineural loss is rarely associated with abnormalities on the head and neck examination, except by coincidence.

Cranial Nerves

Both skull base tumors and head trauma can cause hearing loss in conjunction with cranial nerve abnormalities. Thus, the function of the third through twelfth cranial nerves are ordinarily tested as part of a complete otologic examination. This includes tests for eye movement, facial sensation, facial motion, palate and vocal cord movement, and tongue, shoulder, and neck movement.

Balance

Inner ear disorders may disrupt the vestibular system as well as the auditory system. Extensive balance system assessment is outside the scope of this book, but the otologic physical examination ordinarily includes a cursory assessment of balance. The patient's gait and stance are observed; usually tests are performed with eyes open and also with eyes closed to more effectively challenge the vestibular system and other components of balance control. The *Romberg* test is a simple examination of postural stability standing upright, comparing eyes open to eyes closed. The Romberg may be made more difficult by having the patient assume a tandem stance, with one foot in front of the other. The Fukuda marching test is a somewhat more sensitive test for vestibular function asymmetries, in which the patient is asked to march in place with the eyes closed, and is observed for instability or rotation over time.

Cerebellar Tests

Because balance can be affected by brain disorders, especially in the cerebellum, as well as by inner ear balance organ disease, many otologists routinely add cerebellar tests to their physical examination. These include tests of fine motor coordination, as well as tests of the patient's ability to determine the spatial positions of body parts without vision.

AUDIOMETRY

Chapter 3 discussed basic audiometric tests in an introductory fashion. For medical-legal hearing assessment, a minimum audiometric battery would include pure-tone air conduction and bone conduction tests, speech thresholds and suprathreshold speech discrimination scores, tympanometry, and recording of acoustic reflexes. As indicated in Chapters 3 and 4, the audiometric tests must be evaluated against one another and against history and physical examination findings for consistency. In particular, inconsistencies between pure-tone and speech thresholds usually indicate functional hearing loss. Prior hearing tests, if available, should be reviewed prior to audiometry so that any discrepancies can receive special attention.

Comparing a patient's tinnitus to audiometric tones or noises ("matching") may be helpful in assessing a complaint of tinnitus. Noise-induced tinnitus is usually at or above 3 kHz (Hinchcliffe and King, 1992), or at least no more than an octave below the noise-affected frequencies (Coles, 2000). Its loudness is rarely more than 15 dB above audiometric threshold (Coles, 2000; Meikle and Taylor-Walsh, 1984), and usually varies by no more than 2 dB on multiple measurements within a single session (Vernon, 1996). Most people are surprised to learn that tinnitus loudness is not a reliable indicator of annoyance or disability; thus, these matching tests have potential value only in documenting the existence and cause of tinnitus, not its severity.

LABORATORY AND IMAGING TESTS

Significant asymmetries on the audiograrn often require further testing, which may include evoked potential tests and imaging (computerized tomography or magnetic resonance imaging) to rule out acoustic neuroma. Electrocochleography (an evoked potential test of cochlear function) is often used in the diagnostic assessment of possible Ménière's disease or perilymph fistula, as is glycerin dehydration testing. Some otologists frequently order blood tests for thyroid disease, diabetes, hyperlipidemia, and the like, although these conditions all have at best tenuous associations with hearing loss. In the absence of rapidly progressive or asymmetric sensorineural hearing loss, laboratory and imaging tests are only occasionally indicated, and rarely contribute to diagnosis.

RECOMMENDATIONS TO THE PATIENT

The medical-legal evaluation visit does not necessarily, or even usually, initiate a doctor-patient relationship in which treatment or even counseling can be expected. It may not be possible or appropriate to discuss diagnostic conclusions at the time of the medical-legal assessment; this may require obtaining additional outside records of noise exposure and old hearing tests, or it may require some deliberation and calculation after the visit. Nevertheless, there is usually no reason not to discuss the audiometric results with the patient. The type and severity of the hearing loss can be explained. If there are indications of possible functional hearing loss, this may require subsequent visits, and this can be related to the patient in a tactful fashion by explaining that the results so far have been inconsistent and inconclusive and that further tests need to be done. As indicated in Chapter 4, it is almost never appropriate to confront a patient directly with a suspicion of untruthfulness.

If a patient will require further diagnostic tests, or should embark on treatment of some sort, this can and should be discussed. However, these interventions may be the financial responsibility of a different payer (the patient or his health insurance company) than the source of the medical-legal referral (attorney, employer, or liability insurance company). Hearing protectors should be recommended if appropriate, and any restrictions or limitations should also be discussed with the patient (these will be taken up in more detail in Chapter 14).

REFERENCES

Alberti, Peter W. 1987. Noise and the ear. In *Scott-Brown's Otolaryngology: Volume 2—Adult Audiology*, 5th ed., ed. Dafydd Stephens, pp. 594–641. London: Butterworths.

Coles, Ross R.A. 2000. Medicolegal issues. In *Tinnitus Handbook,* ed. Richard S. Tyler. San Diego, CA: Singular Publishing Company.

Dobie, Robert A. and Robert J. Archer. 1981. Otologic referral in industrial hearing conservation programs. *J. Occup. Med.* 23(11):755–761.

Ferrari, R. and A. S. Russell. 1999. Epidemiology of whiplash: An international dilemma. *Ann. Rheum. Dis.* 58:1–5.

Hinchcliffe, R. and P. F. King. 1992. Medicolegal aspects of tinnitus. III. Assessment of claimants with tinnitus. *J. Audiol. Med.* 1:127–147.

Kerr, Alan G. and Gordon D. L. Smyth. 1987. Ear trauma. Chap. 7 in *Scott-Brown's Otolaryngology, Volume 3,* 5th ed., ed. Alan Kerr and John B. Booth. London: Butterworths.

Levine, Robert A. 1999. Somatic (craniocervical) tinnitus and the dorsal cochlear nucleus hypothesis. *Am. J. Otolaryngol.* 20:351–362.

Meikle, M. B. and E. Taylor-Walsh. 1984. Characterization of tinnitus and related observations in over 1800 tinnitus clinic patients. *J. Laryngol. Otol.* (Suppl. 9):17–21.

Vernon, Jack A. 1996. Is the claimed tinnitus real and is the claimed cause correct? In *Proceedings of the Fifth International Tinnitus Seminar,* ed. G. E. Reich and J. A. Vernon. Portland, OR: American Tinnitus Association.

NOISE EXPOSURE QUESTIONNAIRE

Name: _____

Referred By: _____

A. Hearing Loss and Medical History

1. How old are you? _____ years

2. When did your hearing loss begin? _____
   Was it sudden? _____   or gradual? _____
   Does it change from day to day? _____
   Is it getting worse? _____

3. How would you evaluate your hearing?
   Good _____ Fair _____ Poor _____
   Describe any trouble you have hearing. _____
   _____

   _____

4. From which ear do you hear better?
   Left _____ Right _____ No difference _____

5. Do you hear better in a quiet or in a noisy place?
   Quiet _____ Noisy _____

6. Do you hear well over the telephone?
   Yes _____ No _____

7. Can you hear the telephone ring from the next room?
   Yes _____ No _____

8. Have you ever noticed a *temporary* (for minutes or hours) decrease in your hearing after noise exposure?

Yes _____ No _____

If yes, describe the noise that it followed:

_____

9. Did you have any problem hearing before the date stated in question A2?

Yes _____ No _____

10. Have you ever worn a hearing aid?

Yes _____ No _____

11. Do you have any ringing in your ears?

Yes _____ No _____

If yes:

a. When did you first notice it? _____

b. Describe what it sounds like:

_____

c. Does it bother you? If so, how?

_____

12. Have you ever noticed a *temporary* (for minutes or hours) ringing in your ears after noise exposure?

Yes _____ No _____

If yes, describe the noise that it followed:

_____

13. Have you ever had any drainage from your ears?

Yes _____ No _____

If yes, describe:

_____

_____

_____

14. Have you ever had any dizziness?

Yes _____ No _____

If yes, describe:

_____

_____

_____

15. Have you ever had any ear infections?

Yes _____ No _____

If yes, describe:

_____

_____

_____

16. Have you ever had your hearing tested before?

Yes _____ No _____

If yes, when was your first test? _____

17. Have you ever seen a doctor about your hearing?

Yes _____ No _____

If yes,

a. Doctor's name: _____

b. What did your doctor say was wrong? _____

_____

_____

18. Have you ever taken or been given any of the following medications?

	Yes	No
a. Antibiotics by shot	____	____
b. Aspirin on a daily basis	____	____
c. Any medicine on a long-term basis	____	____

If yes, what was it? _____

_____

19. List all surgeries you have had (if any):

_____

_____

_____

20. List all hospitalizations (if any):

_____

_____

_____

21. Have you ever had any of the following:

	Yes	No		Yes	No
ear surgery	—	—	sudden change in		
ear injury	—	—	hearing	—	—
earaches	—	—	mumps	—	—
scarlet fever	—	—	measles	—	—
head injury	—	—	high fever	—	—
loss of consciousness	—	—	any chronic illness	—	—

22. Do your parents, brothers, or sisters have a hearing loss?

Yes _____ No _____

23. Has any member of your family had ear surgery?

Yes _____ No _____

B. Employment

1. Who is your present (or most recent) employer? _____

_____

2. What is (or was) your job title? _____

3. How long have you worked there? _____

4. What loud noise do you have there? _____

_____

_____

5. Do you have to shout to communicate at arm's length while at work?

Yes _____ No _____

6. If so, how often or what percent of the time? _____

7. When did you start wearing ear protection? _____

8. Do you use muffs or plugs?

Muffs _____ Plugs _____

9. List the places you worked *before* your present employer (most recent employer first).

Employer	Location	Type of Work	Length of Employment (years)	Noise Exposure Yes No	Ear Protection Yes No
1. _____	_____	_____	_____	__ __	__ __
2. _____	_____	_____	_____	__ __	__ __
3. _____	_____	_____	_____	__ __	__ __
4. _____	_____	_____	_____	__ __	__ __
5. _____	_____	_____	_____	__ __	__ __

C. Military Service

1. Were you in the military service?

Yes _____ No _____

If no, skip to Question D1

2. What service were you in?

Army _____ Navy _____ Air Force _____

Marines _____ Other _____

3. What was your job in the service? _____

_____

_____

4. Were you in combat? _____

Yes _____ No _____

5. Were you exposed to noise beyond basic training?

Yes _____ No _____

D. Nonoccupational Noise

1. Have you ever been exposed to any of the following outside of your work?

	Yes	No		Yes	No
snowmobile	—	—	small engines	—	—
motorcycle	—	—	firing range	—	—
chain saw	—	—	farm machinery	—	—
power tools	—	—	heavy equipment	—	—
hunting	—	—	trap shooting	—	—
loud music	—	—	racing	—	—
explosion	—	—	private aviation	—	—

2. If you have shot rifles or shotguns, from which shoulder (right or left)?

_____

3. Do you wear ear protection during these activities?

Yes _____ No _____

If yes:

Muffs _____ Plugs _____

E. General

1. How much time was there between your last exposure to noise and your filling out this questionnaire?

_____ minutes _____ hours _____ days

2. How long did your most recent noise exposure last?

_____ minutes _____ hours

3. Did you wear ear protection during your most recent noise exposure?

Yes _____ No _____

4. Do you grant permission for a report to be sent to the person or organization that referred you, including information from this questionnaire as well as the results of interviews, examinations, and tests performed?

Yes _____ No _____

Date _____

Signature _____

Chapter 13

Diagnosis and Allocation

DIAGNOSIS

After obtaining a history, performing a physical examination, and reviewing audiometric data and outside records, the otolaryngologist proceeds to diagnosis: "the art or act of identifying a disease from its signs and symptoms; also: the decision reached" (Merriam-Webster, 1993). Diagnosis thus refers both to the *process* of identifying the cause or causes of the patient's hearing loss and to the *causes* that have been identified (e.g., otosclerosis). Sometimes, the word diagnosis is qualified to distinguish different goals: *Etiologic diagnosis* means identifying causes (disease, trauma, degeneration, etc.); *functional diagnosis* means identifying and measuring the patient's impairment and handicap (for example, mild vs. severe hearing handicap); and site-of-lesion diagnosis means categorizing the approximate anatomic locus of the disorder (middle ear vs. cochlear vs. retrocochlear, in the case of hearing loss). However, both common usage and the dictionary indicate that "diagnosis" without qualifiers means "etiologic diagnosis": Is the hearing loss caused by noise, by otosclerosis, by ototoxic drugs, and so on.

"Hearing loss," "tinnitus," and "vertigo" are not diagnoses, but symptoms. "Profound hearing loss" or "retrocochlear hearing loss" comes closer, but still says nothing about causation. Of course, it is not always possible to identify a cause, even after extensive examination and testing. The term *idiopathic hearing loss* then indicates that the diagnostic process was at least undertaken. Sometimes a chain of causes can be identified. A conductive hearing loss may be caused by middle ear effusion, which was caused by eustachian tube obstruction, which was caused by a carcinoma in the nasopharynx, which was in turn caused by smoking or by viral infection in the remote past. It is the physician's job to elucidate as much of that process as possible.

Reasonable Medical Certainty

Diagnoses can be made with varying levels of certainty. Some findings are *pathognomonic*, that is, they are seen only in the disease or disorder in question. For example, if an incision through the eardrum yields clear or mucoid fluid, the diagnosis of middle ear effusion can be made with near-certainty (the probability of an effusion is approximately 100 percent). If a biopsy of a nasopharyngeal tumor in the same patient reveals a particular microscopic cellular pattern, the pathologist can diagnose a carcinoma with the same level of near-certainty. While errors and misinterpretations are possible, pathognomonic findings permit diagnosis "beyond a reasonable doubt."

A second level of certainty exists when the particular constellation of findings, (history, physical examination, audiogram, and other tests) *usually* indicates a particular diagnosis. A widened, eroded internal auditory canal (IAC seen on a computed tomography (CT) scan, or a mass in the IAC seen on magnetic resonance imaging (MRI), usually indicates the presence of an acoustic neuroma. However, other diagnoses are possible, for example, meningioma. When the probability of a particular diagnosis exceeds 50 percent, that is, it is more likely than not that the disease or disorder is present—the legal system often refers to a "reasonable medical probability" or even a "reasonable medical certainty."

This confuses physicians for two reasons. First, common sense does not equate "certainty" with "more probable than not"; and second, the 50 percent probability criterion, while legally important, is not particularly relevant in clinical practice.

Decisions to perform additional tests or to treat are based on many factors in addition to the physician's estimate of the probability of disease X. If further workup is imprecise, expensive, risky, or painful, and if treatment for disease X is cheap, effective, and safe, the physician may recommend treatment even though the probability of disease X is quite low; an example is the use of penicillin for a red, sore throat without a culture to prove streptococcal infection. Conversely, no otologist would proceed to intracranial surgery based on a CT showing an enlarged IAC, even though a tumor is "probably" present; MRI demonstration of an IAC tumor would be required, pushing the probability of acoustic neuroma much closer to 100 percent

The third category of diagnostic certainty, from the legal point of view, includes cases in which the probability of disease X is less than 50 percent. There may be findings that are many times more common in patients with disease X than in other people (e.g., unilateral hearing loss and acoustic reflex decay in acoustic tumor patients). However, unless disease X is rather common, most patients with those findings will not be found to have the disease (most pro basketball players are over 6'4", but most people over 6'4" are not pro basketball players).

Differential Diagnosis Versus Multiple Diagnoses

When a diagnosis is not obvious, physicians integrate their clinical findings with their knowledge of the relative frequency (prevalence) and characteristics of different diseases to construct a list of possible causes. The process of constructing, prioritizing, and narrowing (by exclusion) that list is called *differential diagnosis*. Additional tests may eliminate some causes and make others more likely or even certain. Ultimately, the physician usually arrives at a working diagnosis and embarks on treatment, if indicated.

It is axiomatic in medicine that one should always seek to identify a single cause for all of a patient's symptoms, when possible. However, even a single symptom can have multiple causes, and this is certainly the case for sensorineural hearing loss (SNHL). We have seen in Chapters 6 through 8 that both age-related hearing loss (ARHL) and noise-induced hearing loss (NIHL) are very common and that they combine in an approximately additive fashion. Even in isolation, their audiometric characteristics are quite similar (exceptions: ARHL lacks the "notch" seen in NIHL; ARHL accelerates over time, while NIHL decelerates). When we see a middle-aged or elderly patient with a history of decades of unprotected hazardous noise exposure, and a high-frequency SNHL, we can usually diagnose *both* ARHL and NIHL on a "more-probable-than-not" basis.

Diagnosis of Noise-Induced and Age-Related Hearing Loss

As pointed out by the American College of Occupational Medicine (ACOM), the diagnosis of NIHL requires clinical consideration of the noise exposure history along with the audiometric characteristics of NIHL (ACOM, 1989; see Chapter 7). Chapters 6 and 7 presented some of the data available to estimate pure-tone thresholds for populations of varying age, sex, and noise exposure history. The most convenient and authoritative are those published by the International Organization for Standardization (ISO-1999, 1990) and the American National Standards Institute (ANSI S3.44, 1996); their models are identical except that ANSI S3.44 includes a new database (Annex C) screened to exclude only occupational noise exposure. The ISO/ANSI model can be quite helpful in supporting (or undermining) a diagnosis of NIHL (with ARHL present as well). Figures 13–1 and 13–2 show median and 95th percentile audiograms constructed using this model for various combinations of age and noise exposure. These figures used database B (better ears, unscreened) aging values for men, and assume exposures beginning at age 20. All hearing level (HL) values were corrected using the compression term recommended by ISO and ANSI. Together, these figures give some idea of the shape and magnitude of audiometric findings to be expected in noise-exposed

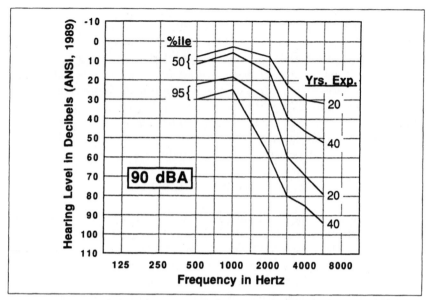

Figure 13–1. Median and extreme audiograms predicted (ISO-1999) after 20 and 40 years of exposure at 90 dBA (database B, male).

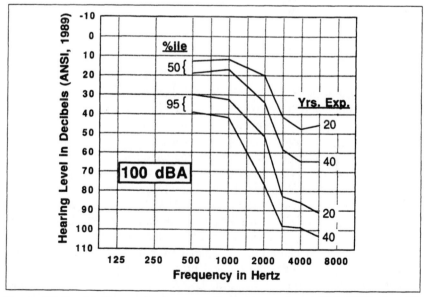

Figure 13–2. Median and extreme audiograms predicted (ISO-1999) after 20 and 40 years of exposure at 100 dBA (database B, male).

populations. Remember that 50 percent of subjects will have *better* hearing than the 50th percentile curves. An individual's audiogram can easily be compared with the curves; values beyond the 95th percentile make a simple diagnosis of NIHL plus ARHL unlikely (Macrae, 1987), and suggest that other factors are present (e.g., exaggerated hearing loss, other otological diseases). To make comparisons for individuals with very different profiles (e.g., a 60-year-old woman with a 20-year noise exposure history), graphs of median and 90th percentile thresholds can be constructed from tables in Chapter 6 and 7. If 95th percentile thresholds are desired, these are easily calculated from the median ($T_{.5}$) and 90th percentile ($T_{.9}$) thresholds:

$$T_{.95} = 1.28T_{.9} - 0.28T_{.5}$$

Audiometric notching (with improvement at 8 kilohertz [kHz]) is seen in most cases of NIHL, but the ANSI/ISO model does not include 8 kHz for comparison. Coles et al. (2000) note that notches apparent early in a career are sometimes effaced by age-related changes, but that these cases will still show "bulges," that is, hearing in the 3–6 kHz range that is worse than would be predicted by drawing a line between thresholds at 1 and 8 kHz.

As the ACOM criteria point out, NIHL audiograms "are usually similar bilaterally." Robinson (1985) suggests that NIHL is unlikely when six-frequency averages (0.5 to 6 kHz) differ by more than 12 decibels (dB) between ears.

Audiograms falling outside the expected limits are discussed in a later section (Extreme Audiograms).

ALLOCATION

In many cases, the issue is not to choose one diagnosis and exclude the other, but to determine the relative contributions each has made to that individual's hearing loss; this process is called *allocation* (others have used the terms *attribution* and *apportionment*). Aging and noise are the usual contributors, but head injury, ototoxic drugs, or any other otologic disorder can be relevant in particular cases. Sometimes it is also important to allocate hearing loss to different time periods, for example, different employers.

The American Medication Association (AMA, 2000) *Guides to the Evaluation of Permanent Impairment* states that "estimation of the relative contributions of various causes of binaural hearing impairment is a clinical process (apportionment or allocation) that is separate from the calculation of binaural hearing impairment." Like the clinical process of diagnosis, allocation is probabilistic and judgmental, requiring knowledge and experience as well as the integration of different types of data, of varying quality and consistency. These may include serial audiograms, multiple exposure level measurements, military records, hearing conservation program records, medical records, and history (from the claimant as well as others) of hearing protection use, non-occupational noise exposure, and so forth (of course, insistence on the clinical nature of allocation for individuals does not preclude use of epidemiological models to estimate the evolution of hearing loss in large groups of people).

In some legal settings (many state workers' compensation board hearings, for example), a defendant is liable for a plaintiff's hearing loss if he was responsible for causing any part of the loss, no matter how small. Allocation then seems irrelevant if it doesn't matter whether a given injury or noise exposure caused 10 percent or 90 percent of the hearing loss. In other settings, the plaintiff may be required to prove that the defendant caused a "substantial" part of his hearing loss, and the size of a monetary judgment may hinge on the magnitude of that contribution. Here, it is both medically and legally relevant to estimate the contributions of the different disorders present.

Allocation is relatively straightforward when an event capable of causing hearing loss occurs, and audiograms have been obtained before and after that event. Assuming negligible aging changes between the two audiograms and no other known cause for hearing loss in that interval, we can blame any additional hearing loss on the event in question, if the change is of the expected type and magnitude. Whatever the cause(s) of any prior hearing loss, the additional hearing loss is easy to allocate because the harmful event was *non-simultaneous* (re: any preexisting loss) and was audiometrically *bracketed*. Allocation among two or more such events is equally straightforward if each is bracketed; we have called this *interval allocation*.

In contrast, ARHL and NIHL proceed simultaneously and can't be completely separated by audiometric bracketing. Some, including many state workers' compensation programs, have dealt with this by "age correction," subtracting a certain decibel value based on a person's age from the audiometric threshold prior to estimating hearing handicap. This may result in a handicapping (and compensable) hearing loss being "downgraded" below the threshold for compensation. "Age correction" is fundamentally unfair, implying that because a worker would have had no compensable handicap in the absence of ARHL, *all* of his handicap is to be blamed on ARHL (American Academy of Otolaryngology–Head and Neck Surgery [AAO–HHS], 1998; AMA, 2000). It would be equally unfair to state that because there would have been no compensable handicap without NIHL, all of the handicap is attributable to NIHL.

Davis (1971) noted the unfairness of age correction, and suggested that epidemiological data on ARHL could provide the basis for a fairer approach. His major insight was that estimation of hearing handicap (referred to as binaural hearing impairment in AMA documents) and estimation of relative contributions of ARHL and NIHL (allocation) are separate processes. One must first, in Davis' words, "see how big the pie is" (estimate hearing handicap), then "cut the pie" (allocate blame based on the relative contributions of the different causes).

We will describe methods for "cutting the pie," recognizing that the results from these quantitative methods are only one input into the clinical allocation process, and that a clinician's best estimate may differ from these results, based on other data. To offer useful decision support, an allocation method should be scientifically sound (logically derived from refereed or professional consensus publications), should incorporate exposure level information when appropriate, and should be unbiased (not systematically blaming too much on aging or noise, or on early or late exposures). It should be clinically sound, in harmony with clinical experience and common sense. It should be separate from, and independent of, any method of estimation of hearing handicap (AMA, 2000; AAO–HNS, 1998).

We will consider first the relatively simple case of nonsimultaneous events "bracketed" by pre- and postevent audiograms, then the more difficult issue of different etiologies that occur simultaneously or are not audiometrically bracketed. Multiple examples will illustrate these problems, as well as the issues of database and audiogram selection, changing exposure levels, unusually flat or severe audiograms, asymmetry, and allocation methods appropriate in different situations. The examples in this chapter are coordinated with the report examples in the next chapter (e.g., Example 8 in each chapter refers to the same case). Finally, the assumptions and limitations of the methods presented will be discussed.

Nonsimultaneous, Bracketed: Interval Allocation

Consider a young man with normal hearing who is unlucky enough to suffer two accidents, the first causing deafness in his right ear, the second causing deafness in his left ear. His hearing handicap (HH), using the American Academy of Otolaryngology (AAO, 1979) method (or any other method) is now 100 percent (he is deaf). How shall we allocate the blame?

On one hand, we can say that each accident destroyed half of his previously excellent hearing, and thus the two accidents were equally responsible. On the other hand, his HH, initially 0 percent, was only 17 percent after the first accident (because of the 5:1 weighting in favor of the better ear), increasing to 100 percent after the second accident, so one could argue that the second accident was five times as injurious as the first. The choice between these points of view is more legal than medical; both are medically defensible. In this case, it is easy to present the analysis both ways and let the legal system decide.

A more challenging scenario would involve simultaneous insults to the two ears, with the same result (total deafness). As before, we can say that each event was responsible for half of the total damage, but an analysis based on sequential consideration of the two events is now ambiguous. Applying a HH subtraction method (removing one cause or event, then recalculating the HH), we can say that "but for the event that damaged his left ear, he'd have only a 17 percent HH, therefore this event is responsible for 83 percent of his HH which is now 100 percent." The problem is that we can with equal justice make the same statement about the right-ear event. Obviously, the two events cannot each be responsible for 83 percent of his HH. The order in which we do the subtraction makes a big difference; such "order effects" are inherent in using the HH subtraction method. In this chapter, we will emphasize methods that are not subject to order effects, but will easily permit HH subtraction as a final step when the legal context requires it; this is illustrated in Example 1.

EXAMPLE 1

Assume that a previously healthy 40-year-old woman enters the hospital after a motor vehicle accident causing severe abdominal injuries. After surgery, an infection develops that requires the prolonged use of gentamicin, an ototoxic antibiotic. Her physician obtains a pretreatment audiogram (Figure 13–3, dotted lines), which shows a symmetrical mild conductive hearing loss probably attributable to otosclerosis. After prolonged gentamicin therapy, she recovers and goes home, but is found one month later to have a much more severe hearing loss than before (Figure 13–3, solid lines) in both ears. Posttreatment bone-conduction scores showed that the conductive part of the loss was unchanged and there was now a significant sensorineural component.

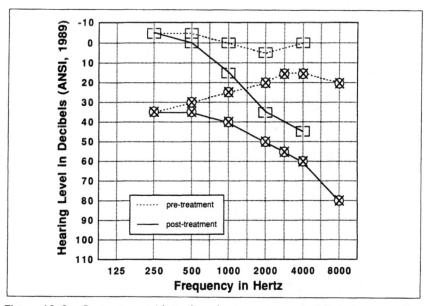

Figure 13–3. Pretreatment (dotted) and posttreatment (solid) audiograms, Example 1.

Since only a month has passed between audiograms, aging could not be blamed for any significant portion of the change. It is most reasonable to divide her total hearing loss into two parts: a conductive component present on her pretreatment test, and a drug-induced component equal to the difference between the two tests. At 8 kHz (kilohertz), for example, the otosclerotic portion is 20 dB, and the drug-induced portion is 60 dB (total posttreatment loss = 80 dB HL).

If the loss were limited to 8 kHz, it would be inconsequential. For most people, the most important consequence of hearing loss is difficulty hearing and understanding speech. As discussed in Chapter 5, the AAO-1979 rule for estimating hearing handicap (HH) is both widely used and reasonable, basing HH on the pure-tone average of 0.5, 1, 2, and 3 kHz (PTA-5123), with a 25 dB "low fence" and a 1.5 percent per dB growth rate. In this chapter, we will use the AAO-1979 rule, but with the caveat that the allocation methods discussed would work equally well with any other set of frequencies, low fence, or growth rate.

Before Drug Therapy (Right and Left Ears)

0.5 kHz	—	30 dB HL
1 kHz	—	25 dB HL
2 kHz	—	20 dB HL
3 kHz	—	15 dB HL

$$\text{PTA-5123} \quad = \quad \frac{30 + 25 + 20 + 15}{4} \quad = \quad 22.5 \text{ dB HL}$$

Impairment = 0%

After Drug Therapy (Right and Left Ears)

0.5 kHz	—	35 dB HL
1 kHz	—	40 dB HL
2 kHz	—	50 dB HL
3 kHz	—	55 dB HL

$$\text{PTA-5123} \quad = \quad \frac{35 + 40 + 50 + 55}{4} \quad = \quad 45 \text{ dB HL}$$

Impairment = (45 − 25) 1.5% = 30%

Hearing Handicap (HH)

$$\text{HH} \quad = \quad \frac{5 \text{ (better ear impairment)} + \text{worse ear impairment}}{6}$$

$$= \quad \frac{5(30) + 30}{6} \quad = \quad \frac{180}{6}$$

$$= \quad 30\%$$

In this example, the patient's PTA-5123s before and after the drug therapy were 22.5 and 45 dB HL, respectively. From one point of view, her HH scores were 0 percent pretreatment (because PTA $<$ 25 dB) and 30 percent posttreatment. From the other, it would be misleading to conclude that all her HH was caused by the drug treatment, because she had already suffered half the total hearing loss prior to this event. As Lebo and Reddell (1972) suggested, since the two etiologies (otosclerosis and ototoxicity) were each responsible for 50 percent of the total hearing loss, they should be assigned equal portions of the HH: 15 percent each, of the total 30 percent HH. As shown in the corresponding report in Chapter 14 (Example 1), both points of view can be represented.

In this example, the pretreatment audiogram was not, in retrospect, entirely necessary from the medical-legal point of view. The hearing losses attributable to the two etiologies could have been distinguished even on the posttreatment audiogram, because otosclerosis causes a primarily conductive loss and ototoxicity a sensorineural loss. Otosclerosis can cause sensorineural loss as well, but it would be unlikely to be responsible for the sensorineural component of this patient's loss, given the history.

Simultaneous or Unbracketed Exposures: The Median-Ratio Method

Simultaneous and/or unbracketed exposures can include any of the causes of hearing loss. In rare cases, one disorder causes conductive loss and the other sensorineural loss, permitting audiometric separation. Much more frequently, both cause sensorineural loss. The most common cases requiring allocation for simultaneous exposures involve noise and aging, causes for which, fortunately, we have good "dose-response" information regarding noise-induced and age-related permanent threshold shifts (NIPTS, ARPTS).

As discussed in Chapter 7, most evidence favors a model of decibel additivity (with compression) to explain the interaction of ARHL and NIHL. ISO-1999 and ANSI S3.44 incorporate such a model, and explicitly propose a method for predicting hearing levels of groups of people; Johnson (1988) has demonstrated the method with clearly worked-out examples. It is our thesis that the same model (and data sets) can be used to work backwards from an individual with known hearing levels, age, gender, and noise exposure, to estimate the relative contributions of simultaneously accruing ARHL and NIHL to that individual's hearing loss. The National Institutes of Health Consensus Conference on Noise and Hearing Loss (NIH, 1990) supported this approach:

> The typical levels of presbycusis at various ages have recently been incorporated as Annex A in International Organization of Standardization Standard 1999.2 (1989). That standard may be used to estimate the

portion of overall hearing loss that is attributable to exposure to excessive noise.

ANSI S3.44 states that the standard "shall not be used to predict or assess the hearing impairment or hearing handicap of individual persons except in terms of statistical probabilities." In other words, one cannot precisely predict an individual's hearing levels, or resultant handicap, given his or her age and noise exposure data (obviously, an audiogram is needed to do that). However, the standard does not address the issue of *retrospective* analysis for allocation purposes, except to say that "For a single individual, it is not possible to determine precisely which changes in hearing threshold level are caused by noise and which changes are caused by other factors. In doubtful individual cases, the data in this Standard might provide an additional means for estimating the most probable causes in audiological diagnosis."

As noted elsewhere (Dobie, 1993),

> Ultimately, the question is not whether to allocate but how best to do it. The legal system quite properly asks us whether occupational noise (or some other insult) contributed to a person's hearing loss, and if so, how much. When faced with a sparse audiometric record, a final audiogram which is consistent with noise and/or aging, and an otherwise negative clinical evaluation, a competent clinician uses personal experience and knowledge of epidemiology to estimate relative contributions. If daily noise exposures were less than 85 dBA [decibels, A-weighted], for example, the NIPTS contribution is negligible; conversely, 40 years of daily steady-state exposure above 100 dBA usually justifies a conclusion that a worker's loss is mostly noise-induced. It would be unfair to lump these two cases together and adopt an agnostic posture that since we can't be sure of the exact contributions of aging and noise, we will say nothing.

In cases like these (ANSI's "doubtful individual cases") we will emphasize the use of the median-ratio method, as demonstrated in Examples 2–7. When the development and progression of hearing loss are well-documented by a series of audiograms, the audiometric trajectory (Example 8) should usually be given greater weight.

EXAMPLE 2
Consider a 60-year-old man who has been exposed to a 100 dBA time-weighted average (TWA) workplace for 40 years. He has never hunted or engaged in any sort of noisy recreational activity. His audiogram is shown in Figure 13–4; no prior audiograms are available. Otologic evaluation reveals no cause for his hearing loss other than the obvious ones: noise and aging. What were the contributions of each?

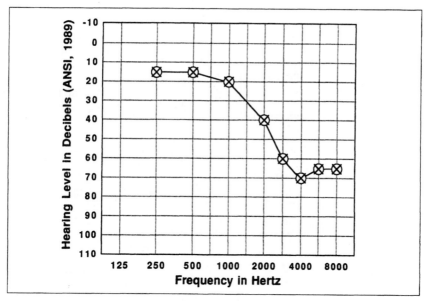

Figure 13–4. Retirement audiogram; Example 2. Bone-conduction thresholds are omitted for clarity, but showed no air-bone gap.

To answer this question, we can begin by asking the ISO/ANSI data set how much hearing loss is expected for a 60-year-old male and how much loss can be expected from 40 years of exposure at 100 dBA. Figures 13–5 and 13–6 show ISO/ANSI data in a somewhat different format than shown in Chapters 6 and 7: Median (fiftieth percentile) and extreme (tenth and ninetieth percentile) values are plotted for PTA-5123. Figure 13–5 shows ARPTS distributions, while Figure 13–6 shows NIPTS distributions for exposures from 85 to 100 dBA. These figures are nearly identical to Figures 1 and 2 in Dobie (1992), except for the correction of three misprint errors in ISO-1999 noted by Clark and Bohl (1992). (The equations used to plot these figures are given in Tables 13–1 and 13–2.) Database A is for a highly screened population, while database B is representative of the better ears of an unscreened U.S. population sample. Turning to database B, we find the expected median hearing level to be about 14 dB for a 60-year-old man (choice of database is discussed later in this chapter). Next, we turn to the 100 dBA graph and find an expected median value for 40 years of 20 dB. The expected total hearing level would be the sum (34 dB); since the sum is less than 40 dB HL, we don't need to use the compression term referred to in Chapter 7.

Returning to our subject, his average hearing level in each ear is 33.75 dB—almost exactly as expected at the median. Since his total loss

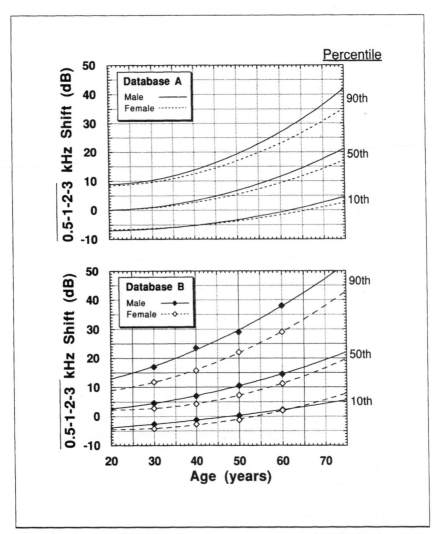

Figure 13–5. Speech-frequency age-related permanent threshold shift (ARPTS) as a function of age for men and women; 10th, 50th, and 90th percentiles; databases A and B (ISO-1999). The curves for database B are quadratic fits to the indicated data points (diamonds).

matches the population median, it is intuitively attractive to conclude that his ARPTS and NIPTS components are also at the median: about 14 and 20 dB, respectively. Of course, it is possible that he had more ARPTS and less NIPTS than expected; but it's just as likely that he had less ARPTS and more NIPTS. Our best estimate—the one most likely

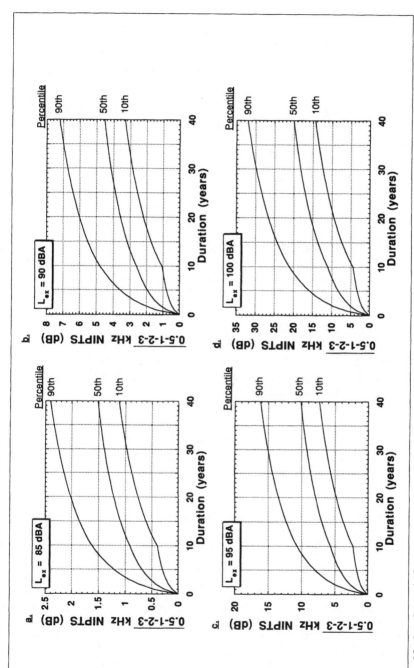

Figure 13–6. Speech frequency noise-induced permanent threshold shift (NIPTS) as a function of duration; 10th, 50th, and 90th percentiles (ISO-1999). Exposure levels of 85-100 dBA are shown in separate graphs.

TABLE 13–1
ARPTS (PTA-5123) as a Function of Age (A, in years)

Database	Median	$\sigma_u{}^a$	$\sigma_L{}^b$
Male			
A	$0.00650(A-18)^2$	$6.81 + 0.00289(A-18)^2$	$5.45 + 0.00231(A-18)^2$
B	$1.17 - 0.00250A$ $+0.00375A^2$	$5.26 + 0.115A$ $+0.00195A^2$	$5.15 - 0.0429A$ $+0.00195A^2$
Female			
A	$0.00525(A-18)^2$	$6.54 + 0.00200(A-18)^2$	$5.23 + 0.00187(A-18)^2$
B	$5.42 - 0.277A$ $+0.00625A^2$	$1.83 + 0.142A$ $+0.000975A^2$	$6.07 - 0.0669A$ $+0.00146A^2$

[a]Upper standard deviation.
[b]Lower standard deviation.

to be true—is that ARPTS, NIPTS, and the total were all at the median. The ratio of median NIPTS to total hearing loss (20/34) is about 0.59; thus, we would conclude that most of his loss is noise-induced.

EXAMPLE 3

Consider now another man with the same age and history (including noise exposure); the only difference is that his hearing levels are much higher (Figure 13–7). In fact, he is near the ninetieth percentile overall, with pure-tone averages of 53.75 dB in each ear; only about 10 percent of workers his age with similar noise exposure will have a greater degree of hearing loss.

The median-ratio method, first suggested by Corso (1980), considers that this man, with the same age, sex, and exposure history as his less-severely affected colleague in Example 2, has the same relative contributions of

TABLE 13–2
NIPTS[a] (PTA-5123) as a Function of Duration (D, in years)

dBA	Median	$\sigma_u{}^b$	$\sigma_L{}^c$
85	$1.005 \log D - 0.089$	$0.244 \log D + 0.306$	$-0.160 \log D + 0.564$
90	$3.231 \log D - 0.623$	$0.630 \log D + 1.126$	$-0.423 \log D + 1.630$
95	$7.450 \log D - 1.772$	$1.344 \log D + 2.553$	$-0.812 \log D + 3.462$
100	$14.958 \log D - 3.922$	$2.596 \log D + 5.230$	$-1.298 \log D + 6.445$

[a]Valid for $10 \leq D \leq 40$; for $0 < D < 10$, use:

$$\overline{\text{NIPTS}} = \left(\frac{\log(D+1)}{\log(11)} \right) \overline{\text{NIPTS}}_{D=10}$$

[b]Upper standard deviation.
[c]Lower standard deviation.

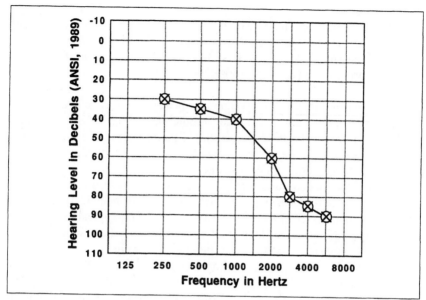

Figure 13–7.   Retirement audiogram; Examples 3 and 4.

ARPTS and NIPTS (about 41 percent and 59 percent, respectively). The extension of median ratios to individuals with more severe hearing loss requires justification, and can be approached at least two ways:

1. What are the most likely relative contributions of ARPTS and NIPTS for individuals beyond the median? As will be discussed in the next section, the answer depends on the degree to which susceptibility to NIHL is correlated with susceptibility to ARHL. The median-ratio method usually produces estimates that are intermediate between those produced by methods assuming either perfect correlation of susceptibilities or no correlation at all.

2. How can we estimate the relative contributions of ARPTS and NIPTS averaged across an entire population of noise-exposed individuals? The ISO/ANSI model shows both ARPTS and NIPTS (and total hearing loss as well) to be skewed distributions, with more spread above the median than below the median, so the medians do not equal the population averages. However, for both ARTPS and NIPTS, averages (means) tend to be higher than medians by similar amounts, and in most cases the ratio of medians is therefore usually very close to the ratio of means. The median ratio method does tend to slightly overestimate the contribution of NIPTS in a population; for example, for the population described in Examples 2 and 3, the means for NIPTS and ARPTS are 22 and 18 dB, respectively

(cf. medians of 20 and 14 dB), and the NIPTS contribution averaged across the entire population would thus be 22/40=55 percent (cf. median-ratio estimate of 59 percent). Nevertheless, the ratio of median NIPTS to median hearing loss is a good estimate of the contribution of NIPTS to total hearing loss in a noise-exposed population.

(Those wishing to calculate population means from the ISO/ANSI tables in Chapters 6 and 7 can use a simple formula: mean=0.38 (median) + 0.31 (10th percentile) + 0.31 (90th percentile). This formula is derived from Mc-Nemar's (1962) definition of the "average deviation," applied separately to the two halves of the skewed distribution.)

Applying the median-ratio method to Example 3, we estimate that about 22 dB of his speech-frequency loss is due to ARHL, and about 32 dB to NIPTS.

It is important to remember that a statistical/epidemiological estimate like this is only one input to a judgmental clinical process. For example, if this man's 8 kHz threshold (not shown in Figure 13–7) were 100 dB HL (no audiometric notch), and a series of audiograms showed his loss to have accrued mostly in the last decade despite stable or even decreasing noise exposures, the median-ratio estimate should be discarded in favor of a clinical diagnosis that his loss was primarily age-related. (See discussion of trajectory analysis later in this chapter.) Conversely, a deep audiometric notch usually justifies a conclusion that an individual's loss is primarily noise-induced. An individual's true ARPTS curve (the audiogram that would have existed in the absence of noise exposure) is unlikely to be worse than the curve created by connecting the 1 kHz and 8 kHz thresholds by a straight line (Coles et al., 2000, describe a similar method). If the speech-frequency ARPTS from this curve is less than the median-ratio estimate, then the median-ratio estimate should usually be discounted.

Alternative Methods

Lebo and Reddell (1972) were probably the first to propose a method meeting Davis' criterion that allocation and estimation of hearing handicap should be separated. They suggested that the contribution of ARHL be estimated by the median dB values expected for a given age, with the remainder attributed to NIHL. King et al. (1992) espoused a similar method, as does an Iowa workers' compensation law passed in 1998 (Myrna Stephens, personal communication, 1998). These methods tacitly assume that age-related changes are the same for all workers of a given age and that all the variability in their hearing levels is due to noise-induced damage. These methods could be considered unbiased if applied to all workers with a given age, sex, and noise exposure history (or to a random cross-section of such workers). However, applicants for compensation are not randomly selected; individuals with more severe hearing loss are more likely to file claims. Assuming median ARPTS in such cases implies that these people have above-average susceptibility to NIHL. Since the opposite assumption (above-average susceptibility to ARHL) is equally likely to be true, these methods are biased for most claimants, assigning too much blame to NIHL and too little to ARHL. Another weakness of these methods is that they fail to consider an individual's noise exposure history.

Robinson (1991) described the median-ratio method but instead preferred a different approach. Specifically, he recommended first finding the appropriate aging-plus-noise population (e.g., 60-year-old men with 40 years of exposure at 100 dBA), then finding the percentile in that population that matched the individual's measured thresholds, then using the ARPTS and NIPTS values at the same percentiles to estimate relative contributions. His method assumes that there is perfect correlation between individuals' susceptibilities to ARHL and to NIHL. In other words, if you are highly susceptible to one, you will be equally highly susceptible to the other. Robinson's method systematically assigns less blame to NIHL than does the median-ratio method. Dobie (1992) described an approach assuming no correlation of susceptibilities, that is, a person who was unusually susceptible to one cause (say, NIHL) was not assumed to have above-average susceptibility to the other (ARHL). This method usually assigned slightly more blame to NIHL than did the median-ratio method, and its calculation was very complex. Although there is clear evidence for correlated genetic susceptibilities to NIHL and ARHL in animals (see Chapter 7), the correlation in humans is unlikely to be either perfect or totally absent. Since the median-ratio method usually assigns blame as if susceptibilities were positively but imperfectly correlated, and since it is easily calculated, it is preferable to either of the other methods described in this paragraph.

In this discussion, susceptibility refers to an individual's tendency to develop more or less ARHL or NIHL than others similarly aged or given similar lifetime noise exposure. It is probably mostly genetically determined, and is to be clearly distinguished from the effects of prior hearing loss. Any person, whether possessed of tough ears or tender ears, who has had 30 years of exposure at 100 dBA will have developed almost all the NIHL that that person is capable of developing. An additional 10 years of exposure will have little effect, but that phenomenon (deceleration) is unrelated to susceptibility.

Johnson (1998) described a method in which the contributions of ARHL and NIHL were allocated by a variable ratio of "decibels over the fence." This is equivalent to estimating the average AMA hearing handicap in populations of a certain age and sex, with and without a specified noise exposure, then assigning blame to NIPTS and ARPTS accordingly. Unlike the median-ratio method, it does not permit an estimate of an *individual's* speech-frequency ARPTS, or an individual's likely hearing handicap in the absence of noise exposure.

Choice of Aging Database and Dealing
with Nonoccupational Exposure

Table 13–3 shows median ARPTS and NIPTS values, rounded to the nearest decibel, for PTA-5123. Median-ratio allocation is easy using this table; just select the appropriate values for ARPTS and NIPTS, then use these numbers to calculate the median hearing level and to estimate the relative contributions of noise and aging.

In our examples, we have used ISO-1999 database B, derived from the 1960–62 U.S. Public Health Service survey. These are unscreened data, including some occupationally-noise-exposed subjects; they are also better-ear data. Database A, on the other hand, presents highly screened data, some collected with laboratory rather than clinical techniques, excluding subjects with any significant history, physical examination findings, and even "abnormal" audiograms (Robinson and Sutton, 1979). The more recently published American standard (ANSI S3.44, 1996) offers a third aging database (Annex C), as mentioned earlier, with values slightly worse than those in database B (for whites). Occupationally exposed populations rarely hear as well as would be predicted by database A, even at the beginning of their noise-exposed careers. Perhaps this is caused by unreported nonoccupa-

TABLE 13–3
Median Speech-Frequency (0.5, 1, 2, 3 kHz) ARPTS and NIPTS,
in Decibels (ANSI-S3.44)

				ARPTS		
				Age		
Gender	Database/Annex	30	40	50	60	70
M	A	1	3	7	11	18
M	B	4	7	10	14	19
M	C (white)	6	8	12	17	24
M	C (black)	2	3	6	10	15
F	A	1	3	5	9	14
F	B	3	4	7	11	17
F	C (white)	5	7	11	16	22
F	C (black)	4	5	7	9	12

			NIPTS	
			Duration	
Level				
(dBA-TWA)	10	20	30	40
85	1	1	1	2
90	3	4	4	5
95	6	8	9	10
100	11	16	18	20

tional noise exposure or to subtle effects of socioeconomic status (as described in Chapters 6 and 7). In any case, database A combined with ISO/ANSI NIPTS estimates does a poor job predicting hearing threshold levels of noise-exposed populations (Royster et al., 2000). Robinson and Lawton (1996) recommend that unscreened ARHL databases be used in medical-legal evaluation; for American workers, either database B or Annex C would usually be appropriate.

Figure 13–8 gives some idea of the effects of choosing databases A and B on the relative contributions of aging and noise, using median-ratio allocation. We assume the (male) individual began work at age 20 and remained in the specified noise level workplace until the age of interest (or age 60, whichever is earlier). The graph shows the proportion of total HL (aging plus noise) attributable to aging, based on PTA-5123. As expected, the older the individual, the *higher* the percentage of HL attributed to aging; and the higher the noise level, the *lower* the percentage of ARPTS. The "aging" allocation is always higher for database B; again, this is no surprise, since database B predicts greater HL for any given age in the absence of occupational noise exposure. For both databases A and B, aging is responsible for the majority of the HL at age 60 for levels of 85, 90, and 95 dBA; only at 100 dBA is ARPTS less than 50 percent at age 60.

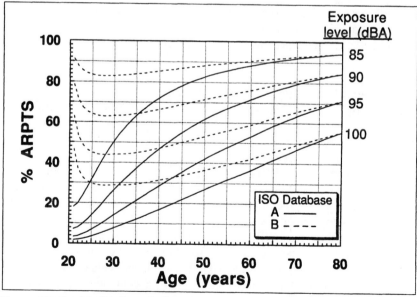

Figure 13–8. Median-based allocation to ARPTS for different combinations of age and exposure level, based on assumption of beginning exposure at age 20 and retirement by age 60. Databases A and B (ISO-1999), male.

The allocation curves for database B show a curious anomaly between ages 20 and 30. Recall from Figure 13–5 that even at age 20, database B predicts median HLs of about 3 dB; on day 1 of the job, the HL will be 100 percent attributable to ARPTS. In the first 10 years, NIPTS grows rapidly and the percentage of ARPTS falls; later, NIPTS decelerates, ARPTS accelerates, and percentage of ARPTS grows. We don't see this anomaly for database A because median ARPTS is assumed to be essentially zero at age 20.

When dealing with individuals with substantial history of shooting or other nonoccupational noise exposure, it is worth noting that Johnson and Riffle (1982) found that shooters had as much additional hearing loss, compared to nonshooters, as people exposed for 20 years at 89 dBA. "Above-average" shooters have even more NIHL, but unfortunately (see Chapter 8) we lack good "dose-response" data for shooting.

EXAMPLE 4

Let us reconsider the 60-year-old man from Example 3 (his audiogram is shown in Figure 13–7), but change his history to include 20 years of annual deer hunts without use of hearing protectors. While we cannot precisely predict the amount of NIPTS to be expected from this nonoccupational exposure from any good epidemiological data, it is reasonable to expect that his shooting caused some hearing loss. Twenty years of annual hunting at 89 dBA would add about 3 dB to median ARPTS; this is also the difference between annex C (white) and database B. Using 17 dB for ARPTS and 20 dB (as before) for NIPTS, we now estimate that occupational NIPTS contributed 54 percent (20 dB ÷ 37 dB) of the total loss, less than the 59 percent NIPTS contribution calculated earlier.

Audiogram Shape: Allocation by Frequency

Some audiogram shapes are incompatible with NIHL; in Ménière's disease, for example, one often sees an ascending pattern of SNHL, with normal hearing at 2 kHz and above. Flat hearing losses cannot be caused primarily by NIHL; there must be other components (often functional) responsible for most or all of the loss. ARHL and NIHL combine to produce down-sloping audiograms, but with somewhat different contours (as seen in Chapters 6 and 7). For a specified degree of high-frequency loss (say, 50 dB HL at 4 kHz), ARPTS tends to involve the lower frequencies (500 and 1,000 Hertz) to a greater degree than does NIPTS. This difference is especially prominent for women and for noise exposures under 10 years. All other things being equal (age, gender, noise exposure, and PTA-5123), an individual with a gently sloping audiogram probably has a larger ARPTS component and a smaller NIPTS component than an individual with a steeply sloping audiogram.

The allocation methods previously discussed use PTA-5123 and implicitly assume that the audiometric shape is appropriate for the ARHL-NIHL combination. When the slope is unusually flat or steep, it is preferable to perform separate allocations for each frequency prior to calculating PTA-5123.

EXAMPLE 5

A 60-year-old man has the audiogram (assumed to be valid) shown in Figure 13–9 after 40 years of workplace exposure at 90 dBA-TWA. Median PTA-5123 value for a male aged 60 (database B) is 14 dB, and 40 years at 90 dBA yields 5 dB at the median (Figures 13–5 and 13–6 or Table 13–3). The median-based allocation method would therefore attribute 26 percent (5 dB ÷ 19 dB) to NIPTS.

However, this audiogram is flatter than we'd normally expect for ARHL plus NIHL (see Figure 13–1), so we will calculate median-ratio allocations by frequency. Referring back to Tables 6–2 and 7–2, we can estimate the following median expected shifts:

Freq. (kHz)	ARPTS	NIPTS	Total	%NIPTS
0.5	12	0	12	0
1	6	0	6	0
2	10	6	16	38
3	30	12	39	31

The fifth column, %NIPTS, is simply the NIPTS divided by the total expected HL (ARPTS + NIPTS, with a compression correction at 3 kHz).

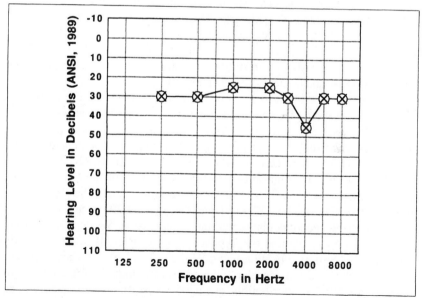

Figure 13–9.   Retirement audiogram, Example 5.

When these percentages are applied to this man's audiogram and PTA-5123 is calculated, the overall allocation is different from that obtained from median PTA-5123 values:

Freq. (kHz)	dB HL	%NIPTS	NIPTS(dB)
0.5	30	0	0
1	25	0	0
2	25	38	9.5
3	30	31	9.3
PTA-5123	27.5		4.7

Based on individual frequency allocations, we estimate that 17 percent (4.7 dB ÷ 27.5 dB) of his HL (PTA-5123) is attributable to NIPTS. This is less than the 26 percent calculated directly from PTA-5123, as we expected, because of his unusually flat audiogram. Note also that this allocation percentage cannot be obtained by averaging the %NIPTS values for the individual frequencies directly.

When should median-ratio allocation by frequency be used? No precise criterion can be offered; if audiometric shape differs "substantially" from expectation, but the diagnoses of ARHL and NIHL are still appropriate, consider using this method. Specifically, if there is significant low-frequency loss, that is, at 0.5 and 1 kHz, and exposure levels were 90 dBA or less (where no loss is expected below 2 kHz), allocation by frequency will usually (and appropriately) result in a lower noise allocation than allocation using PTA-5123.

Obviously, our subject's audiogram (Figure 13–9) is much flatter than expected. In fact, were it not for the notch at 4 kHz, it would be reasonable to discount NIHL entirely. For audiograms close to the expected shape, allocation by frequency will give results essentially identical to those obtained using PTA-5123, and is therefore unnecessarily complex.

It could be argued that allocation by frequency is preferable because it often (as in this example) involves a compression correction at one or more frequencies, in cases where the PTA-5123 medians don't require the correction. When a correction is required (simple sum of ARPTS and NIPTS > 40), it should be considered to have been taken from the ARPTS component, because in the evolution of a typical case, most of the NIPTS occurs early and most of the ARPTS occurs later. In the example, the NIPTS contribution at 3 kHz is 12 ÷ 39 = 31 percent, not the 29 percent (12 ÷ 42) that would have been calculated without compression. While allocation by frequency (for audiograms of "typical" shape) generally blames a little more on NIPTS than allocation using PTA-5123, it is usually unnecessary, especially when we consider that the median-ratio method already tends to overestimate NIPTS contributions averaged across an entire population, as previously discussed.

Occasionally, one sees an audiogram with an unusually prominent notch in the 3–6 kHz region and much better hearing at 8 kHz. Allocation by frequency may then result in an ARPTS curve that also has a prominent notch. If there is a history of substantial nonoccupational noise exposure or head injury, this notch will not be unexpected. However, without such a history, it is likely either that the individual's exposure history is incomplete, or that he or she is more susceptible to noise than to aging. The latter scenario can be modelled by selecting an ARPTS curve of median or other susceptibility that will fit the individual's audiogram, that is, 6 kHz ARPTS will not exceed the 8 kHz threshold for the individual. The difference between this ARPTS curve and the audiometric curve then provides an NIPTS estimate that can be compared to NIPTS curves from ISO-1999 for plausibility.

Range of Exposure Levels or Unknown Exposure Levels

Sound level or dosimeter measurements may sometimes define an individual's exposure only within a range. In that case, simply obtain median-ratio allocation estimates for the upper and lower limits of that range. Ideally, a noise control engineer, industrial hygienist, or other noise measurement specialist will specify a "more probable than not" range of exposures.

EXAMPLE 6

Consider a 50-year-old black woman who has worked for 20 years in a factory where she has to shout to communicate with coworkers. She has never worn personal hearing protective devices and has a completely negative history for nonoccupational noise exposure. No other cause for hearing loss is discovered and an audiogram reveals symmetrical high-frequency SNHL with PTA-5123 of 35 dB.

Her occupational exposures varied from 95–100 dBA. From Table 13–3 (Annex C), we obtain the following median values:

ARPTS (50-year-old black woman)   = 7 dB
NIPTS (20 years at 100 dBA)   = 16 dB (hearing level = 23 dB)
NIPTS (20 years at 95 dBA)   = 8 dB (hearing level = 15 dB)

The NIHL allocation for 100 dBA is 70 percent ($16 \div 23$); for 95 dBA, it is 53 percent ($8 \div 15$). Her estimated speech-frequency thresholds in the absence of noise exposure would be 11 dB (for the 100 dBA case, i.e., 30 percent of 35 dB) or 16 dB (for the 95 dBA case, i.e., 47 percent of 35 dB); in either case, we estimate that her HH would have been zero were it not for her noise exposure.

In the absence of exposure measurements for an individual, Appendix A permits estimates of noise-exposure levels for many occupational environments.

In most cases, even potentially hazardous exposures are in the lower ranges of hazard (see Table 13–4 for an estimate of the distribution of exposures for the U.S. workforce). Although these are 1981 estimates, they agree well with Franks' (1988) estimate of about five million American workers with exposures above 85 dBA-TWA. When no other exposure estimates are available, it may be helpful to calculate allocation estimates for a variety of exposure levels, such as 85 and 95 dBA (relatively few workers are exposed above 95 dBA).

Change in Exposure Level and Allocation over Time: Curve-Walking

How do we deal with the individual whose workplace exposure changes mid-career (assuming there is no valid audiometric "bracketing" of the two exposures)? An obvious strategy would be to simply add the corresponding median NIPTS values for the two exposures to predict the expected median NIPTS of the combined exposure. As we will see, this strategy would be wrong. The next example will demonstrate an approach that assumes that a worker moves along the median NIPTS curve appropriate to the first exposure, then takes his accrued NIPTS with him to the second job; he then moves along the median NIPTS curve for that exposure, but joins that curve not at zero years, but at the number of years matching the NIPTS "transferred" from the first job.

EXAMPLE 7

A 52-year-old man has worked for 20 years for one company. If the worker had spent 10 years at 100 dBA and 10 years at 95 dBA (perhaps because he began to wear earplugs with 5 dB attenuation), we'd be tempted to add 11 dB and 6 dB (from Figure 13–6) to get about 17 dB expected median NIPTS for PTA-5123. However, if this approach were correct, we could also use it to add NIPTS values for separate exposures

TABLE 13–4
Noise Exposure in 19 U.S.A. Industries[a]

Level (dBA)	Workers (thousands)	% of Total
<80	6987.0	46.88
80–85	2793.0	18.74
85–90	2244.5	15.06
90–95	1636.5	10.98
95–100	815.2	5.47
>100	427.7	2.87

[a]Machinery, transportation equipment, electrical machinery, fabricated metals, food, apparel, primary metals, textiles, printing and publishing, utilities, lumber and wood, rubber and plastics, stone and glass, chemicals, paper, furniture and fixtures, petroleum and coal, tobacco, leather.
Source: OSHA 1981.

at the *same* noise level; median NIPTS for 20 years at 95 dBA would be twice the NIPTS for 10 years, that is, about 12 dB. Reinspection of Figure 13–6 shows, to the contrary, that the rate of growth of NIPTS declines after 10 years, and the expected 20-year NIPTS at 95 dBA is only about 8 dB. In other words, NIPTS values are not simply additive; as exposure continues, the rate of loss decreases. Furthermore, for a given exposure level, median NIPTS eventually approaches a plateau (about 10 dB for 95 dBA, for PTA-5123). It seems logical that this plateau represents the maximum NIPTS this level of noise can produce for the average person; if the individual already has a larger NIPTS from prior exposure at a higher level, we would predict no further NIPTS from the lower-level exposure. Thus, we conclude that the hypothetical worker can expect about 11 dB NIPTS from his 10 years at 100 dBA, and no NIPTS from his subsequent 10 years at 95 dBA. Since his median expected ARPTS was also about 11 dB (Figure 13–5, database B), we'd allocate half his loss to ARPTS, half to exposure 1 (100 dBA), and none to exposure 2 (95 dBA).

What if the order of exposures is reversed? After 10 years at 95 dBA, we expect 6 dB NIPTS, which (referring again to Figure 13–6) is equivalent to about three years exposure at 100 dBA. We can now simply "walk" 10 years to the right on the 100 dBA median curve, from 3 to 13 years, and find an expected final NIPTS of about 13 dB (6 dB from the initial 95 dBA exposure, plus 7 dB more from the exposure at 100 dBA). Assuming a median ARPTS of 11 dB, as before, we would allocate his total loss as follows:

Exposure 1 (95 dBA)	6 dB ÷ 24 dB (25%)
Exposure 2 (100 dBA)	7 dB ÷ 24 dB (29.2%)
ARPTS	11 dB ÷ 24 dB (45.8%)

Note that we are still using the median-ratio method; we simply use curve-walking to estimate median NIPTS.

Figure 13–10 reproduces the relevant curves from Figure 13–4 with the arrows indicating the steps taken in this example:

1. Follow the curve for the first exposure to determine the median expected NIPTS for that exposure level and duration.
2. Move horizontally to intersect the curve for the second exposure at an equivalent NIPTS.
3. Follow the curve for the second exposure moving as far to the right as required by the second exposure duration.
4. The total expected NIPTS can be read at the ordinate.

From this second example, we can see that when a less intense exposure is followed by a more intense exposure, each may contribute substantially. However, when the more intense exposure comes first, the less intense exposure may be insignificant. This pattern may occur when a worker changes jobs, even within the same company; many workers move up to foreman or supervisor jobs requiring far less noise exposure. Equally common is the worker who began to use personal hearing protection devices effectively halfway through his career, halting the accumulation of NIPTS.

The approach described above was introduced by Robinson (1991); detailed formulae for computer implementation on a frequency-by-frequency, percentile-specific basis are given by Lutman (1996). The choice between graphic estimation as presented in Figure 13–10, versus software-based estimation (with a marginal improvement in accuracy) is left to the reader. It may be worthwhile to look at individual frequencies, however, if (as in Example 7) a second exposure is predicted to add no NIPTS at all. Referring to Table 7–2, we see that for 0.5, 1, and 3 kHz, our predictions are the same (10-year NIPTS for 100 dBA is greater than even 40-year NIPTS for 95 dBA), but the situation is different for 2 kHz. A frequency-by-frequency curve-walk predicts that the second exposure (10 years at 95 dBA) would actually add 3 dB NIPTS at 2 kHz (less than 1 dB NIPTS for the pure-tone average).

Johnson (1987) proposed a method of converting exposures like those discussed above into energy-equivalent stable exposures (e.g., 10 years at

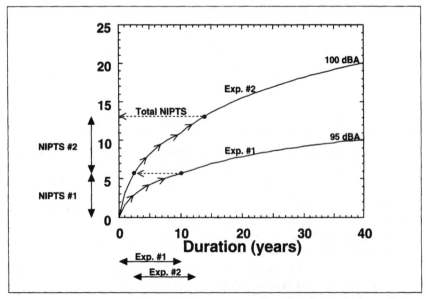

Figure 13–10. Speech-frequency NIPTS curves for 95 and 100 dBA are shown, as used in the curve-walking method of allocation (Example 7).

95 dBA plus 10 years at 100 dBA is equivalent in total acoustic energy to 20 years at 98.2 dBA). In most cases, this method gives results very similar to the curve-walking method (Royster et al., 2000).

King et al. (1992) offer a very simple method in which the contribution of each exposure period is deemed proportional to the difference between its level and 84 dBA, multiplied by its duration. Unfortunately, this method fails to incorporate the preemptive effect that prior high-level exposure has on subsequent lower-level exposure, as acknowledged by Lutman (1992).

Obviously, a similar but simpler approach can be used to allocate NIPTS within a period of *stable* exposure. Figure 13–6 shows nearly identical NIPTS trajectories for 85 to 100 dBA: for all levels, the median curve reaches about 60 percent of its 40-year maximum by 10 years, while the ninetieth percentile curves show about 67 percent of total NIPTS occurring in the first 10 years. Based on these curves, the relative contributions of various periods are easy to estimate. For example, if a worker was at company A for 10 years, then company B for 30 years, with no substantial change in noise exposure over the years, it would be reasonable to allocate 60 to 67 percent of his occupational NIHL to company A.

The curves in Figure 13–6 can be used to analyze growth of NIPTS in groups of workers as well as in individuals. Henderson and Saunders (1998) showed that longitudinal growth of NIPTS in noise-exposed railroad workers matched the ISO/ANSI curves well. Their data support the use of this model in large groups, such as may be involved in an insurance case where an employer had different liability policies in different years, and each insurer was only responsible for damage (hearing loss) accruing during a particular coverage year.

Simultaneous or Unbracketed Exposures: Allocation by Trajectory

Occasionally, we see patients who have had multiple hearing tests throughout their noise-exposed careers. We can then plot the "trajectory" of hearing level over time as an aid to inferring the relative contributions of noise and aging. When such a record exists, trajectory analysis should usually be given greater weight than median-ratio estimates of the relative contributions of noise and aging. Recall that ARPTS shows *acceleration* over time, while NIPTS shows *deceleration*. When NIPTS and ARPTS have made roughly equal contributions, one might expect these tendencies to cancel each other, with a resultant linear trajectory, that is, a constant growth rate of HL in decibels per year. When NIPTS predominates, one would expect a decelerating curve; an accelerating curve would suggest ARPTS predominance.

Figure 13–11 illustrates these concepts using ISO-1999 functions (database A, male). As expected, the trajectory for 40 years at 95 dBA, beginning at age 20, is nearly linear, since ARPTS and NIPTS after 40 years are so

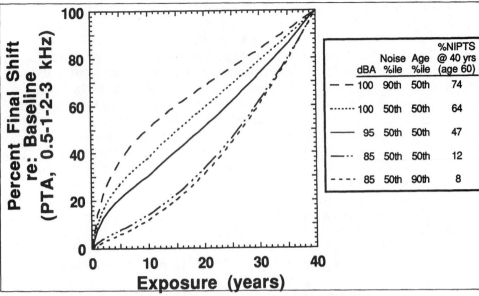

Figure 13–11. Predicted speech-frequency audiometric trajectories, as percentages of final shift, for various combinations of exposure level and susceptibility to aging and noise-induced shifts (database A, male).

nearly equal. At 85 dBA, ARPTS predominates (accelerating curve), and at 100 dBA, most (64 percent) of HL is attributable to NIPTS (decelerating curve). In addition to trajectories for median NIPTS and ARPTS, we have graphed curves with unequal susceptibilities to show more extreme cases. For example, if ninetieth percentile NIPTS (most susceptible 10 percent) for 100 dBA is added to fiftieth percentile ARPTS, the resultant curve shows even stronger deceleration than when median NIPTS and ARPTS are added. However, the differences in trajectory due to varying susceptibilities are smaller than those due to different noise-exposure levels.

EXAMPLE 8

Consider a hypothetical 60-year-old man who received multiple audiograms during 40 years of exposure at unknown noise levels. His PTA-5123 values for each of these audiograms are plotted in Figure 13–12. Hearing levels worsened rapidly during the first 10 years, then the decline decelerated; this suggests that most of his loss is due to NIPTS. About two thirds of his loss was accrued during the first 20 years. Compare this to the 100 dBA curves in Figure 13–12. It would be reasonable to conclude that he had high-level exposures (either at work or at play) or that he was highly susceptible to NIPTS.

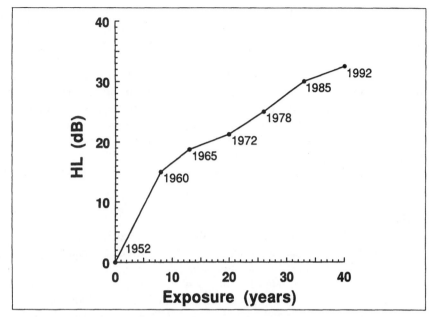

Figure 13–12. Speech-frequency audiometric trajectory, Example 8.

This is a complex approach relying heavily on professional judgment, especially regarding the quality of the serial audiometric data and the evolving audiometric shape (not just the time course of PTA-5123).

Simultaneous or Unbracketed Exposures: Extreme Audiograms

ISO-1999 and ANSI S3.44 purport to be valid only within the fifth and ninety-fifth percentiles. This constraint does not place absolute upper (or lower) bounds on the hearing levels associated with aging and noise, but indicates poor statistical precision for the 10 percent of the population who are most (and least) susceptible to both. The least susceptible individuals are of little concern; they have negligible handicap even at advanced age and very high exposure. However, otologists will fairly frequently encounter patients with audiograms worse than the appropriate ninety-fifth percentile curves in Figures 13–1 and 13–2 who have no apparent etiology for their hearing loss other than ARHL and NIHL.

Several possibilities must be considered. Most obviously, such persons may be very highly susceptible to noise, aging, or both. However, most otologists, including the author, believe that NIHL is never profound; excluding acoustic trauma, thresholds rarely if ever exceed 60 dB for PTA-5123. Otologic diseases such as autoimmune inner ear disease, hereditary degeneration, or viral labyrinthitis may have escaped diagnosis, but the same is true of the populations included in studies of ARHL (which includes nosoacusis as a category for undiagnosed otologic disease). Conversely, a small number of individuals in any population lose all of their hearing in adulthood for no apparent cause, without any apparent relationship to noise exposure. The natural conclusion is that the more extreme the severity of the hearing loss, the less likely it is that NIHL made a significant contribution. Certainly, it is unlikely in these cases that NIHL's contribution, if any, was as large as would be calculated using the median-ratio allocation method advocated for less extreme examples.

EXAMPLE 9

Consider a 40-year-old woman with bilateral profound SNHL (>95 dB HL) that accrued gradually over 20 years, during which she had a noisy job (90 dBA). Assume that the prevalence of idiopathic (i.e., no known cause) adult-onset profound loss at age 40 is 5:100,000 in the general population and that noise-exposed workers have a profound loss prevalence of 8:100,000. These hypothetical prevalences, if true, would suggest that five eighths of profound deafness cases in the noise-exposed population were idiopathic and about three eighths were related to (and presumably at least partly caused by) noise exposure. For the woman in question, we would not be able to conclude, on a "more probable than not" basis, that her deafness was noise-related. In general, the prevalence of a disorder must be *twice* as great in the exposed population to permit an inference of probable causality.

Unfortunately, this discussion required the use of hypothetical prevalence estimates, because no data of the kind we would like to see are known to the author. Nevertheless, it seems unlikely that profound losses are twice as prevalent in noise-exposed workers as in the general population. In contrast, profound losses are relatively common after head injury, ototoxic drugs, meningitis, and almost every other cause of sensorineural hearing loss listed in Chapter 10. When any of these is found, it is more likely to be the cause of profound loss than noise exposure. Even when no such cause is discovered otologically, it is probably inappropriate to attribute profound loss to NIHL.

Whether or not to attribute a *part* of such a loss to NIHL will be a matter of judgment. If noise exposure preceded the period of severe to profound loss, it is fair to assign a median NIPTS (about 4 dB, for 20 years at 90 dBA); if audiograms bracket these periods, one can be even more precise. Conversely, if noise exposure occurred *after* severe to profound loss, it is highly unlikely that substantial further loss was due to NIHL—a noise must be audible to be hazardous.

Asymmetry

Our examples up to now have all involved symmetrical audiograms, both for simplicity of illustration and because most medical-legal cases involving noise and aging display minimal differences between ears. We have calculated allocations for noise, aging, and other events on the assumption that if the contribution of a particular etiology was 25 percent for each ear, it would also be 25 percent for the person's overall hearing handicap.

The simplest and most often appropriate noise-aging allocation method, median-ratio allocation using PTA-5123, is unaffected by moderate degrees of asymmetry. As long as both ears show audiograms within the ninety-fifth percentile for age and noise exposure, the proportions attributed to noise and aging will be the same for each ear, based on the ratio of median expected shifts.

However, the other allocation methods may yield different allocations for each ear when the audiograms are asymmetrical. These differences are usually small and inconsequential, but a method of dealing with substantial asymmetries will be illustrated. Unlike many other methods, it gives reasonable estimates across a wide range of scenarios and is not subject to order effects (Dobie, 1990). The principles are simple:

1. The relative contributions of each *etiology* (noise, aging, etc.) must be estimated for each ear, using the allocation methods previously described.
2. The relative contributions of each *ear* to the person's hearing handicap must be estimated (as will be described).
3. The contribution of a particular etiology to hearing handicap is then the sum of the products of the proportions calculated in Steps 1 and 2.

For example, if occupational noise were responsible for 25 percent of right ear hearing loss and 50 percent of left ear hearing loss (Step 1); and the right and left ears were responsible (respectively) for 60 percent and 40 percent of overall hearing handicap (Step 2), the contribution of occupational noise to hearing handicap would be calculated as follows:

$$(0.25)(0.60) + (0.50)(0.40) = 0.15 + 0.20 = 0.35$$

We would conclude that 35 percent of this person's hearing handicap was due to occupational noise.

How do we obtain the "ear contributions" in Step 2? This is best illustrated by an example of unilateral injury.

EXAMPLE 10

Assume that a 60-year-old man suffers a severe head injury. Pre- (dotted lines) and postinjury audiograms are shown in Figure 13–13. His pre-injury PTA-5123s were 35 dB in each ear, resulting in a HH of 15 percent. Only the right ear shows an additional loss on the postinjury test, to 65 dB; his HH postinjury is 22.5 percent (15 percent monaural impairment [MI] for the left ear, 60 percent for the right ear, with a 5:1 weighting in favor of the better ear, as specified by the AAO-1979 rule). It is reasonable to assume that the head injury was responsible for none of the left ear loss (no change), and almost half (30 dB ÷ 65 dB) of the right ear loss. What part of the HH (15 percent preinjury, 22.5 percent postinjury) is attributable to the injury?

Briefly, we assume that if hearing is symmetrical, each ear contributes equally to the total HH. Before the injury, for example, this man's HH was 15 percent of which each ear contributed 7.5 percent; the additional loss in the right ear raises the HH to 22.5 percent. Since the left ear loss is unchanged, it still contributes 7.5 percent HH and the right ear must contribute 15 percent HH (two thirds of the total). In general, if MI_B is the monaural impairment of the better ear, the HH contributions of the better and worse ears can be calculated as follows:

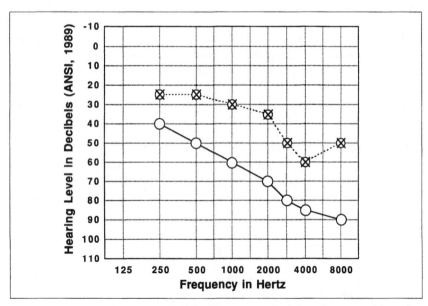

Figure 13–13. Preinjury (dotted) and postinjury (solid, right ear only) audiograms, Example 10.

$$HH_B = \frac{MI_B}{2} = \frac{15}{2} = 7.5\%$$

$$HH_W = HH - HH_B = 22.5 - 7.5 = 15\%$$

Although the injured ear is responsible for two thirds of the total HH, only 46 percent (30 dB ÷ 65 dB) of that ear's loss is caused by the injury; 46 percent of 15 percent is 6.9 percent. Thus, our final conclusion is that, of his new total HH of 22.5 percent, a little less than one third (6.9 percent) is attributable to the head injury.

In this hypothetical example, we had both pre- and postinjury audiograms. Many patients do not have the foresight to obtain preinjury hearing tests, but if the injury is purely unilateral, one can use the contralateral, uninjured ear to estimate preinjury hearing in the injured ear. This would not be appropriate for head injury, blast injury, or any systemic insult (each of these can affect both ears), but would be acceptable in the case of direct trauma to one ear.

From a medical-legal standpoint, asymmetrical hearing losses are far more common than unilateral injuries. Interaural differences greater than about 10 to 15 dB for PTA-5123 are unusual in occupational NIHL and usually reflect either nonoccupational exposure (especially shooting) or other otologic disorders. A simple and logical approach when large asymmetries are present is to divide the better ear into two components (ARHL and occupational NIHL), while the worse ear has these two components plus a third—equal to the interaural difference—attributable to "other" causes.

EXAMPLE 11

Figure 13–14 shows a very asymmetric audiogram in this 67-year-old worker who has had 20 years exposure at 90 dBA. His PTA-5123 thresholds are 62.5 dB HL (right ear) and 42.5 dB HL (left ear). His hearing handicap is 31 percent. We assume that some nonaging, nonoccupational noise etiology caused the considerable additional loss in the right ear. Median ARPTS for a 67-year-old man (database B) is about 18 dB HL (PTA-5123), while median NIPTS for 20 years at 90 dBA is only about 4 dB HL (18 percent of the sum of ARPTS and NIPTS). The expected contribution of occupational NIPTS in *each* ear is the product of the median allocation (18 percent) and the *better* ear PTA-5123 (42.5 dB HL), that is, about 8 dB HL. We can now use the asymmetry method described previously to calculate that 15 percent of his total HH is caused by occupational NIHL:

%NIPTS, left ear = 8 dB ÷ 42.5 dB = 18%
%NIPTS, right ear = 8 dB ÷ 62.5 dB = 12%

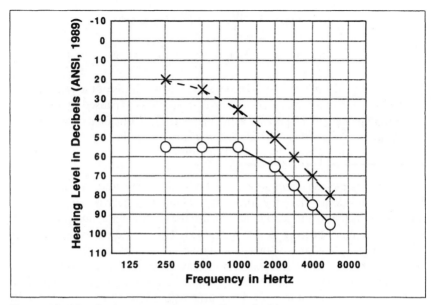

Figure 13–14. Retirement audiogram, Example 11.

MI, left	$= (42.5 - 25)1.5 = 26.25\%$
MI, right	$= (62.5 - 25)1.5 = 56.25\%$
HH (total)	$= 31.25\%$
HH_B (left)	$= 26.25 \div 2 = 13.125\%$
HH_W (right)	$= 31.25\% - 13.125 = 18.125\%$

HH due to NIPTS $= (0.18)(13.125) + (0.12)(18.125) = 2.4 + 2.2 = 4.6\%$. 4.6% (HH due to NIPTS) is about 15% of 31.25% (total HH).

Choice of Audiograms

Some audiometric patterns are highly unlikely to represent valid measurements. Very steep up-slopes (improving more than 20 dB/octave) and isolated thresholds more than 15 dB better or worse than their nearest frequency neighbors on either side are common examples. Audiograms much worse than tests taken just before or after the date in question may represent fluctuations due to temporary threshold shift (TTS), but are often invalid. Frequently, an applicant for workers' compensation benefits has had several audiograms within a short period after retiring from the noisy job. Even after professional review to exclude any tests that are probably invalid, there may remain several competing audiograms; which should be used in estimating hearing handicap? If the tests differ substantially from one another, it is highly likely that those showing worse hearing have been contaminated by TTS, by functional hearing loss, or by some other source of fluctuating loss; ARHL and NIHL do not demonstrate fluctuations. The audiogram showing the best hearing is also the audiogram that best represents the true hearing (AAO–HNS, 1988).

If several audiograms are similar (say, within 5 dB for PTA-5123), they may all be valid, varying only because of random test-retest error. The best estimate would then be based on an *average* of these measurements.

In general, the baseline audiogram for a given exposure should be the last test done prior to the onset of that exposure. However, if a subsequent valid test (even after the exposure begins) shows better hearing, it is likely that the original "baseline" was contaminated by TTS or functional loss or that learning effects are being seen; the audiogram showing the best hearing after exposure onset would be a better choice for the baseline.

A CAVEAT: Audiograms done prior to about 1964 were based on the old American Standards Association (ASA) 1951 calibration standard; between 1964 and 1970, either standard may have been used (the record should indicate which). After 1970, the American National Standards Institute (ANSI-1969, 1970) standard can be assumed. Valid comparisons between audiograms done with different standards are possible, but require prior conversion to the ANSI-1969 format using the correction values in Table 3–1.

Role of Systemic Disease

The controversies surrounding the possible roles of diabetes, hypertension, cardiovascular disease, and other systemic diseases in causing hearing loss, either alone or synergistically with noise exposure, have been discussed in Chapters 6, 7, and 10. Briefly, the effects are questionable; if they are real, they are, on the average, small and uncorrelated with the severity of the underlying systemic disease. Further research may establish the existence and magnitude of these possible effects more certainly. At this time, it is probably inappropriate to allocate an individual's hearing loss (or part of it) to any of these systemic diseases unless there is strong circumstantial evidence, for example, a sudden hearing loss coincidental with some other vascular event. In the typical case involving an allegation of NIHL, the postulated effects of systemic disease, even if real, would tend to cancel out. If hypertension (for example) were an independent cause of hearing loss, one would decrease the proportion of loss allocated to noise; if hypertension increased susceptibility to NIHL, the opposite would be true.

Allocation Estimates and "Medical Certainty"

The standard of proof for "reasonable medical certainty" in most litigation is "more probable than not," that is, the probability of a statement's truth is greater than 50 percent. Numbers such as audiometric thresholds, hearing handicap, and allocations are "point estimates." For example, we may estimate, based on an audiogram, that a person's hearing handicap is 15 percent. To say that this is true "more probably than not" is artificial; repeated audiograms, each valid on its own merits, might produce HH estimates ranging from 10–20 percent. What is needed here is a confidence interval, within which one feels reasonably certain the truth lies (for normally distributed variables, "probable errors" fall within about two thirds of a standard deviation above and below the mean). For median-ratio allocation estimates, one relatively large source of variability is uncertainty regarding exposure levels. Another source of variability is the presumably imperfect correlation of susceptibility between NIHL and ARHL. For the worst-case assumption (zero correlation), error ranges in dB can be calculated based on the standard deviations of ARPTS and NIPTS (Dobie, 1993). For exposure levels up to 90 dBA, these ranges will be ± 5 dB or less, applied to the individual's estimated NIPTS (not to the median NIPTS). Ultimately, when such a confidence interval is requested, it is up to the clinician to estimate the range within which the truth is likely to be found, considering all relevant sources of variation. For example: "I am reasonably certain that some of the loss, but less than half, was caused by the noisy job," or "I believe the job caused most of the loss, but the job-related portion could be as little as 40 percent or as much as 80 percent of the total."

SUMMARY

Diagnosis is a complex clinical process, requiring the judgmental integration of multiple lines of evidence against a background of knowledge and experience. In the case of NIHL and ARHL, that knowledge should include epidemiological evidence, such as is incorporated in the ISO/ANSI model (Figures 13–1 and 13–2). When more than one cause has contributed to hearing loss, the question of allocation arises; this is also a clinical process.

When two causes are audiometrically bracketed, that is, when one cause acts alone within an interval marked by both "before" and "after" audiograms, allocation is relatively straightforward. In the more common case of simultaneous age-related and noise-induced changes, a careful analysis of audiometric patterns over time (a "trajectory" analysis) often provides the best evidence of the relative contributions of noise and aging, or of different periods of noise exposure. Especially when the audiometric record is scanty, the median-ratio method can provide useful allocation estimates, which is be considered along with audiometric shape and severity and other evidence.

The basic premise of the median-ratio method is that the relative amounts of NIPTS and ARPTS for PTA-5123 at the median for a given age, gender, and exposure level and duration usually represent the best estimates for the relative contributions of each in individual cases of hearing loss. Median-ratio allocation is straightforward. The steps are as follows:

1. Select an aging database (usually B or C).
2. Find the expected median ARPTS for the subject's age and gender (see Figure 13–5 or Table 13–3).
3. Find the expected median NIPTS for the subject's exposure level and duration (see Figure 13–6 or Table 13–3).
4. Add median ARPTS and median NIPTS to determine the expected sum (apply a compression correction if the sum is greater than 40 dB).
5. Noise allocation % = (median NIPTS) ÷ (expected sum) × 100%.

This simple procedure will be appropriate in most instances, but it can be elaborated on as needed to suit specific circumstances. For audiograms with atypical shapes, allocation by frequency may be preferable. When changes in exposure level are documented, a curve-walking method is helpful. Methods for dealing with asymmetrical and extreme hearing loss, as well as unknown exposure levels, have also been discussed.

The role of professional judgment cannot be overemphasized. Many issues in diagnosis and allocation involve decisions that may be difficult and controversial, regarding validity of audiograms, definitions of "large" asymmetries and "reasonable" audiometric shapes, and exposure level estimates at different times in a worker's career. Multidisciplinary input may be needed, and allocation estimates may need to be calculated for various scenarios or hypothetical sets of facts.

Several assumptions and limitations need to be remembered. The median-ratio method assumes that ARPTS and NIPTS are additive (with or without compression) and have at least partially correlated susceptibilities, as discussed in a previous paper (Dobie, 1992). In other words, individuals who are destined to have above-average ARHL are expected to have at least average susceptibility to NIHL and vice versa. This method is applicable only for losses not exceeding ninety-fifth percentile HLs, according to ISO-1999, and should be used only *after* a well supported diagnosis of NIHL has been made on clinical grounds. NIPTS estimates are unavailable for levels exceeding 100 dBA, as well as for high-level impulse noise and acoustic trauma, precluding the straightforward use of the median-ratio method in such cases.

REFERENCES

1993. *Webster's Tenth New Collegiate Dictionary.* Springfield, MA: Merriam-Webster, Inc.

American Academy of Otolaryngology–Committee on Hearing and Equilibrium and the American Council of Otolaryngology–Committee on the Medical Aspects of Noise. 1979. Guide for the evaluation of hearing handicap. *JAMA* 241(19):2055–2059.

American Academy of Otolaryngology–Head and Neck Surgery. 1998. *Evaluation of People Reporting Occupational Hearing Loss.* Alexandria, VA: AAO–HNS.

American College of Occupational Medicine (Noise and Hearing Conservation Committee). 1989. Occupational noise-induced hearing loss. *J. Occup. Med.* 31:996.

American Medical Association. 2000. *Guides to the Evaluation of Permanent Impairment.* 5th edition. Chicago: AMA.

American National Standards Institute. 1970. *American National Standard Specifications for Audiometers, ANSI S3.6-1969.* New York: Acoustical Society of America.

———. 1996. *Determination of Occupational Noise Exposure and Estimation of Noise-Induced Hearing Impairment.* ANSI S3.44-1996. New York: Acoustical Society of America.

American Standards Association. 1951. *Audiometers for General Diagnostic Purposes, ASA Z24.5-1951.* New York: American Standards Association, Inc.

Clark, William W. and Carl D. Bohl. 1992. Corrected values for Annex B of ISO 1999. *J. Acoust. Soc. Am.* 91(5):3064–3065.

Coles, R. R. A, M. E. Lutman, and J. T. Buffin. 2000. Guidelines on the diagnosis of noise-induced hearing loss for medicolegal purposes. *Clin. Otolaryngol.* 25:264–273.

Corso, John F. 1980. Age correction factor in noise-induced hearing loss: A quantitative model. *Audiology* 19:221–232.

Davis, Hallowell. 1971. A historical introduction. In *British Acoustical Society Special Series: Volume 1—Occupational Hearing Loss*, ed. D. W. Robinson, pp. 7–12. New York: Academic Press.

Dobie, Robert A. 1990. A method for allocation of hearing handicap. *Otolaryngol. Head Neck Surg.* 103(5 Pt. 1):733–739.

———. 1992. The relative contributions of occupational noise and aging in individual cases of hearing loss. *Ear & Hearing* 13(1):19–27.

———. 1993. Confidence intervals for hearing loss allocation estimates. *Ear & Hearing.* 14:315–21.

Franks, John R. 1988. Number of workers exposed to occupational noise. *Semin. Hear* 9(4):287–298.

Henderson, D., and S. S. Saunders. 1998. Acquisition of noise-induced hearing loss by railway workers. *Ear & Hearing* 19:120–130.

International Organization for Standardization. 1990. *Acoustics: Determination of Occupational Noise Exposure and Estimation of Noise-Induced Hearing Impairment, ISO-1999.* Geneva, Switzerland: International Organization for Standardization.

Johnson, Daniel L. 1987. Predicting hearing loss for noise-exposed populations using ISO-1999. *J. Acoust. Soc. Am.* 81(Suppl. 1):S23.

———. 1988. Risk of hearing loss from noise. *Semin. Hear.* 9(4):279–285.

———. 1998. Evaluation of different approaches for determining age corrections for monetary compensation for noise-induced hearing loss. *J. Occup. Hear. Loss* 1:39–50.

Johnson, Daniel L. and Carol Riffle. 1982. Effects of gunfire on hearing level for selected individuals of the Inter-Industry Noise Study. *J. Acoust. Soc. Am.* 72(4):1311–1314.

King, P. F., R. R. A. Coles, M. E. Lutman, and D. W. Robinson. 1992. *Assessment of Hearing Disability: Guidelines for Medicolegal Practice.* London: Whurr Publishers.

Lebo, Charles P. and Rayford C. Reddell. 1972. The presbycusis component in occupational hearing loss. *Laryngoscope* 82(8):1399–1409.

Lutman, Mark E. 1992. Apportionment of noise-induced hearing disability and its prognosis in a medicolegal context: A modelling study. *Br. J. Audiol.* 26(5):307–319.

Lutman, Mark E. 1996. Estimation of noise-induced hearing impairment for compound noise exposures based on ISO-1999. *J. Audiol. Med.* 5:1–7.

Macrae, J. 1987. A procedure for assessing occupational hearing loss. *Austr. J. Audiol.* 9:69–72.

McNemar, Q. 1962. *Psychological Statistics.* New York: John Wiley and Sons.

National Institutes of Health–Office of Medical Applications of Research. 1990. Consensus conference: Noise and hearing loss. *JAMA* 263(23): 3185–3190.

Robinson, Daniel W. and G. J. Sutton. 1979. Age effect in hearing: A comparative analysis of published threshold data. *Audiology* 18(4):320–334.

Robinson, Douglas W. 1985. The audiogram in hearing loss due to noise: A probability test to uncover other causes. *Ann. Occup. Hyg.* 29:477–493.

———. 1991. Relation between hearing threshold level and its component parts. *Br. J. Audiol.* 25:93–103.

Robinson, Douglas W. and B. W. Lawton. 1996. Concept of the notional person in the assessment of hearing disability. *Br. J. Audiol.* 30:45–54.

Royster, Larry H., Julia D. Royster, and Robert A. Dobie. 2000. Prediction and analysis of the hearing characteristics of noise-exposed populations or individuals. In *The Noise Manual,* ed. Elliott H. Berger, Larry H. Royster, Julia D. Royster, Dennis P. Dirscoll, and Martha Layne. Fairfax, VA: American Industrial Hygiene Association.

U.S. Department of Labor—Occupational Safety and Health Administration. 1981. Occupational Noise Exposure: Hearing Conservation Amendment. *Federal Register* 46(11; January 16, 1981):4078–4179.

Chapter 14

Reporting

An otologist's report to a physician colleague can usually be focused and brief. Indeed, many referring physicians prefer to know just the facts that are relevant to their continued involvement: the diagnostic impressions, management recommendation, and plans for follow-up. A medical-legal report is a different matter. While the physician is not an advocate (except for the truth as he or she sees it), the physician's findings and opinions may be used to support one point of view in an adversarial setting in which the other side will try to discredit them. The entire process will work more efficiently and reach more appropriate judgments if these reports are complete, well documented, and well reasoned.

Written reports are not always necessary. Attorneys and insurance companies sometimes request a physician to review medical records and related documents without seeing the patient they pertain to. In some states (e.g., Oregon), attorneys are not required to disclose their experts prior to trial and may prefer telephone or face-to-face discussions, which can remain confidential as "attorney work product," whereas a written report is discoverable by opposing counsel. In other instances, the attorney may not wish to incur the cost of preparing a report. However, when a patient is seen and examined, a medical record is created that would itself be discoverable; a written report is then usually appropriate.

This chapter will describe and illustrate the medical-legal report in hearing loss cases. Referrals from occupational hearing conservation programs may not be of immediate medical-legal significance and usually require a less detailed report than referrals from attorneys and insurance companies. After a brief discussion of consent issues and an outline of the elements of the typical report, several examples will be offered.

CONSENT

The Doctor-Patient Relationship

When a person sees a physician in the expectation of receiving evaluation and management of a medical problem, and the physician agrees to provide those services for the patient's benefit, a doctor-patient relationship is said to exist, creating both rights and duties for both parties. For example, the doctor has a right to be paid and the patient has a duty to pay him. The patient's rights include competent medical care, access to the information in his or her medical records, and confidentiality; the information must not be shared with others without the patient's permission (there are several exceptions to this general rule, e.g., a physician's statutory duty to report infectious diseases). When a physician refers a patient to another physician for whatever reason, the patient's agreement to see the other physician constitutes tacit consent for an exchange of medical information (including reports and copies of medical records) between the referring physician and the consultant. Persons referred by employers, attorneys, and so on, for examination regarding employment, litigation, or compensation usually do not establish a doctor-patient relationship with the examining physician. By consenting to the examination, they might be assumed to consent to a report to the referring party, but it is probably wise to obtain consent anyway (see history questionnaire, Chapter 12).

The ACOEM Code of Ethical Conduct

The American College of Occupational and Environmental Medicine (ACOEM, 1994) has endorsed the employee's right to confidentiality regarding medical records held in occupational settings. ACOEM states that an employer has no right to a worker's detailed medical records except "when required by law" or at the employee's request, but is entitled to information relevant to a worker's job fitness. Thus, obtaining consent is especially important for referrals from employers.

ELEMENTS OF THE REPORT

The report should begin by documenting the patient's identity, with full name plus some other unique identifier, such as date of birth, social security number, medical record number, or case number. Unless the patient was referred by his or her physician, it may be worthwhile to document consent for the report to be sent, either by a written consent in the chart or by a statement of the patient's oral consent in the report itself. The introductory material should also document the date of the examination. The presence of accompanying persons (see Chapter 12) requires documentation; if any of them offered information on behalf of the patient, this should be stated.

History

In occupational noise-induced hearing loss (NIHL) cases, most of a patient's history can usually be dictated directly from the form in Chapter 12, with additions and amendments as needed. If a form is not used, the physician should still obtain and report a history of the present illness, past history, occupational history, family history, social history, and a relevant review of systems. This is usually the longest section of the report.

Physical Examination

Abnormal findings should be listed first, followed by recitation or summary of pertinent negative findings. Any inconsistent findings should be described in a factual manner in this section, without interpretation.

Audiologic Examination

A copy of the audiogram, with a statement of its validity, is essential. The report narrative should document the examiner (including ASHA certification), the instrument used (including, for U.S. Department of Labor reports, the date of the most recent calibration), and, if NIHL is at issue, the patient's most recent noise exposure (to determine whether the audiogram could be contaminated by temporary threshold shift). The examiner's opinion regarding the test's validity and reliability is relevant here. If there were reasons to doubt the test's validity (for example, pure tone-speech threshold discrepancies, as discussed in Chapter 4), these should be described factually. Straightforward interpretive statements regarding site-of-lesion (conductive vs. sensorineural) and severity of loss are not out of place here if the results were apparently valid and internally consistent. This would include a statement of the hearing handicap, calculated by the 1979 American Academy of Otolaryngology (AAO) rule or other method as appropriate.

Differential Diagnosis

The likely cause or causes of the patient's hearing loss should be stated along with an explanation of the otologist's rationale for these choices. Remember that in civil cases the critical question is whether the disease or disorder in question is "more probably than not" present and responsible—at least in part—for the hearing loss. Less likely diagnoses can be mentioned; in fact, it may be essential to recommend further testing to rule out an unlikely but dangerous problem such as an acoustic neuroma.

The otologist should attempt to resolve any inconsistencies in the data or recommend obtaining additional data as needed; this might include repeat hearing tests, other tests, previous audiograms and medical records, and occupational records to document noise exposure. It may be appropriate to offer tentative conclusions, modifiable depending on additional data.

When the data could be interpreted to support more than one set of conclusions, it is advisable to specifically justify the conclusions reached. What data support this? What data support alternate explanations? Why are some data given greater weight than others in selecting the most likely explanation of the patient's hearing loss? In this section, the otologist may refer not only to the data obtained from the patient, but also to clinical experience, the medical literature, and other sources of information useful in forming an informed medical opinion.

Prognosis

If the disorder causing the hearing loss is expected to be progressive or unstable, discuss this. What is the range of expected outcomes over time?

Allocation

For middle-aged or older patients, hearing loss almost always includes an age-related component. In addition, a worker may have had more than one noisy job, an illness or injury capable of causing hearing loss, and a noisy hobby. It is inappropriate to demand that a single cause of hearing loss be identified when several have contributed; as shown in Chapter 13, the relative contributions of each can often be estimated, a process referred to as *allocation*. In referrals from hearing conservation programs, when there is no active claim for compensation, a quantitative allocation estimate is usually unnecessary, and it will be irrelevant in some legal settings, as discussed earlier. It is best to ask the referring party whether allocation would be helpful in advance of the patient's visit. However, this can be done just as well at a later date, using the methods described in Chapter 13, assuming that the relevant data were collected and documented at the time of the patient's visit. In fact, as discussed in Chapter 12, differential diagnosis and allocation can be done without seeing the patient at all if the relevant audiological and otological facts, collected by others, are not in dispute.

Recommendations

Further Tests
If additional tests, including repeat audiometry, are necessary, this will have been mentioned in the "Differential Diagnosis" section; restate it here.

Treatment
Any treatment that would be offered to the patient in the otologist's own practice should be stated. Most often, this will pertain to conductive hearing loss and need not delay the process of diagnosis and allocation; hearing handicap can be stated "as is" and as it would be if the conductive loss were corrected. Not all conductive losses can be fully corrected by medical and surgical treatments, so one can't assume that the bone conduction thresholds accurately represent what the patient's loss would be after treatment. In fact, they may not even accurately represent the sensorineural component of the hearing loss; in otosclerosis, the true sensorineural component is usually somewhat *less* than indicated by the bone conduction thresholds.

Treatment will sometimes be recommended partially as a *diagnostic* maneuver. If a middle ear effusion or negative pressure can be cleared with treatment, the subsequent audiogram will more accurately reflect the true sensorineural loss than the pretreatment audiogram's bone conduction thresholds.

Prevention
Obviously, the otologist must reinforce the need for personal hearing protection devices (PHPDs) for patients with potentially hazardous noise exposures, whether occupational or recreational. Some workers don't need to wear PHPDs (those with bilateral profound deafness or severe conductive losses), and some need to avoid certain types of PHPDs (workers with chronic ear drainage should use earmuffs instead of earplugs). In rare cases, the otologist will recommend avoidance of specific drugs, especially for a worker with kidney disease or prior drug-induced hearing loss.

Job Restrictions and Precautions

Chapter 5 discusses the relationship between hearing loss and job fitness. Where no statutory or regulatory limits apply, the otologist and audiologist will usually have to rely on clinical judgment to determine whether a hearing-impaired worker can perform a job effectively and safely. This task has become even more difficult with full implementation of the Americans with Disabilities Act passed by Congress in 1990 (see Chapter 5). This law requires that "reasonable accommodation" be made in the workplace for those with problems such as hearing loss. This might include noise reduction, the provision of communication headsets, use of visual warning signals, or other ways to permit a hearing-impaired worker to do a job he couldn't otherwise do.

Some workers with recurrent infections need to keep their ears dry and dust-free. This might require the use of cotton plugs in dirty but noise-free environments, avoidance of wet or humid workplaces, and so forth.

Hearing loss caused by Ménière's disease and many other inner ear disorders may be associated with dizziness and poor balance. Some affected workers need to avoid driving, working at heights, and tasks requiring good balance. Medications prescribed for control of dizziness may be sedatives, which will also affect safety in many of the same situations.

EXAMPLES

Examples 1 to 11 are based on (and correspond numerically to) the examples from the previous chapter. The reader may wish to refer back to Chapter 13 for fuller explanation of the rationale for allocation using the different methods in each case.

EXAMPLE 1: NONSIMULTANEOUS, BRACKETED: INTERVAL ALLOCATION

> Re: Mary Brown
> MR# 0165-3383

Dear Mr. Jones:

Thank you for asking me to see your client, Mrs. Mary Brown. She was examined on March 23, 1989, and asked that I send this report to you. Mrs. Brown is a 40-year-old attorney who has complained of bilateral hearing loss for several years, worse since July 1988, when she was hospitalized after a motor vehicle accident.

Mrs. Brown was driving her sedan on July 2, 1988, when it was struck from the left side by another vehicle. She suffered injuries to her abdomen and left hip, but denies any head injury or loss of consciousness. After urgent abdominal surgery and hip repair, she did well until July 7, when she developed infections that required the use of gentamicin intravenously. Because she had been aware of mild hearing loss of gradual onset over the past 5 to 10 years, her physician obtained audiograms prior to beginning gentamicin therapy and one month after discharge. These were available for my review, as were her hospital records documenting a total gentamicin dose of 3 gm over 10 days, with "trough" blood levels up to 2.5 mcg/ml and serum creatinine levels up to 1.5 mg%.

During her hospitalization, Mrs. Brown noted progressively worsening hearing loss, dysequilibrium, and tinnitus. Since discharge, the dysequilibrium has become less troublesome, bothering her only in conditions involving poor visibility, unsteady support surfaces, or rapid head movements. Her tinnitus does not interfere with sleep, work, recreation, or social activities. However, her hearing loss makes even face-to-face conversations difficult, especially in the presence of background noise. She has recently been fitted with binaural hearing aids, which reduce her communicative difficulties substantially. If she tries to use the telephone without her hearing aids, she must ask for frequent repetitions.

Mrs. Brown is an otherwise healthy woman who denies significant medical illness, allergies, head injuries, or regular use of any medications. She is a nonsmoker and had a Caesarean section in 1978. She has no family history of hearing loss or ear surgery. She had rare ear infections in early childhood, but denies any otologic symptoms or treatment since then, except as described earlier.

Physical examination of the head and neck is unremarkable except for an asymptomatic nasal septal deviation. Specifically, the tympanic membranes are normal and mobile. Cranial nerves III to XII are normal, as is the Romberg test. Audiometry was performed by Mr. Charles Robinson, M.S., CCC-A, using a Beltone Model CR5000 audiometer calibrated January 12, 1989, and the results were felt to be reliable; a copy is enclosed [see Figure 13–3]. There is a symmetrical mixed hearing loss, unchanged since the test performed one month after hospital discharge. Tympanometry is normal, but acoustic reflexes are absent. Comparison with her pretreatment audiogram reveals that the conductive component is unchanged, but that there is now a sensorineural component that was not present before. Pretreatment, her pure-tone averages (0.5, 1, 2, and 3 kHz) were 22.5 dB HL in each ear, with a hearing handicap of 0 percent, using the AAO-1979 method. At present, her pure-tone averages are 45 dB HL bilaterally and her hearing handicap is 30 percent. Electronystagmography was normal except for bilaterally reduced caloric responses.

I believe her hearing loss was caused by otosclerosis (preceding her accident and hospitalization) and to toxic injury to her inner ears from gentamicin administered in July 1988. Each of these disorders is responsible for about half of her hearing handicap. She has recently been fitted with hearing aids and appears to be doing well with these. Her otosclerosis may well progress, but the ototoxic injury is now stable. She understands that stapes surgery is an option for hearing improvement in either ear (or both); the pros and cons, including the small chance of deafness in the operated ear, were discussed. For now, she wishes to continue with her hearing aids. Annual followup with audiometry is recommended.

Her dysequilibrium was also caused by toxic injury by gentamicin, in this case involving the inner ear balance organs. She is reasonably well compensated, but should use a night-light, carry a penlight, and take special care when walking on uneven surfaces.

Thank you again for the opportunity of seeing Mrs. Brown. Please let me know if I can be of further assistance.

Sincerely,

COMMENT   *The report begins with identification, date, and documentation of the patient's consent. This patient is probably suing either the doctor who prescribed the ototoxic drug or the other driver, who set in motion the chain of events that led to her needing the drug. However, the otologist is not called upon to comment on the possible negligence of any party (any medical negligence would be outside the sphere of otology), but rather to determine the cause(s) of her hearing loss. The history is straightforward, with some additional detail regarding her reported degree of handicap from her symptoms. The audiometric tester, instrument calibration date, and degree of reliability are included in the report; this information can also be provided on the audiometric form, but must be available one way or another. Differential diagnosis is rather simple here; both otosclerosis and ototoxicity would be identified by almost any otologist, given the set of facts, with greater than 90 percent certainty. Since the otosclerosis accrued prior to ototoxic injury and the latter was bracketed by pre- and postinjury audiograms, we were able to use interval allocation to determine that the two etiologies were equally responsible for her 45 dB HL pure-tone average and the resultant 30 percent hearing handicap. We have also noted that her hearing handicap was 0 percent prior to the ototoxic injury; we leave it up to the legal system to decide which point of view is appropriate in the event monetary compensation is to be awarded.*

EXAMPLE 2: SIMULTANEOUS EXPOSURE: MEDIAN-RATIO ALLOCATION

Re: John Smith
D.O.B.: 2-20-30

Dear Dr. Anderson:

Thank you for referring Mr. John Smith for evaluation. He was seen on June 5, 1990; a copy of his consent for this report is enclosed. Mr. Smith is a 60-year-old man who worked as a welder for Acme Shipyards for 40 years prior to his retirement three months ago; he complains of hearing loss for at least 10 years, of gradual onset.

Mr. Smith hears better in quiet places and has some difficulties conversing on the telephone, although he can usually hear the phone ring from the next room. During the 1950s and 1960s he noted temporary hearing loss and tinnitus at the end of his shifts; he has had tinnitus, which is continuously noticeable in quiet places, since about 1980, although this is tolerable and does not interfere with his activities. He has never used a hearing aid, and has had no otologic or audiologic evaluation or treatment prior to his visit here.

Mr. Smith denies otalgia, otorrhea, or dizziness. He has had mumps and measles, but denies antibiotic injections, daily aspirin, or any long-term medications. He had an outpatient inguinal hernia repair in 1965. Family history is negative.

He began working for Acme after a series of clerical and menial jobs that did not involve significant noise exposure. At work, he was exposed to welding equipment noise, chipping, scaling, and hammering, in and around ships under construction and repair. Only occasionally could he converse with coworkers without shouting. He never used hearing protective devices, although these were made available about 1980 in the workplace. He has had no military service and denies hunting, target shooting, or any other nonoccupational noise exposure. Workplace noise surveys provided by your firm's industrial hygiene department indicate that his time-weighted average exposures ranged from 96 to 102 dBA during his tenure at Acme.

His tympanic membranes were scarred, but mobile. The remainder of the head and neck examination was within normal limits.

Audiometry was performed by Dr. Carol Hammond, CCC-A, using a Grason-Stadler 1701 audiometer calibrated April 5, 1990 [see Figure 13–4]. The results were felt to be reliable and showed a symmetrical high-frequency sensorineural hearing loss; a copy is enclosed. He has had no significant noise exposure within three months prior to this hearing test. Using the AAO-1979 method, his hearing handicap is 13 percent.

Mr. Smith probably has hearing loss caused by both aging and occupational noise exposure. Based on epidemiological studies (ANSI S3.44, database B), and given his age (60) and noise exposure (40 years at about 100 dBA), my best estimate is that about 60 percent of his hearing handicap is attributable to occupational noise, and about 40 percent is attributable to aging. This is a permanent loss that cannot be medically treated; however, he is a candidate for hearing aid use. Thank you for referring Mr. Smith.

Sincerely,

COMMENT *A glance back at Chapter 12 will show that most of the very detailed history was dictated directly from the patient's signed noise questionnaire. His audiogram is almost exactly what would be expected of a 60-year-old man after 40 years working in 100 dBA (time-weighted average); since ANSI S3.44 (database B) indicates that aging and noise are responsible for 41 percent and 59 percent respectively, of median loss for this combination of age, gender, exposure level, and exposure duration, we can reasonably allocate blame in his case in the same proportions.*

To conserve space, most of the other examples in this chapter have been abbreviated, but these first two examples show the appropriate degree of detail in a medical-legal report.

EXAMPLE 3: SIMULTANEOUS EXPOSURE: MEDIAN-RATIO ALLOCATION

Re: John Smith
D.O.B.: 2-20-30

This report would be identical to Example 2 except for the audiogram showing more hearing loss (Figure 13–7): his hearing handicap is 43 percent (compared to 13 percent in Example 2). The history might include more severe complaints and use of hearing aids. However, using median-ratio allocation, we still consider 59 percent of his loss to be attributable to occupational noise, and 41 percent to aging.

EXAMPLE 4: DEALING WITH NONOCCUPATIONAL EXPOSURE

Re: John Smith
D.O.B.: 2-20-30

Dear Dr. Anderson:

[Mr. Smith's history is modified as follows:]

. . . Mr. Smith engaged in at least one deer-hunting trip each year during the 1950s and 1960s, using a .30 caliber rifle without hearing protectors. He also "sighted-in" his weapon each year at a firing range without hearing protectors.

[The final paragraph is also modified:]

. . . Based on epidemiological studies (ANSI S3.44, database C), and given his age (60) and noise exposure (40 years at about 100 dBA), approximately

54 percent of his hearing handicap is attributable to occupational noise, and about 46 percent is attributable to other causes (including aging and nonoccupational noise exposure).

COMMENT   *The different allocation figures are attributable to his history of significant nonoccupational noise exposure, as discussed in Chapter 13.*

EXAMPLE 5: AUDIOGRAM SHAPE: ALLOCATION BY FREQUENCY

                                        Re: James Carter
                                              D.O.B. 3-8-32
Dear Dr. Wood:
Thank you for referring Mr. Carter, who was seen on September 23, 1992. This 60-year-old man complains of hearing loss noticeable since his retirement two years ago. . . .

[The detailed history and physical examination will not be reproduced here, except for the relevant positive findings.]

. . . The reports from your firm's medical department indicate that Mr. Carter had 40 years of exposure at time-weighted average levels about 90 dBA. While earplugs and muffs were made available about 1985, he used them sporadically—less than 20 percent of his shift hours, by his own estimate. In addition to his workplace exposure, Mr. Carter has been an occasional hunter since his youth. . . .

. . . The audiogram [see Figure 13–9] shows a symmetrical, rather flat, sensorineural hearing loss. Hearing handicap (AAO-1979 method) is 3.75 percent. The audiogram was felt to be valid and reliable, with good agreement between pure-tone and speech measures. . . .

. . . I believe that Mr. Carter has a hearing loss caused by a combination of aging, occupational noise exposure, and nonoccupational noise exposure (shooting). While his audiometric contour is unusually flat, this is not inconsistent with the etiologies mentioned, given the notch at 4 kHz. Using epidemiological data (ANSI S3.44, database B) and the median-ratio allocation by frequency method, I estimate that about one sixth of Mr. Carter's hearing loss is attributable to his occupational noise exposure.

                                                          Sincerely,

COMMENT *Although there was no overt evidence of exaggeration in this case, functional or exaggerated hearing loss commonly results in elevation of low-frequency thresholds, and a flatter-than-expected audiogram. Allocation by frequencies reduces the impact of such exaggeration, if present, and is appropriate whether or not there is any exaggeration. If the usual median-ratio allocation method had been used, we would have attributed 26 percent to NIPTS, compared to 17 percent in this report.*

EXAMPLE 6: RANGE OF EXPOSURE LEVELS

Re: Susan Scott
MR# 6616-1348

Dear Mr. Moore:

Thank you for referring Ms. Scott, who was seen in my office on April 3, 1992. She is a 50-year-old black woman who worked for 20 years on the assembly line at the now-defunct Wonder Widget Company and complains of bilateral hearing loss. She never wore personal hearing protection devices, although she states it was loud enough (because of the noise of the pneumatic lines and the clatter of the widgets) that she had to shout to communicate at arm's length in the factory. Sound level measurement records indicate that her typical exposures were between 95 and 100 dBA, time-weighted average.

[The remainder of the history and examination is noncontributory and is omitted for brevity.]

. . . Her pure-tone averages (0.5, 1, 2, and 3 kHz) are 35 dB HL in each ear, and her hearing handicap (AAO-1979 method) is 15 percent.

I believe her hearing loss was caused by a combination of occupational noise and aging. Without occupational noise exposure, her speech-frequency pure-tone averages would probably have been below 20 dB HL. Based on ANSI S3.44 (database C) and an exposure level of 95 dBA, a little more than half her loss is noise-induced; based on 100 dBA, about 70 percent is noise-induced.

Sincerely,

COMMENT *Median-ratio estimates were calculated for a range of exposure levels; this will often be appropriate.*

EXAMPLE 7A: CHANGE IN EXPOSURE LEVEL

Re: Thomas Dunbar
MR# 6823-1124

Dear Mr. Allison:

We saw Mr. Dunbar at your request on April 23, 1989. A copy of his consent for this report is enclosed.

Mr. Dunbar is a 52-year-old man who has worked 20 years as a welder at Dynamic Corporation. He complains of bilateral hearing loss of gradual onset over the past 10 years. During his first 10 years at Dynamic, he used no hearing protection, but when these were made available, he began to use earplugs regularly. During the past 10 years, he states that he has used earplugs at all times on the job. . . .

[The remainder of the history and examination is omitted, but was noncontributory. His audiogram showed a high-frequency sensorineural hearing loss, consistent with NIHL plus ARHL, and well within the ninety-fifth percentile limits for expected hearing loss. See Figure 13–2.]

. . . Mr. Dunbar's hearing loss was probably caused by both aging and occupational noise exposure, in about equal proportions. After 10 years of unprotected exposure at 100 dBA, his effective use of personal hearing protective devices probably prevented any additional significant noise-induced damage during the second decade of exposure. Even if his earplugs had only reduced his exposure to 95 dBA, epidemiological data indicate that it is unlikely that further damage would have ensued. . . .

Sincerely,

COMMENT *Expected ARPTS (database B) and NIPTS (10 years at 100 dBA) are each 11 dB; thus the equal allocation. The second 10 years, at lower levels, was probably essentially harmless, since even 40 years at 95 dBA gives a median expected NIPTS of only 10 dB, less than the 11 dB accrued from the first 10 years. Estimating degree of attenuation from hearing protectors is difficult. The Noise Reduction Rating (NRR) used by manufacturers probably overstates "real-world" protection by about a factor of two, that is, most users obtain 10 to 15 dB of protection with full-time use (see Chapter 9 for a more complete discussion). Part-time use is even less protective: an earplug giving 15 dB attenuation in full-time use reduces time-*

weighted average exposure by less than 5 dB if used 50 percent of work hours. However, in this case, the history supports full-time and effective use, and even a 5 dB exposure reduction sufficed to render the second exposure period harmless.

EXAMPLE 7B: CHANGE IN EXPOSURE LEVEL: CURVE-WALKING

Re: Thomas Dunbar
MR# 6823-1124

Dear Mr. Allison:

[The history is modified to reverse the order of exposure.]

. . . Following 10 years at Dynamic Corporation, he transferred to McDouglas Aircraft Company, where he continued as a welder, but in a noisier plant. Hearing protectors were not used by him in either job. Dosimetry data provided by both employers indicates that his typical time-weighted average exposures were 95 dBA at Dynamic and 100 dBA at Mc-Douglas. . . .

. . . Epidemiological data (ANSI S3.44) indicate that median expected noise-induced shift from 10 years at 95 dBA is 6 dB (for the 0.5, 1, 2, 3 kHz pure-tone average). This is equivalent to three years at 100 dBA. An additional 10 years at 100 dBA yields an additional 7 dB expected shift. Combining these estimates with the 11 dB age-related shift expected for this man (database B), we conclude that his loss is most appropriately allocated as follows:

Dynamic	25%
McDouglas	29%
Aging	46%

Sincerely,

COMMENT   *This curve-walking approach can obviously also be used when allocation between jobs is necessary, but exposure levels don't change. Since NIPTS decelerates with time, the earlier years of exposure will always cause more damage than later years at the same level.*

EXAMPLE 8: SERIAL AUDIOGRAMS: ALLOCATION BY TRAJECTORY

Re: John Chambers
MR# 1266-8255

Dear Mr. Allman:

Mr. Chambers was seen at your request on August 2, 1992 and asked that I send you this report. He is a 60-year-old gentleman who has been employed as a welder for 40 years. During that time, he had several audiograms, which were provided for me to review. However, no dosimetry or other noise-exposure level data are apparently available. He reports that spoken communication was apparently impossible on the job, because of the constant noise level. . . .

[The remainder of the history and examination and most of the audiometric discussion are omitted.]

. . . His audiograms show speech-frequency thresholds (0.5, 1, 2, 3 kHz average) increasing quite rapidly in the first 10 years of employment, then less rapidly, as shown in the following table:

Year	PTA-5123 (dB HL)
1952	0*
1960	15*
1965	18.75*
1972	21.25
1978	25
1985	30
1992	32.5

*Corrected from ASA-1951 standard to ANSI-1969.

Although his exposure levels are undocumented, the decelerating trajectory of his hearing levels over time, along with the typical audiometric shapes, the history of speech interference in the workplace, and the absence of other detectable causes for hearing loss, strongly suggest that most of his hearing loss is attributable to his occupational noise exposure.

Sincerely,

COMMENT   *As mentioned in Chapter 13, this approach requires careful exercise of professional judgment with respect to the quality of the audiometric data and the evolving audiometric shape. The trajectories expected for different combinations of ARHL and NIHL are similar enough (see Figure 13–11) that one cannot really go beyond semiquantitative estimates of relative contributions with this method.*

EXAMPLE 9: EXTREME AUDIOGRAM

Re: Jane Wilson
MR# 8247-0883

Dear Dr. Stewart:

Thank you for asking me to see your patient, Mrs. Jane Wilson, on October 12, 1992. As you know, she is a 40-year-old woman who has suffered from a progressive bilateral sensorineural hearing loss, first noticed about 20 years ago. A series of audiograms done, beginning in 1975, shows an initially mild loss with irregular progression in each ear and some acceleration in the past five years. There were no audiometric notches in the 3 to 6 kHz region. Since 1972, she has been employed as a quality control inspector in a bottling plant where, according to dosimetry reports, her typical exposure was 90 dBA, time-weighted average.

Mrs. Wilson has no other otologic complaints. Her hearing loss has now become quite severe, and even with her new and very powerful hearing aids, she has great difficulty using the telephone, conversing in noisy settings, or when she can't see the speaker's face. Her past history is otherwise unremarkable. She is a nonsmoker who has no systemic diseases, takes no drugs, and denies head injury, nonoccupational noise exposure, ototoxic exposures, and family history of hearing loss. On two previous occasions she has been otologically evaluated with no etiology found. A brief course of steroids was given in 1988 because of rapidly progressing loss, without benefit.

. . . Physical examination was unremarkable. Audiometry was reliable and showed a symmetrical severe-to-profound sensorineural hearing loss, with pure-tone averages of 97.5 dB HL in each ear. Using the AAO-1979 method, her hearing handicap is 100 percent. . . .

Mrs. Wilson's hearing loss is much too severe to have been caused by her age, her occupational noise exposure, or even these two etiologies combined. The average person exposed for 20 years at 90 dBA in the workplace would suffer only about a 4 dB change in the 0.5, 1, 2, 3 kHz pure-tone average (ANSI S3.44). It would thus be reasonable to attribute about 4 percent of her loss to her occupational noise exposure. However, the bulk of her loss is idiopathic, caused by an inner ear disorder of unknown type and causation.

She should continue to have annual audiograms to monitor her hearing, and to turn her hearing aids off and wear hearing protectors while at work. Please let me know if we can be of further assistance.

Sincerely,

COMMENT *In this case, we have assumed that the patient suffered some noise-induced cochlear damage along with the idiopathic damage. If she had already had a severe-to-profound loss in 1975, it would have been quite unlikely that her occupational exposure (barely audible without hearing aids) contributed at all.*

EXAMPLE 10: ASYMMETRY (UNILATERAL INJURY)

Re: William Fletcher
MR# 3832-1132

Dear Dr. Peters:

Thank you for referring Mr. Fletcher, who was seen on June 5, 1991. Mr. Fletcher is a 60-year-old man who was involved in a motor vehicle accident on October 12, 1990, suffering a right temporal bone fracture. He had a temporary facial nerve paralysis and a cerebrospinal fluid leak, which also resolved spontaneously, and was discharged 10 days after the accident. His only apparent sequela is right-sided hearing loss, which he states is much worse than before the injury.

Mr. Fletcher has been employed as a postal worker for 35 years and denies any noisy employment. However, he admits to an extensive history of hunting and trapshooting without hearing protection. Indeed, he was seen by Dr. Richards only four months prior to his injury for evaluation of bothersome tinnitus. At that time, an audiogram showed a symmetrical sensorineural hearing loss, with pure-tone average hearing levels of 35 dB HL in each ear. . . .

[Past history and physical examination were unremarkable.]

. . . Audiometry today [Figure 13–13] reveals that the left ear is unchanged, while the right ear now is at 65 dB HL. His hearing handicap (AAO-1979 method) was 15 percent prior to the injury; it is now 22.5 percent. The right ear is responsible for two thirds of his hearing handicap, and the head injury was responsible for 46 percent (30 dB ÷ 65 dB) of the right ear hearing loss. Accordingly, 31 percent of his overall hearing handicap (two thirds of 46 percent) is attributable to the head injury; the remaining 69 percent is attributable to aging and nonoccupational noise exposure. . . .

Sincerely,

COMMENT *Refer to Chapter 13 for discussion of the rationale and methods for determining the relative contributions made by aging, noise, and the head injury.*

Example 11: Asymmetry (Unknown Cause)

Re: Donald Riley
MR# 6656-5732

Dear Mr. Curtis:

Thank you for asking us to see Mr. Riley. He was seen on June 6, 1991; a copy of his consent for this report is enclosed. Mr. Riley is a 67-year-old gentleman who worked for 20 years on the assembly line at Acme Products (dosimetry records indicate daily exposures between 88 and 91 dBA), retiring in 1985. Prior to his employment at Acme, he worked in a variety of sales jobs. He has noted hearing loss for about 10 years, initially symmetrical, but worse in the right ear for at least five years.

His past history is unremarkable and yields no clue to explain his hearing loss. He denies any nonoccupational noise exposure, specifically hunting and shooting. Physical examination was also unremarkable.

. . . Audiometry revealed an asymmetrical sensorineural hearing loss [see Figure 13–14]. Pure-tone averages (0.5, 1, 2, 3 kHz) were 42.5 dB HL (left) and 62.5 dB HL (right). His hearing handicap (AAO-1979 method) is 31 percent. . . .

I believe the hearing loss in Mr. Riley's left ear is caused by aging plus occupational noise exposure. However, some unknown (idiopathic) third factor probably accounted for much of the loss in the right ear, for two reasons: first, the right ear hearing loss is much worse than could be expected, based on epidemiological studies (beyond the ninety-fifth percentile; ANSI S3.44); second, the degree of asymmetry is much greater than usually seen with age-related and/or noise-induced hearing loss. Based on the ratio of median shifts for aging (67-year-old male, database B) and noise (20 years at 90 dBA), I believe it is reasonable to allocate the hearing loss in each ear as follows:

	Left	Right
Aging	34.5 dB	34.5 dB
Occupational noise exposure	8 dB	8 dB
Idiopathic factor	0 dB	20 dB

Occupational noise-induced hearing loss would then be responsible for 18 percent of his left ear loss, 12 percent of his right ear loss, and 15 percent of his hearing handicap.

Sincerely,

COMMENT. *In this case, the large asymmetry is attributable to some id-iopathic cause, but the most common cause of large asymmetries is probably shooting rifles and shotguns. Right-handed shooters usually develop greater losses in their left ears (the right ear is partially shielded from the muzzle blast by the "head shadow").*

REFERENCES

American Academy of Otolaryngology–Committee on Hearing and Equilibrium and The American Council of Otolaryngology–Committee on the Medical Aspects of Noise. 1979. Guide for the evaluation of hearing handicap. *JAMA* 241(19):2055–2059.

American College of Occupational and Environmental Medicine. 1994. The new ACOEM Code of Ethical Conduct. *J. Occup. Med.* 36:27–30.

Chapter 15

The Expert Witness

Any clinician who sees patients with medical-legal problems will eventually have to testify, at trial or in a deposition. An elementary understanding of legal procedures can make the first few encounters less stressful. This chapter is primarily aimed at otolaryngologists and audiologists who may have to serve as expert witnesses, but it is hoped that attorneys and insurance professionals will also find items of interest, especially in the sections on qualifications of experts, interprofessional cooperation, and compensation.

The author is not an attorney, and nothing in this chapter is intended, nor should it be construed, as legal advice. Rather, this is a descriptive account of selected aspects of the expert witness experience. Individuals must seek competent counsel for answers to personal legal questions.

TORTS

If you break a law, you offend the state (or city or nation) and may face *criminal* prosecution. Your opponent will be the government, you must be found guilty "beyond a reasonable doubt," and, while you may be ordered to make restitution to your victims, you also face incarceration and/or a fine.

Civil law is different. A civil offense violates a duty you owe to your neighbor (not to the state); such offenses, other than breaches of contract, are called *torts*. The tort of negligence is familiar to physicians as the basis for nearly all malpractice and personal injury suits: Basically, the plaintiff claims that the defendant failed to exercise due care and caused an injury that requires compensation. To prevail, the injured party must establish that

1. The defendant had a duty to the plaintiff (e.g., to drive carefully, or to perform surgery in a competent manner, or to manufacture a safe product).

2. The defendant neglected that duty.
3. An injury or loss occurred.
4. The injury was caused by the defendant's negligence.

In criminal trials, the power of the state is somewhat counterbalanced by the burden of proving guilt "beyond a reasonable doubt"; a "probably guilty" defendant should be set free. The standard of proof is much more symmetrical in civil trials. Usually, the plaintiff need only prove that his or her claim is probably true—"more probably than not"—to win the case.

THE ROLE OF THE EXPERT WITNESS

Most witnesses in criminal trials are *fact* (or *material*) witnesses who may have (for example) seen the crime or sold the defendant the murder weapon. Such a witness possesses no special qualifications, but happens to have unique information about the case needed by the court, and must testify as a matter of civic duty. A physician who treated the victim of a crime is a fact witness; no other physician can testify as well regarding the medical facts he or she observed.

An expert witness, on the other hand, is different in three important ways: expertise in some field important for the case at hand, lack of unique information about the case, and the ability to state an opinion. The first is obvious: In cases involving complex issues of engineering, medicine, or banking, for example, both sides will need expertise to support their points of view. The second is more subtle. In almost any field of interest, no matter how narrow, there will be several experts from whom the attorneys can choose their expert witnesses. Because none of these possesses *unique* information or expertise, none has an obligation to testify, and they may charge for their services in testifying. Finally, the expert witness is ordinarily allowed to express opinions and conclusions, unlike fact witnesses, who must simply present the facts as they saw them.

These boundaries are not absolute. A fact witness can also be a potential expert, as in the case of a treating physician. In this situation, some physicians accept the obligation to appear as a fact witness and to state their observations and findings, but refuse to express opinions and conclusions requiring expertise unless paid as expert witnesses, claiming that otherwise they would be deprived of valuable property without due compensation. Obviously, it could be hard to draw the line between fact and opinion, and few attorneys balk at paying appropriate fees in these circumstances.

The expert should resist the temptation to think of the attorney who has contracted for services as "his" attorney. The attorney's obligation is to his or her own client, the plaintiff or defendant, not to the expert. For clarity in the discussions to follow, we will frequently refer to the "client-attorney" (the one who usually pays the expert's fees) and the "opposing attorney." Rarely, an expert is hired not by either side, but directly by the judge, as happened in a group of silicone breast implant cases. (Hulka et al., 2000)

Not infrequently, the expert will play a background role, helping the client-attorney prepare the case through teaching and consultation, but not testifying in court. The attorney may have several different reasons for using an expert in this way. The expert may have some opinions that are more likely to hurt than to help the attorney's cases. The attorney may want to minimize the number of experts presenting a complex case, or cost may be an issue.

TRIALS AND DEPOSITIONS

In our adversarial legal system, the judge or jury decides the winner, but does not actively pursue information. Instead, each side presents its case as vigorously and convincingly as possible, without any expectation that these presentations will be impartial or balanced. Our hope is rather that out of the combat of two opposing points of view, a fair conclusion will emerge and make itself known to the judge or jury. For the expert witness, this means being interviewed, not once by an impartial inquisitor, but by two attorneys who seek to shape one's testimony to fit opposite views of reality.

Direct Examination

The expert witness will usually be questioned first by the client-attorney. After being called to the stand, the expert is typically led through a series of questions intended to establish qualifications (training, experience, etc.) as an expert. Often, this is followed by questions about the relevant science and medicine ("How does the ear work?"; "How does noise damage the ear?"). Courts often allow considerable latitude during the qualification and didactic parts of the expert's testimony, permitting very general questions and long narrative answers.

Questions and answers must be narrower and more specific as the facts of the case at hand are approached. Ultimately, the expert will be asked for opinions on one or more of the key elements of a tort: duty, negligence, damage, and liability. In a malpractice case, the physician may be asked to express opinions about all elements, determining whether the standard of care was violated, whether an injury occurred, and whether the two are causally related. Conversely, in a personal injury case, the physician may only testify about the injury and its cause without expressing an opinion about possible negligence. The attorney may ask the expert to assume certain facts (which may or may not have been established) in forming opinions; these hypothetical questions are relevant if the attorney can subsequently convince the judge or jury of this version of the facts.

In an adversarial system, it is the client-attorney's right (indeed, it is his or her *duty*) to present the expert's testimony in a way that is most favorable to the client. For example, an expert may believe that the attorney's client (defendant) was not at all negligent, but that the plaintiff suffered significant harm from other causes. The attorney may wish to argue that his client was not negligent *and* that there were no significant damages. If there is a second expert who believes there were no damages, the attorney may choose to ask the first expert only about the issue of negligence. The expert witness's obligation is only to answer the questions that are asked. Even when the witness believes that additional information would be *helpful* to the attorney, it is best not to answer questions that have not been asked. Ultimately, it is the responsibility of the attorneys on both sides to determine the questions they want answered.

Cross-Examination

The opposing attorney's job is to impeach (reduce or eliminate the effect of) the expert's testimony, choosing from strategies that include attacks on the expert's qualifications, knowledge, experience, reasoning, judgment, impartiality, and consistency, as well as attempts to show that the expert relied on incorrect or incomplete versions of the facts of the case. The opposing attorney may also try to establish that the expert is reflecting a controversial point of view from the fringes of the scientific or medical community.

Attacks on an expert's qualifications and experience can be mitigated by careful presentation during direct examination. The expert should neither understate nor exaggerate his or her qualifications. Potential weaknesses are usually best brought out during direct examination. However, if the client-attorney chooses not to deal with some of these issues on direct examination, the expert should be prepared to respond to them on cross-examination, forthrightly and positively, with explanation but without defensiveness or apology.

Some questions, although framed so as to demand a "yes" or "no" answer, should *never* be answered that way. For example, if the expert believes that a plaintiff's hearing loss was caused by both noise exposure and aging, the question "Did noise cause his hearing loss?" must be answered positively, but with qualification. If the expert is responsive and avoids evasiveness and rambling, the court will almost always permit complete answers, regardless of the phrasing of the questions. However, in cross-examination as in direct examination, the expert witness should answer only those questions that are asked.

The expert witness must be prepared to explain his or her reasoning clearly and simply. Conclusions and opinions must be supported by facts and logic; it is not enough to invoke one's authority as a physician. The opposing attorney will often have acquired a considerable command of the professional and scientific literature, and may try to undermine the expert's conclusions by references to contrary facts and opinions in "authoritative" books and journal articles. This strategy is particularly effective when the expert under cross-examination has previously identified these sources as "authoritative."

Questions about "authoritative" or "well accepted" books, authors, or organizations are best handled cautiously. A long list will invariably include material contradicting at least some of an expert's testimony in controversial areas; but if the expert says "there are no authoritative references," this casts doubt on the erudition of both the field and the expert. The court should learn instead that while there is extensive literature in the field in question, there are areas of both consensus and controversy. Before listing a book or author as "generally authoritative," it is best to qualify this answer by stating that there may be areas of disagreement. Of course, the expert must be prepared to defend any such disagreement; usually this can be done by reference to equally authoritative books and authors! This task is more difficult when most or all the "authorities" hold a different view than the expert. Opposing attorneys will then argue that the expert is on the fringes of (or outside of) the range of accepted professional opinion. This doesn't necessarily make the expert's opinions wrong, but may undermine his or her credibility.

An expert's impartiality can be attacked by showing that he or she regularly or exclusively testifies on behalf of a particular class of clients or has a conflict of interest in the case. The best defense against the latter charge is simply innocence: An expert should never participate in a case where he or she could directly profit from a victory by either side. The expert should be equally available to attorneys representing plaintiffs or defendants, regardless of the type of case. However, the nature of an individual's expertise and opinions may make him or her much more attractive to one side than to the other in a series of related cases; this does not in and of itself establish bias. Opposing attorneys will sometimes ask about the expert's fees, implying that being paid creates bias. The expert should make it clear that it is *time* and not one's opinion that is being paid for. Occasionally, the client-attorney will defuse this issue by dealing with it on direct examination.

One of the most effective ways to impeach an expert's testimony is to show inconsistencies with previous testimony, writings, or pronouncements. The expert should assume that the opposing attorney has read everything relevant in the expert's *curriculum vitae* (C.V.), as well as transcripts of prior depositions and trials, newspaper interviews, and so forth. (Bibliographic services can provide the names, dates, and venues of all cases in which an expert has testified; transcripts can then be obtained.) When testifying, the expert should think before speaking, correct any misstatements as soon as they are realized as such, avoid overgeneralization, make assumptions explicit, and (obviously) answer truthfully, remembering that what is said will be available for use in future cases. Where there is controversy or the expert has some uncertainty, this should be stated. Often, it is helpful to offer a range of possibilities and a level of certainty. This is an area where it is important to remember that the client-attorney is not the expert's attorney. The client-attorney's interests are in presenting the strongest case for the plaintiff or defendant, even if that involves pushing the expert into a "black or white" position that will be uncomfortable at a later date. The expert's interest is, above all, to protect his professional integrity and reputation; this interest may not always coincide with that of the client-attorney.

Opposing attorneys will sometimes try to impeach an expert's testimony by quoting from the expert's writings or testimony out of context, to create an *apparent* inconsistency. If the quotation does not sound right, the expert should insist on seeing the quoted material, then explain why there is really no inconsistency. Reading the longer passage aloud to show context is often effective.

Inconsistencies may be justifiable if new scientific data or accumulated clinical experience have caused a change of heart since the previous testimony or writing. An expert should, if possible, keep track of these evolutions, both in the professional field and in personal opinion, and discuss them with the client-attorney; if potentially embarrassing, they may be better dealt with on direct examination.

The opposing attorney may contend that the expert was given erroneous or incomplete information on which to base his conclusions. If important facts are at issue (for example, did the plaintiff fire a weapon without hearing protection?), the expert may be asked to reformulate his opinions based on a different hypothetical scenario than was provided on direct examination. A competent and ethical opposing attorney cross-examining a competent and ethical expert witness will focus primarily on this type of attack, attempting to show that the version of the facts he hopes to sell to the jury would lead the expert to a different conclusion, one favorable to his client.

A somewhat less honorable version of this fact-based strategy involves attacking the expert because he or she didn't personally see the plaintiff as a patient. This has great emotional appeal; all other things being equal, juries assume the doctor who saw the patient is better able to form correct opinions than one who didn't. However, it frequently happens that the medical *facts* (history, physical examination, audiogram) are well-established, often based on two or more independent and near-identical evaluations, and could be agreed to by both sides. An expert would not have to see such a patient to reach a well-reasoned opinion. Nevertheless, many client-attorneys prefer an additional examination simply to deter this line of attack.

Redirect/Recross

The client-attorney is permitted to try to repair any damage done during cross-examination, and the opposing attorney is then permitted another opportunity as well. This cycle can be repeated *ad nauseam*, but the opposing attorney always gets the last word.

Depositions

A deposition consists of transcribed testimony taken under oath, in the presence of attorneys representing both parties and a court reporter (often a videotape is also made), for possible introduction as evidence during a later trial. Depositions may take place anywhere; often, the offices of an attorney or witness are used. In the absence of a judge, attorneys may object to their opponents' questions, but the witness must usually answer regardless. If the judge subsequently excludes the objectionable question, the answer will not be read at the trial.

Depositions are of two types. Most common is the *discovery* deposition, called by the opposing attorney to find out what the expert will say at trial. If, at trial, the expert deviates from or goes beyond his deposition testimony, the opposing attorney can read the contradictory parts of the deposition into the trial record as a way of impeaching the expert. In many cases, the *opposing* attorney, who requested the deposition, pays the expert's fee.

The second type of deposition is called by the client-attorney to *perpetuate* the expert's testimony for use in court, in the event he or she is unavailable during the trial. This proceeds more like a trial, with the client-attorney conducting the direct examination.

Exhibits can be entered during depositions and perpetuated for trial. For example, if the expert illustrates a point by drawing a picture or referring to a textbook, either counsel may request that the original or a copy be made an exhibit. Files and notes are also subject to "capture" during a deposition. It is best to ask the client-attorney (regardless of who called the deposition) what to bring to the deposition.

A deposition should be conducted with as much decorum as a trial, but in the absence of a judge and jury, some opposing attorneys will resort to abusive tactics in an attempt to weaken an expert's testimony. The client-attorney can object, but without immediate effect other than to give the witness a chance to collect his thoughts. Repetitious and argumentative questioning can extend a deposition well past three to four hours in duration, making it difficult to remain calm and collected. The witness may ask for breaks at any time and may confer with the client-attorney during these breaks. Really abusive behavior may merit on-the-record complaints from the client-attorney or even from the witness. If the deposition goes past the witness' level of tolerance, a recess can be requested and a second session can be rescheduled. If all else fails and the record shows multiple objections by both the expert and the client-attorney, the deposition can be terminated without the consent of the opposing attorney, but at the risk of a later contempt citation if the judge eventually finds that the deposition should have been permitted to continue.

At the end of the deposition, the court reporter will offer the expert the opportunity to read and correct the transcript, once it's available, prior to submitting it to the court. Substantive errors are common enough to make this a worthwhile task.

QUALIFICATIONS OF THE EXPERT WITNESS

The Board of Regents of the American College of Surgeons (ACS) has recently approved a "Statement on the physician expert witness" (Spencer and Guice, 2000). While its context is malpractice litigation, most of this statement is also applicable to hearing loss cases and to expert testimony in general. Following a preamble bemoaning recent increases in malpractice cases and awards, the statement outlines both qualifications and guidelines for behavior:

I. Recommended qualifications for the physician expert witness
   A. The physician expert witness must have a current, valid, and unrestricted license to practice medicine in the state in which he or she practices.
   B. The physician expert witness should be a diplomate of or have status with a specialty board recognized by the American Board of Medical Specialties, as well as be qualified by experience or demonstrated competence in the subject of the case.
   C. The specialty of the physician expert witness should be appropriate to the subject matter in the case.
   D. The physician expert witness should be familiar with the standard of care provided at the time of the alleged occurrence and should be actively involved in the clinical practice of the specialty or the subject matter of the case during the time the testimony or opinion is provided.
   E. The physician expert witness should be able to demonstrate evidence of continuing medical education relevant to the specialty or the subject matter of the case.
   F. The physician expert should be prepared to document the percentage of time that is involved in serving as an expert witness. In addition, the physician expert should be willing to disclose the amount of fees or compensation obtained for such activities and the total number of times the physician expert has testified for the plaintiff or defendant.

II. Recommended guidelines for behavior of the physician expert witness
Physicians have an obligation to testify in court as expert witnesses when appropriate. Physician expert witnesses are expected to be impartial and should not adopt a position as an advocate or partisan in the legal proceedings.
   A. The physician expert witness should review the medical information in the case and testify to its content fairly, honestly, and in a balanced manner. In addition, the physician expert witness may be called upon to

draw an inference or an opinion based on the facts of the case. In doing so, the physician expert witness should apply the same standards of fairness and honesty.

B. The physician expert should be prepared to distinguish between actual negligence (substandard medical care that results in harm) and an unfortunate medical outcome (recognized complications occurring as a result of medical uncertainty).

C. The physician expert witness should review the standards of practice prevailing at the time of the alleged occurrence.

D. The physician expert witness should be prepared to state the basis of his or her testimony or opinion, and whether it is based on personal experience, specific clinical references, evidence-based guidelines, or a generally accepted opinion in the specialty field. The physician expert witness should be prepared to discuss important alternate methods and views.

E. Compensation of the physician expert witness should be reasonable and commensurate with the time and effort given to preparing for deposition and court appearance. It is unethical for a physician expert witness to link compensation to the outcome of a case.

F. The physician expert witness is ethically and legally obligated to tell the truth. Transcripts of depositions and courtroom testimony are public records, and subject to independent peer reviews. The physician expert witness should be aware that failure to provide truthful testimony exposes the physician expert to criminal prosecution for perjury, civil suits for negligence, and revocation or suspension of his or her professional license.

These guidelines would seem to imply that the most appropriate physician expert witness in hearing loss cases would be certified by the American Board of Otolaryngology. A board-certified occupational physician could also be an appropriate expert, especially with respect to standards of practice in hearing conservation, but occupational physicians are not usually skilled in otological diagnosis.

Attorneys seeking expert witnesses will want to go beyond these minimal criteria to find experts who can provide the best possible service. Recognized expertise can be documented by peer-reviewed publications in relevant areas, by invited lectures, and by invited service on national and regional committees, boards, et cetera, in related areas. Perhaps most important are word-of-mouth references from other clients who can speak to a reputation for competence, integrity, communication skills, and cooperation.

Fellowship training and a practice limited to otology enhance an expert's credibility a little, but are less important than interest, expertise, and activity in medical-legal assessment. The same can be said for society memberships.

WORKING WITH THE ATTORNEY

The preliminary interview helps the potential expert determine whether to participate in the case. Any real or apparent conflict of interest is cause to withdraw. It is important to be forthcoming about one's areas of expertise; many cases require experts from other disciplines. For example, few otolaryngologists can make acoustical measurements, or comment on their adequacy if the data are questioned. This initial discussion allows both parties to make a tentative determination whether they can work together, based on style, values, and other intangibles. The attorney should want to learn about the expert's opinions and positions, especially with respect to the case at hand; the expert should make them known as early as possible, so the attorney can determine whether the expert will be helpful to the case. Attorneys often try to persuade their experts to modify their preliminary opinions at this stage, and they sometimes succeed by providing new data and arguments that the expert hadn't properly considered. This is perfectly appropriate. However, if the attorney persists in trying to coerce a change in position after all facts and reasoning have failed to persuade, the wise expert will withdraw.

Good two-way communication is crucial at every stage of the attorney-expert interaction and may require some teaching in both directions. Many attorneys need tutoring in the scientific and medical background of hearing loss cases, and most otolaryngologists are naive about the legal issues that are important in individual cases. Actually, it is my hope that this book will help to smooth this path for both professions.

The expert witness needs to let the attorney know what options exist in case analysis. The attorney may or may not want a written report, literature reviews, a physical evaluation of the patient by the expert, and so forth. If the expert would need to carry out library research or other investigations to perform adequately, the magnitude of this work should be estimated. A frank discussion of fees at this point may help the attorney decide what level of work is needed at the outset.

Communication with opposing counsel should be limited to logistical matters (time, place, and so forth.) surrounding a deposition. It is inappropriate to discuss the case with opposing counsel except with the permission of the client-attorney.

Most cases settle before trial. If a trial seems likely, the expert witness will need to review notes, reports, and important background material. If a deposition took place, the transcript should be reviewed carefully; more than a year may have gone by, and the expert can avoid personal embarrassment and damage to his client's case by revisiting his previous remarks.

The expert should bring to trial at least his or her C.V., any written reports made on the case and the records required to substantiate those reports; the client-attorney will indicate any other materials required. The C.V. will be helpful during the qualification phase of direct examination, providing a listing of relevant achievements and experience.

ON THE STAND

Testifying in court can be a little scary, at least the first few times. Even with experience, it should not be approached casually; the expert witness must discharge his or her duties to the court in a serious and respectful manner. The stakes are high for the parties (otherwise, the case would not be in court and the expert would not be there); they deserve the best efforts of all concerned.

Demeanor

The expert witness must defer to the judge, listen to the attorney asking the questions, and talk to the jury. The judge is the absolute monarch of the courtroom; his orders to respond or not to respond to a question must be obeyed without argument (the attorneys may argue with the judge up to a point, but witnesses may not). An attorney asking a question deserves full attention, including eye contact; to do otherwise—glancing around the courtroom—is rude. If a short answer is appropriate, conversational contact with the questioning attorney should be maintained. However, any answer requiring or allowing elaboration should be directed to the jury, which will after all decide the outcome.

The effective expert witness projects a demeanor that is relaxed and confident, giving careful and thoughtful attention to the issues at hand. Humor should be used very carefully, if at all; it's better to err in the direction of being too solemn than to introduce unwanted levity. Above all, be yourself: natural is better than contrived.

Courtesy and respect are absolutes. Even when mistreated by opposing counsel, a firm but polite rejoinder always goes over better than an angry outburst. Many attorneys are skilled at feigning anger without losing control and effectiveness; few witnesses acquire this skill. When the expert must disagree with statements made by the plaintiff, defendant, or by other witnesses, this should be done tactfully. It is rarely possible or necessary to know the causes and motives for errors and misstatements, and one should avoid calling others dishonest, incompetent, or careless; such conclusions are beyond the expertise of medical expert witnesses, anyway.

Teaching the Jury

A good client-attorney will often organize the direct examination to include a brief tutorial from expert to jury. Since juries usually include at least some poorly educated people, most attorneys recommend presenting material at the sixth-to-eighth-grade level. The expert may be asked to discuss the nature of sound, the workings of the ear, ear disorders, or other related topics. Whatever the topic, the presentation must be simple and reasonably brief.

Visual aids are doubly useful. First, they help any audience grasp difficult concepts more quickly. Second, they allow the expert to get off the witness stand and interact more closely and naturally with the jury, while drawing on or pointing to the visual material.

A plain flip chart on an easel is an excellent visual aid, large enough for the small (12-member) audience to see well, and interactive—the expert can draw on a blank sheet, or can mark up a prepared chart or graph to make a point. The expert may want to bring anatomical charts, audiograms, and the like; copy centers can enlarge them to poster size on short notice, and they can be placed on the same easel as the flip chart. Any such demonstration materials will probably be marked as exhibits for the jury to examine later, at their leisure.

Overhead transparency projectors are less suitable for courtroom use. Fiddling with cords and dimming lights can be distracting. Slides are even worse; the darker it gets, the less contact between expert and jury. Neither medium is convenient for the jury's use during their deliberations.

Three-dimensional models, such as skulls and ear models, work well if they are large enough and lighting is good. The expert needs to discuss with the client-attorney whether the models will become exhibits and whether they will be returned after the trial.

Audio demonstrations can play a special role in cases involving hearing loss. One can attempt to reproduce the sounds of the noisy workplace, the effects of background noise on speech communication, the contribution of lipreading to communication in the presence of noise and/or hearing loss (using an audio-visual display), the effects of excluding high frequency energy from speech signals, and other medically and legally relevant phenomena. However, their use is limited by several severe constraints. First, the accuracy of recording and reproduction must be established. Second, the demonstration must be shown to be truly representative of the real-world event being simulated. Finally, the acoustics of the courtroom and the possible hearing losses of judge and/or jurors can have unpredictable effects on almost any such demonstration. Several professionally-produced compact discs are now available to simulate many real-world noise and communication situations (Etymotic Research, Elk Grove, IL; Aearo Company, Indianapolis, IN; Resound Corporation, Redwood City, CA; National Aeronautics and Space Administration, Cleveland, OH).

COMPENSATION

The distinction between fact witnesses and expert witnesses has already been discussed. Fact witnesses possess unique information needed by the court, almost always obtained prior to the filing of the legal case, and owe their testimony as a matter of civic duty. They are entitled to a nominal witness fee in most jurisdictions, regardless of training or expertise. An expert witness, on the other hand, possesses no unique information about the case, but has expertise that can be brought to bear to assist the court in understanding or interpreting the facts of the case. Many courts have held that an expert witness has a constitutionally protected property right in his or her expertise, and that it can no more be taken without compensation than any other piece of property. The expert witness is thus entitled to charge a reasonable fee for time spent in reviewing, discussing, reporting, testifying, et cetera.

It is the time spent (combined with knowledge, skill, and experience), rather than the opinions given, that justifies the fee. The dishonesty of changing one's professional opinions for a fee is so obvious that it is almost offensive to have to mention it. However, opposing attorneys may imply such an arrangement by asking "Are you being paid for your testimony in support of the plaintiff (or defendant)?" A simple "yes" from the expert witness may seem to admit guilt; a better answer is that one is paid for one's expertise and time, regardless of the opinions arrived at, the outcome of the case, or whether one is called to the stand or not.

Most experts bill by the hour, and base their fees on several factors. An obvious point of reference for a clinician is lost revenue from office or surgical practice; since overhead expenses (rent, salaries, etc.) continue in the doctor's absence, *gross* hourly revenue is the appropriate yardstick. An expert may consider the marketplace: What do others with similar expertise charge for similar work? Remember that systematic sharing of fee information among a group of experts could constitute anticompetitive behavior subject to the antitrust laws. An expert who has more demands for medical-legal services than desired can raise fees to deliberately reduce those demands; this is not anticompetitive as long as other experts are available. The expert's prestige within a professional field may justify higher fees as well. Ultimately, expert witnesses can usually set fees as high or as low as desired.

Some expert witnesses charge different hourly rates for different types of services (travel, record review, consultation, reporting, deposition, testimony at trial, etc.) because of the variable levels of effort and stress involved. Usually, travel is the least demanding service, and testimony at trial the most demanding. Substantial expenses, such as transportation and hotel charges, are of course reimbursable in addition to professional fees. Since trial dates are *usually* rescheduled at least once, or canceled altogether, it is reasonable to charge a cancellation fee for scheduled appearances at trial (or deposition) that are changed within some specified interval. This partially compensates the expert for his inability to fill his office schedule with income-producing activity on short notice.

Although fixed hourly fees, perhaps at different levels for different services, are most commonly used by expert witnesses, they are not universal or required. An expert may charge a particular client more or less based on factors such as the magnitude of the case, the plaintiff's or defendant's ability to pay, or pure whim (again, assuming other experts are available and there is no collusion among them regarding fees). Some experts charge a flat fee for consulting and testifying on a particular case, based on their estimation of the magnitude of work and its value to the client. This approach is a bit of a gamble for both expert and client, since the actual work may be much more—or less—than estimated.

Plaintiffs' attorneys typically charge contingency fees: a percentage of the award or settlement, if any. As indicated earlier in the ACS statement, it is unethical for physician expert witnesses to accept contingent fee arrangements in which compensation is linked to the outcome of a case. Such an arrangement would undermine impartiality and should be avoided by experts from any profession.

The responsibility to pay the expert witness technically lies with the plaintiff or defendant, not with the client-attorney. It is not rare for an expert to be left with an uncollectible bill against a losing party on whose behalf he or she has testified. While attorneys are not permitted to pay costs, such as expert fees, for their clients, they can and do *advance* these expenses for their clients in the hope of being reimbursed later. The prudent expert witness will settle this issue early in the relationship with a client-attorney. First, the expert's fee schedule should be discussed; documented written notification creates a strong presumption that the client-attorney accepts those fees. Second, payment should be guaranteed in advance of any substantial work. A verbal guarantee will suffice from an established and reputable law firm, insurance company, or other organization. As an alternative, an exchange of letters establishes a contract between the expert, who agrees to perform certain duties, and the client-attorney, who agrees to advance payment on behalf of his or her client. Such an exchange of letters should incorporate the expert's fee schedule, and should specify whether payments will be made as work is done (e.g., monthly), or as a lump sum when the case closes. Since cases can drag on for years, with long periods of inactivity, the former "pay-as-you-go" option is clearly in the expert's best interest.

A retainer—a flat fee, usually nonrefundable, prepaying for a certain amount of work—is appropriate in some circumstances, for example, if the expert is reluctant to accept even a written guarantee of payment of fees. This is rarely necessary: A letter to the local or state bar association will almost always elicit prompt payment of a legitimate expert fee if the attorney has guaranteed payment. A more appropriate setting for a retainer occurs when a client-attorney has decided, after initial consultations, and with the expert's permission, to include the expert in tentative trial plans. At this point, very little usually happens for a period of months from the expert's point of view, but the client-attorney has obtained certain benefits: First, the expert is unavailable for consultation with other parties to the litigation, except by deposition; second, the expert has promised to be available for trial and for intervening consultation; third, the expert's name can be used as ammunition in settlement negotiations. These benefits are not automatic (an expert can decline, after the initial consultations, to agree to these conditions), and it is reasonable to charge for them, just as an attorney charges a retainer after agreeing to take a case. A retainer may be a set fee for a particular case, regardless of the duration of delays, or it may be a periodic (quarterly or annual) fee to guarantee the expert's continued availability to the client-attorney (and unavailability to others).

LIABILITY AS AN EXPERT WITNESS

Courts in the United States have tried to protect witnesses from legal liability in order to encourage forthright and complete testimony. A truthful answer given under oath, even a sincere but clumsily expressed opinion that could publicly harm someone ("Dr. So-and-So is a charlatan and a quack"), is generally protected and cannot be the basis for a successful slander suit. However, nothing is really absolute in law, and Dr. So-and-So could still file a lawsuit and cause the expert witness considerable nuisance and legal expense. The expert's opinions expressed in medical-legal reports are less clearly protected; certainly, any malicious actions or statements intended to harm either litigant or a third party could be cause for action, although malice is hard to prove.

Most physicians who are in private practice are well protected; their malpractice policies cover their medical-legal activities as well. However, physicians employed by hospitals, universities, clinics, or other entities need to consider their coverage carefully. Frequently, the employer's policy covers only activities done for the employer's benefit, or it may specifically exclude any activity resulting in direct payment to the individual. Acceptance of consultation and expert witness fees directly, rather than through the employer, may void coverage. Other professionals, such as audiologists and engineers, are similarly at some risk when testifying. The author is unaware of any *reasonable* way to obtain coverage for the probably negligible risk of medical-legal work. The usual options include purchasing full professional liability coverage (prohibitive for salaried physicians doing only occasional medical-legal work) and "going bare." In rare instances, it may be appropriate to ask the plaintiff or defendant on whose behalf one is testifying to agree to pay for counsel and to indemnify the witness in the event of a subsequent suit.

REFERENCES

Hulka, B. S., N. L. Kerkvliet, and P. Tugwell. 2000. Experience of a scientific panel formed to advise the federal judiciary on silicone breast implants. *N. Engl. J. Med.* 342:812–815.

Spencer, F. C. and K. S. Guice. 2000. The expert medical witness: Concerns, limits, and remedies. *Bull. Am. Coll. Surgeons* 85(6):22–25.

Appendix A

Typical Noise Levels/Explosures

This appendix lists typical sound levels, or ranges of levels, for various types of equipment or exposures. Most values are dBA, but impulse noise levels are given in peak sound pressure level (SPL), some impact and fluctuating levels are expressed as L_{eq} (levels that, if constant, would contain as much sound energy as the time-varying exposures under consideration), and only linear SPL values (usually several dB higher than A-scale) are available for some exposures. While these measurements are from published references, they are not all of equal quality. The variability seen in the wide range of levels measured for some noise sources has several causes. Often, the measurements are for a *class* of items, for example, .30-caliber rifles; even for a single make and model, noise levels often vary according to use factors (type of ammunition, power settings, etc.), state of repair, and environment (size of room, reverberation characteristics). Most measurements are at or near the ear of the user; otherwise, distances are specified.

Many of the references contain more detailed information regarding sources of variability. However, in a particular occupational or medical-legal setting, direct measurements of actual exposure levels and durations, often including dosimetry, by a person experienced in noise measurement are much better than relying on published data from similar exposures.

The Canadian Centre for Occupational Health and Safety (www.ccohs.ca) makes available a large database on industrial noise levels, via diskette or CD-ROM.

Occupation/ Noise Source	Level (dBA)	Reference
HOUSEHOLD		
Blender	64–87	EPA (1974)
Disposal	67–93	"
Dryer	50–72	"
Refrigerator	46–68	"
Screaming baby	100–117	Davis et al. (1985)
Toy walkie-talkie	83–135	Orchik & Wark (1995)
Vacuum cleaner	60–86	EPA (1974)
Washing machine	47–78	"
Window air conditioner	60–73	"
WORKSHOP AND CONSTRUCTION		
Boring machine	94	NIOSH (1972)
Compressed air hammer	106–116	Kenney & Ayer (1975)
Drill press	87	O'Neil (1986)
Electric drill	94	McClymont & Simpson (1989)
Jointer	98–101	O'Neil (1986)
Molder	100	NIOSH (1972)
Planer	102	O'Neil (1986)
"	106	NIOSH (1972)
Pneumatic chipper	93–113	Sinclair & Haflidson (1995)
Router	98–108	O'Neil (1986)
"	93	NIOSH (1972)
Sander		
Belt Sander	96	O'Neil (1986)
Orbital sander	100	McClymont & Simpson (1989)
Sander	97	NIOSH (1972)
Saw		
Bandsaw	95	O'Neil (1986)
Cut-off saw	112	NIOSH (1972)
Jig saw	97	McClymont & Simpson (1989)
Portable circular saw	113	McClymont & Simpson (1989)
Power saw	95–112	Clark & Bohne (1984)
Radial-arm saw	102–110	O'Neil (1986)
"	98	NIOSH (1972)
Saber saw	108	O'Neil (1986)
Skilsaw	108	"
Tablesaw	92	"
Shaper	95	"
"	104	NIOSH (1972)
Shop vacuum	78–92	Clark & Bohne (1984)

Occupation/ Noise Source	Level (dBA)	Reference
OUTDOORS		
Chain saw	103–116	EPA (1974)
Electric mower	103	McClymont & Simpson (1989)
Hedge cutter	95	McClymont & Simpson (1989)
Model airplane	106–117	Clark & Bohne (1984)
Power lawnmower	80–95	EPA (1974)
Snow blower	84–92	Clark & Bohne (1984)
Snowmobile	85–109	EPA (1974)
"	85–120	Curtis & Sauer (1973)
MUSIC AND RECREATION		
Arcade games	84–111	Davis et al. (1985)
"Boom cars"	84–108	Ramsey & Simmons (1993)
Classical musicians	79–99	Royster et al. (1991)
Discotheques	95–98	Davis et al. (1985)
Personal stereo systems	74–128	Clark (1991)
Race car @ 15–20 m	90–107	Davis et al. (1985)
Rock music (live)	89–119	Clark (1991)
TRANSPORTATION		
Aircraft		
Aircraft cabin (jet)	82–93	Clark & Bohne (1984)
Aircraft flyover (1000 ft)	92–102	"
Commercial aircraft	76–92	Bray (1974)
Helicopters	93–112	House (1975)
Single engine aircraft cabin	88–90	Hughes & Koonce (1986)
"	87–96	Harling (1987)
Armored personnel carrier	113	Price et al. (1989)
Personal and Other Public		
Car @ 50 ft	60–90	EPA (1974)
Car passenger	60–90	"
Intercity bus	74–84	Bray (1974)
Motorcycle	80–110	EPA (1974)
Motorcycle (no helmet, 30–60 mph)	108–119	Davis et al., 1985
Motorboat	74–114	EPA (1974)
"	65–105	Campbell (1972)
Subway	80–114	EPA (1974)
Trains		
Diesel locomotive @ 50 ft	87–102	EPA (1974)
Intercity rail	60–75	Bray (1974)
Locomotive crew		
Diesel engine	84–89	Kilmer (1980)

Occupation/ Noise Source	Level (dBA)	Reference
TRANSPORTATION (continued)		
Trains (continued)		
Horn	92–111	Kilmer (1980)
Brake (vented into cab)	85–115	"
Train passenger	72–91	EPA (1974)
Trucks		
Heavy truck @ 50 ft	77–89	EPA (1974)
1-ton truck	70	NIOSH (1972)
5-ton truck	73	"
20-ton truck	92	"
Sleeper cab	79–84	Casali et al. (1998)
WEAPONS AND EXPLOSIVES		
M16 @ 4.5 m	155 (peak)	Price (1983)
105 mm Howitzer @ 5 m	164 (peak)	"
Explosive-actuated tools	150–160 (peak)	Smith (1971)
Other Recreational		
Cap guns @ 50 cm	143–152 (peak)	Axelsson & Jerson (1985)
Firecrackers @ 3 m	150 (peak)	Gupta & Vishwakarma (1989)
"	125–156 (peak)	Axelsson & Jerson (1985)
Toy guns @ 25 cm	145–160 (peak)	Hodge & McCommons (1966)
Sports Weapons		
12 g shotgun	163–173 (peak)	Odess (1972)
16 g shotgun	166–169 (peak)	"
20 g shotgun	166–168 (peak)	"
410 g shotgun	164–169 (peak)	"
.22 cal rifle	143–158 (peak)	"
.30 cal rifle	168–172 (peak)	"
INDUSTRIAL		
Canning Food Products		
Can filling machine	100	NIOSH (1972)
Can making body operation	95	"
Canning punch press	97	"
Drop Forging		
Hammer operator	108	Taylor et al. (1984)
Press operator	99	"
Farm Equipment		
Grain roller mill	85	NIOSH (1972)
One-row beet puller	94	"
Pneumatic conveyor	100	"
Tractor	98	"
Tractors	97–114 (linear)	Simpson & Deshayes (1969)
Two-row corn picker	106	NIOSH (1972)

Occupation/ Noise Source	Level (dBA)	Reference
INDUSTRIAL (continued)		
Fishing Trawler		Szczepanski & Weclawik (1991)
Engine room	97–104	"
Processing	84–97	"
Glass Products		
Corrugated band saw	99	NIOSH (1972)
Inflation of containers	106	"
Heavy Equipment (Earthmoving)	110	NIOSH (1972)
Bulldozer		
Double scraper	92	"
Road grader	95	"
Scraper	117	"
Mining, Open Pit		
Crusher	96	NIOSH (1972)
Jumbo drill	107	"
Locomotive	85	"
Oxygen torches	120	"
Rotary drill	93	"
Mining, Underground		
Axial vane fan	107	NIOSH (1972)
Continuous miner	99	"
Conveyor belt	93	"
Jackhammer drill	113	"
Loader (gathering arm)	96	"
Roof bolter	103	"
Stopper drill	115	"
Offshore Oil and Gas Platforms		
Diesel generators	100–120	Pelton (1974)
Gas lift compressors	105–110	"
Gas turbines	100–112	"
Pipe noise	95–105	"
Pumps	100–115	"
Valves	104–120	"
Wellhead rooms	90–95	"
Paper Products		
Bag and handle former	89	NIOSH (1972)
Paper cutter	96	"
Petroleum Refining		
Can seaming	96	NIOSH (1972)
Furnace heating distilling columns	100	"

Occupation/ Noise Source	Level (dBA)	Reference
INDUSTRIAL (continued)		
Petroleum Refining (continued)		
Furnace high-speed		
rotating equipment	100	NIOSH (1972)
Furnace pumps	103	"
Steam let-down	130	"
Printing and Publishing		
Binder	86	NIOSH (1972)
Folding machines	85	"
Keyboard monotype	84	"
Mono-casting	91	"
Newspaper press	97	NIOSH (1972)
Offset press	88	"
Postcard press	91	NIOSH (1972)
Small offset press	82	"
Steel Products		
160" mill	98	NIOSH (1972)
Basic oxygen furnace	91	"
Blast furnace	100	"
Coke oven	83	"
Electric furnace (150 tons)	112	"
Textile Mill		
Cotton spinning	83	NIOSH (1972)
Loom	106	"
Various Metal Products		
4" hand grinder	85	NIOSH (1972)
Automatic punch press	95	"
Forge drop hammer	105	"
Milling machine	90	"
Pneumatic chisel	101	"
Riveting machine	110	"
Turret lathe	90	"
Welding		
CO_2 welding arc	91–95	Hermanns (1982)
Inert gas–metal arc	95–102	"
Plasma cutting	98–110	"
Slag chipping	92–105	"
Tungsten inert gas	65–74	"
Welding arc	84–92	"

REFERENCES

Axelsson, Alf and Tomas Jerson. 1985. Noisy toys: A possible source of sensorineural hearing loss. *Pediatrics* 76(4):574–578.

Bray, Don E. 1974. Noise environments in public transportation. *Sound and Vibration* 8(4):16–20.

Campbell, Richard A. 1972. A survey of noise levels on board pleasure boats. *Sound and Vibration* 6(2):28–29.

Casali, J. G., S. E. Lee, and G. S. Robinson. 1998. *Evaluation of the FHWA hearing requirement for truck drivers.* Presentation to National Hearing Conservation Association, February 21, 1998, Albuquerque, NM.

Clark, William W. 1991. Noise exposure from leisure activities: A review. *J. Acoust. Soc. Am.* 90(1):175–181.

Clark, William W. and Barbara A. Bohne. 1984. The effects of noise on hearing and the ear. *Medical Times* (December).

Curtis, Jack and Richard C. Sauer. 1973. An analysis of recreational snowmobile noise. *Sound and Vibration* 7(5):49–50.

Davis, A. C., H. M. Fortnum, R. R. A. Coles, M. P. Haggard, and M. E. Lutman. 1985. *Damage to hearing arising from leisure noise: A review of the literature.* MRC Institute of Hearing Research, Nottingham, England.

Gupta, Deepak and S. K. Vishwakarma. 1989. Toy weapons and firecrackers: A source of hearing loss. *Laryngoscope* 99(3):330–334.

Harling, C. C. 1987. Noise hazard for crews of light aircraft. *Aviation Medicine Quarterly*, 93–99.

Hermanns, Ingo. 1982. Noise problems when welding: Causes, effects and prevention. *Schweissen und Schneiden* (English translation) 34(2):E44-E45.

Hodge, D. C. and R. B. McCommons. 1966. Acoustical hazards of children's "toys." *J. Acoust. Soc. Am.* 40(4):911.

House, John W. 1975. Effects of helicopter noise on pilots' hearing. *Transactions of the Pacific Coast Oto-Ophthalmological Society Annual Meeting.* 56:175–186.

Hughes, Stanley T. and Jefferson Koonce. 1986. Cabin noise levels in single engine general aviation aircraft. *Proceedings of the Human Factors Society—30th Annual Meeting*, pp. 1381–1385.

Kenney, G. D. and H. E. Ayer. 1975. Noise exposure and hearing levels of workers in the sheet metal construction trade. *Am. Ind. Hyg. Assoc. J.* Aug., 1975:626–632.

Kilmer, Roger D. 1980. *Assessment of locomotive crew in-cab occupational noise exposure.* Washington, DC: U.S. Department of Transportation–Federal Railroad Administration.

McClymont, L. G. and D. C. Simpson. 1989. Noise levels and exposure patterns to do-it-yourself power tools. *J. Laryngol. Otol.* 103(12):1140–1141.

Odess, John S. 1972. Acoustic trauma of sportsman hunter due to gun firing. *Laryngoscope* 82(11):1971–1989.

O'Neil, Joy. 1986. Workshop noise: Are machines damaging your hearing? *Fine Woodworking* (July/August):62–65.

Orchik, D. J. and D. J. Wark. 1995. Hearing hazard of toy cellular telephones and walkie talkies. *Clin. Pediatr.* 34:278–280.

Pelton, H. K. 1974. *Noise control engineering experience with offshore oil and gas platforms and related refinery and process equipment.* New York: American Society of Mechanical Engineers.

Price, G. Richard. 1983. Relative hazard of weapons impulses. *J. Acoust. Soc. Am.* 73(2):556–566.

Price, G. Richard, Joel T. Kalb, and Georges R. Garinther. 1989. Toward a measure of auditory handicap in the Army. *Ann. Otol. Rhinol. Laryngol. Suppl.* 98[Suppl. 140](5 Pt. 2):42–52.

Ramsey, K. L. and F. B. Simmons. 1993. High-powered automobile stereos. *Otolaryngol. Head Neck Surg.* 109:108–110.

Royster, Julia Doswell, Larry H. Royster, and Mead C. Killion. 1991. Sound exposures and hearing thresholds of symphony orchestra musicians. *J. Acoust. Soc. Am.* 89(6):2793–2803.

Simpson, E. W,. Jr. and I. L. Deshayes. 1969. Tractors produce ear damaging noise. *J. Environ. Health* 31(4):347–350.

Sinclair, J. D. N. and W. O. Haflidson. 1995. Construction noise in Ontario. *Appl. Occup. Environ. Hyg.* 10:457–460.

Smith, L. K. 1971. Explosive-actuated tools: An impulse noise hazard? *Am. Ind. Hyg. Assoc. J.* 32(3):346–350.

Szczepanski, C. and Z. Weclawik. 1991. Exposure of the crew of a fishing trawler–factory ship to noise. *Bull. Inst. Maritime Trop. Med. Gdynia.* 42:67–70.

Taylor, William, Barry Lempert, Peter Pelmear, Ian Hemstock, and Jeffrey Kershaw. 1984. Noise levels and hearing thresholds in the drop forging industry. *J. Acoust. Soc. Am.* 76(3):807–819.

U.S. Department of Health, Education, and Welfare–National Institute of Occupational Safety and Health. 1972. *Occupational exposure to noise.* Washington, DC: U.S. Government Printing Office.

U.S. Environmental Protection Agency. 1974. *Information on levels of environmental noise requisite to protect public health and welfare with an adequate margin of safety, EPA 550/9-74-004.* Washington, DC: U.S. Government Printing Office.

Appendix B

Workers' Compensation Practices in the United States and Canada

[The text and references of this Appendix are excerpted and reprinted with permission of the American Industrial Hygiene Association from Chapter 18, "Workers' Compensation," by Robert A. Dobie and Susan C. Megerson, in *The Noise Manual*, 5th ed., ed. Elliot H. Berger, Larry H. Royster, Julia D. Royster, Dennis P. Driscoll, and Martha Layne. AIHA: Fairfax, VA, 2000. Brackets [ ] have been used to indicate text insertions made for the purpose of this Appendix.]

Table 18.1 [B-1] provides a summary of WC [workers' compensation] practices and awards throughout the United States and Canada. Data were obtained in late 1998 and early 1999 by a written survey of WC officials. In some cases, the state or province supplied a copy of relevant statutes *in lieu* of completing the written survey. In these instances, the authors extracted the appropriate data from the materials provided. In cases where the written survey appeared to conflict with the statutes, the authors utilized information from the official published document.

In general, almost all states and all Canadian provinces indicated that hearing loss is compensable in their jurisdictions. The following four states reported that only work-related hearing loss caused by injury (single event) is compensable: Idaho, Indiana, Louisiana, and Virginia. Michigan responded that compensation is considered only if an injury to the ear (single event), which may or may not result in hearing loss, causes a loss of wages. Georgia reported that in cases of monaural loss, awards are provided only in the presence of pre-existing deafness in the other ear. Ohio stated that only total hearing loss in one or both ears is compensable.

All states, provinces, territories, and agencies were surveyed regarding specific statutes and practices for assessing hearing-loss claims and awarding compensation within their jurisdictions. A number of states compensate all work-related hearing loss but follow different procedures for hearing loss resulting from injury and resulting from long-term noise exposure (considered a disease process). In many states and provinces, the written statutes provide little information specific to hearing loss. Actual WC practices in these jurisdictions are heavily dependent upon interpretation of general WC standards and case law (which is flexible in application and can evolve over time). A number of states reported that statutes have been revised over the years, and individual claims are evaluated using different criteria depending upon date of injury or date of claim.

Due to the many special circumstances and qualifiers surrounding processing of a WC claim for hearing loss, it is important for those involved to become completely familiar with regulations and procedures within their jurisdiction. In practice, WC claim evaluations are subject to many nuances that require an in-depth understanding of applicable regulations and practices. Readers are cautioned not to rely on Table 18.1 [B-1] as a definitive single source of information. Professionals should contact the appropriate WC office to request the most current and comprehensive information available.

Results of the recent survey (Table 18.1) [B-1] revealed that the most popular method for calculating binaural impairment is the AAO-79 [American Academy of Otolaryngology, 1979] method. It is notable that a full third of jurisdictions surveyed stated that they do not specify a formula to be used (impairment ratings are based on "medical evidence"). Of those jurisdictions that do require a certain method for determining impairment, 68 percent of U.S. states/territories and 25 percent of Canadian provinces responded that they utilize the AAO-79 formula by specific reference or by virtue of a requirement to follow the most recent AMA [American Medical Association] guideline for determining impairment (which specifies the AAO formula). Six states are still utilizing the AAOO-59 [American Academy of Ophthalmology and Otolaryngology, 1959] formula and several states and provinces have adopted other variations (see Table 18.1 [B-1], Column 7).

Awards

The process for determining awards is typically based on applying the impairment rating to some sort of schedule for lump sum payments or extended payments based on a percentage of the individual's wages. There is a great deal of variation across states and provinces in the amount of awards available. Depending on the state, a totally deaf worker could receive as little as $9000 or as much as $150,000 over and above replacement of wage losses (see Table 18.1 [B-1]). Once again, the reader is cautioned to contact local WC offices for the most definitive and up-to-date information available.

Some employers find benefit in tracking total "potential liability" for hearing loss claims for a given plant, division, or company. An example of the computation of potential claims is provided by Berger (1985).

Other Considerations

Beyond the key issues of the BI formula that a state uses and the maximum dollar payments available, a number of additional factors can effect the potential compensation. They are discussed in the following sections.

Adjustments for Age

It is generally recognized that hearing deteriorates with the passage of time, even without noise exposure. This age effect, often termed presbycusis (but which also includes sociocusis and nosoacusis—see Chapter 4 [Chapter 6 in this book]) is characterized by a gradual, yet significant loss of hearing at all frequencies—usually, the higher the frequency, the greater the degree of loss. For most WC laws, an individual's total impairment is compensable as long as an occupational noise exposure substantially contributed to the overall impairment. However, many states do consider aging effects.

Over 40 percent of states and provinces (Table 18.1 [B-1]) indicated that some type of deduction in impairment/award may be made for presbycusis. A number of jurisdictions deduct 0.5 dB [decibel] from the person's average hearing level for every year of the person's age beyond 40, prior to the calculation of BI [binaural impairment]. This is called "age correction." It can have the effect of making an otherwise compensable loss noncompensable. For this reason, age correction prior to BI calculation is often considered unfair (AAO–HNS [American Academy of Otolaryngology–Head and Neck Surgery] 1998). In contrast, allocation or apportionment refers to a process in which BI is calculated first, followed by an estimation or calculation of the relative contributions of occupational noise, aging, and other factors. For example, Iowa requires that the initially calculated BI score be reduced by a factor equal to the ratio of median expected age-related threshold shift (for the 0.5, 1, 2, and 3 kHz pure-tone average) during the period of employment to the final pure-tone average. Pennsylvania permits expert testimony regarding the contribution of aging and other causes, and awards are frequently adjusted or denied based on such testimony. AAO–HNS (1998) has published a monograph on the evaluation of noise-exposed workers that includes a discussion of allocation from the medical point of view.

Waiting Period

WC laws require that hearing impairment be both occupationally related and *permanent.* In the process associated with sensory damage from noise exposure, there is a temporary threshold shift that disappears upon termination of the exposure. Although there is considerable variation in recovery time depending on the level and duration of the noise insult, most of the temporary effect is gone within 48 hours in a quiet environment. For economic reasons, longer recovery periods have been assumed in some states, and an employee may not be able to pursue a claim until six months of nonexposure have passed. Seventy percent of U.S. states and provinces surveyed indicated that no waiting period is necessary for filing a WC claim. For those jurisdictions that do impose a waiting period, reported time-frames range from 3 days to 6 months. Ironically, such provisions usually do not apply to traumatically-induced hearing loss, which often *can* require three to six months for full stabilization (Segal et al., 1988).

Use of Hearing Protection Devices (HPDs)

Most WC laws do not address the question of personal hearing protection. It is not generally clear whether the wearing of adequately-fitted hearing protection constitutes removal from exposure, although in at least one state, the law specifically adopts such a provision. Over 40 percent of the U.S. jurisdictions surveyed indicated that claims would be denied or an award penalty assessed if an individual was found to have willfully disregarded a requirement to wear HPDs [hearing protection devices]. Canadian provinces reported no such provisions.

Statute of Limitations

Most WC laws were originally established to compensate employees for traumatic injury, and contain a provision encouraging timely filing of claims. The provision, called a statute of limitations, also applies to NIHL [noise-induced hearing loss] claims and requires that a date of injury be established. In some states, the date of injury is "the last day exposed," while in others it is the date the employee became aware of hearing loss or its work relatedness. The statute of limitations varies from state to state, and can be as short as 30 days to as long as 5 years.

Apportionment or Allocation Among Employers

The WC system was originally established on the principle that at the time of the employee's injury, the employer should pay for the loss of earnings of the employee. However, in a case of NIHL, where several employers might be involved, a new approach was necessary. This led to the inclusion of an apportionment clause in the acts of many states. For example, if the last employer at the date of injury can establish that the employee began employment with hearing loss, prior employers (or a special fund) may be tapped for any NIHL present at the time of employment.

Allocation among employers does have the effect of encouraging preplacement audiometry, and can be a costly potential liability in the purchase of manufacturing operations. The survey summarized in Table 18.1 [B-1] reported that only 17 percent of WC jurisdictions reported that they have no provision for apportionment of pre-existing hearing loss.

Hearing Aids

In most states, hearing impairment is evaluated without consideration of the effect a hearing aid or other prosthesis might have on the claimant's ability to understand speech. Most states and all Canadian provinces now include some provision for hearing aids as part of the compensation. However, the award for NIHL is generally based on a pure-tone audiogram in the absence of such a device.

Tinnitus

Although tinnitus (ringing or head noises) typically accompanies NIHL, it often occurs in the absence of noise exposure. As shown in Table 18.1 [B-1] tinnitus is recognized in a number of states, and the award for compensation may be modified by its presence. Over half the states and provinces responding to the WC survey indicated that awards may be made for tinnitus. Many of these jurisdictions qualified that the award is available only in combination with hearing impairment, not for tinnitus alone. There are no objective measurements for tinnitus, and the award (if any) is based on the claimant's symptoms and on the physician's opinion.

Duration and Level of Exposure

Many states include a provision that excludes an NIHL claim where the occupational noise exposure is below a specified level. In the U.S., the most commonly specified minimum exposure is 90 dB (or 90 dBA time-weighted average [TWA]). In Canada, provinces require a minimum of from 85 to 90 dB exposures for claims to be considered. Other states require that the noise exposure duration must exceed a minimum number of days in order to file a valid claim. Other characteristics, such as A-weighting or TWA, may also be addressed in the WC law.

REFERENCES

American Academy of Opthamology and Otolaryngology. 1959. Committee on Conservation of hearing: Guide for the evaluation of hearing impairment. *Trans. Am. Acad. Ophthalmol. Otolaryngol.* 63:236–238.

American Academy of Otolaryngology. 1979. Committee on Hearing and Equilibrium and the American Council of Otolaryngology Committee on the Medical Aspects of Noise: Guide for the evaluation of hearing handicap. *JAMA* 241(19):2055–2059.

American Academy of Otolaryngology–Head and Neck Surgery (1998). *Evaluation of people reporting occupational hearing loss.* Alexandria, VA.

Berger, Elliott H. 1985. "EARLog #15—Workers' Compensation for Occupational Hearing Loss." *Sound and Vibration* 19(2):16–18.

Segal, S., M. Harell, A. Shahar and M. Englender. 1988. Acute acoustic trauma: Dynamics of hearing loss following cessation of exposure. *Am. J. Otol.* 9(4):293–298.

TABLE B-1
Hearing loss statutes in the United States and Canada.

Jurisdiction	1. Is occupational hearing loss compensable?	2. Is minimum noise exposure required for filing?	3. Schedule in weeks (one ear).	4. Schedule in weeks (both ears).	5. Maximum compensation (one ear).	6. Maximum compensation (both ears).	7. Hearing impairment formula.	8. Waiting period.	9. Is deduction made for presbycusis?	10. Is award made for tinnitus?	11. Provision for hearing aid?	12. Credit for improvement with hearing aid?	13. Is hearing loss prior to employment considered in compensation claim?	14. Statute of limitations for hearing loss claim.	15. Penalty for not wearing hearing protection devices?	16. Self-assessment of hearing impairment considered in rating/award?	Comments
Alabama	Yes	No	53	163	$11,660	$35,860	ME	No	No	Yes-I	Yes	No	Yes	2 yrs.	Yes-D	Poss	3-6: awards based on temporary disability and permanent partial impairment according to AMA guidelines; 12: unless hearing aid enables worker to return to work; 13: as long as there has been substantial aggravation at work.
Alaska	Yes	No	*	*	*	*	AAO-79	No	No	Yes-I	Yes	No*	No*	2 yrs.	No	No	
Arizona	Yes	No	86	260	$23,100	$69,300	ME	No	No	Yes-I	Yes	No	Yes	1 yr.	No	No	14: statute of limitations and other hearing loss issues currently before Board of Appeals.
Arkansas	Yes	No	42	158	$11,296	$42,502	AAO-79	No	Poss	No	Poss	No	No*	Yes*	No	No	
California	Yes	No	50*	311*	$8,040*	$58,863*	AAO-79	No	No	Yes	Yes	Yes	Yes	1 yr.	Yes-P	Yes	3-6: awards modified by age and occupation at time of injury.
Colorado	Yes	No	35	139	$5,250	$20,850	AAO-79	No	Yes	Yes	Yes	No	Yes	Yes	Yes-P	No	
Connecticut	Yes	No	35	104	*	*	ME*	3 days	Poss	Poss	Poss	Poss	Poss	1 yr.	Yes-P	Poss	5-6: no maximum reported—award is number of weeks scheduled benefit at claimant's compensation rate; 7: case law has supported AAO-79.
Delaware	Yes	No	75	175	$30,833	$71,944	ME	No	No	No	Yes	Yes	No	2 yrs.	No	No	
District of Columbia	Yes	No	39	150	$34,880	$134,170	AAO-79	6 mo.	Poss	Poss	Poss	Poss	Poss	1 yr.	Poss	Poss	
Florida	Yes	No	18	105	$8,892	$51,870	AAO-79	No	No	Yes-I	Yes	No	No	2 yrs.	Yes-P	No	
Georgia	Yes*	Yes*	NA	150	NA	NR	AAOO-59	6 mos.	NR	No	NR	NR	Yes	NR	Yes-D	NR	1: no awards granted for monaural hearing loss unless pre-existing deafness in other ear; 2: 90 dBA for 90 days.
Hawaii	Yes	Yes	52	200	$26,416	$101,600	AAOO-59	No	No	Yes	Yes	No	No	2 yrs.	No	No	

State							Formula										Comments
Idaho	Yes*	No	NR	175	NR	$42,639	ME	No	No	Yes-I	No	No	Yes	1 yr.	No	No	1: only hearing loss due to work-related trauma/injury is considered.
Illinois	Yes*	Yes*	50-100	200	$43,989	$87,978	Other*	No	No	Yes-I	No	No	Yes	2-3 yrs.	No	No	2: 90 dBA TWA; 7: avg > 30 dB at 1000, 2000, and 3000 Hz, 1.82% per dB.
Indiana	Yes*	No	*	*	$12,500	$39,500	ME	No	Yes	NR	No	NR	Yes	2 yrs.	Yes-D	Yes	1: only hearing loss due to work-related trauma/injury is compensable, but case law evolving–likely to consider NIHL in future; 3-4: awards paid for temp. disability (up to 500 wks) or permanent partial impairment based on % of max. awards.
Iowa	Yes	Yes	50	175	$43,600	$152,600	AAO-79	1 mon.	Yes	Yes	Yes	Yes	Yes	2 yrs.	Yes-D	No	
Kansas	Yes	No	30	110	$10,980	$40,260	AAO-79	No	Yes	Yes-I	Yes	Yes	Yes	200 days	Yes-D	No	
Kentucky	Yes	No	520	Life-time	*	*	ME	No	No	No	No	No	No	3-5 yrs.	No	No	5-6: award based on % impairment and average weekly wage.
Louisiana	Yes*	No	100	100	NR	$36,700	ME	No	No	Yes-I	No	No	Yes	1 yr.	Yes-D	No	1: only hearing loss due to work-related trauma/injury is considered.
Maine	Yes	Yes	50	200	$20,100	$80,400	AAOO-59	30 days	Yes*	Yes-I	Yes	Yes	Yes	Yes	Yes-D	No	9: 1/2 dB for each year over 40 yrs. of age.
Maryland	Yes	Yes*	125	250	NR	NR	AAOO-59	Yes	Poss	Poss	No	No	Yes	Yes	NR	Poss	2: exposure to harmful noise for 90 days or more.
Massachusetts	Yes	No	*	*	*	*	ME	No	Yes	Yes	NR	NR	Yes	Yes	Yes	No	3-6: based on statewide average wage — maximum $700/week.
Michigan	No*																1: no compensation for occupational hearing loss — employees are compensated only if an injury to the ear (that may or may not result in hearing loss) causes a loss of wages.
Minnesota	Yes	No					AAO-79	3 mos.	No	Yes	Yes	No	Yes	3 yrs.	No	No	3-6: hearing loss compensation is based on a percentage of whole body impairment (max for one ear, 6% whole body; for both ears, 35% whole body).
Mississippi	Yes	No	40	150	$11,191	$41,967	ME	No	No	Yes	No	No	Yes	Yes	No	Yes	
Missouri	Yes	No	49	180	$14,442	$53,051	AAOO-59	6 mo.	Yes*	Yes	Yes	No	Yes	No	Yes-P*	No	9: 1/2 dB per year over age 40 yrs.; 15: results in 15% penalty.
Montana	Yes	Yes*	40	200	NR	NR	AAOO-59	6 mo.	Yes*	No	Yes	No	Yes	No	No	No	2: 90 dB daily for 90 days or more; 9: 1/2 dB per year over age 40 years.
Nebraska	Yes	No	50	*	$22,200	*	ME	No	No	Poss	Yes	No	Yes	2 yrs.	No	No	4 and 6: average weekly wage x life expectancy.
Nevada	Yes	No	*	*	*	*	AAO-79	No	Poss	Yes	Yes	No	Yes	No	Yes-P	No	3-6: awards determined according to AMA guide and state statute.

table continued on next page.

Data compiled in 1998/1999 by Susan Megerson with assistance from Cyd Kladden.

KEY: **Poss** - possible; **NA** - non-applicable; **NR** - no response; * - see comments; **AAOO-59** - avg. > 25 dB at 500, 1000, and 2000 Hz; **AAO-79** - avg. > 25 dB at 500, 1000, 2000, and 3000 Hz; **ME** - medial evidence, hearing loss formula at discretion of consulting physician; **I** - only if impairment also present; **D** - claim denied; **P** - penalty applied.

TABLE B-1—continued
Hearing loss statutes in the United States and Canada.

Jurisdiction	1. Is occupational hearing loss compensable?	2. Is minimum noise exposure required for filing?	3. Schedule in weeks (one ear).	4. Schedule in weeks (both ears).	5. Maximum compensation (one ear).	6. Maximum compensation (both ears).	7. Hearing impairment formula.	8. Waiting period.	9. Is deduction made for presbycusis?	10. Is award made for tinnitus?	11. Provision for hearing aid?	12. Credit for improvement with hearing aid?	13. Is hearing loss prior to employment considered in compensation claim?	14. Statute of limitations for hearing-loss claim.	15. Penalty for not wearing hearing protection devices?	16. Self-assessment of hearing impairment considered in rating/award?	Comments
New Hampshire	Yes	No	30	123	$25,200	$103,320	ME	No	No	No	Yes	No	Yes	2 yrs.	No	No	2: 90 dB TWA; 7: avg. > 30 dB at 1000, 2000, and 3000 Hz, 1.5% per dB.
New Jersey	Yes	Yes*	60	200	$8,280	$48,200	Other*	4 wks.	No	Yes	Yes	Yes	Yes	2 yrs.	Yes-D	Yes	2: exposure to harmful noise for 90 days or more.
New Mexico	Yes	No	40	150	$15,039	$56,397	ME	7 days	No	No	No	No	Yes	1 yr.	Poss-P	No	
New York	Yes	Yes*	60	150	$24,000	$60,000	AAO-79	3 mos.	No	Yes	No	No	Yes	90 days	No	No	2: 90 dBA for at least 90 days; 7: if hearing loss due to injury, then "medical evidence" is utilized.
North Carolina	Yes	Yes*	70	150	$37,240	$79,800	AAO-79*	6 mos.	No	No	Yes	No	Yes	2 yrs.	Yes-D	No	
North Dakota	Yes	No	5	100	$695	$13,900	AAO-79	No	Poss	Yes-I	Yes	No	Yes	No	No	No	1: only permanent total hearing loss in one or both ears is compensable.
Ohio	Yes*	No	25	125	$13,525	$67,625	ME	No	No	No	Yes	No	No	2 yrs.	No	Yes	10: up to 5% for tinnitus in cases of unilateral hearing loss.
Oklahoma	Yes	No	104	312	$22,194	$66,583	AAO-79	No	No	Yes*	Yes	No	Yes	2 yrs.	Yes-D	No	
Oregon	Yes	No	*	*	$27,240	$87,168	Other*	No	Yes	Yes	Yes	No	Yes*	1 yr.	No	No	3-4: one time permanent partial disability award based on impairment; 7: avg > 25 dB at 500, 1000, 2000, 3000, 4000, and 6000 Hz, 1.5% per dB; 13: if baseline completed within 180 days of hire.
Pennsylvania	Yes	No*	60	260	*	*	AAO-79	No	No	No	No	No	Yes*	3 yrs.	No	No	2: case law has adopted OSHA standards as employer defense; 5 and 6: # weeks x 2/3 average wage; 13: only if pre-employment testing was performed at employer's expense.

State/Province																	Comments
Rhode Island	Yes	Yes	17*	100*	$1,530*	$9,000*	AAO-79	6 mos.	Yes	Poss-I	Poss	No	No*	2 yrs.	No	No	**3:** 60 weeks if loss due to trauma; **4:** 200 weeks for trauma; **5:** $5400 for trauma; **6:** $18,000 for trauma; **13:** current employer is solely responsible for occupational loss.
South Carolina	Yes	No	80	165	$38,678	$79,773	AAO-79	No	No	No	No	No	Yes	No	No	No	
South Dakota	Yes	Yes*	50	150	$20,400	$61,200	AAO-79	No	Yes*	No	Yes	No	Yes	2 yrs.	Yes-D	No	**2:** 90 dBA TWA; **9:** 1/2 dB for each year over 45 yrs.
Tennessee	Yes	No	75	150	$38,625	$77,250	ME	No	Yes	Yes-I	Yes	Poss	Yes	1 yr.	Poss-D	Yes	**3-6:** no maximum scheduled awards.
Texas	Yes	No	*	*	*	*	AAO-79	No	No	No	No	No	Yes	30 days	No	No	
Utah	Yes	Yes*	NR	109	NR	$35,425	AAO-79	6 wks.	NR	NR	NR	NR	Yes	180 days	NR	NR	**2:** 90 dBA TWA or impact/impulsive noise 140 dB or greater.
Vermont	Yes	No	24	142	$17,448	$103,052	ME	No	No	Yes-I	Yes	No	No	Yes	Yes-D	No	**1:** only hearing loss due to work-related trauma or injury is considered; **5-6:** # weeks x average weekly wage.
Virginia	Yes*	No	50	100	*	*	AAO-79	No	No	No	Poss	No	No	2-5 yrs.	No	No	
Washington	Yes	No	N/A	N/A	$10,837	$65,023	AAO-79	No	No	Yes-I	Yes	No	Yes	2 yrs.	No	No	**3-6:** hearing loss compensation is based on a percentage of whole body impairment (max for both ears, 22.5% whole body).
West Virginia	Yes	No	*	*	*	*	AAO-79	2 mos.	Yes	No	Yes	No	Yes	3 yrs.	No	No	
Wisconsin	Yes	No	36	216	*	*	Other*	7 days	No	No*	Yes	No	Yes	No	No	No	**5-6:** depends on year of retirement; **7:** avg. ≥ 30 dB at 500, 1000, 2000, and 3000 Hz; **10:** not compensable since 1/1/92.
Wyoming	Yes	No	*	*	*	NR	ME	No	No	NR	No	No	Yes	Yes	Yes-D	NR	**3-6:** based upon rating of impairment.
U.S. DOL –FECA	Yes	Yes	52	200	NR	NR	AAO-79	No	No	No	Yes	No	No	3 yrs.	No	No	FECA - federal employees compensation act
U.S. DOL – Longshoremen	Yes	No	52	200	*	*	AAO-79	No	No	No	Yes	No	No	1 yr.	No	No	**5-6:** based upon compensation rate, increases annually.
Guam	Yes	No	52	200	$13,000	$50,000	ME	No	Yes	Yes-I	Yes	No	Yes	1 yr.	No	No	**2:** 85 dBA for 8 hrs.
Alberta	Yes	Yes*	NA	NA	$3,184	$19,105	NR	No	No	Yes-I	Yes	No	Yes	5 yrs.	No	No	
British Columbia	Yes	Yes*	NA	*	NR	*	Other*	No	No	No	Yes	No	No	No	No	No	**2:** 85 dB L_EX,8h for 2 yrs.; **5-6:** based on % of annual wage; **7:** avg > 28 dB at 500, 1000, and 2000 Hz; 2.5% per dB
Manitoba	Yes	Yes*	NA	*	*	*	Other*	No	Yes*	No	Yes	No	Yes	No	Poss-D	No	**2:** 85 dB for 2 yrs.; **5-6:** lump sum paid based on %; **7:** avg ≥ 35 dB at 500, 1000, 2000, and 3000 Hz; **9:** 1/2 dB per year over 60 yrs. of age.

table continued on next page.

Data compiled in 1998/1999 by Susan Megerson with assistance from Cyd Kladden.

KEY: **Poss** - possible; **NA** - non-applicable; **NR** - no response; ***** - see comments; **AAO-59** - avg. > 25 dB at 500, 1000, and 2000 Hz; **AAO-79** - avg. > 25 dB at 500, 1000, 2000, and 3000 Hz; **ME** - medial evidence, hearing loss formula at discretion of consulting physician; **I** - only if impairment also present; **D** - claim denied; **P** - penalty applied.

TABLE B-1—continued

Hearing loss statutes in the United States and Canada.

Jurisdiction	1. Is occupational hearing loss compensable?	2. Is minimum noise exposure required for filing?	3. Schedule in weeks (one ear).	4. Schedule in weeks (both ears).	5. Maximum compensation (one ear).	6. Maximum compensation (both ears).	7. Hearing impairment formula.	8. Waiting period.	9. Is deduction made for presbycusis?	10. Is award made for tinnitus?	11. Provision for hearing aid?	12. Credit for improvement with hearing aid?	13. Is hearing loss prior to employment considered in compensation claim?	14. Statute of limitations for hearing-loss claim.	15. Penalty for not wearing hearing protection devices?	16. Self-assessment of hearing impairment considered in rating/award?	Comments
New Brunswick	Yes	No	NA	NA	*	*	ME	No	No	Yes-I	Yes	No	Yes	Yes*	No	No	**5-6**: depends on percent of disability; **14**: prior to retirement.
NW Territories	Yes*	Yes*	*	*	$147/month	$887/month	Other*	Yes*	No	No	Yes	No	Yes	1 yr.	No	No	**2**: 90 dB for 8 hrs/day for 2 yrs.; **3-4**: no maximum time period; **7**: avg ≥ 30 dB at 500, 1000, 2000, and 3000 Hz; **8**: when removed from exposure.
Nova Scotia	Yes	Yes*	*	*	*	*	Other*	No	Yes*	Yes*	Yes	No	Yes	5 yrs.	No	No	**2**: 85 dB for 8 hrs for 5 yrs.; **3-6**: awards based on pre-injury wages and % impairment with no maximums; **7**: avg ≥ 35 at 500, 1000, 2000 and 3000 Hz; **9**: 1/2 dB per year over age 60 yrs.; **10**: 2-5% awarded if specific criteria are met.
Ontario	Yes	Yes*	NA	NA	*	*	AAO-79	No	Yes*	Yes	Yes	No	Yes	6 mo.	No	No	**2**: 90 dB for 5 yrs.; **5-6**: lump sum awards based on % impairment, age at date of accident and maximum medical recovery; **9**: 1/2 dB per year over age 60 yrs.
Prince Edward Island	Yes*	Yes*	*	*	*	*	ME	No	Yes*	Yes*	Yes	No	Yes	No	No	No	**2**: 2 yrs. minimum; **3-6**: lump sum awards based on % impairment; **9**: 1/2 dB per year over age 60 yrs.; **10**: 2% maximum.
Quebec	Yes*	Yes*	*	*	*	*	ME	No	Yes	No	Yes	No	Yes	No	No	NR	**2**: 90 dB for 8 hrs/day for 2 yrs.; **3-6**: lump sum award based on % impairment and age at time of injury.
Saskatchewan	Yes	No	*	*	$1,130	$13,560	Other*	No	No	Yes-I	Yes	No	Yes	No	No	No	**3-4**: lump sum pension and hearing aid costs; **7**: avg ≥ 30 dB at 500, 1000, 2000, and 3000 Hz.
Yukon	Yes*	Yes*	*	*	*	*	AAO-79	2-5 yrs.	Yes*	Yes-I	Yes	No	Yes	No	No	No	**2**: 85 dB for 30 dB at 500, 1000, 2000, and 3000 Hz; **9**: maximum 2% for each year over age 45 yrs.

Appendix C

List of Abbreviation

A	A-weighted
AAO	American Academy of Otolaryngology
AAO–HNS	American Academy of Otolaryngology–Head and Neck Surgery
AAOO	American Academy of Ophthalmology and Otolaryngology
ABR	auditory brainstem response
AC	air conduction
ACGIH	American Conference of Governmental Industrial Hygienists
ACOEM	American College of Occupational and Environmental Medicine
ACOM	American College of Occupational Medicine
ACS	American College of Surgeons
ADA	Americans with Disabilities Act
ADBA	audiometric database analysis
A-duration	duration of the initial or principal pressure pulse
AI	articulation index
AIHA	American Industrial Hygiene Association
AMA	American Medical Association
AMIA	American Mutual Insurance Alliance
ANSI	American National Standards Institute
AOM	acute otitis media
ARHL	age-related hearing loss
ARPTS	age-related permanent threshold shift
ASA	American Standards Association

ASHA	American Speech-Language-Hearing Association
BADGE	Békésy ascending-descending gap evaluation
BAEP	brainstem auditory evoked potential
BAER	brainstem auditory evoked response
BC	bone conduction
B-duration	20-dB decay time
BI	binaural impairment
BSER	brainstem evoked response
CHABA	Committee on Hearing, Bioacoustics, and Biomechanics
cm	centimeter(s)
cm^2	centimeters squared (square centimeters)
CO_2	carbon dioxide
COM	chronic otitis media
cps	cycles per second
CROS	contralateral routing of signal (type of hearing aid)
CT	computerized tomography
C.V.	curriculum vitae
DAF	delayed auditory feedback
dB	decibel(s)
dBA	decibels measured using A-weighting network of a sound level meter
dBA-TWA	decibels measured using A-weighting network of a sound level meter, time-weighted average
DOL	Department of Labor
DPOAE	distortion product otoacoustic emission
EDA	electrodermal audiometry
EHL	exaggerated hearing loss
EPA	Environmental Protection Agency
FAA	Federal Aviation Administration
FELA	Federal Employers Liability Act
FRA	Federal Railroad Administration
ft	foot or feet
g	gram(s)
GSR	galvanic skin response
HCP	hearing conservation program
HH	hearing handicap
HHIE	Hearing Handicap Inventory for the Elderly
HL	hearing level
HPD	hearing protection device
Hz	hertz
I	intensity
IAC	internal auditory canal
in	inch(es)

ISO	International Organization for Standardization
IQ	intelligence quotient
kHz	kilohertz
L_{ex}	equivalent continuous A-weighted sound pressure level
lb	pound(s)
log	logarithm
LOT	lengthened off-time
m	meter(s)
m^2	meters squared (square meters)
mcg	microgram(s)
mg%	milligram(s) per 100 ml
ml	milliliter(s)
MRI	magnetic resonance imaging
msec	millisecond(s)
MSHA	Mine Safety and Health Administration
mW	milliwatts
µPa	microPascal(s)
µV	microvolt(s)
NHCA	National Hearing Conservation Association
NIH	National Institutes of Health
NIHL	noise-induced hearing loss
NIOSH	National Institute for Occupational Safety and Health
NIPTS	noise-induced permanent threshold shift
NRA	National Rifle Association
NRR	Noise Reduction Rating
NU-6	Northwestern University Auditory Test No. 6
OAE	otoacoustic emission
OE	otitis externa
OME	otitis media with effusion
ONAC	Office of Noise Abatement and Control
OSH	Occupational Safety and Health
OSHA	Occupational Safety and Health Administration
P	pressure
PCB	polychlorinated biphenyl
PEL	permissible exposure level
PGSA	psychogalvanic skin response audiometry
PHPD	personal hearing protective device
PI	performance-intensity
PLF	perilymph fistula
ppm	parts per million
PTA	pure-tone average
PTA-123	pure-tone average at 1, 2, and 3 kHz
PTA-1234	pure-tone average at 1, 2, 3, and 4 kHz

PTA-124	pure-tone average at 1, 2, and 4 kHz
PTA-234	pure-tone average at 2, 3, and 4 kHz
PTA-512	pure-tone average at 0.5, 1, and 2 kHz
PTA-5123	pure-tone average at 0.5, 1, 2, and 3 kHz
PTA-5124	pure-tone average at 0.5, 1, 2, and 4 kHz
PTS	permanent threshold shift
R	reproducibility
rad	radiation absorbed dose
sec	second(s)
SES	socioeconomic status
SF	subject fit
SIL	speech interference level
SIP	Sickness Impact Profile
SL	sensation level
SNHL	sensorineural hearing loss
SNR	signal-to-noise ratio
SPAR	sensitivity prediction from the acoustic reflex
SPL	sound pressure level
SRT	speech reception threshold
ST	spondee threshold
STS	standard threshold shift
SVR	slow vertex response
TEOAE	transient-evoked otoacoustic emission
TM	tympanic membrane (eardrum)
TTS	temporary threshold shift
TTS_2	temporary threshold shift at 2 minutes after cessation of exposure
TWA	time-weighted average
Type A	normal tympanogram
Type B	flat tympanogram
Type C	normally shaped tympanogram, but presence of negative or positive middle ear pressure
USPHS	U.S. Public Health Service
V	volume velocity
VA	Veterans Administration
W-22	Central Institute for the Deaf Auditory Test W-22
WC	Workers' Compensation
WHO	World Health Organization
WRT	word recognition test
Z	acoustic impedance

Author Index

Subject Index